Enterprise Application Architecture with .NET Core

An architectural journey into the Microsoft .NET open source platform

Ganesan Senthilvel
Ovais Mehboob Ahmed Khan
Habib Ahmed Qureshi

BIRMINGHAM - MUMBAI

Enterprise Application Architecture with .NET Core

First published: April 2017

Production reference: 1210417

Published by Packt Publishing Ltd.
Livery Place
35 Livery Street
Birmingham
B3 2PB, UK.

ISBN 978-1-78646-888-8

www.packtpub.com

Credits

Authors
Ganesan Senthilvel
Ovais Mehboob Ahmed Khan
Habib Ahmed Qureshi

Copy Editor
Sonia Mathur

Reviewer
Adwait Ullal

Project Coordinator
Prajakta Naik

Commissioning Editor
Aaron Lazar

Proofreader
Safis Editing

Acquisition Editor
Nitin Dasan

Indexer
Aishwarya Gangawane

Content Development Editor
Siddhi Chavan

Graphics
Tania Dutta

Technical Editor
Abhishek Sharma

Production Coordinator
Aparna Bhagat

About the Authors

Ganesan Senthilvel is a passionate IT leader with two decades' experience in architecture, design, and implementing cutting edge solutions to the address business opportunities of enterprise applications. He has earned a Master's degree in Computer Science and Master's degree in Business Administration. Now, he is pursuing a doctorate program in Big Data. He is a consistent technical contributor via COE, Blog, Whitepaper, Summit, Certification, and so on. Highly skilled at providing coaching and mentoring to internal teams and external institutes, he maintains his weekly blog at http://ganesansenthilvel.blogspot. in. He has published double dozens of technology articles on CodeProject and LinkedIn Pulse. He has earned industry certifications in Big Data, Microsoft (MCP, MCAD), and the financial domain.

Writing this book was a rewarding experience with a high degree of learning. I highly appreciate the sacrifices of my wife, Hema, and my boys, Vaishak and Vishwak, while I worked on the book. I'm blessed with the support of my parents, friends, and mentors. Big thanks go out to the Packt team.

Ovais Mehboob Ahmed Khan is a seasoned programmer and solution architect with more than 14 years of software development experience. He has worked in different organizations across Pakistan, the USA, and the Middle East. Currently, he is working for a government entity based in Dubai, and also provides consultancy services to a Microsoft gold partner firm based in New Jersey.

He is a Microsoft MVP in Visual Studio and Development Technologies and specializes mainly in Microsoft .NET, Cloud, and Web development. He is a prolific writer and has published numerous technical articles on different websites, such as MSDN, TechNet, DZone, and so on; he also has a personal blog at http://OvaisMehboob.com and is an author of another book named as *JavaScript for .NET Developers, published by Packt*. He is an active speaker and group leader of Microsoft Developers UAE Meetup, Microsoft Technology Practices, and Developers and Enterprise Practices user groups, and has presented various technical sessions at various events and conferences. In short, Ovais is a passionate developer and architect who is always interested in learning new technologies. He can be reached at ovaismehboob@hotmail.com, and on Twitter at @ovaismehboob.

I would like to thank my family for supporting me, especially my mother, wife, and brother, who have always encouraged me in every goal of my life. My father, may he rest in peace, would have been proud of my achievements.

Habib Ahmed Qureshi is an integration architect and lead developer with over 14 years of professional experience in the software industry working with the cutting edge technologies. He has worked globally with on-site, off-site, and remote teams in Karachi, Dubai, Copenhagen, London, and Basel. He is a go-getter, and his teams always look to him for technical reviews and solutions.

He has worked extensively with C++, .NET (C#/VB), Java, TIBCO, and various other middlewares on Windows and other platforms.

You can connect to him on Twitter at `@habib_a_qureshi`.

I would like to appreciate the support from my family, especially my wife, to help me achieve writing this book.

About the Reviewer

Adwait Ullal is an Enterprise Architect with cloud skills, having assisted Fortune 100 companies assess the public cloud environments and migrate applications and infrastructure to the cloud. He is a presenter at the local SQL Saturdays and Code Camps and has also reviewed books for Wrox and Manning. He can be contacted on Twitter at `@adwait`.

I would like to thank my wife, Suchitra, for her enormous patience while I am engaged in multiple projects as well as the staff at Packt for keeping me on point.

www.PacktPub.com

For support files and downloads related to your book, please visit www.PacktPub.com.

Did you know that Packt offers eBook versions of every book published, with PDF and ePub files available? You can upgrade to the eBook version at www.PacktPub.com and as a print book customer, you are entitled to a discount on the eBook copy. Get in touch with us at service@packtpub.com for more details.

At www.PacktPub.com, you can also read a collection of free technical articles, sign up for a range of free newsletters and receive exclusive discounts and offers on Packt books and eBooks.

https://www.packtpub.com/mapt

Get the most in-demand software skills with Mapt. Mapt gives you full access to all Packt books and video courses, as well as industry-leading tools to help you plan your personal development and advance your career.

Why subscribe?

- Fully searchable across every book published by Packt
- Copy and paste, print, and bookmark content
- On demand and accessible via a web browser

Customer Feedback

Thanks for purchasing this Packt book. At Packt, quality is at the heart of our editorial process. To help us improve, please leave us an honest review on this book's Amazon page at `https://www.amazon.com/dp/1786468883`.

If you'd like to join our team of regular reviewers, you can e-mail us at `customerreviews@packtpub.com`. We award our regular reviewers with free eBooks and videos in exchange for their valuable feedback. Help us be relentless in improving our products!

I would like to dedicate this book to two of my inspirations, Grady Booch and Martin Fowler.

- Habib Ahmed Qureshi

Table of Contents

Preface

This book contains various topics for the development of enterprise applications architecture for diversified applications. Whether it's a layered architecture, service-oriented architecture, microservices architecture, or a cloud-specific solution, you will learn best practices in developing enterprise application architecture with .NET Core. It also covers emerging fields, such as DevOps and Big Data, for the broader perspective. This book starts with a brief introduction to enterprise architecture (EA) and the key components in EA practice. It then takes you through the SOLID principles and design patterns in software development and explains the various aspects of distributed computing to keep your applications efficient and scalable. These chapters act as a catalyst to start the practical implementation for the designing and development of applications using various architectural approaches. Gradually, you will explore different approaches to implement security in your applications and explore various authentication models and authorization techniques. In the end, you will learn the concepts of the emerging fields and practices of DevOps, Containerization, Big Data, Artificial Intelligence, and more.

What this book covers

Chapter 1, *Enterprise Architecture Concepts*, helps you understand the fundamental concepts of enterprise architecture and its related business need and benefits. As the best practice in the industry, enterprise architecture is expected to have the responsibility to perform the strategic steps in alignment with the business vision. An enterprise architecture has few strong fundamental blocks, namely, agility, durability, efficiency, and effectiveness. An enterprise architecture is the discipline of addressing business needs with people, process, and technology, with the definition of purpose, intent, and structure of enterprise applications.

Chapter 2, *Principles and Patterns*, provides an introduction to SOLID principles and design patterns, but also provides C# .NET Core-based implementations to some of the famous design patterns, including GoF patterns and Dependency Injection.

Chapter 3, *Distributed Computing*, explains that the reader will get an opportunity to understand the fundamentals of this computing and application in the enterprise world. It starts from the definition, followed by its core characteristics, such as concurrency, scalability, transparency, security, and more. In the modern world, distributed computing plays a vital role.

Chapter 4, *Software Development Life Cycle*, covers SDLC, which is a term used in systems engineering, information systems, and software engineering as a process. This tutorial elaborates on various methodologies, such as Waterfall, Spiral, Agile, and so on. At the end of this chapter, you will understand the fundamental concepts of Enterprise Architecture and its related business needs and benefits. It has started from the traditional Waterfall model and traversed through multi-iteration Spiral model, trendy Agile model with the specific Scaled Agile Framework (SAFe). On traversing through various timelines and related methodologies, it has been easy to understand the necessity of the improvement and related adoption.

Chapter 5, *Enterprise Practices in Software Development*, explains the enterprise practices in the software development life cycle with the popular ALM tools and techniques. After reading this chapter, the reader will know different ways to measure the performance of .NET Core applications and see how enterprises can create their own custom project templates using the .NET CLI tool.

Chapter 6, *Layered Approach to Solution Architecture*, teaches you a few best practices that can be used while designing n-tier architecture. We will implement a few patterns, such as Repository, Unit of Work, and Factory, in the data access layer that decouples the dependencies and uses them in business layer for database manipulation. We will explore certain benefits of keeping entities and other helper classes in the common layer, which can be used throughout the layers and, in the service layer, we will develop few controllers to show how business managers can be developed and injected. We will also learn how logging and exception handling can be implemented and, finally, in the presentation layer, we will use Angular 2 as a frontend framework to bring responsive user experience.

Chapter 7, *SOA Implementation with .NET Core*, talks about taking the top-down approach, taking you from theoretical aspects to implementation-related information. It introduces how to approach a SOA platform from an enterprise architecture perspective, how to model an architecture in step-by-step approach, and what elements to look for and take care of at the time of implementation of a SOA architecture.

Chapter 8, *Cloud-Based Architecture and Integration with .NET Core*, teaches you about cloud computing and using Microsoft Azure as the cloud platform. We will focus on Azure App Services and see how simply we can develop and deploy .NET Core applications on the cloud. Scalability is an essential key, and we will learn how easy it is to scale out or scale up our applications running on Azure following with the techniques to increase performance. Finally, you will learn about logging and monitoring options in Azure and see how we can use Application Insights with web applications running on the cloud to monitor application performance.

Chapter 9, *Microservices Architecture,* builds on SOA concepts and architectural artifacts and utilizes the right information from the cloud-based architecture and fits it to the right level to design the microservices-based architecture. We will design a high-level architecture using microservices and introduce you to some of the key elements from Azure-based offerings in order to design a sample serverless architecture.

Chapter 10, *Security Practices with .NET Core,* teaches you about the security frameworks ASP.NET Core Identity and IdentityServer4 in order to handle easy and complex scenarios, customize and extend the existing Identity model using Entity Framework Core, and use middleware to authenticate users using Facebook, 2FA, and OpenID Connect. Moreover, we will develop a basic Central Authentication System (CAS) that provides multiple applications to connect using the same protocol and implement single sign-on. You will also learn different techniques of securing Web API and MVC Controllers and Actions using attributes, or imperatively by writing custom code and then, finally, we will discuss how we can store application secrets using user secrets.

Chapter 11, *Modern AI Offerings by Microsoft,* explains the emerging architecture practices of the industry in a succinct and concise way with .NET Core environment. In the software industry, things can change quickly. You will learn DevOps concepts as well as the implementation of a simple microservices-based architecture in depth using Docker-based containers, and deploy them onto the Azure cloud using the relevant Azure offerings for the multi-container based implementation. The chapter covers virtual machines and containerization, Docker, DevOps, Continuous Integration and Continuous Delivery, sample app based on Docker containers, Big Data in Microsoft, Business Intelligence (BI), and an introduction to Artificial Intelligence (AI).

What you need for this book

- Development Environment: Visual Studio 2015/2017 Community Edition
- Execution Environment: .NET Core
- OS Environment: Oracle VM VirtualBox with Windows or Linux
- Microsoft Azure Account

Who this book is for

This book assumes that the readers are either senior developers or software solution architects who want to design and develop enterprise applications with .NET Core as the development framework and quickly get their hands on enterprise architecture, patterns, SOA, and microservices following the .NET Core in the cloud.

With this book, you will get to know modern architectures and patterns in a summarized form within a short period of time.

Conventions

In this book, we follow the C# coding style as is followed by the .NET Core community here: `https://github.com/dotnet/corefx/blob/master/Documentation/coding-guidelines/coding-style.md`.

In this book, you will find a number of text styles that distinguish between different kinds of information. Here are some examples of these styles and an explanation of their meaning.

Code words in text, database table names, folder names, filenames, file extensions, pathnames, dummy URLs, user input, and Twitter handles are shown as follows: "Logging can be enabled by injecting the `ILoggerFactory` instance through the `Configure` method of the `Startup` class, and then using that to add providers."

A block of code is set as follows:

```
using System;

namespace Chapter2.SRP.Decorator
{
  public class Student
  {
    public string Name;
    public string Id;
    public DateTime DOB;

  }
}
```

Any command-line input or output is written as follows:

```
yum install -y gcc-c++ make
```

New terms and **important words** are shown in bold. Words that you see on the screen, for example, in menus or dialog boxes, appear in the text like this: "Logic App can be created by selecting the **Web + Mobile** option in the search pane and by then selecting the **Logic App** option."

Warnings or important notes appear in a box like this.

Tips and tricks appear like this.

Reader feedback

Feedback from our readers is always welcome. Let us know what you think about this book-what you liked or disliked. Reader feedback is important for us as it helps us develop titles that you will really get the most out of.

To send us general feedback, simply e-mail `feedback@packtpub.com`, and mention the book's title in the subject of your message.

If there is a topic that you have expertise in and you are interested in either writing or contributing to a book, see our author guide at `www.packtpub.com/authors`.

Customer support

Now that you are the proud owner of a Packt book, we have a number of things to help you to get the most from your purchase.

Downloading the example code

You can download the example code files for this book from your account at `http://www.packtpub.com`. If you purchased this book elsewhere, you can visit `http://www.packtpub.com/support` and register to have the files e-mailed directly to you.

You can download the code files by following these steps:

1. Log in or register to our website using your e-mail address and password.
2. Hover the mouse pointer on the **SUPPORT** tab at the top.
3. Click on **Code Downloads & Errata**.
4. Enter the name of the book in the **Search** box.
5. Select the book for which you're looking to download the code files.
6. Choose from the drop-down menu where you purchased this book from.
7. Click on **Code Download**.

Once the file is downloaded, please make sure that you unzip or extract the folder using the latest version of:

- WinRAR / 7-Zip for Windows
- Zipeg / iZip / UnRarX for Mac
- 7-Zip / PeaZip for Linux

The code bundle for the book is also hosted on GitHub at `https://github.com/PacktPubl ishing/Enterprise-Application-Architecture-with-NET-Core`. We also have other code bundles from our rich catalog of books and videos available at `https://github.com/P acktPublishing/`. Check them out!

Downloading the color images of this book

We also provide you with a PDF file that has color images of the screenshots/diagrams used in this book. The color images will help you better understand the changes in the output. You can download this file from `https://www.packtpub.com/sites/default/files/down loads/EnterpriseApplicationArchitecturewithNETCore_ColorImages.pdf`.

Errata

Although we have taken every care to ensure the accuracy of our content, mistakes do happen. If you find a mistake in one of our books-maybe a mistake in the text or the code-we would be grateful if you could report this to us. By doing so, you can save other readers from frustration and help us improve subsequent versions of this book. If you find any errata, please report them by visiting `http://www.packtpub.com/submit-errata`, selecting your book, clicking on the **Errata Submission Form** link, and entering the details of your errata. Once your errata are verified, your submission will be accepted and the errata will be uploaded to our website or added to any list of existing errata under the Errata section of that title.

To view the previously submitted errata, go to `https://www.packtpub.com/books/content/support` and enter the name of the book in the search field. The required information will appear under the **Errata** section.

Piracy

Piracy of copyrighted material on the Internet is an ongoing problem across all media. At Packt, we take the protection of our copyright and licenses very seriously. If you come across any illegal copies of our works in any form on the Internet, please provide us with the location address or website name immediately so that we can pursue a remedy.

Please contact us at `copyright@packtpub.com` with a link to the suspected pirated material.

We appreciate your help in protecting our authors and our ability to bring you valuable content.

Questions

If you have a problem with any aspect of this book, you can contact us at `questions@packtpub.com`, and we will do our best to address the problem.

1
Enterprise Architecture Concepts

This section starts with the core concepts and frameworks of the industry-wide adopted **Enterprise Architecture** (**EA**). EA is an industry framework to align the enterprise with the execution of disruptive and emerging changes. Strategically, it supports the targeted (or) desired vision and outcomes of the business. By design, EA is the fundamental block of the business, domain, and technology vision of an enterprise.

By the end of the chapter, you will understand the fundamental concepts of enterprise architecture, and its related business needs and benefits.

In this chapter, we will cover the following topics:

- Understanding the definition of an enterprise architect and their related stakeholders
- Knowing the real need of Enterprise Architecture to attain business benefits
- Knowing the clear segregation between **Solution Architecture** and Enterprise Architecture
- Details of four segregation types of Enterprise Architecture
- Understanding the commonly known EA Frameworks--**The Open Group Architecture Framework** (**TOGAF**) and **Zachman**

Why do we need Enterprise Architecture?

As this book is focused on the enterprise level, it is expected to provide a few core points to understand enterprise architecture easily.

In my personal experience, it was confusing to understand the role of an enterprise architect because people used to refer to so many architectural roles and terms, such as architect, solution architect, enterprise architect, data architect, blueprint, system diagram, and so on. My work experience clarified the underlying concepts and motivated me to write this section.

In general, the industry perception is that an IT architect role is to draw a few boxes with a few suggestions; the rest is with the development community. They feel that the architect role is quite easy, just drawing a diagram and not doing anything else. As said earlier, it is completely a perception of a few associates in the industry. This perception leads me to a different view about the architecture role:

However, my enterprise architect job has cleared this perception and I understand the true value of an enterprise architect.

Definition of Enterprise Architecture

In simple terms, an enterprise is nothing but human endeavor. The objective of an enterprise is where people are collaborating for a particular purpose supported by a platform. Let me explain with an example of an online e-commerce company. Employees of that company are people who work together to produce the firm's profits using their various platforms, such as infrastructure, software, equipment, building, and so on.

Enterprise has the structure/arrangements of all these pieces/components to build the complete organization. This is the exact place where enterprise architecture plays its key role. Every enterprise has an enterprise architect.

EA is a process of architecting that applies the discipline to produce the prescribed output components. This process needs experience, skill, discipline, and descriptions. Consider the following image, where EA anticipates the system in two key states:

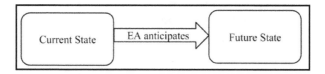

Every enterprise needs an enterprise architect, this is not optional. Let me give a simple example. When you need a car for business activities, you have two choices, either drive yourself or rent a driver. Still, you will need the driving capability to operate the car. EA is pretty similar to this.

As depicted in the preceding diagram, EA anticipates the system in two key states, which are as follows:

- How it currently is
- How it will be in the future

Basically, they work on options/alternatives to move from the current to a future state of an enterprise system. In this process, Enterprise Architecture does the following:

- Creates the frameworks to manage the architecture
- Details the descriptions of the architecture
- Road maps to lay the best way to change/improve the architecture
- Defines constraints/opportunities
- Anticipates the costs and benefits
- Evaluates the risks and values

In this process of architecting, the system applies the discipline to produce the prescribed output components.

Stakeholders of Enterprise Architecture

Enterprise Architecture is so special because of its holistic view of management and evolution of an enterprise holistically. It has a unique combination of specialist technologies, such as architecture frameworks and design pattern practices.

Such a special EA has the following key stakeholders/users in its ecosystem:

S.No.	Stakeholders	Organizational actions
1	Strategic planner	• Capability planning • Set strategic direction • Impact analysis
2	Decision makers	• Investment • Divestment • Approvals for the project • Alignment with strategic direction
3	Analyst	• Quality assurance • Compliance • Alignment with business goals
4	Project managers	• Solution development • Investigate opportunities • Analysis of existing options

Business benefits

Though many organizations intervened without EAs, every firm has the strong belief that it is better to architect before creating any system. It is integrated in a coherent fashion with a proactively designed system instead of a random ad hoc and inconsistent mode.

In terms of business benefits, cost is the key factor in the meaning of **Return on Investment** (**RoI**). That is how the industry business is driven in this highly competitive IT world. EA has the opportunity to prove its value for its own stakeholders with three major benefits, ranging from tactical to strategic positions. They are as follows:

- Cost reduction by technology standardization
- **Business Process Improvement** (**BPI**)
- Strategic differentiation

 Gartner's research paper on *TCO: The First Justification for Enterprise IT Architecture* by Colleen Young is a good reference to justify the business benefits of an Enterprise Architecture.
Check out
`https://www.gartner.com/doc/388268/enterprise-architecture-benef its-justification` for more information.

In the grand scheme of cost saving strategy, technology standardization adds a lot of efficiency to create indirect benefits. Let me share my experience in this space. In one of my earlier legacy organizations, it was noticed that the variety of technologies and products were built to serve the business purpose due to historical acquisitions and mergers.

All businesses have processes; a few life examples are credit card processing, employee on-boarding, student enrollment, and so on. In this methodology, there are people involved with few steps for the particular system to get things done. During rapid business growth, the processes become chaotic, which leads to duplicate efforts across departments. In turn, stakeholders do not leverage the collaboration and cross learning.

BPI is an industry approach that is designed to support the enterprise for the realignment of the existing business operational process into the significantly improved process. It helps the enterprise to identify and adopt in a better way using industry tools and techniques.

BPI was originally designed to induce a drastic, game-changing effect on enterprise performance instead of bringing changes in incremental steps.

In the current, highly competitive market, **Strategic Differentiation** efforts make a firm create the perception in customers minds of receiving something of greater value than is offered by the competition. An effective differentiation strategy is the best tool to highlight a business's unique features and make it stand out from the crowd.

As the outcome of strategic differentiation, the business should realize the benefits of Enterprise Architecture investment. Also, it makes the business institute new ways of thinking to add new customer segments along with new major competitive strategies.

Knowing the role of an architect

When I planned to switch my career to the architecture track, I had too many questions in mind. People were referring to so many titles in the industry, such as architect, solution architect, enterprise architect, data architect, infra architect, and so on that I didn't know where exactly do I needed to start and end. The industry had so many confusions to opt for. To understand it better, let me give my own work experience as the best use cases.

In the IT industry, two higher-level architects are named as follows:

- **Solution architect (SA)**
- **Enterprise architect (EA)**

In my view, Enterprise Architecture is a much broader discipline than Solution Architecture, with the sum of **Business Architecture**, **Application Architecture**, **Data Architecture**, and **Technology Architecture**. It will be covered in detail in the subsequent section:

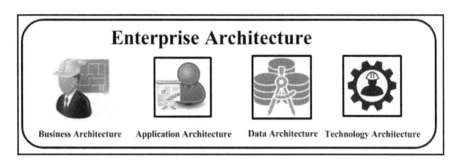

SA is focused on a specific solution and addresses the technological details that are compiled to the standards, roadmaps, and strategic objectives of the business. In comparison with SA, EA is a more senior level. In general, EA takes a strategic, inclusive, and long term view of goals, opportunities, and challenges facing the company. However, SA is assigned to a particular project/program in an enterprise to ensure technical integrity and consistency of the solution at every stage of its life cycle.

Role comparison between EA and SA

Let me explain the working experiences of two different roles--EA and SA. When I played the SA role for an Internet based telephony system, my role was to build tools, such as code generation, automation, and so on around the existing telephony system. It needed the skill set of the Microsoft platform technology and telephony domain to understand the existing system in a better way and then provide better solutions to improve the productivity and performance of the existing ecosystem. I was not really involved in the enterprise-level decision making process. Basically, I was pretty much like an individual contributor to building effective and efficient solutions to improvise the current system.

As the second job, let me share my experience in the EA role for a leading financial company. The job was to build the enterprise data hub using emerging big data technology.

Degree of Comparisons

If we plot EA versus SA graphically, EA needs higher degree of strategy focus and technology breath, as depicted in the following image:

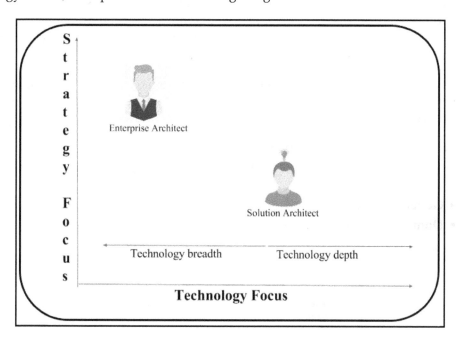

In terms of roles and responsibilities, EA and SA differ in their scope. Basically, the SA scope is limited within a project team and the expected delivery is to make the system quality of the solution for the business. At the same time, the EA scope is beyond SA by identifying or envisioning the future state of an organization.

With the degree of experience, expertise, responsibility, and much more. EA is superior to SA. EA has the vision of end-to-end broader system knowledge; but SA is bound to a specific problem statement. In terms of enterprise role, EA role is pretty close to Chief Architect, whereas SA is at the Senior Architect level.

Commonly known EA Frameworks

In the real-world scenario, the **Enterprise Architecture Framework (EAF)** inspires software development processes in the industry. It is essential to fulfill the mission of the associated enterprise.

In a nutshell, EA serves as the blueprint for the system and the project that develops it. An EAF can describe the underlying infrastructure, thus providing the groundwork for the hardware, software, and networks to work together.

With the usage of EAF, the organization will be in a situation to understand and analyze the weaknesses or inconsistencies to be identified and addressed. As per the fundamentals of computing, a framework is often a layered structure indicating what kind of programs can or should be built, and how they will interrelate.

To my knowledge, there are a few established EAFs available in the industry today. Some of them were developed for a very specific area, whereas others have a broader coverage with complete functionality.

In my view, there are two common types of EAFs used in the industry, which are as follows:

- **General Purpose Framework**
- **Domain Specific Framework**

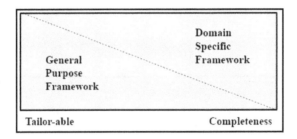

General Purpose Frameworks

As the name describes, these frameworks are designed by being agnostic to any specific implementation. They have no specific business drivers in terms of an enterprise specific scenario, but rather, they are capability based. Some of the well-known general purpose EA Frameworks are TOGAF and Zachman.

Domain Specific Frameworks

As self-described, these frameworks are derived from the common EA effort, in turn referred to as domain specific. By design, they are derived with a predefined set of business conditions and concerns because they may have originated from an Enterprise Architecture team or process improvement effort. On rolling out to the industry, these frameworks are mostly driven by government agencies or other geographies.

Based on the types of industry of the EA Frameworks, the type charter is depicted as follows:

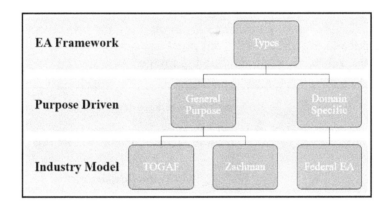

By design, the EA Framework provides a conceptual framework to explain the following:

- How the key terms are related to each other conceptually for architectural description
- The following are the number of scenarios for the enterprise architectural activities during the software life cycle:
    - Evolutionary system
    - Existing architecture
    - Architectural evaluation
- The role of the stakeholders in the creation and use of an architecture description

In this book, we will cover the foundations of two commonly known, general purpose EA Frameworks, which are as follows:

- TOGAF
- Zachman Framework

We will look into their details after the layers of Enterprise Architecture section as follows:

Architecture segregation

In 1992, Steven H. Spewak defined **Enterprise Architecture Planning (EAP)** as the process of defining architectures for the use of information in support of the business and the plan for implementing those architectures.

In highly distributed computing, a layered architecture is recommended for a simple reason--to allocate the different responsibilities of the system to the respective layers. With the same principle, Enterprise Architecture is built on the same layer design concept. It is inspired with the idea to execute the relevant processes and services of the layer and its related components. Take a look at the following image:

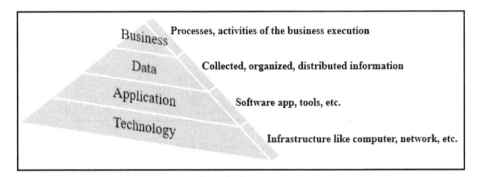

As defined in the preceding image, each layer, namely **Business**, **Data**, **Application**, and **Technology**, is designed to delegate its execution to the underlying layer. It means that the top layer, **Business**, is coarse-grained level, whereas the bottom layer, **Technology**, is a fine-grained level.

Business Architecture

Business Architecture is nothing but a blueprint of the enterprise. It helps you understand the organization and supports you to align the long-term strategic objectives and short-term tactical demands. Basically, it is the bridge between enterprise strategy and business functionality, as depicted in the following image:

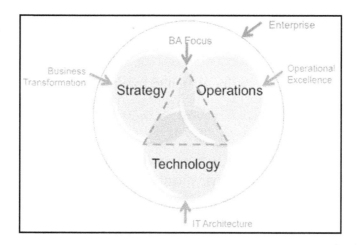

As shown in the preceding image, Business Architecture has three dimensions at its core--**Strategy**, **Operation**, and **Technology**. The success factors of a Business Architecture are directly proportional to the business transformation, using strategy, a stable platform via technology, and exhibited excellence in the business operation.

In essence, the key aspect of the represented business by Business Architecture is tabulated as follows:

S.No.	Query raised	Target delivery	Sample
1	Who?	• Stakeholders	End customers, senior managers.
2	Why?	• Strategy • Tactics	Vision, mission, objectives of the business.
3	How?	• Initiatives • Projects	Innovative development, operational excellence.
4	When?	• Events	Business critical moments.
5	What?	• Products • Services	Manufacturing output, customer facing service.
6	Where?	• Policies • Regulations	Governing body, corporate policy, company process.
7	How well?	• Metric • Measurement	Financial report, revenue trend, profit sharing.

Business Architecture is directly based on business strategy. By design, it is the foundation for subsequent architectures, where it is detailed into various aspects and disciplines of the business.

 One of the relevant Business Architecture case studies by Oracle is available at
`http://www.oracle.com/technetwork/articles/entarch/oea-case-stud`
`y-brinks-2012-1883032.pdf`.

In my view, an ideal business architect delivers the framework of services and artifacts, which enables customers to rapidly deliver quantifiable business value with realistic, technology enabled, business solutions.

Data Architecture

Data Architecture is the key contract between the business and technology in an enterprise. I experienced the value of Data Architecture during my tenure of the **Enterprise Data Hub** development initiative.

Data Architecture is designed in such a way that the real business data is handled smoothly across the layers of the enterprise architecture. It plays the key role/artifact to develop and implement governance supporting the enterprise data strategy. It collaborates/connects with the various enterprise objects, such as hardware, applications, networks, tools, technology choices, and data.

To support a variety of the commonly used enterprise applications and business improvement activities, the framework/layers of the Data Architecture is designed as follows:

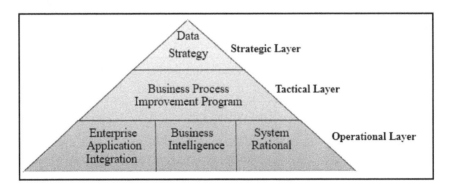

As depicted in the preceding image, Data Architecture has three layers of components based on its operational strategy, namely **Strategic, Tactical**, and **Operational**. As self-described, most of the ground-level operations are executed in the lower components-- **Enterprise Application Integration (EAI), Business Intelligence (BI)**, and **System Rationalization**. Data is tactically architecture at the middle layer using the BPI program. The top layer of Data Architecture is getting involved in the **Data Strategy** of the underlying enterprise.

Let me illustrate with a real life example to easily understand enterprise data architecture. Our business use case is to build the inventory management system of a production factory. Consider the following image:

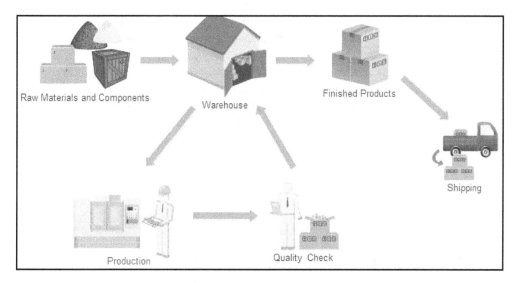

As depicted in the preceding image, the inventory management workflow is aimed towards the process of supervising and controlling stock items for the production in an efficient way. Let's get into the details of Data Architecture with this example.

In operation level, raw material information is fed into the inventory core system (**Warehouse**) in different formats/sources. EAI (tools such as Informatica) is the core component to ingest the incoming source data in a clean/expected layout. Rationalization is the process of extraction of the master data from the various systems of record of both internal and external systems. After processing, to produce the cleansed raw data using EAI and Rationalization in **Warehouse**, the BI layer takes the execution responsibilities. BI analyzes the enterprise's raw data from the various sources of the system.

Therefore, the lower operational layer of Data Architecture deals with the processing of inventory data from end to end, ranging from raw material to shipping the finished products. Thus, the operational layer cuts across the entire phase of the business.

The next tactical layer BPI is used to improve the existing business operation to accomplish significant improvement in production. In our use case, let's say the raw materials are sourced from various locations around the globe. In doing the various analysis methodologies, the BPI system can come up with an efficient way of sourcing the raw materials for the inventory. Of course, the existing raw data is essential for any prediction/analysis. Effective BPI generates promising results operational efficiency and customer focus, which in turn improves the productivity and profitability of the business.

By definition, enterprise data strategy is the comprehensive vision and actionable foundation for an organization's ability to harness data-related or data-dependent capability. To emphasize the importance of Data Strategy, let me share an interesting answer by Bill Gates of Microsoft. When he was asked a question--"What is the most important asset of your company?" he replied--"Data". In our use case, by doing Data Strategy of the inventory system, it drives the business to be a customer-centric data driven culture. In general, legacy systems produce data silos that will get in the way of understanding customers. This is a big challenge; without a Data Strategy, it is next to impossible for any inventory system. Due to the characteristic of relevancy, which is contextual to the organization, evolutionary, and expected to change on a regular basis, enterprise data strategy is essential to build the comprehensive strategies necessary to make a real difference for the organization.

Application Architecture

In general, software application is designed to meet an organizational need in reality mode. As the business model is quite common in a similar industry, it obviously expects the software application to build with the common architecture to satisfy the business requirements of an enterprise. As a result, Application Architecture is built in a generic way to create the business system, which is required to meet the specific requirements of the business.

By definition, Application Architecture specifies the leveraging technologies. Technologies are easily used to implement information systems, such as data, processes, and interfaces. On top of that, Application Architecture describes the details of the internal components and the way they interact to build the complete information system.

In terms of the engineering principle, Application Architecture exhibits the execution steps and methods in the model of the system blueprint into the reality of the leveraging enterprise.

Applications are generally categorized in the following listed types, along with their related characteristics. The categorization is based on the nature of the business process:

S.No.	Application processing type	Characteristics	Sample
1	Data	It is completely data-centric without explicit user manual intervention	• Customer store • Payroll application
2	Transaction	On the receipt of user requests, system-centric data is updated with the received information in a system database	• E-commerce application • Financial trade app
3	Event	This system is based on the receipt of the interested events from the system environment; it is not necessary to process non-interested data points	• Traffic control system • Real-time dashboard
4	Language	Users' interventions are specified in a formal language to be processed by the underlying system. It is mostly involved in system programming	• Compilers and interpreter • Command processor

Irrespective of the preceding types of application, Application Architecture is designed into the logical groupings of the software components. These logical layers help you differentiate between the different kinds of tasks performed by the components. In turn, the system is easier to support the design principle of reusability across the platform.

 Earlier, I was so confused about using the terms **Layers vs. Tier**. Now, my understanding is that layer describes the logical groupings of the functionality/components in an application. However, tier describes the physical distribution of the functionality/components on the underlying hardware systems.

Each layer can be implemented as a large scale component running on a separate server. It is the most commonly used web-based architectural model in the industry. As a common practice, six layers are designed in the Application Architecture of the industry, which are as follows:

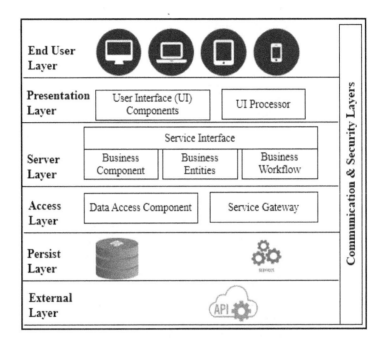

- **End User Layer**: This is an individual who uses the product after it is fully developed and marketed. This layer is around the usage pattern of the end user. As a result of rapid technology growth in recent times, the End User Layer is essential to build for desktop, web, mobile, pad, and so on.
- **Presentation Layer**: This contains the end user oriented functionality responsible for managing user interaction with the core system. In general, it consists of components that provide a common bridge between the end user and core business logic encapsulated in the business layer. Presentation Layer consists of UI components to render the user output and UI processor for local processing.
- **Server Layer**: This implements the core functionality of the target system by encapsulating the relevant business logic. In modern design, this layer consists of components, some of which may expose service interfaces that other callers can use. It is termed as the heart of the system.

- **Access Layer**: This layer is a bridge between the core business/server layer and the persisted store layer. It is designed using the best access pattern and practices of the enterprise architecture. It has two key components, namely the **Data Access Component** (**DAC**) and **Service Gateway** (**SG**). DAC allows programmers to have a uniform and comprehensive way of developing applications that can access almost any data store. The SG component encapsulates the low-level details of communicating with a service by means of service interfaces. Moreover, SG provides an ideal location to provide common features, such as asynchronous invocation, caching, and error handling.
- **Persistence Layer**: As the application data is persisted in this layer, it provides access to data hosted within the boundaries of the system and data exposed by other networked systems. By design, data is accessed through services in modern Application Architecture.
- **External Layer**: This layer is designed to expose the functionality of the application as the services to the external customer. API is the popular term in the industry, through which business services are exposed externally to earn the profit by sharing the best services.

In conclusion, Applications Architecture is the art and science of ensuring the suite of enterprise applications to create the composite architecture with the characteristics of scalability, reliability, availability, and manageability.

Technology Architecture

Technology/Infrastructure architecture principles are defined in collaboration with operational staff. It is the duty of the application architect to correct any wrong assumptions that the team might make with regard to enterprise infra architecture. Traditionally, it covers the servers, desktops, storage, network, and so on.

In the current distortive and emerging technology world, collaboration is the key for success. On connecting and cooperating with various groups, it is easy to adapt into the latest trends instead of reinventing the wheel again on our own. Technology Architecture is highly influenced by this principle.

On playing the enterprise architect role, my experience educated me to insist on a high degree of collaboration with other types of architects in the system. It is expected to have a closer working experience with a solution architect to roll out the implementation of the specific technology and platform as part of the role. In fact, architecture is not at all specifically associated with a particular release of the software. If so, then it is probably not considered architecture:

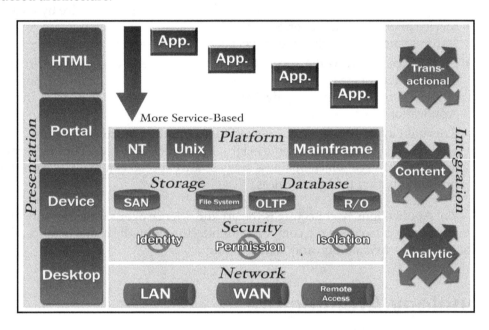

As depicted in the preceding image, Technology Architecture layers start from the **Network** layers of **LAN**, **WAN**, or **Remote Access**. On top of the **Network** layer, the **Security** principles are laid with **Identity**, **Isolation**, and **Permission** models. **Storage** layer is designed on top of **Network** and **Security** layers. **Platform** resides on top of the **Storage** layer and is the foundation for any type of software application, which reaches/touches the end customer. Take a look at the following model:

OSI Model		Examples
Application Layer Facilitates communiation between software applications like Outlook, IE	7	Web Application
Presentation Layer Data representation and encryption	6	HTTP
Session Layer Interhost communication	5	80
Transport Layer End to end connection and reliability	4	Transmission Control Protocol (TCP)
Network Layer Path determination and logical addressing	3	Internet Protocol (IP)
Data Link Layer Mac and LLC - Physical addressing	2	Ethernet
Physical Layer Media, signal and binary transmission	1	CAT5

(Data: layers 7, 6, 5 · Segments: 4 · Packets: 3 · Frames: 2 · Bits: 1)

The **Open System Interconnection (OSI)** model is an interesting area in Technology Architecture. It defines a networking framework to implement protocols in seven layers. As the lower/deep technical details, control is passed from one layer to the next, starting from the **Application Layer** to the bottom most **Physical Layer** of bits. The communication passes over the channel to the next station and back up the hierarchy.

Technology Architecture deals with these various layers and its essentials.

Introduction to TOGAF

TOGAF is one of the well-known leading Enterprise Architecture Frameworks used in the industry. As per the common goal, TOGAF is leveraged to make the enterprise for implementing and improving business efficiency. As the name stands, TOGAF insists the industry's architecture standard using the consistent methods, processes, and communication with the group of Enterprise Architecture professionals. In turn, the openness culture supports architecture practitioners to avoid the industry pain of proprietary lock mode.

Evolution of TOGAF 9.1

TOGAF's first version was developed during mid-1990s and continuously maintained by it based on experience and exposure from the *United States Department of Defense*, namely **Technical Architecture Framework for Information Management (TAFIM)**. Later, the forum started releasing successive versions based on the fundamental blocks. Consider the following image:

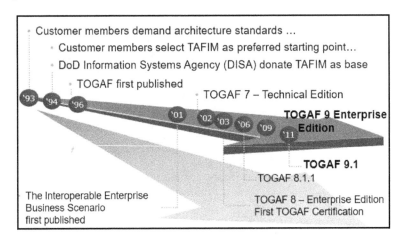

The preceding image is a view of the timeline for the growth of TOGAF until the latest version, 9.1. This illustrates the long maturation cycle.

 TOGAF 9 Technical Corrigendum 1 can be obtained from
www.opengroup.org/bookstore/catalog/u112.htm.

As TOGAF has become more mature, the time period between publications has also increased.

Core components

TOGAF's core components construct the strong fundamentals of this open architecture framework. It is depicted in the following diagram:

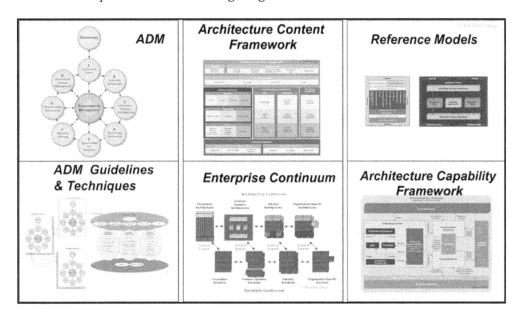

The preceding diagram shows the structure in a graphical overview format calling out the main components, which are briefed as follows:

Architecture Development Method (**ADM**) is a kind of circular flow chart aimed to building an enterprise-level architecture. It has a set of resources and the related governance to support the enterprise applications development.

The **Architecture Content Framework** uses the following three categories to describe the type of architectural work product within the context of use:

- Deliverables
- Artifacts
- Building blocks

Deliverables are the output of the project to be agreed and signed off by the enterprise stakeholders. Artifacts are represented as the content of the architectural repository of the firm. Building blocks are commonly represented as the reusable components of the enterprise platform.

As we know, architecture repository contains the enterprise designs, policies, framework, and so on. **Enterprise Continuum** is the method or mode to classify the repository content.

TOGAF 9 provides an **Architecture Capability Framework** that is a set of reference materials and guidelines to establish an architecture function or capability within an organization.

 Core components of ADM and related topics are covered in details at Open Group site. It is a great industrywide reference artifact, available at `http://pubs.opengroup.org/architecture/togaf9-doc/arch/chap05.html`

Industry usage

TOGAF is highly adopted/used in the industry. The following statistical points make them pretty clear:

- More than 150k downloads
- Individual certifications near 60k, with foundation of 18k and certified of 42k
- Around 400 corporate members of TOGAF
- Over 60k TOGAF series books shipped
- Association of enterprise architects membership at more than 75k

The continental wide usage of TOGAF is depicted in the right-hand diagram, whereas the top-10 countries is on the left-hand side:

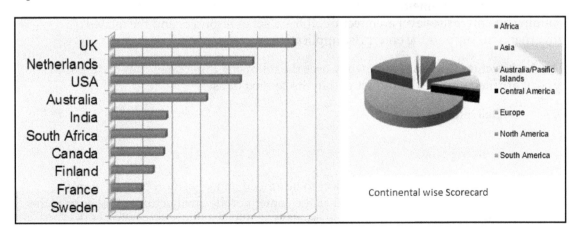

Introduction to Zachman

In the space of Enterprise Architecture, Zachman Framework is the veteran being the initial member. It was the brainchild of John Zachman during the year 1987. In the system journal of IBM, he released this technical paper in the name of--*A framework for information systems architecture.*

By design, Zachman Framework has the logical structure, which is intended to make the comprehensive illustration of an information technology enterprise. In fact, it exhibits the multiple perspectives and categorization of the business artifacts.

Evolution

In 1987, John Zachman published a different approach to the elements of system development. Instead of representing the process as a series of steps, he organized it around the points of view taken by the various players of an enterprise.

Zachman's first paper, titled--*A framework for information systems architecture* IBM Systems Journal, Volume 26, Number 3, 1987, is cited at `http://dl.acm.org/citation.cfm?id=33596.`

In the history of Enterprise Architecture evolution, the Zachman Framework is the early-bird player, as depicted in the following image:

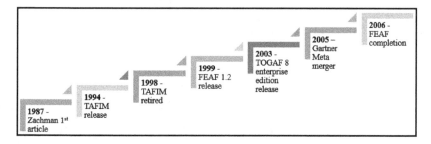

Core components

On analyzing the history, Zachman originally defined his IT taxonomy using the building domain/industry as an analogy. Interestingly, architectural artifacts are implicitly designed using a two-dimensional matrix in the building domain.

In a subsequent paper with Sowa, Zachman proposed a different strategy of six descriptive namely data, function, network, people, time, and motivation, and six player perspectives, namely planner, owner, designer, builder, subcontractor, and enterprise

 J.A. Zachman and J.F. Sowa published the subsequent version titled *Extending and Formalizing the Framework for Information Systems Architecture.* IBM Systems Journal, Volume 31, Number 3, 1992.

By design, the Zachman Framework is represented in a 6 x 6 matrix, as depicted in the next image. On noticing, the table's column represents the interrogatives of the communication channel, namely What, How, Where, Who, When, and Why. At the same time, the row represents the philosophical concepts of reification, namely scope, model, design, build, and configuration.

The details of the Zachman Framework are clearly drawn in the following diagram:

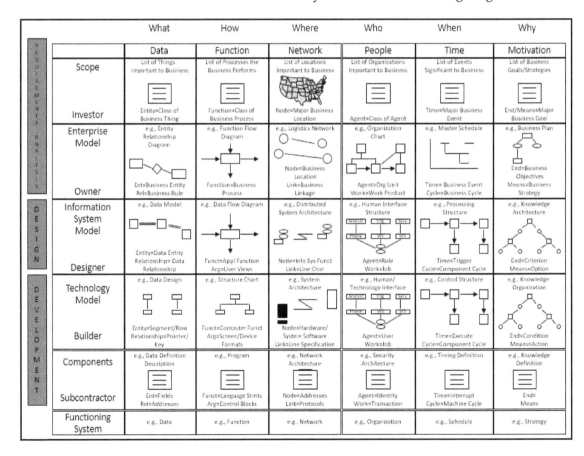

With the support of the appropriate artifacts in every cell, it is pretty much very simple to depict the sufficient amount of detail. Zachman provided the following rules to assist the reader in understanding the system of the enterprise applications. Fundamentally, it contains six major rules, which are as follows:

1. The columns have no order
2. Each column has a simple, basic model
3. The basic model of each column must be unique
4. Each row represents a distinct perspective
5. Each cell is unique
6. Combining the cells in one row forms a complete model

After 26 years at IBM, John founded Zachman International as a company dedicated to the research and advancement of the state of the art in Enterprise Architecture by his principle. It helps the industry adopt his framework in a massive way, from a scientific perspective.

Summary

As the best practice in the industry, Enterprise Architecture is expected to have the responsibility to perform strategic steps in alignment with business vision. EA has few strong fundamental blocks, namely agility, durability, efficiency, and effectiveness.

EA is the discipline of addressing business needs with people, process, and technology, with the definition of the purpose, intent, and structure of any system.

In the next chapter, we will discuss the most commonly used fundamental design patterns and practices, being It is getting used on to build Enterprise Application across the industry.

2
Principles and Patterns

In this chapter, we will take a concise, quick, and solid look into the most common and fundamental software industry patterns and practices applied to enterprise grade as well as medium-sized applications.

In this chapter we will learn about the fundamental and modern design & development principles that are essential to the quality and maintainable code for a stable and flexible application design. We will go through some of the frequently used design patterns from the *GoF* (*Gang of Four*) and look at their implementation using the .NET Core code.

The topics that we will primarily cover in this chapter include:

- SOLID design principles
- Dependency injection
- GoF design patterns

The code that we will use here will be simple, straightforward and will be used primarily to show the main idea of the pattern.

Getting started with principles and patterns

Before we directly jump into defining the principles and talk about the important and most common design patterns, let's question the basics of what designs are patterns and why we should have software development principles.

Why follow design principles?

No individual, group, or organization wants a software product whose code looks complex, hard-to-change, fragile, and nonreusable. All of us want the code to remain flexible, robust, and reusable. Therefore, we follow some of the core design principles that are eventually essential to the quality of a software product.

What are design patterns?

Design patterns are basically best practices in software engineering using **object-oriented design** (**OOD**) that describe general reusable solutions to common problems in software design within a given context. These are not the finished or final designs readily transformed into live software product but a description or a template of how to solve a given problem that can be used in many different situations. Design patterns are formalized best practices that can be used to solve common problems when designing a solution.

Why use design patterns?

Design patterns provide a way to solve problems related to software development using a proven solution. They not only make communication between designers more efficient, but they also make the code more tangible, clear, efficient, and reusable.

GoF design patterns are generally considered the foundation for all other patterns. Software professionals can immediately picture high-level design when they refer to the name of the pattern used to solve a particular problem.

SOLID design principles

SOLID design principles are a set of basic OOD design principles. These principles were first published by Robert C. Martin, popularly known as Uncle Bob. He is also a coauthor of the *Agile Manifesto*.

S.O.L.I.D stands for five primary class design principles:

- **Single Responsibility Principle** (SRP): A class should have only one reason to change, which means that a class should have only one primary job to do; an extension can be added, for example, inheritance.
- **Open Closed Principle** (OCP): A class should be designed in such a way that it is open for the extension of its behavior but is closed for modification in itself.
- **Liskov Substitution Principle** (LSP): All of the derived classes should be substitutable (replaceable) with their parent class.
- **Interface Segregation Principle** (ISP): Interfaces should be fine-grained and client-specific. Let's say that a client should never be forced to implement an interface that they don't need or use.
- **Dependency Inversion Principle** (DIP): Depend only on abstractions rather than on concretions. Abstractions should not depend on details (or implementations); instead, details should depend on the abstractions.

SRP - Single Responsibility Principle

"A class should have one, and only one, reason to change."

This primarily means that a class should have one main task, that is, a specific interface or a single responsibility to achieve. A class with one specific responsibility and objective is easier to code and maintain as it's clearer. Any further changes to the objectives should either be a separate interface that is implemented separately or a derived class, or they should be implemented in a way that the addition of behavior is added in a separate class.

SRP example - The decorator pattern

For the practical demonstration of SRP, I will provide you with a solid example using a *GoF* design pattern. The *Decorator pattern* is one of the structural design patterns that dynamically adds/overrides behavior in the existing method of an object. It allows functionality to be divided between classes with unique areas of concern, that is, single responsibility. The behavior can be added to an individual object either statically or dynamically without affecting the behavior of other objects from the same class.

Consider the following UML diagram:

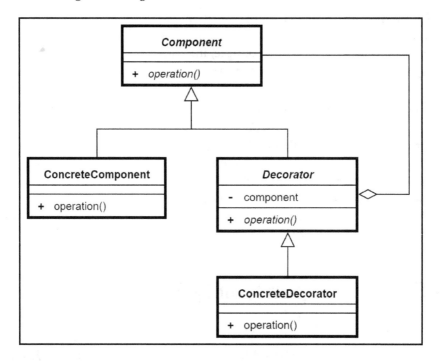

UML diagram for the Decorator pattern

The preceding figure depicts the UML diagram for the decorator pattern. I will, instead, provide the example where a decorator pattern is applied, which will help you practically understand this UML as well as the single responsibility principle by looking at the additional changes/behavior added separately instead of modifying the same class again.

In the real world, you sometimes face a scenario where you need to change the database from the SQL server to Oracle or vice versa. Let's say you have a persistence functionality written in a class and you either may change the code in the class or follow the SRP and design in a way that the new persistence functionality is handled by another class without modifying the original class. To achieve this, we follow the decorator pattern in our tiny example persistence layer:

```
using System;

namespace Chapter2.SRP.Decorator
{
  public class Student
  {
    public string Name;
```

```
    public string Id;
    public DateTime DOB;

}
}
```

Let's say we have a simple `Student` entity class, which we want to persist in various forms, for example, to XML, JSON, or DB. Here are the basic classes defined to setup the decorator:

```
public interface IPersistor<T>
{
    bool Persist(T objToPersist);
}

public class DefaultPersistor<T> : IPersistor<T>
{
    public bool Persist(T objToPersist)
    {
      Trace.WriteLine("DefaultPersistor.Persist gets called");

      return true; //Do nothing, eat up.
    }
}
```

In the following code, you see a simple implementation for the `XMLPersistorDecorator` class, and `OraclePersistorDecorator` and `SQLPersistorDecorator` follow the same pattern:

```
namespace Chapter2.SRP.Decorator
{
    public class XMLPersistorDecorator<T> : PersistorDecorator<T>
    {
        public XMLPersistorDecorator(IPersistor<T>
        objectToBeDecorated) : base(objectToBeDecorated)
          { }

        public override bool Persist(T objToPersist)
        {
            //stacking up functionality of the decorator pattern -
            which basically ensures that main functionality is
            achieved and this decorator adds up new functionality.

            if (base.Persist(objToPersist))
            return DoXMLPersistence();
            return false;
        }

        private bool DoXMLPersistence()
```

```
        {
            //Does XML conversion and persistence operation..

            Trace.WriteLine("DoXMLPersistence gets called");

            return true;
        }
    }
}
```

Now you see the case where the decorator pattern is applied, satisfying the single responsibility principle:

```
[Fact]
    public void Test_SRP_Decorator()
    {
        var student = GetFakeStudent();

        IPersistor<Student> studentPersistence = new
            OraclePersistorDecorator<Student>(new
            XMLPersistorDecorator<Student>(new
                DefaultPersistor<Student>()));

        Assert.True(studentPersistence.Persist(student));
    }
```

From this code, you can see how changes to the functionality are achieved by various classes instead of by modifying the single class with multiple responsibilities. The preceding sample code is basically persisting to all persistence layers.

OCP - Open Closed Principle

"Classes should be open for extension but closed for modification."

This principle simply means that a class should not allow modification in its code due to a change in functionality. It should only allow you to extend the functionality in some form, for example, by inheritance.

Once again, this principle is satisfied in our decorator example, where our persistence decorator (derived) classes implement the abstract base class to extend (and add up) the functionality instead of modifying the existing class.

LSP - Liskov Substitution Principle

"Functions that use pointers or references to base classes must be able to use objects of derived classes without knowing it."

This means that all of the derived classes should retain the existing behavior of the base class as expected by the client while extending the functionality as fulfilled by the parent class. This also means that the client code that consumes a specific class or interface should be able to use a derived class or a different implementation of the interface without affecting or having to change its internal behavior, which ultimately minimizes the impact on the consumer code as a result of a change added by the derived class.

Let's demonstrate this principle with an example. We create the interface for settings when we have different types of settings, such as `UserSettings`, `MachineSettings`, and `ReadOnlySettings`. Settings would be required to be loaded and saved. We will first show the example violating the LSP and then do the correction and adhere to the LSP. Let's have our simple setting interface:

```
public interface ISettings
{
    void Load();
    void Save();
}
```

Let's have our sample classes implementing the `ISettings` interface:

```
public class UserSettings : ISettings
{
    public void Load()
    {
        //Loads the user settings
    }

    public void Save()
    {
        //Saves the user settings
    }
}
public class MachineSettings : ISettings
{
    public void Load()
    {
        //Loads the machine settings
    }

    public void Save()
```

```
        {
            //Saves the machine settings
        }
    }
    /// <summary>
    /// Says this class holds readonly or constant settings /
    configuration parameters to the software
    /// </summary>
    public class ReadOnlySettings : ISettings
    {
        public void Load()
        {
            //Loads some readonly/constant settings
        }

        public void Save()
        {
            throw new NotImplementedException();
        }
    }
```

Now let's look at a sample client code making use of these settings classes and realize how it breaks the principle:

```
[Fact]
    public void Test_Client_Violating()
    {
        List<ISettings> allSettings = new List<ISettings>();

        ISettings setting = new LSP.Bad.UserSettings();
        allSettings.Add(setting);

        setting = new LSP.Bad.MachineSettings();
        allSettings.Add(setting);

        setting = new LSP.Bad.ReadOnlySettings();
        allSettings.Add(setting);

        //Load all types of settings
        allSettings.ForEach(s => s.Load());

        //Do some changes to settings objects..

        //Following line fails because client (actually)
        does not know it has to catch
        allSettings.ForEach(s => s.Save());
    }
```

The last line in this code fails because the client code does not expect to catch (and possibly ignore) the exception. Otherwise, it has to put a specific case to work to detect whether the class is ReadOnlySettings; then, it does not call its Save() method, which is clearly a very bad practice.

Now let's look at how to solve this problem and adhere to the Liskov Substitution Principle:

```
public interface IReadableSettings
{
    void Load();
}
public interface IWriteableSettings
{
    void Save();
}
public interface ReadOnlySetting : IReadableSettings
{
    public void Load()
    {
        //Loads the machine settings
    }
}
```

Here, you can see that we have divided the interfaces according to their correct purpose or need and then implemented the ReadOnlySettings class using only the required interface, that is, IReadableSettings.

What we did here is basically segregate the interfaces.

Let's now take a look at the sample client code using the various types of settings classes:

```
[Fact]
    public void Test_Client_NonViolating()
    {
        var allLoadableSettings = new List<IReadableSettings>();
        var allSaveableSettings = new List<IWriteableSettings>();

        var userSettings = new LSP.Good.UserSettings();
        allLoadableSettings.Add(userSettings);
        allSaveableSettings.Add(userSettings);

        var machineSettings = new LSP.Good.MachineSettings();
        allLoadableSettings.Add(machineSettings);
        allSaveableSettings.Add(machineSettings);

        var readOnlySettings = new LSP.Good.ReadOnlySettings();
        allLoadableSettings.Add(readOnlySettings);
```

```
//allSaveableSettings.Add(readOnlySettings); Cannot
  compile this line;
readOnlySettings is not save-able/writable settings

//Load all types of settings
allLoadableSettings.ForEach(s => s.Load());

//Do some changes to settings objects..

allSaveableSettings.ForEach(s => s.Save()); //Now this
line clearly does not fail :)
    }
```

From the preceding code, it's evident that loading and saving setting interfaces are segregated cleanly according to their responsibilities and the code works as expected by the client.

From this example, you can understand how a neatly designed code follows the fundamental OOD principles and how closely related these SOLID principles are in the sense that usually, when trying to adhere to one SOLID principle, you automatically follow one or more of the other principles. Once a mature programmer starts following SOLID principles, he/she does not need to remember them--over a period of time, it becomes part of their nature or a good coding habit.

ISP - Interface Segregation Principle

"Interfaces should be fine-grained and client-specific."

In other words, this means that if the class has various use cases, then it should have a specific interface for each of its use cases.

Once again, our preceding example in LSP shows how the interface segregation principle is achieved by splitting the ISettings interface into two separate interfaces-- IReadableSettings and IWriteableSettings.

DIP - Dependency Inversion Principle

Depend only on abstractions rather than on concretions.

Dependency Inversion Principle is the last principle of SOLID design principles. Here, I quote directly from the source (Uncle Bob), as it is beautifully written:

- *High-level modules should not depend on low-level modules. Both should depend on abstractions.*
- *Abstractions should not depend on details. Details should depend on abstractions.*

Basically, this means that your code should never depend on the implementation, but it should only depend on the interfaces (or abstract classes).

This will enable you to change or replace any implementation with just another implementation, and none of the client code needs to change or worry about it since it only depends on the interfaces.

Here, I first give you a bad example that violates the DIP:

```
public class OrderProcessor : IOrderProcessor
{
    public void Process(IOrder order)
    {
        //Perform validations..
        if (new OrderRepository().Save(order))
          new OrderNotifier().Notify(order);
    }
}
```

This is bad example because the OrderProcessor class depends upon the actual implementation of OrderRepository and OrderNotifier. The client code will need to change if, say, we need to have a different repository persistence layer tomorrow or we need a different notification mechanism than SMS or e-mail.

Now we provide you with the good example by correcting the bad one:

```
public class OrderProcessor : IOrderProcessor
{
    private readonly IOrderRepository _orderRepository;
    private readonly IOrderNotifier _orderNotifier;

    public OrderProcessor(IOrderRepository orderRepository,
      IOrderNotifier orderNotifier)
    {
```

```
        _orderRepository = orderRepository;
        _orderNotifier = orderNotifier;
    }

    public void Process(IOrder order)
    {
        //Perform validations..
        if (_orderRepository.Save(order))
            _orderNotifier.Notify(order);
    }
}
```

With these changes, our `OrderProcessor` class does not have dependencies on the actual implementations anymore; instead, it only relies on the interfaces--`IOrderRepository` and `IOrderNotifier`. Now if we want to change the way notifications are sent, we will need to have a new implementation of `IOrderNotifier` and pass that implementation to `OrderProcessor` without any code changes to the `OrderProcessor` class.

Dependency injection

In modern coding patterns, factory level containers that help assemble components eventually into a cohesive application have become very important. Beneath such type of containers, there is a common pattern which defines how to perform the wiring of different components together and is known as **Inversion of Control** (**IoC**). The pattern coming out of it is more specifically known as Dependency Injection.

Introducing dependency injection

Dependency Injection design pattern fulfills the dependency inversion principle of the SOLID design principles. There are three main forms of dependency injection:

- **Constructor injection**: An example of this is shown in the *DIP* section
- **Setter injection**: Let's look at an example code for setter injection:

```
public class OrderProcessorWithSetter : IOrderProcessor
{
    private IOrderRepository _orderRepository;
    private IOrderNotifier _orderNotifier;

    public IOrderRepository Repository
    {
        get { return _orderRepository; }
```

```
        set { _orderRepository = value; }
    }

    public IOrderNotifier Notifier
    {
        get { return _orderNotifier; }
        set { _orderNotifier = value; }
    }

    public void Process(IOrder order)
    {
        //Perform validations..
        if (_orderRepository.Save(order))
            _orderNotifier.Notify(order);
    }
}
```

Now we look at an example client code using the setter injection:

```
[Fact]
    public void Test_DI_With_Setter()
    {
        var someOrder = new DIP.Order();
        var op = new DIP.Good.OrderProcessorWithSetter();
        op.Repository = new DIP.OrderRepository();
        op.Notifier = new DIP.OrderNotifier();

        op.Process(someOrder);
    }
```

- **Interface injection**: Let's take a look at an example code for interface injection. The following are the two interfaces that will be used for our sample injection:

```
public interface InjectOrderRepository
{
    void SetRepository(IOrderRepository orderRepository);
}
public interface InjectOrderNotifier
{
    void SetNotifier(IOrderNotifier orderNotifier);
}
```

And here is the `OrderProcessorWithInterface` class that implements the interfaces that are used for injection (usually via a DI framework):

```
public class OrderProcessorWithInterface : InjectOrderRepository,
InjectOrderNotifier, IOrderProcessor
{
    private IOrderRepository _orderRepository;
    private IOrderNotifier _orderNotifier;

    public void SetRepository(IOrderRepository orderRepository)
    {
        _orderRepository = orderRepository;
    }

    public void SetNotifier(IOrderNotifier orderNotifier)
    {
        _orderNotifier = orderNotifier;
    }

    public void Process(IOrder order)
    {
        //Perform validations..
        if (_orderRepository.Save(order))
            _orderNotifier.Notify(order);
    }
}
```

Let's have a look at the client code that uses the simple example of interface injection:

```
[Fact]
    public void Test_DI_With_Interface()
    {
        var someOrder = new DIP.Order();

        var op = new DIP.Good.OrderProcessorWithInterface();
        //Creation of objects and their respective dependencies
        (components/services inside) are usually done by the
        DI Framework
        op.SetRepository(new DIP.OrderRepository());
        op.SetNotifier(new DIP.OrderNotifier());

        op.Process(someOrder);
    }
```

Knowing about the Service Locator pattern

Injection isn't the only way to loosen the components/service dependencies. Another way is to use the service locator.

Basically, a service locator is a sort of a registry object (a factory) that knows how to create the services or components that an application might need. For obvious reasons, this primarily shifts the burden of object creation from an individual class to the factory and we still have to get the locator object inside the classes using it, which results in the dependency of the locator itself.

We can also have more than one type of service locator inside an application. For example, `FakeServiceLocator`, whose purpose is just to provide the fakes that can be tested in the testing framework.

Your service locator can internally use the *abstract factory* pattern or the *builder* pattern, as appropriate. It can also be a static or dynamic service locator, where in the dynamic service locator, it may keep the object with string keys, for example, by maintaining the objects in `Hashmaps`.

A simple code for the dynamic service locator implemented as a singleton factory catalog would be as follows inside `OrderProcessor`:

```
IOrderRepository repository = (IOrderRepository)
serviceLocator.Instance.getService("OrderRepository");
```

More conceptual information on dependency resolutions
There are discussions separately on service locator that it does not completely follows SOLID design principles and good OO practices, but we leave that discussion out of this book.
For more information on dependency resolution, refer to *Inversion of Control Containers and the Dependency Injection pattern* on Martin Fowler's website `https://martinfowler.com/articles/injection.html`.

Dependency injection support with .NET Core

Microsoft has now supplied support for dependency injection directly with .NET Core in the form of extensions with the `Microsoft.Extensions.DependencyInjection` NuGet package. The support for DI in .NET Core is in a way that you can either use the provided DI implementation, or you can use given DI interfaces in `Microsoft.Extensions.DependencyInjection.Abstractions` and use it with the DI framework implementation of your choice, for example, **Ninject**.

Just to give you an idea of the .NET Core direction, a similar behavior or style is also designed with a logging framework in .NET Core using the `Microsoft.Extensions.Logging.Abstractions` package.

Let's look at an example to see the Microsoft DI in motion with .NET Core.

The sample code needs to call an airport interface in order to get the list of arrival flights, and it also needs to do the logging in between; so both of these dependencies need to be injected. Consider the following code:

```
public class ScheduleWorker
{
    private IServiceProvider _provider;
    private ILogger _logger;

    public ScheduleWorker(IServiceProvider provider,
    ILogger logger)
    {
        _provider = provider;
        _logger = logger;
    }

    public void ExecuteSchedules()
    {
        _logger.LogInformation("Executing schedules at {UTCTime}",
          DateTime.UtcNow);

        IAirportFlightSchedules airportFlightSchedules =
          _provider.GetRequiredService<IAirportFlightSchedules>();

        _logger.LogInformation("Getting schedules..");
        var arrivalSchedules = airportFlightSchedules.
          GetDailyArrivalSchedules(DateTime.UtcNow.Date);

        _logger.LogInformation("{FlightCount} schedules found",
          arrivalSchedules.Count);
    }
}
```

From the preceding code, you can see that the dependencies are injected via the constructor. Moreover, another business interface object is retrieved via `IServiceProvider` DI supplied interface, which shows the way that's similar to service locator pattern. Consider the following code:

```
public class AirportFlightSchedules : IAirportFlightSchedules
{
    private ILogger _logger;

    public AirportFlightSchedules(ILogger logger)
    {
        _logger = logger;
    }

    public IList<string> GetDailyArrivalSchedules(DateTime date)
    {
```

From this preceding code, you can see that even `AirportFlightSchedules` needs the logger dependency to be injected.

Let's take a look at how the DI container was configured in order to insert interfaces:

```
public class DICTests
{
    private static IServiceProvider Provider { get; set; }

    [Fact]
    public void Test_Simple_DIC()
    {
        RegisterServices();
        ExecuteScedule();
    }

    private void RegisterServices(bool bUseFactory = false)
    {
        IServiceCollection services = new ServiceCollection();

        //Adding required dependencies to the DI Container
        //Note: DebugLogger only available when Debugger
          is attached
        services.AddTransient<ILogger, DebugLogger>(provider =>
          new DebugLogger(typeof(DICTests).FullName));
        services.AddTransient<IAirportFlightSchedules,
          AirportFlightSchedules>();
        services.AddSingleton(typeof(ScheduleWorker));

        if(bUseFactory) ConfigureServices(services);
```

```
                Provider = services.BuildServiceProvider();
        }
```

Notice that the DI container even allows you the capability to turn a normal class into a singleton very easily so that the same instance/object is given back to the client/consumer who needs its interface. Please ignore `bUseFactory` we see it next as it is used to control the injection of an **abstract factory** class.

Our client code looks so simple and neat:

```
        private void ExecuteScedule()
        {
            var scheduleWorker =
                Provider.GetRequiredService<ScheduleWorker>();
            scheduleWorker.ExecuteSchedules();
        }
```

Upon this call, all the dependencies are automatically injected into the `scheduleWorker` object as well as all the dependent object's hierarchy in the usage.

Now let's come to the Abstract Factory injection part, why would we need it? There could be some situations where we would need to create objects via the relevant abstract factory object and also some logic may need to be performed when creating new object(s) via such a factory in each call to the factory. In such situations, instead of binding the abstract factory class directly with the client code, we can better use the DI to inject our desired abstract factory class and the client retrieves the factory interface from the DI to create the objects it needs. This does not only decouple the factory object from the client but also gives the capability to inject the different abstract factory for a different configuration; a fake factory for instance.

I will provide you with another example, adding to this DI sample code in order to show the factory method pattern in its own section more clearly. Here, you will see how the factory class is inserted and configured as a singleton and used in a client code to create the specific object for the given interface. Let's take a look at the following code:

```
        private void ConfigureServices(IServiceCollection
          serviceCollection)
        {
            serviceCollection.AddSingleton<IAirportFlightSchedulesFactory,
              AirportFlightSchedulesFactory>();
        }

        [Fact]
            public void Test_Simple_DIC_WithFactory()
            {
                RegisterServices(true);
```

```
        ExecuteSceduleWithFactory();
    }

    private void ExecuteSceduleWithFactory()
    {
        var scheduleWorker = Provider.
          GetRequiredService<ScheduleWorker>();
        scheduleWorker.ExecuteSchedulesUsingFactoryViaDI();
    }
```

Look at the client code using the factory to create the required objects based on the
IAirportFlightSchedules interface:

```
public void ExecuteSchedulesUsingFactoryViaDI()
{
    _logger.LogInformation("Executing schedules at {UTCTime}",
      DateTime.UtcNow);

    var factory = _provider.GetRequiredService
      <IAirportFlightSchedulesFactory>();
    IAirportFlightSchedules airportFlightSchedules =
      factory.CreateAirportFlightSchedules();

    _logger.LogInformation("Getting schedules..");
    var arrivalSchedules =
      airportFlightSchedules.GetDailyArrivalSchedules(
        DateTime.UtcNow.Date);

    _logger.LogInformation("{FlightCount} schedules found",
      arrivalSchedules.Count);
```

That's enough about dependency injection, and I hope you learned and enjoyed it just like I
did. Let's jump onto lots of other design patterns.

GoF design patterns

*A software design pattern is a general reusable solution to a commonly occurring problem
within a given context in software design. It is not a finished design that can be
transformed directly into the source or machine code. It is a description or a template for
how to solve a problem that can be used in many different situations. Design patterns are
formalized best practices that the programmer can use in order to solve common problems
when designing an application or a system.*

What are software design patterns?

Design patterns were formally introduced in the book *Design Patterns: Elements of Reusable Object-Oriented Software*, first published in 1994 by the four authors Erich Gamma, Richard Helm, Ralph Johnson, and John Vlissides, with a foreword by Grady Booch. These authors are usually referred to as the *Gang of Four*. The book contains the most popular 23 design patterns; hence, the 23 patterns are known as *GoF* design patterns. These design patterns are fundamentally the crux of **object-oriented analysis and design** (**OOAD**).

Here, we will cover some of the most commonly used *GoF* design patterns and look at their implementation in C# using the latest version of .NET Core.

23 *GoF* design patterns are divided into three main categories. I will write the names and a one-liner explanation about them and after that, I will go into detail about the selected ones:

Creational patterns		
These design patterns deal with object creational mechanisms in a suitable manner under a given situation		
1	Abstract factory	Provides an interface that can create families of related classes
2	Builder	Separates complex object construction from its representation
3	Factory method	An interface used to create an object without specifying the exact class to be created
4	Prototype	Creates fully initialized objects by copying or cloning an existing object
5	Singleton	A class whose only a single instance can exist

Structural Patterns

These design patterns are the best practice used to identify a simple way to realize relationships between entities in a given situation

6	Adapter	Converts the interface of a class into another interface client except by wrapping it's own interface around that of an already existing class
7	Bridge	Separates an object's interface from its implementation so that the two can vary independently
8	Composite	Composes zero or more similar objects in a tree structure so that they can be manipulated as one object to represent part or whole hierarchies
9	Decorator	Dynamically adds/overrides behavior in an existing object
10	Facade	Provides a unified interface to a set of interfaces in a subsystem
11	Flyweight	Efficient sharing of a large number of similar objects
12	Proxy	An object acting as a placeholder for another object to control access to it and reduce complexity

Behavioral patterns

They identify common communication patterns between objects and increase the flexibility in carrying out the communication between them

13	Chain of responsibility	Decouples the request sender from the request receiver by chaining more than one receiver object in a way that if one receiver object does not handle the request, it passes on to the next until the request has been handled
14	Command	Encapsulates a request/action/event along with parameter as an object
15	Interpreter	Specifies a way to interpret/evaluate sentences in a given language
16	Iterator	Sequentially accesses the elements present in an aggregate object without exposing its underlying representation/Structure
17	Mediator	Promotes loose coupling by encapsulating (and often centralizing) the communication/interaction between various objects
18	Memento	Provides the capability to snapshot the object's internal state in order to restore to this state later
19	Observer	An observable object sends events to many observing objects; sort of defines a one-to-many dependency between objects
20	State	Allows the changes in the object's behavior based on the change in its state

We just gave an almost single line definition for all 23 *GoF* design patterns. Some of them would be obvious to understand, while others might be difficult, if not confusing. So when we get into the details of certain patterns, their intent, design, and reference implementation should be clearer.

We have already covered the decorator pattern as an example of SRP earlier. In the remainder of the chapter, we will cover the following design patterns:

Four creational design patterns are as follows:

- Singleton
- Factory method
- Abstract factory
- Builder

Three structural design patterns are as follows:

- Adapter
- Bridge
- Flyweight

Six behavioral design patterns are as follows:

- The template method
- Observer
- Chain of responsibility
- Visitor
- Strategy
- State

Creational patterns

Creational design patterns are those software design patterns that deal with the mechanism of object creation in a flexible, maintainable manner under certain situations or scenarios.

Let's jump on to the individual creational pattern to see its detail.

The singleton pattern

The singleton pattern is perhaps the most common pattern used by developers across the globe. This pattern basically defines a class for which only one (single) instance can exist.

You can have a class that is either global or static with all static methods so that you do not need to create any instance of this class and use it directly. This is okay but not considered a best practice generally, unless you are defining a stateless interface to expose an underlying OS APIs, such as subset `win32` APIs or a native DLL or system library exposing its one-off APIs.

Singleton - If you want to have a stateful class whose only one instance should exist in the given software, then what you need is a singleton class. An example of this class can be a configuration class, which is accessed by many other client classes from within the application layer.

Moreover, some of the other design patterns can themselves be singletons in their implementation, for example, factory, builder, and prototype patterns. The façade pattern can also be implemented as a singleton since in most of the cases, only one façade object is required to be created. You will understand more when we read more about these other patterns as we move further in this chapter.

The following code shows a simple implementation of a singleton pattern:

```
/// <summary>
/// A very simple Singleton class
/// Its a sealed class just to prevent derivation that
could potentially add instances
/// </summary>
public sealed class SimpleSingleton
{
    /// <summary>
    /// Privately hidden app wide single static
      instance - self managed
    /// </summary>
    private static readonly SimpleSingleton instance = new
      SimpleSingleton();

    /// <summary>
    /// Private constructor to hinder clients to create
    the objects of <see cref="SimpleSingleton"/>
    /// </summary>
    private SimpleSingleton() { }

    /// <summary>
    /// Publicly accessible method to supply the only
```

```
    instace of <see cref="SimpleSingleton"/>
    /// </summary>
    /// <returns></returns>
    public static SimpleSingleton getInstance()
    {
        return instance;
    }
}
```

Variations on the singleton pattern

There are some commonly used variations of the singleton pattern that are applicable based on the given situation. Out of these, the most common ones are *lazy initialization* and the *double check locking* pattern.

Lazy initialization singleton basically creates its one and only instance upon its first call to get an instance instead of pre-creating it. Refer to the following simple code sample:

```
public sealed class LazySingleton
{
    private static LazySingleton instance = null;
    private LazySingleton() { }

    public static LazySingleton getInstance()
    {
        if (instance == null) instance = new LazySingleton();
        return instance;
    }
}
```

The *double check locking* pattern is basically a thread-safe singleton pattern in a multithreaded environment. It ensures that only one instance is created if two or more threads ask for a singleton instance at the same time using the simple synchronization technique. Refer to the following simple code sample for a better understanding:

```
public sealed class DCLockingSingleton
{
    /// <summary>
    /// volatile tells the compiler not to optimze this
    field and a field might be modified by multiple threads
    /// </summary>
    private static volatile DCLockingSingleton instance = null;

    /// <summary>
    /// Single object instance is used to lock all the
    accesses to get the instance of the Singleton
```

```
/// </summary>
private static object syncRoot = new Object();

private DCLockingSingleton() { }

/// <summary>
/// Exposed as a Get only property instead of a method
/// </summary>
public static DCLockingSingleton Instance
{
    get
    {
        if (instance == null)
        {
            lock (syncRoot)
            {
                if (instance == null)
                    instance = new DCLockingSingleton();
            }
        }

        return instance;
    }
}
```

The factory method pattern

The factory method pattern basically specifies the interface to create an object without specifying its exact class. This pattern primarily focuses on creating only one type of object specified by the interface for the object to be created.

For example, in our application, we want to use a weather service to get the current weather of a given city. What we need is a reference to the weather service object, and what the factory method abstracts out is that we need a weather service reference without knowing where this actual object reference is coming from. For example, it can be from Yahoo weather, AccuWeather, or even a fake weather service object that can be used for testing.

In the section for .NET Core dependency injection, we used the IAirportFlightSchedulesFactory factory class, which creates the objects of the IAirportFlightSchedules interface, which the client code uses to get the list of all arrival flights.

Now let's say that we want to get a list of all arrival flights from Geneva airport. What we will do is use the `GenevaAirportFlightSchedulesFactory` class that implements the same interface `IAirportFlightSchedulesFactory` and creates the objects of type `GenevaAirportFlightSchedules`, which implements the same interface, `IAirportFlightSchedules`. Let's take a quick look at the code for this new Geneva factory:

```
public class GenevaAirportFlightSchedulesFactory :
IAirportFlightSchedulesFactory
{
    private ILogger _logger;

    public GenevaAirportFlightSchedulesFactory(ILogger logger)
    {
        _logger = logger;
    }

    public IAirportFlightSchedules CreateAirportFlightSchedules()
    {
        return new GenevaAirportFlightSchedules(_logger);
    }
}
```

Say, if we need flight schedules for a different airport, all we need to do is use the different factory to get the right service object, and in this way, no change is required in the client code at all.

Abstract factory pattern

Abstract factory gives you the ability to create a number of related classes. It provides an interface that encapsulates the capability to create a group of classes that are related in some way.

You are already aware of the factory method pattern. In other words, an abstract factory is an interface that groups together related factory methods.

For example, KTM bikes creates various types of bikes using a number of various factory methods, whereas the abstract factory for KTM brings all these factory methods together and gives you a generic interface so that you can similarly implement an Aprilia bikes abstract factory, and so on.

Let's take a look at the following UML diagram for the abstract factory pattern for our understanding:

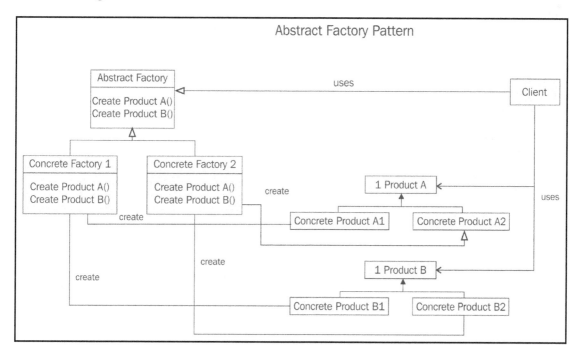

Now let's look at a simple abstract factory pattern example in the code. Here, let's say we want to create a simple application with a user interface. The user interface includes graphical components menu, status bar, and a wizard screen interface.

While these components would be better if created by their own factory methods, for simplicity, we club them altogether in one abstract factory interface, IUIAbsFactory:

```
public interface IUIAbsFactory
{
    IMenu GetMenu();
    IWizard CreateWizard();
    IStatusBar CreateStatusBar();
}
```

You can see that menu, screens, wizards, and status bar are UI components related to each other for a specific app. Based on this abstract factory interface, we can have, for example, DarkUIAbsFactory and LightUIAbsFactory concrete factory classes. We will take a look at the concrete factory implementation in a later section again, where we'll enhance our design further by utilizing the template method pattern.

Builder pattern

The Builder pattern is used in situations where the creation of a complex object is required, and the creation is generally achieved through a number of steps until the final product is ready.

A classic example is that of a car as a final product, which is created in steps by adding the engine, chassis, body, tires, and so on. The main client asks for the product and receives the final product with all the creation steps hidden from it. This is achieved via a Director class.

The basic builder pattern involves a **Director**, **Builder**, and **Product** class, as shown in the following diagram:

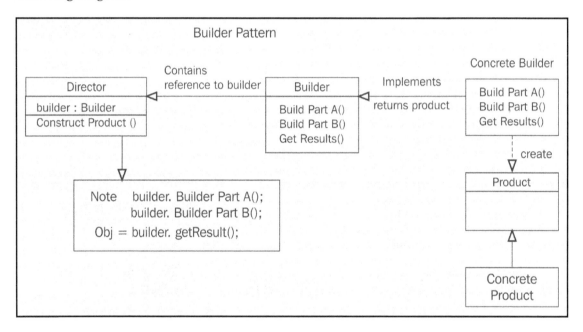

Let's look at an example in the code. We will build up our previous example of a sample GUI app that added the menu, status bar, and wizard screen.

Remember, we had the abstract factory pattern applied in order to build our UI controls, and one of the methods of this factory class was `CreateWizard()`. For the example, we suppose that creating the wizard means adding a couple of screens to create one flow of a wizard operation common in some types of user applications. Therefore, creating a wizard is achieved through a number of steps internally by the `CreateWizard()` method, and these steps are essentially the builder pattern, that is, to simplify the creation of a complex product.

Let's take a look at the interface of our builder class:

```
public interface IWizardBuilder
{
    void CreateWizardSteps(int screenSteps);
    void AddFrontScreen();
    void AddFinalScreen();

    IWizard GetResult();
}
```

The code that uses the builder object to create the product in correct steps is basically done by Director according to the builder pattern, which in our example is the code inside the `CreateWizard()` method of the abstract factory:

```
/// <summary>
/// Internal code demonstrates the use of Builder pattern
/// </summary>
/// <returns></returns>
public IWizard CreateWizard()
{
    //Director code for builder pattern
    var wizardBuilder =
      _provider.GetRequiredService<IWizardBuilder>();

    wizardBuilder.CreateWizardSteps(4);
    wizardBuilder.AddFrontScreen();
    wizardBuilder.AddFinalScreen();

    var wizard = wizardBuilder.GetResult();

    ApplyThemeOnWizard(wizard);

    return wizard;
}
```

Note that the following line is retrieving the correct build object using the DI container:

```
var wizardBuilder =
  _provider.GetRequiredService<IWizardBuilder>();
```

You do not need to go into its detail; this DI container is explained in the *Dependency injection support with .NET Core* section within this chapter.

From the preceding code, you can see how the `wizard` in our example application is actually created in steps using the builder pattern.

A commentary on creational patterns

Sometimes, some creational patterns overlap each other, while other times, they compliment each other. For example, an abstract factory is commonly implemented as a singleton pattern itself so as to have a single instance of the abstract factory object. Abstract factory can store the prototypes from which it can return the newly created cloned objects. Abstract factories are often implemented as a number of factory methods (which is what I prefer as well) that promote creation through inheritance and give you dual flexibility with both abstract factory and factory method at the same time. Some abstract factories can also be implemented using the prototype pattern internally that promotes creation through delegation, as prototypes would be contained inside the abstract factory or otherwise implemented as singleton.

Structural patterns

These design patterns are best practices to identify a simple way to realize relationships between entities and their structure in a given situation.

Let's jump on to our selective structural patterns individually to look at their detail.

Adapter pattern

The adapter pattern, as the name suggests, is the pattern for a class that adapts the interface of another considerably complicated or inconsistent class. It's basically just a wrapper class. It wraps the interface of another class to an interface that is simpler, consistent to the software design, and is what the client is expecting.

The following diagram shows the adapter pattern in general and the one used for our example:

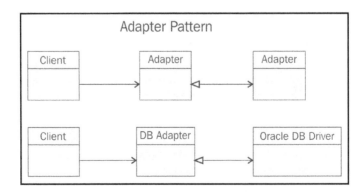

It is one of the simplest *GoF* design patterns with the purpose of simplifying the interface.

In the example scenario, we have an Oracle database hypothetical DB driver class with a complex and inconsistent API interface in contrast to our own application design. Therefore, in order to simplify things and make them uniform to use in our application, we define our adapter interface, which our client code will use to access the actual database objects without knowing the details of how to use Oracle DB driver.

Let's take a look at our imaginary code. The following is our hypothetical and not-so-simple OracleDBDriver interface:

```
public interface OracleDBDriver
{
    bool Initialize(string parameters);

    IOracleDBConnection CreateNewConnection();
    IOracleDBConnection CreateNewPooledConnection();

    bool ValidateSQL(string validSQL);

    SomeDBFormat ExecuteSQL(IOracleDBConnection dbCon,
        string validSQL);
    int ExecuteScalarSQL(IOracleDBConnection dbCon, string
        validSQL);
}
```

To simply the interface of OracleDBDriver, we write our simplified adapter, as shown here:

```
public class DBAdapter
{
    private OracleDBDriver dbDriver = null;
    private bool bDBInitialized;
    private readonly string initializationDBParameters;

    public DBAdapter()
    {
        //dbDriver = new OracleDBDriverImpl();
        initializationDBParameters = "XYZ, ABC";
    }

    public DataTable ExecuteSQL(string strSQL)
    {
        if (string.IsNullOrWhiteSpace(strSQL)) throw new
         InvalidSQLException();

        if (!bDBInitialized) bDBInitialized =
```

```
            dbDriver.Initialize(initializationDBParameters);

            if(!dbDriver.ValidateSQL(strSQL)) throw new
                InvalidSQLException();

            var dbConnection = dbDriver.CreateNewPooledConnection();

            SomeDBFormat dbData = dbDriver.ExecuteSQL(dbConnection,
                strSQL);

            return TransformDBDataType(dbData);
        }

        private DataTable TransformDBDataType(SomeDBFormat dbData)
        {
            DataTable dbTable = null;

            //dbTable = dbData; do some conversions

            return dbTable;
        }
    }
}
```

From the preceding code, you can easily see how our adapter class is hiding the complexity of database driver initialization and connection pooling logic as well as transforming the db format into a simplified one, as desired.

Bridge pattern

The purpose of the bridge pattern is to create a separation between an interface that the client uses from the actual implementation. This will allow the client's interface (abstraction) to vary independently from the actual implementation. The bridge primarily uses aggregation to separate the responsibilities exposed by the interfaces.

Let's say we have a simple interface that provides the capability to perform an addition operation. We create a new interface and expose it to the client that also provides the multiply operation. And we implement the new interface by aggregating the object of the existing interface in a way that we call our actual implementation logic by calling the addition operation a number of times to achieve the correct result of the multiply operation.

The following diagram shows the general diagram for the bridge pattern as well as the diagram to show another near real-world example:

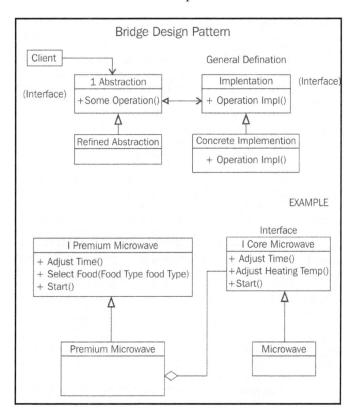

Our example in the code talks about the core microwave implementation that works very well, but then we add a layer of abstraction on top of it, which is exposing the premium version of the microwave interface but internally, in fact, it uses the same core microwave implementation.

The following code shows our core microwave interface, which is a complete and perfectly working one in its own right:

```
/// <summary>
/// Core Implementation Interface
/// </summary>
public interface ICoreMicrowave
{
    //0 seconds to 1800 seconds
    void AdjustTime(int seconds);
```

```
//0 to 10 steps (10=200 degree)
void AdjustHeatingTemperature(int temperature);

void Start();
}
```

We already have a `Microwave` class that implements this `ICoreMicrowave` interface.

Let's say we create an abstraction by creating a new interface that is presented to the client for use:

```
/// <summary>
/// It gives one touch functionality
/// </summary>
public interface INewPremiumMicrowave
{
    void SelectFood(FoodType foodType);
    void Start();
}
```

Take a look at its implementation; it basically uses an existing implementation in a smart way and proves that an abstraction can vary quite independently from its core implementation:

```
public class NewPremiumMicrowave : INewPremiumMicrowave
{
    private ICoreMicrowave _microwave;
    private int[] _temperatureValuesForFood;
    private int[] _timeValuesForFood;

    public NewPremiumMicrowave(ICoreMicrowave microwave)
    {
        _microwave = microwave;

        //Storage of pre-determined values
        _temperatureValuesForFood = new int[] { 180, 180, 150,
            120, 100, 90, 80 };
        _timeValuesForFood = new int[] { 300, 240, 180, 180, 150,
            120, 60 };
    }

    public void SelectFood(FoodType foodType)
    {
        _microwave.AdjustTime(_temperatureValuesForFood[
            (int)foodType]);
        _microwave.AdjustHeatingTemperature(
            _temperatureValuesForFood[(int)foodType]);
    }
```

```
public void Start()
{
    _microwave.Start();
}
}
```

In the sample implementation, you can see that the `NewPremiumMicrowave` class fundamentally uses the same microwave implementation just by smartly pre-setting some of the heating temperature and time duration values and by efficiently utilizing the existing microwave engine.

You can see that, when such kind of feature (that is, enhancement in the interface is needed without necessarily changing the implementation) needs to be implemented, the bridge pattern is the right way to do it.

Flyweight pattern

The flyweight pattern enables the sharing of information in a resource-efficient way. You use it when you typically have the same information segment in a large number of objects and you decide to share this information between all of these large number of objects instead of having the same copy of information contained inside all of them.

For example, let's say in a software application, you have a list of a million employee records for a group of companies, and several thousands of employees belong to the same company and thus have similar information for their employer. Instead of having this information repeatedly copied into all of the employee objects, we share the common information into a separate object and let all those employees refer to the same object. In this way, we save a lot of memory space. Note that this is almost the way in which we design and relate entities in the relational database.

In most of the popular programming languages, there are some types that are immutable, for example, strings and other primitive types. This means that, if there is another object with the same value (the same characters) of the string, it will not have its own copy of strings; rather, they refer to the same string in memory as managed by the runtime. The string is immutable in .NET as well as in Java.

It is quite common to have flyweight objects to be immutable objects so that they automatically share the same memory space, such as the string value of the company name.

In general implementations, we have a flyweight factory that provides the flyweight objects that are then shared across. The client code uses this factory to get/add the flyweight objects in a way that this factory actually acts as memory storage or holder of the flyweight (shared) objects.

Let's look at the flyweight's general UML diagram:

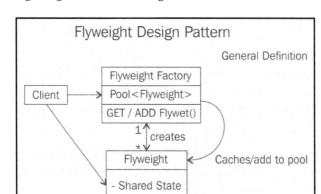

We will now consider a practical example of the flyweight pattern. Let's say we have a flight reservation system that has a list of flights, passengers booked in them, and the reservation records.

Since the flight number and its meta information is shared across various reservations and passengers, we create the flyweight of the flight objects; all the flight objects are immutable objects (basically carrying only the string members) so that they become resource-efficient for sharing. Consider the following diagram:

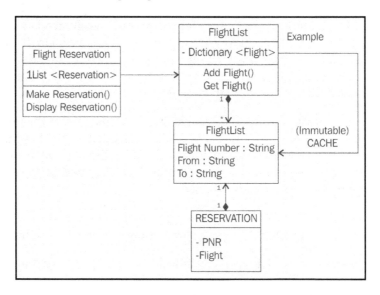

Let's jump into the code and look at how classes actually look like in C# for .NET Core. We first look at the flyweight factory class, its design, and the sample code:

```
public class FlightList
{
    /// <summary>
    /// Thread-safe internal storage
    /// </summary>
    private readonly ConcurrentDictionary<string,
    Flight> _cache = new ConcurrentDictionary<string, Flight>();

    public FlightList()
    {
        PopulateFlightList(); //List of available flights
        by the given carrier (airline)
    }

    /// <summary>
    /// Returns immutable (and shareable flyweights) instances
    /// </summary>
    /// <param name="flightNumber"></param>
    /// <returns></returns>
    public Flight GetFlight(string flightNumber)
    {
        Flight flight = null;
        if (_cache.TryGetValue(flightNumber, out flight))
        return flight;
        throw new FlightDoesNotExistException();
    }

    public void AddFlight(string flightNumber, string from,
    string to, string planeType)
    {
        var flight = new Flight(flightNumber, from, to,
          planeType);
        _cache.AddOrUpdate(flightNumber, flight,
        (key, oldFlight) => flight);
    }
}
```

The factory object allows the adding and retrieving of the flight (flyweight) objects and holds them in a thread-safe dictionary. We have added a dummy code fragment to populate a few dummy flights just for demo purposes. You can see them in the actual code, but it's not important for the pattern.

Here is our `Flight` class, which is an immutable `flyweight` object:

```
public class FlightList
{
    /// <summary>
    /// Thread-safe internal storage
    /// </summary>
    private readonly ConcurrentDictionary<string, Flight> _cache =
      new ConcurrentDictionary<string, Flight>();

    public FlightList()
    {
        PopulateFlightList(); //List of available flights by
        the given carrier (airline)
    }

    /// <summary>
    /// Returns immutable (and shareable flyweights) instances
    /// </summary>
    /// <param name="flightNumber"></param>
    /// <returns></returns>
    public Flight GetFlight(string flightNumber)
    {
        Flight flight = null;
        if (_cache.TryGetValue(flightNumber, out flight))
        return flight;
        throw new FlightDoesNotExistException();
    }

    public void AddFlight(string flightNumber,
    string from, string to, string planeType)
    {
        var flight = new Flight(flightNumber, from, to,
          planeType);
        _cache.AddOrUpdate(flightNumber, flight,
          (key, oldFlight) => flight);
    }
}
```

The following `FlightReservation` class uses the `FlightList` factory class to get the flights for each reservation and binds them into a `Reservation` object:

```
public class FlightReservation
{
    private readonly IList<Reservation> _reservations = new
      List<Reservation>();
    private FlightList _flightList;

    public FlightReservation(FlightList flightList)
```

```
{
    _flightList = flightList;
}

public void MakeReservation(string lastName, string id,
string flightNumber)
{
    int pnr = PNRAllocator.AllocatePNR(lastName, id);

    //Flyweight-Immutable object is returned which will be
    shared between all instances
    Flight flight = _flightList.GetFlight(flightNumber);

    _reservations.Add(new Reservation(pnr, flight));
}

public void DisplayReservations()
{
    //Print Total Reservations: _reservations.Count;
    foreach (var reservation in _reservations)
        reservation.Display();
}
}
```

Take a look at the tiny Reservation class that binds the reservation of a passenger created by FlightReservation:

```
public class Reservation
{
    private readonly int _pnr;
    private readonly Flight _flight;

    public Reservation(int pnr, Flight flight)
    {
        _pnr = pnr;
        _flight = flight;
    }

    public string Display()
    {
        //concat all properties and return as a single string
        return "";
    }
}
```

Finally, let's look at a simple .NET Core XUnit-based test case demonstrating sample usage. I do not think it requires further explanation, as the test code is fairly straight forward. Do not forget to download the whole source code from the *Packt* website:

```csharp
public class FlyweightTests
{
    private static IServiceProvider Provider { get; set; }

    [Fact]
    public void Test_Flyweight_Pattern()
    {
        RegisterServices();
        FlyweightClient();
    }

    /// <summary>
    /// Initializing & populating DI container
    /// </summary>
    private void RegisterServices()
    {
        IServiceCollection services = new ServiceCollection();

        //Adding required dependencies to the DI Container
        services.AddSingleton<FlightList>();
        services.AddTransient<FlightReservation>();

        Provider = services.BuildServiceProvider();
    }

    private void FlyweightClient()
    {
        var flightReservationSystem =
          Provider.GetRequiredService<FlightReservation>();

        flightReservationSystem.MakeReservation("Qureshi",
          "NRJ445", "332");
        flightReservationSystem.MakeReservation("Senthilvel",
          "NRI339", "333");
        flightReservationSystem.MakeReservation("Khan",
          "KLM987", "333");

        flightReservationSystem.DisplayReservations();
    }
}
```

A commentary on structural patterns

Like creational patterns, structural patterns are sometimes implemented interchangeably. For example, a bridge pattern is often implemented using the adapter pattern. Flyweight does not necessarily have to be implemented only as an immutable object; it can be a single instance (using, for example, a singleton) that is shared in various other classes in different scopes.

Also, note that, although adapter and bridge patterns match very much in terms of implementation design, their intent is different: one is to simplify and unify, while the other is to create further abstractions (that do not necessarily simplify) on top of an existing implementation.

Behavioral patterns

These design patterns are best practices to identify a simple way to realize relationships between entities in a given situation.

Let's jump on to our selective behavioral patterns one by one in order to see them in detail.

The template method pattern

The template method pattern basically defines the steps of an algorithm inside a class as a contract while deferring some of the steps (methods) to be implemented by the derived classes; hence, it primarily defines the structure via an abstract base class.

We will explain its implementation using an example in continuation of our sample for a GUI app we created earlier for the abstract factory pattern. In fact, within the same example app, we cover abstract factory, builder, and template method patterns.

In the abstract factory example, we presented the `IUIAbsFactory` interface and mentioned two of the possible implementations as `DarkUIAbsFactory` and `LightUIAbsFactory` concrete factory classes. Since the difference in our supposed implementation is basically only the color factor between the two themes, `DarkUIAbsFactory` and `LightUIAbsFactory`, we do not need to fully implement all the methods of `IUIAbsFactory`. Therefore, what we will do is create a partial implementation as an abstract class and leave the specific parts of the code algorithm which deals with the coloring part to the further derived classes; that is, we apply the template method pattern.

For our example code, this `ThemeableUIAbsFactory` abstract base class looks like the following:

```
public abstract class ThemeableUIAbsFactory : IUIAbsFactory
{
    protected IServiceProvider _provider;
    private IMenu menu;

    public ThemeableUIAbsFactory(IServiceProvider provider)
    {
        _provider = provider;
    }

    #region IUIAbsFactory abstract factory interface
    public IStatusBar CreateStatusBar()
    {
        var statusBar = new StatusBar();
        //StatusBar creation Preprocessing..
        ApplyThemeOnStatusBar(statusBar);
        //StatusBar creation Post-processing..
        return statusBar;
    }

    /// <summary>
    /// Internal code demonstrates the use of Builder pattern
    /// </summary>
    /// <returns></returns>
    public IWizard CreateWizard()
    {
        //Director code for builder pattern
        var wizardBuilder = _provider.
          GetRequiredService<IWizardBuilder>();

        wizardBuilder.CreateWizardSteps(4);
        wizardBuilder.AddFrontScreen();
        wizardBuilder.AddFinalScreen();

        var wizard = wizardBuilder.GetResult();

        ApplyThemeOnWizard(wizard);

        return wizard;
    }

    public IMenu GetMenu()
    {
        //sort of Singleton resource behaviour
        if (menu != null) return menu; //only one menu
```

```
    resource will be created

    menu = new Menu();
    //Menu creation Preprocessing..
    ApplyThemeOnMenu(menu);
    //Menu creation Post-processing..
    return menu;
}
#endregion

#region Template Methods
public abstract void ApplyThemeOnStatusBar(IStatusBar
  statusBar);

public abstract void ApplyThemeOnWizard(IWizard wizard);

public abstract void ApplyThemeOnMenu(IMenu menu);
#endregion
}
```

ThemeableUIAbsFactory is an abstract base class that implements IUIAbsFactory. It implements almost all of the interface methods and carefully delegates the responsibility of filling the gaps, that is, applying themes of colors to the derived classes. It has provided a template to be followed by the derived classes, in our case, DarkUIAbsFactory and LightUIAbsFactory, so let's look at the code for one of them; the other is similar:

```
public class DarkUIAbsFactory : ThemeableUIAbsFactory
{
    public DarkUIAbsFactory(IServiceProvider provider) :
      base(provider)
    {
    }

    public override void ApplyThemeOnMenu(IMenu menu)
    {
        //specific implementation
    }

    public override void ApplyThemeOnStatusBar(IStatusBar
      statusBar)
    {
        //specific implementation
    }

    public override void ApplyThemeOnWizard(IWizard wizard)
    {
        //specific implementation
```

```
        }
    }
```

From the implementation of `DarkUIAbsFactory`, you can see that it only has to fill the template of the abstract methods and does not have to worry about implementing the complete `IUIAbsFactory` interface again.

The observer pattern

The observer pattern is a pattern to enable the publisher/subscriber scenario between the classes of an application. In this pattern, there is an observable object that sends events to many observing objects registered to it for receiving events.

Let's take a look at the class diagram for the example implementation of the observer pattern:

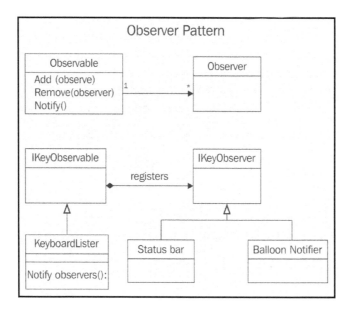

So, our example is basically talking about a scenario in a user interface-based application where you have a `KeyboardListener` class that is listening to keyboard events and then there are some other classes that need to know about certain key events, for example, Caps Lock, Num Lock. In this case, our `KeyboardListener` class is a publisher of the event class, and our observers are subscriber classes that are interested in receiving the key events. In our example, our events that receive the observers are `StatusBar` and `BalloonNotifier`.

First, we show you the code of the important `IKeyObserver` interfaces for the observer:

```
public interface IKeyObserver
{
    void Update(object anObject);
}
```

This is the code of `IKeyObservable` for the observable:

```
public abstract class IKeyObservable
{
  private IList<IKeyObserver> _observers = new
    List<IKeyObserver>();

  public void AddObserver(IKeyObserver observer)
  {
    _observers.Add(observer);
  }

  public void RemoveObserver(IKeyObserver observer)
  {
    _observers.Remove(observer);
  }

  public void NotifyObservers(object anObject)
  {
    foreach (IKeyObserver observer in _observers)
    {
      observer.Update(anObject);
    }
  }
}
```

Now let's take a look at the implementation of the code for our observable class, that is, `KeyboardListener`:

```
public class KeyboardListener : IKeyObservable
{
    public void SartListening()
    {
        ListenToKeys(); //Normally it would be a
          continous process..
    }

    /// <summary>
    /// Listen and notify only the interested keys
    /// </summary>
    private void ListenToKeys()
```

```
        {
            ObservedKeys key;

            //Got the key, we are interested in..
            key = ObservedKeys.NUM_LOCK;

            NotifyObservers(key);
        }
    }
```

This is the code for our simple observing class `StatusBar` that receives events to show their key status in the display area of the status bar control:

```
public class StatusBar : IKeyObserver
{
    public void Update(object anObject)
    {
        Trace.WriteLine("StatusBar - Key pressed: " +
            anObject.ToString());
    }
}
```

Now take a look at our sample client test code:

```
public class ObserverTests
{
    [Fact]
    public void Test_Observer_Pattern()
    {
        var listener = new KeyboardListener();
        var statusBar = new StatusBar();
        var balloonNotifier = new BalloonNotifier();

        listener.AddObserver(statusBar);
        listener.AddObserver(balloonNotifier);

        listener.SartListening();

        listener.RemoveObserver(balloonNotifier);
        listener.SartListening(); //trigger a new
            notification again
    }
}
```

This code produces the following outcome:

```
StatusBar - Key pressed: NUM_LOCK
BalloonNotifier - Key pressed: NUM_LOCK
```

```
StatusBar - Key pressed: NUM_LOCK
```

The output confirms that when a key event, NUM_LOCK, is triggered, it is received by all the observers waiting for the key event, and we can dynamically add and remove the observers. This summarizes our sample for the observer pattern.

The chain of responsibility pattern

The chain of responsibility pattern promotes loose coupling by separating the request senders from the request receivers and processors. It works like how a sender sends a request to be fulfilled to one of the receiver objects, and this object either fulfills the request and returns, or it partially fulfills the request, does not process the request, and sends the request to the next request receiver/processor object until it has been handled. In this way, all the request receivers, processors, or handlers are chained to each other.

A more common example of this pattern is this: say, we have a request to purchase an item and it requires an approval; it depends on the value of an item whether it can be approved by a manager, SVP, or CEO. So in this scenario, we send the request for approval to a manager first; if he can fulfill the request, it is satisfied there. Otherwise, the manager sends the request to its successor, SVP, and so on to all the connected request receiver objects automatically, while the request sender does not know where it should be actually handled and all the receivers chained together work smoothly until it has been completely handled.

Let's take a look at the UML class diagram for the chain of responsibility pattern:

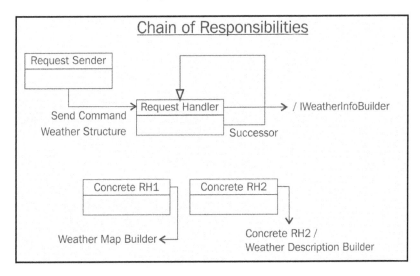

The class diagram is simple; the client who is the request sender basically has the instance of one request and sends the command to it; one request handler keeps the instance of another request handler, and so on. Note that in this way, request handlers are chained together and, therefore, processing can take place only sequentially and only in one direction.

As mentioned earlier, in a chain of responsibility, either the request handler can skip and pass the request to its successor, or it can process it or partially process and pass it forward to the next one in the chain.

We will now take a fairly practical example for the chain of responsibility pattern. Let's say we have some kind of an app that needs to display the weather information containing various attributes such as the map, temperature, and so on. In our example, we will fill the request command object partially by each request handler, and when it reaches the last one, the request is fulfilled.

This is what our example request command object looks like:

```
public class WeatherStructure
{
  public WeatherStructure()
  {
    Temperature = new Temperature();
    Map = new Map();
    WeatherThumbnail = new WeatherThumbnail();
    WeatherDescription = new WeatherDescription();
  }

  public Temperature Temperature;
  public Map Map;
  public WeatherThumbnail WeatherThumbnail;
  public WeatherDescription WeatherDescription;
}
```

We will fill each of the four attributes one by one by four request handlers chained together. The interface for the request handler for our example is as follows:

```
public abstract class IWeatherInfoBuilder
{
  protected IWeatherInfoBuilder _successor;

  public void SetSuccessor(IWeatherInfoBuilder successor)
  {
    _successor = successor;
  }
}
```

```
    public abstract void BuildWeatherObject(WeatherStructure ws);
}
```

One of the request handlers looks like this, while all other request handlers look and work the same way:

```
public class WeatherMapBuilder : IWeatherInfoBuilder
{
  public override void BuildWeatherObject(WeatherStructure ws)
  {
    BuildMap(weatherStructure.Map);

    if (_successor != null)
    _successor.BuildWeatherObject(weatherStructure);
  }

  private void BuildMap(Map map)
  {
    //construct Map appropriately
    map.MapURL = "https://maps.google.com/";
  }
}
```

Note how the request handlers are chained together: first, the successive request handler is taken and saved in SetSuccessor() and used for chained processing; when the request is being handled in BuildWeatherObject() after the handling is done, the successor is invoked because, in this example, we are processing the request command partially by each of the request handlers.

Let's take a look at what the client code looks like and who acts as a request command object sender:

```
public void Test_ChainOfResponsibility_Pattern()
{
  IWeatherInfoBuilder wInfoBuilder1 = new
    WeatherDescriptionBuilder();
  IWeatherInfoBuilder wInfoBuilder2 = new
    WeatherMapBuilder();
  IWeatherInfoBuilder wInfoBuilder3 = new
    WeatherTemperatureBuilder();
  IWeatherInfoBuilder wInfoBuilder4 = new
    WeatherThumbnailBuilder();

  wInfoBuilder1.SetSuccessor(wInfoBuilder2);
  wInfoBuilder2.SetSuccessor(wInfoBuilder3);
  wInfoBuilder3.SetSuccessor(wInfoBuilder4);
```

```
        WeatherStructure weather = new WeatherStructure();
        wInfoBuilder1.BuildWeatherObject(weather);
    }
```

The client code is simple and all the chained request processing is achieved by a single line-- `wInfoBuilder1.BuildWeatherObject(weather);`

Chained request handlers fill each attribute of `WeatherStructure` one by one.

The visitor pattern

The visitor pattern allows you to separate an algorithm via the `visitor` class from an object structure (aggregating elements) so that the new operations can be added without modifying the object structure.

It's a cleaner way by design for an old way of C++ friend class, which is allowed to access the private members of another class.

In simple words, you break the class into two classes, one only with elements/variables, and another only with the methods. In this way, you keep the one with variables the same while varying the methods, that is, algorithms in the other class. You define the methods grouped together in an interface called `visitor` so that you can have more than one implementation of this `visitor` interface, which means that you can have a completely different set of implementations while working on the same set of attributes / variables / elements.

Before we jump into a realistic example code, let's close the definition by the UML class diagram:

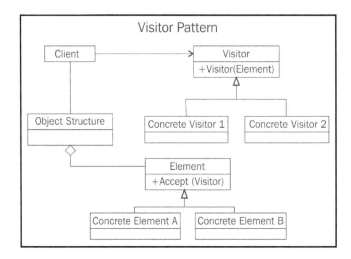

We will use the same example we used for the chain of responsibility pattern, that is, filling up `WeatherStructure`, which is our **Object Structure** for the visitor pattern. It contains four elements `IWeatherElement` mapping to the element of the visitor pattern as `Map`, `Temperature`, `Description`, and `Thumbnail`.

We will have two versions of concrete visitors (`YahooWeatherBuilder`, `ForecastIOWeatherBuilder`); we will also see two ways of visitor (`AnotherWeatherManipulator`) method's signature implementation. Ensure that you download and see the full version of the code for visitor pattern and others.

The interface for the `Element` is as follows:

```
/// <summary>
/// Interface for the Visitable class (The class to be visited
by the visitor class)
/// </summary>
public interface IWeatherElement
{
    void ManipulateMe(IWeatherManipulator weatherManipulator);
}
```

The interface for the `Visitor` class is as follows:

```
/// <summary>
/// Interface for the Visitor object
/// </summary>
public interface IWeatherManipulator
{
    void ManipulateElement(IWeatherElement weatherElement);
}
```

The **object structure** that aggregates the weather elements looks like the following:

```
public class WeatherStructure
{
    private Temperature _temperature;
    private Map _map;
    private WeatherThumbnail _weatherThumbnail;
    private WeatherDescription _weatherDescription;

    private IWeatherManipulator _weatherBuilder;

    public WeatherStructure(IWeatherManipulator weatherBuilder)
    {
        _weatherBuilder = weatherBuilder;

        _temperature = new Temperature();
```

```
        _map = new Map();
        _weatherThumbnail = new WeatherThumbnail();
        _weatherDescription = new WeatherDescription();
    }...
```

Our test client code looks like the following:

```
WeatherStructure weatherStructure = new WeatherStructure(new
YahooWeatherBuilder());
weatherStructure.BuildWeatherStructure();
```

To use the other implementation of the visitor pattern, that is, to apply the different algorithm on the same set of elements, that is, the object structure, we just have to do the following:

```
WeatherStructure weatherStructure = new WeatherStructure(new
ForecastIOWeatherBuilder());
weatherStructure.BuildWeatherStructure();
```

Let's take a look at the simple code for `BuildWeatherStructure()`:

```
void BuildWeatherStructure()
{
    _temperature.ManipulateMe(_weatherBuilder);
    _map.ManipulateMe(_weatherBuilder);
    _weatherThumbnail.ManipulateMe(_weatherBuilder);
    _weatherDescription.ManipulateMe(_weatherBuilder);
}
```

This line, `_temperature.ManipulateMe(_weatherBuilder)`, is basically `element.visit(visitor)`.

A while ago, I mentioned that we could have a slight variation in the visitor interface, and it would look like the following:

```
interface IAnotherWeatherManipulator
{
    void ManipulateElement(Map map);
    void ManipulateElement(Temperature temperature);
    void ManipulateElement(WeatherDescription weatherDescription);
    void ManipulateElement(WeatherThumbnail weatherThumbnail);
}
```

For the first version of the visitor interface, the implementation looks like the following:

```
class WeatherManipulator : IWeatherManipulator
{
    public void ManipulateElement(IWeatherElement weatherElement)
```

```
{
  if (weatherElement is Map)
     BuildMap(weatherElement);
  else if (weatherElement is Temperature)
     BuildTemperature(weatherElement);
  else if (weatherElement is WeatherDescription)
     BuildWeatherDescription(weatherElement);
  else if (weatherElement is WeatherThumbnail)
     BuildWeatherThumbnail(weatherElement);
}
```

This means that we have to check the exact type of element in order to manipulate it effectively; on the other hand, the other variation of the visitor interface as a concrete type is passed into its argument, so the type checking inside the function is not required. Both are valid implementations of the visitor pattern.

If you still have any confusion about this example visitor pattern, take a look at the complete source code and have fun.

The strategy pattern

The strategy pattern basically allows an algorithm to be selected dynamically at runtime without modifying the client code.

For example, if we have lot of input data from past weather information and we need to forecast the weather, we could perhaps infer based on purely statistical values from the past or from an algorithm doing some kind of scientific manipulation or both. After doing the calculations, we would want to compare the results to check the effectiveness, for example. In this scenario, instead of changing the client code each time, we just supply a different algorithm implementation to the client, thus incurring maybe just a single line of code change. So, the strategy pattern lets the algorithm vary independently from clients using it.

The simple UML diagram for the strategy pattern looks like the following:

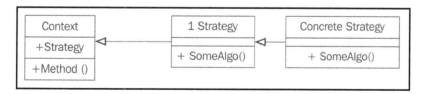

Let's talk about the example code. We want to travel between two points, A and B, on the map and need to calculate the duration. We encapsulate the duration calculation algorithm in the strategy so that we can calculate the duration while traveling in the car and traveling via public transport. Therefore, our class diagram will look like the following for our example code:

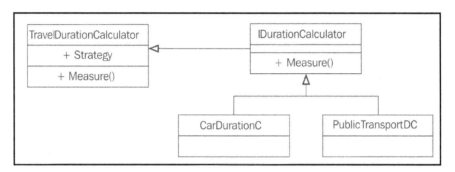

Jumping on to the code, let's look at the code of the context class, that is, `TravelDurationCalculator`:

```
public class TravelDurationCalculator
{
  private IDurationCalculator strategy;

  public TimeSpan Measure(string pointA, string pointB)
  {
    return strategy.Measure(pointA, pointB);
  }

  //Change the strategy
  public void SetCalculator(IDurationCalculator strategy)
  {
    this.strategy = strategy;
  }
}
```

From this class, you know how the flow is controlled, so let's see the interface for our strategy:

```
public interface IDurationCalculator
{
  TimeSpan Measure(string pointA, string pointB);
}
```

Now let's see the simple code for our classes implementing the strategies:

```
/// <summary>
/// Travel duration calculating strategy using car
/// </summary>
public class CarDurationCalculator : IDurationCalculator
{
  public TimeSpan Measure(string pointA, string pointB)
  {
    //Calculate and return the time duration value..
    return new TimeSpan(4, 46, 0);
  }
}
/// <summary>
/// Travel duration calculating strategy using public
transport (bus, tram, train..)
/// </summary>
public class PublicTransportDurationCalculator :
  IDurationCalculator
{
  public TimeSpan Measure(string pointA, string pointB)
  {
    //Calculate and return the time duration value..
    return new TimeSpan(6, 02, 0);
  }
}
```

After seeing this ultimate algorithm for the travel duration calculator, let's look at what the client code would look like the following:

```
public void Test_Strategy_Pattern()
{
  string pointA = "Berlin";
  string pointB = "Frankfurt";
  TimeSpan timeSpan;
  var durationCalculator = new TravelDurationCalculator();

  durationCalculator.SetCalculator(new
    PublicTransportDurationCalculator());
  timeSpan = durationCalculator.Measure(pointA, pointB);
```

```
        Trace.WriteLine(pointA + " to " + pointB + " takes " +
          timeSpan.ToString() + " using public transport.");

        durationCalculator.SetCalculator(new CarDurationCalculator());
        timeSpan = durationCalculator.Measure(pointA, pointB);
        Trace.WriteLine(pointA + " to " + pointB + " takes " +
        timeSpan.ToString() + " using car.");
    }
```

The output of this client test code is as follows:

```
Berlin to Frankfurt takes 06:02:00 using public transport.
Berlin to Frankfurt takes 04:46:00 using car.
```

I hope this wonderful design pattern is well understood now.

The state pattern

The state pattern allows the change in the object's behavior based on the change of its state.

If the state is changing for an object, the behavior automatically changes as well. For example, a person whose state is nervous behaves strangely, while a person whose state is happy behaves in a more positive way.

The state pattern basically implements the state machine in a way that each state is a derived class of a state interface, and they alter between them jumping from one state to another, thus dynamically updating the behavior as per the state.

Let's jump to our example. We want to know the number of days in a season, either summer, winter, autumn, or spring. We will always invoke one single method to know the number of days while we want the object to shift its state automatically to the next season and therefore change its behavior and give us the different number of days on the next call to the same method.

The UML class diagram for the state pattern applied to our example looks like the following:

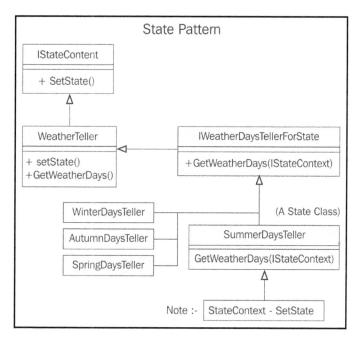

Now it's time to make things more clear, so let's talk code. First of all, I will show you the client code so that we can see the big picture directly, which I might have failed to explain very clearly:

```
public void Test_State_Pattern()
{
  var weatherTeller = new WeatherTeller();

  var weatherDays = weatherTeller.GetWeatherDays();
  Trace.WriteLine(string.Format("Name: {0} - Days: {1}",
    weatherDays.Weather, weatherDays.Days));

  weatherDays = weatherTeller.GetWeatherDays();
  Trace.WriteLine(string.Format("Name: {0} - Days: {1}",
    weatherDays.Weather, weatherDays.Days));

  weatherDays = weatherTeller.GetWeatherDays();
  Trace.WriteLine(string.Format("Name: {0} - Days: {1}",
    weatherDays.Weather, weatherDays.Days));

  weatherDays = weatherTeller.GetWeatherDays();
```

```
        Trace.WriteLine(string.Format("Name: {0} - Days: {1}",
          weatherDays.Weather, weatherDays.Days));

        weatherDays = weatherTeller.GetWeatherDays();
        Trace.WriteLine(string.Format("Name: {0} - Days: {1}",
          weatherDays.Weather, weatherDays.Days));
    }
```

Let's look at the interface for the context and the class implementing the `WeatherTeller` context:

```
    internal interface IStateContext
    {
      void SetState(IWeatherDaysTellerForState newWeatherState);
    }
```

This is the interface for the implanting class:

```
    public class WeatherTeller : IStateContext
    {
      private IWeatherDaysTellerForState weatherDaysTellerState;

      public WeatherTeller()
      {
        weatherDaysTellerState = new SummerDaysTeller();
      }

      public WeatherDays GetWeatherDays()
      {
        return weatherDaysTellerState.GetWeatherDays(this); ;
      }

      /// <summary>
      /// Internal interface IStateContext implementation
      /// </summary>
      void IStateContext.SetState(IWeatherDaysTellerForState
        newWeatherState)
      {
        weatherDaysTellerState = newWeatherState;
      }
    }
```

The interface for the state classes:

```
    internal interface IWeatherDaysTellerForState
    {
      WeatherDays GetWeatherDays(IStateContext stateContext);
    }
```

Finally, here is the code for one of the state classes:

```
internal class SummerDaysTeller : IWeatherDaysTellerForState
{
    public WeatherDays GetWeatherDays(IStateContext stateContext)
    {
        stateContext.SetState(new AutumnDaysTeller());

        return new WeatherDays()
        {
            Weather = "Summer",
            Days = 150 //5 months * 30
        };
    }
}
```

This completes our state pattern. In fact, this is the last design pattern we cover in this chapter.

I imagine you have understood this pattern as well as the others. Download the complete source code and run through the code to get the complete essence.

A commentary on behavioral patterns

Sometimes, some behavioral patterns overlap each other, while other times, they make perfect individual sense uniquely. For example, in terms of the class diagram, the structural implementation state and strategy patterns are quite similar, but they exhibit completely different behavior as well as have their own different intent. Remember, the state pattern always involves a state machine situation.

One could argue that there is an overlap between the chain of responsibility and the decorator pattern; while both satisfy the single responsibility principle, one tackles the addition of the functionality dynamically through the design of the structure and other via its behavior. Also, there is a big difference between the class diagram and implementation of the decorator and the chain of responsibility pattern.

Summary

All of these design patterns satisfy the S.O.L.I.D object-oriented design principles. Going through this chapter not only helped you revise your *GoF* patterns and fundamental S.O.L.I.D principles, but it will also help you keep in mind when you are designing your new classes to solve certain problems and hence increase the quality of your software.

We also covered some fundamentals of Inversion of Control via dependency injection and also went though some examples of DI using .NET Core. You would have also noticed that with the advent of DI, a lot of *GoF* patterns are automatically taken care of by the DI pattern. For example, almost all of the creational patterns can be replaced by the DI, while for many others, DI can complement them by taking care of part of their responsibility with regards to their implementation.

I hope you enjoyed this chapter as much as I did. This chapter provides the solid and essential basis for all of the design and code-heavy chapters in the remainder of this book.

3

Distributed Computing

In the previous chapter, we looked at modern design and development principles that are essential to quality and maintainable code and stable yet flexible application design. Learning is through some of the most used design patterns and their implementation using the .NET Core code. Distributed computing is an art of computing to interact with a collection of independent systems in the field of computer science. In this chapter, you will get an opportunity to understand the fundamentals of this computing and application in the enterprise world. It starts with the definition, followed by its core characteristics, such as concurrency, scalability, transparency, security, and so on. In the modern world, distributed computing has a vital role to play.

This chapter will cover the following topics:

- What are Distributed applications?
- Multithreaded programming
- Concurrency versus parallelism
- Design challenges to build the distribution
- Scalability
- Security

Understanding Distributed applications

To understand distributed applications in a better way, we can start with the definition of the computing, following with comparison points.

Definition

In the early days of computer evolution, mainframe computers were heavily used in the industry. By design, the legacy mainframe was performed on a single system and was called **centralized computing**

A distributed system is a collection of independent computers, interconnected via a network. The core objective of the network is to collaborate and complete a particular task. Fundamentally, distributed computing is computing performed in a distributed system. Consider the following diagram:

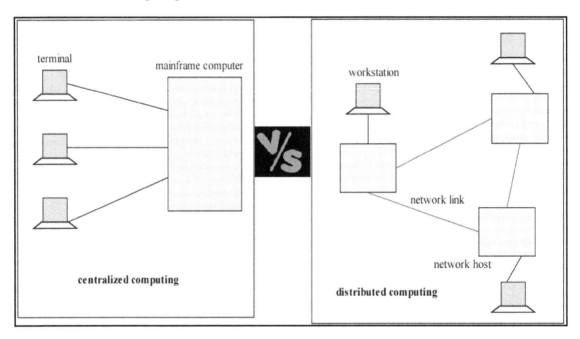

Historically, distributed systems have been successful because of the availability of powerful and cheaper microprocessors in personal computers, embedded systems, personal digital assistant, and so on. Most importantly, the continuous advancement in communication technology has been key to their success.

Comparison

On comparing distributed computing with the traditional centralized computing model, it can be tabulated as follows:

Sr.No.	Centralized	Distributed
1	Monolithic architecture within a single system.	Distributed architecture across the network.
2	In terms of functionality, separate and single function applications are designed.	Integrated applications are designed in terms of functionality.
3	Applications can't share data or other app resources by design.	By design, applications can share all types of resources.
4	Mainframe-based applications are developed using this approach.	Modern multi-layer/tier applications are designed based on this methodology.
5	Proprietary user interfaces are developed here.	Common user interfaces are designed here.

In terms of economics, the distributed system allows the pooling of resources, including CPU cycles, data storage, input and output devices, and services in the enterprise system.

Multiprogramming

Since the advent of the Internet in the 1980s, there has been a steady growth of new enterprise applications being built on distributed processing. In recent times, there has been an explosive growth in network technology expansion. The technical journey goes in the way of intranet, Internet, World Wide Web, wireless network, GPS, RFID (Radio Frequency Identifier), and so on.

In the emerging world of global computing, distributed computing is the core central piece of all computing.

According to the fundamentals of computing, there are four core components, namely:

- Input
- Process
- Storage
- Output

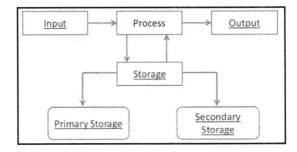

The **Input** phase ingests the data and commands into CPU using one or more input devices. The **Process** phase performs the execution of the input data and turns it into useful information as **Output.** During this process, it persists the useful data into the **Storage** layer.

In general it is a bit confusing between multiprogramming and multithreading in parallelism context. Few simple examples clear the differentiation in a perfect way.

Multiprogramming is the capability of an operating system to execute more than one program on a single machine. A classic example is to run more than one program, such as Excel, Internet Explorer, word, and more, in a Windows operating system:

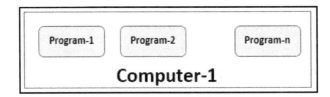

In a similar trend, multithreading has the ability of an operating system to execute different parts of a program, namely--threads. It is depicted in the following diagram:

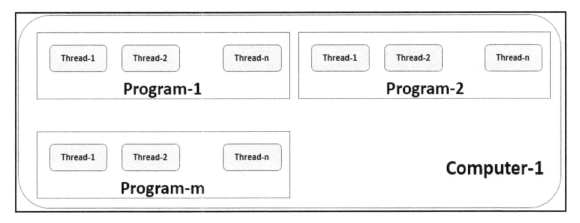

In a different dimension, threads are considered as child processes to share the parent process resources, but execute independently. In terms of parallel execution, multiple threads of a single process shares the single CPU system on time-sliced basis. A classic example is a multiple document process using a single Word process.

Thread synchronization

In my work experience, associates always felt that multithreaded applications provide the illusion that numerous activities are happening at more or less the same time. Interestingly, on observing CPU/system reality, it is considered as **Time Slice** to switch between different threads. It is based on round-robin methodology.

Process-based multitasking handles the concurrent execution of programs, while thread-based multitasking deals with the concurrent execution of pieces of the same program.

In this section, it is essential to highlight the risk factor of thread collision during a multithreading process in an enterprise application. On building any multithreaded application, shared data should be protected from the possibility of multiple thread engagement with its content/value.

Let's illustrate with a simple example:

```
static void Main(string[] args)
{
    Console.WriteLine("Demo of Thread Synchronize");
    Console.WriteLine("#########################");
    Console.WriteLine("Main Thread starts here...");
    WorkerThreadClass p = new WorkerThreadClass();

    /* Group of 7 threads creation
     * for synchronize execution
     */
    Thread[] threadList = new Thread[7];
    for (int i = 0; i < 7; i++)
    {
        threadList[i] = new Thread(new
            ThreadStart(p.SyncThreadProcess));
    }
    foreach (Thread thread in threadList)
    {
        thread.Start();
    }
    Console.WriteLine("Main Thread ends here...");
    Console.ReadLine();
}
```

Now, the key factor is to protect the shared block using the lock option. It requires us to specify a token to acquire by a thread to enter within the `lock` scope:

```
class WorkerThreadClass
{
    // Synchronization Lock object
    private Object ThreadLock = new object();
    public void SyncThreadProcess()
    {
        //Lock to synchronize
        lock (ThreadLock)
        {
            Console.WriteLine("Starting Thread with ID: {0}",
                Thread.CurrentThread.ManagedThreadId);
            Console.WriteLine("Lock the operation of Thread");
            for (int i = 1; i <= 10; i++)
            {
                Console.Write(i + " ");
            }
            Console.WriteLine("n Release the Lock to
                other Thread");
        }
```

```
    }
  }
```

On attempting to lock down an instance-level method, the execution can simply pass the reference to that instance. Once the thread enters into a `lock` scope, the lock token (in our example, the `ThreadLock` object) is inaccessible by other threads until the lock is released or the `lock` scope has exited.

The execution result depicts the process in a clear way, as shown here:

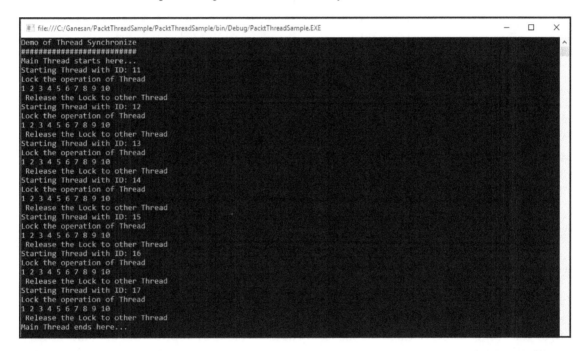

Storage

As there has been rapid development in the electronics and communication space, the industry has released the hardware components with cost-effective and highly efficient modes. In this direction, computer architecture is designed with the interconnected multiple processors types in two forms:

- Tightly coupled system
- Loosely coupled system

In **tightly coupled system**, there is a single system-wide primary memory, which is shared by all the processors in the ecosystem. As the name depicts, any sort of communication is executed in the closed tightly couple environment of the common shared memory route, as defined here:

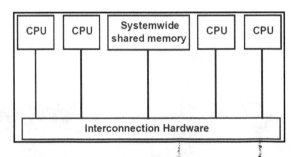

Let's take an example in the multiprocessor environment. Processor 1 writes value 100 into the shared memory address location ADDR1. Subsequent reads by the rest of the processors will be the same value, 100, from the ADDR1 location. It will be valid until there are any further updates on the specific location.

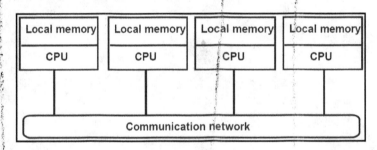

If you take the same scenario in the loosely coupled system, each processor contains its own independent local memory to persist the value. It doesn't share any memory location across the processors. By design, message-bound inter-process communication is established. By architecture, this is termed **Message Driven Architecture** in the computing industry.

With the concept of fundamentals, the first version tightly coupled system is built using parallel computing. The second version Loosely Coupled system is based on distributed computing.

On analyzing the need for hard disk capacity (GB) in personal computers, the plot is interestingly logarithmic. The lesson learned is that the industry fitted line corresponds to exponential growth.

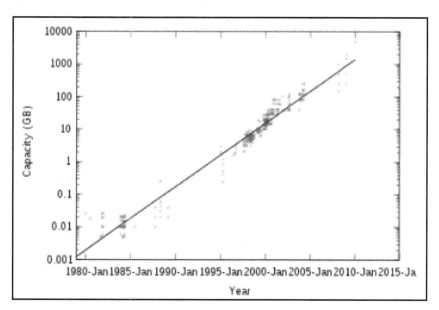

Process

In simple terms, the computing process is defined as an instance of a software program to execute a set of predefined activities to generate the result as the output. In the hardware of the computers, CPU is the core component of the process in which **Control Unit** (**CU**) and **ALU** (**Arithmetic Logic Unit**) are the fundamentals to execute.

Performance is the key success indicator of the process. There are two aspects to a performance improvement scheme. The first is to execute multiples of a single job instance. This refers to concurrency and parallelism. However, both objectives are the same, and they have quite distinct concepts.

The second aspect is the multiple folds at the machine level. It is a foundation for the scaling concepts of scale up and scale out. We will discuss scalability in detail at the end of this chapter.

Concurrency

In concurrent computing, the program is decomposed into multiple threads to execute the control with distinct responsibilities. Multithreads may run either simultaneously or in turn based on the system infrastructure. By design, there are two main concepts. They are as follows:

- How are the processes scheduled to execute?
- How does the coordination process synchronize to produce the result?

Let's take a simple example. The given business problem statement is converted into a software program. Multiple instructions of the program are decomposed into logical independent splits, named **Thread**.

Therefore, the program/problem 'p' is split into 't' threads (**t1, t2,...tN**), the execution target at one CPU processor.

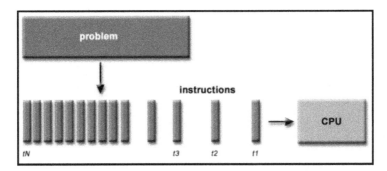

The scheduler component drafts the execution order after making several independent instructions associated with threads. The coordination process is quite interesting in the way that multiple threads of control cooperate to complete the task for producing the end result. Thus, concurrency is virtual parallelism through a shared mode, such as time slicing.

As we know, concurrency systems have several processes that are executing simultaneously. These processes can interact with each other while they are executing. On the flip side, concurrency may trigger indeterminacy among the resulting outcome that leads to issues such as deadlock and starvation. Again, these design challenges are properly addressed during the implementation phase.

As a result, concurrent programming is implemented by splitting the existing task into multiple factors to be executed. Concisely, concurrency achieves logical execution of multiple tasks at once.

Parallelism

Parallel computing has a major design difference with the earlier concurrent computing. Typically, it reduces the execution cycle/timing by taking advantage of the infrastructure/hardware ability to execute/complete more than one task at any point of given time.

Parallel computing leverages various techniques, such as vectorisation, instruction level parallelism named super scalar architecture, multiprocessing using multiple core processors, and so on. At a software level, there is another model in which uniform operations over aggregate data can be speed up. This is achievable by partitioning the data and computing on the partitions simultaneously.

Parallelism is a combination of software and hardware techniques. It is used to allow several processes to run in parallel, physically. The primary objective is used for faster computation in modern enterprise applications. Take a look at the following diagram:

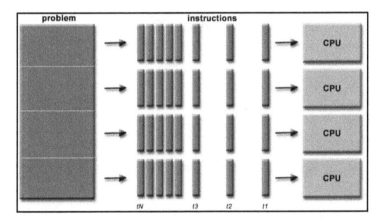

In a nutshell, parallelism achieves the physical execution of multiple tasks at once using multiple processors in the ecosystem.

Multithreading exercise

In computing theory, job execution is programmatically spanned using the control named thread. Each thread defines a unique flow of control, but it is controlled by the main program. If you notice that the application is a time-consuming complicated independent process, it is advisable to leverage thread programming for the efficient execution. Independent is the key for parallelism.

In .NET programming, threads are created by extending `Thread` class of `System.Threading` library. On invoking `Start()` method of the extended `Thread` class, the system kick starts the child thread execution. The life cycle of a thread starts when an object of the `System.Threading.Thread` class is created and ends when the thread is terminated or completes execution.

By design, .NET Core supports multithreaded operations in the following two ways:

- Own threads with `ThreadStart` delegates
- Using ThreadPool framework class

As best practice, it is highly recommended to create a new thread **manually** using `ThreadStart` for long-running tasks, whereas ThreadPool only for brief jobs.

ThreadStart

In terms of implementation, let me explain the details of coding statement and its significance. A thread does not begin executing when it is created in C# program as follows:

```
Thread thread = new Thread(job)
```

In fact, thread execution is scheduled by calling the C# `Start` method as follows:

```
thread.Start();
```

To sequence .NET thread processing, `ThreadStart` delegate is a parameter when creating a new thread instance:

```
ThreadStart job = new ThreadStart(ThreadJob);
```

Generally, worker thread is referred to describe another thread from the one that is doing the work on the current thread, which, in lots of cases, is a foreground or UI thread. It is similar to master slave execution model in computing theory. With these fundamental coding concepts, simple thread program is written with main and worker thread as follows:

```
/// <summary>
/// Main method to kick start Job
/// </summary>
public static void Main()
{
    ThreadStart job = new ThreadStart(ThreadJob);
    Thread thread = new Thread(job);
    thread.Start();
```

```
    for (int i = 0; i < 5; i++)
    {
      Console.WriteLine("Main thread: {0}", i);
      Thread.Sleep(1000);
    }
    Console.ReadKey();
  }

  /// <summary>
  /// Sub or worker thread is getting triggered here
  /// </summary>
  static void ThreadJob()
  {
    for (int i = 0; i < 10; i++)
    {
      Console.WriteLine("Worker thread: {0}", i);
      Thread.Sleep(500);
    }
  }
```

In terms of execution of the preceding code, worker thread counts from 0 to 9 fairly fast (about twice a second) while the main thread counts from 0 to 4 fairly slowly (about once a second). In turn, framework execution has discrepancy of execution between main thread of 1000ms sleep and worker thread of 500ms. As a result, the execution output on one machine looks like the following screenshot:

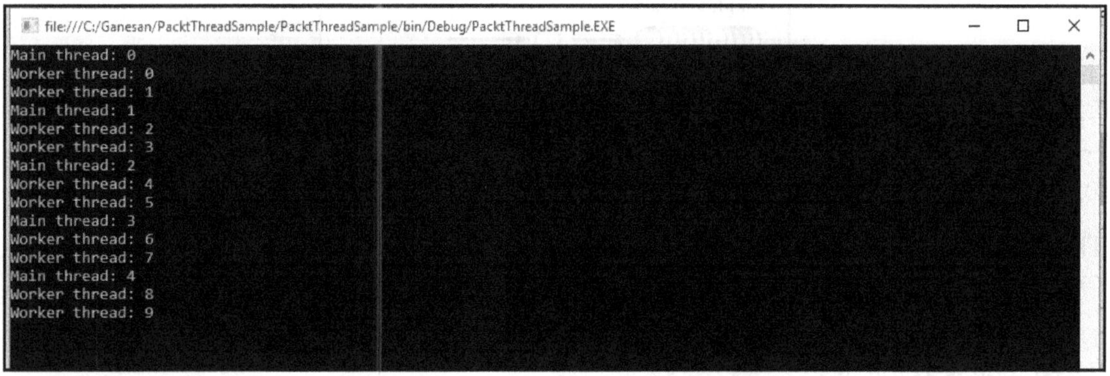

On observing the code execution's result, it is clear indication that the sleeping thread will immediately start running across main and worker threads as soon as the sleep finishes. On thread execution, another thread may be currently running coincidentally on a single processor machine. The impact is that the current thread needs to await until the system thread scheduler shares the processor time during the next round of allocation.

ThreadPool

ThreadPool is an interesting concept and entirely different from the earlier approach. In fact, a collection of threads is created based on the system resources (like memory) availability. By default, the thread pool has 25 threads per processor.

On demand, thread pool size can be scaled up and down to match the code execution. Every thread of ThreadPool is always associated with a specific given task. On completion, the underlying thread will return to the pool manager for further assignments. It has been depicted in the following diagram:

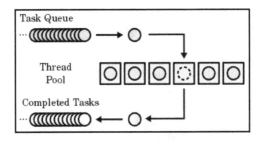

In terms of implementation, the `System.Threading.ThreadPool` class handles the creation of new threads along with the efficient distribution of consumer and management among those threads.

Though there are a number of ways to create thread pool in C#, the simplest way is by calling `ThreadPool.QueueUserWorkItem`.

This method allows us to launch the execution of a function on the system thread pool. Its declaration is as follows:

```
ThreadPool.QueueUserWorkItem(new WaitCallback(Consume));
```

The first parameter specifies the function that we want to execute on the pool. Framework expects to match the delegate of `WaitCallback`, as follows:

```
public delegate void WaitCallback(object state);
```

In terms of implementation, here is a simple example to illustrate the `ThreadPool` concept in .NET C# code:

```
using System;
using System.Threading;

namespace PacktThreadSample
{
  class ThreadPoolTest
  {
    static void Main()
    {
      Console.WriteLine("Before handover to ThreadPool..");
      System.Threading.ThreadPool.QueueUserWorkItem(
        new WaitCallback(WorkerThread), "Content insider Worker
          Thread");

      Console.WriteLine("Right after ThreadPool retrun..");
      // Give the callback wait time of 2 mins after
      WorkerThread trigger
      // Else App might terminate before the control returns
      Thread.Sleep(2000);
      Console.WriteLine("2 minutes dealy after
        ThreadPool retrun..");
    }
    static void WorkerThread (object parameter)
    {
      Console.WriteLine(parameter);
    }
  }
}
```

The only catch in `ThreadPool` is to handle the asynchronous thread execution. As the best practice, the main thread needs to await for the complete worker thread execution. On executing the preceding C# `ThreadPool` code, the result will be as follows:

```
file:///C:/Ganesan/PacktThreadSample/PacktThreadSample/bin/Debug/PacktThreadSample.EXE        —    □    ×
Before handover to ThreadPool..
Right after ThreadPool retrun..
Content insider Worker Thread
2 minutes dealy after ThreadPool retrun..
```

Technically, thread pooling is essential in multithreaded enterprise applications for response time improvement, thread management, optimized thread timing, and more.

`ThreadPool` can only run so many jobs at once, and some framework classes use it internally, so you do not want to block it with many tasks that need to block for other things.

Task Parallel Library (TPL)

TPL is the recent feature in .NET programming for well managed parallel processing. The main purpose is to increase the developer's productivity by simplifying the programming related to parallelism and concurrency to any enterprise applications. In my view, it is a highly recommended approach to write parallel processing code in .NET.

In spite of simplicity at TPL, I recommend the programmers to have a basic understanding of the fundamental threading concepts like deadlocks and race conditions. By doing so, TPL will be effectively used in the source code.

Let's start the implementation of TPL with a simple example by simply adding two Threading namespaces:

```
using System;
using System.Threading;
using System.Threading.Tasks;
```

To demonstrate the execution of TPL, let's write two independent methods to display integer and characters of a string, which will be invoked concurrently using the `Parallel.Invoke()` method:

```
static void PostInteger()
{
  for (int i=0; i<10; i++)
  {
    Console.WriteLine("Integer Post:" + i);
    Thread.Sleep(500);
  }
}
static void PostCharacter()
{
  const String sampleText = "Packt Thread";
  for (int i = 0; i < sampleText.Length; i++)
  {
    Console.WriteLine("Character Post:" + sampleText[i]);
    Thread.Sleep(1000);
  }
```

```
    }
```

Now, it is action time to execute the preceding methods concurrently by the following code base using Parallel class:

```
using System;
using System.Threading;
using System.Threading.Tasks;

namespace PacktThreadSample
{
  class TaskParallel
  {
    static void PostInteger()
    {
      for (int i=0; i<10; i++)
      {
        Console.WriteLine("Integer Post:" + i);
        Thread.Sleep(500);
      }
    }
    static void PostCharacter()
    {
      const String sampleText = "Packt Thread";
      for (int i = 0; i < sampleText.Length; i++)
      {
        Console.WriteLine("Character Post:" + sampleText[i]);
        Thread.Sleep(1000);
      }
    }
    static void Main(string[] args)
    {
      Parallel.Invoke(
        new Action(PostInteger),
        new Action(PostCharacter)
        );
      Console.ReadLine();
    }
  }
}
```

On executing the preceding source code, it is interesting to observe the highly managed parallelism by .NET framework. From the developer's point of view, the independent parallel methods are constructed and just attached in the `Parallel.Invoke` method. Without any issue, the application is able to achieve in-built parallelism using simple implementation. The execution result will be as follows:

```
file:///C:/Ganesan/PacktThreadSample/PacktThreadSample/bin/Debug/PacktThreadSample.EXE          —    □    ×
Character Post:P
Integer Post:0
Integer Post:1
Character Post:a
Integer Post:2
Integer Post:3
Character Post:c
Integer Post:4
Integer Post:5
Character Post:k
Integer Post:6
Integer Post:7
Character Post:t
Integer Post:8
Integer Post:9
Character Post:
Character Post:T
Character Post:h
Character Post:r
Character Post:e
Character Post:a
Character Post:d
```

Thus, TPL supports the well managed parallelism to build .NET enterprise applications. Task parallel library helps the developer community to leverage the full potential of the available hardware capacity. The same code can adjust itself to give you the benefits across various hardware. It also improves the readability of the code and, thus, reduces the risk of introducing challenging parallel process bugs.

Design challenges

By design, the industry always feels it's too difficult to design distributed enterprise applications. With the fundamental concepts of a loosely coupled system, the lack of latest current state and consistent information leads to many synchronization issues in the design of a distributed system design. As we know, the resources of distributed applications are physically separated in their ecosystem. Due to the missing common resource factors, it is highly possible to have a delay in message delivery, and messages could even be lost. Consider the following diagram:

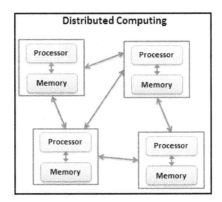

In spite of the previously listed complexities and challenges, distributed applications must be designed to leverage the complete advantages of the design to the end users. By leveraging the built-in concepts of the virtual centralized system, the distributed enterprise application is capable of demonstrating system characteristics such as reliability, transparency, efficiency, security, and easiness.

As a process to mitigate the listed challenges, the distributed applications are developed to deal with resolving several design issues.

Transparency

Spatially separated multiple users consume the distributed applications concurrently. In this condition, it is highly economical to build the sharing concept among the existing system resources for the concurrent execution of the user's request.

By design, one of the existing processes must influence the other concurrently executing process as they might compete for the shared resources. As a result, collision might occur by making concurrent updates in the system. It is highly recommended that you avoid system collision.

Concurrency transparency is a concept in which each user is intended to get a feeling of the sole usage of the resource in the system. To simulate the concept of concurrency transparency, the distributed system is recommended to get the following four properties during the resource sharing processes:

- In terms of **priority-based execution**, it is proposed that you have an event-ordering property. This property ensures access requests to various system resources, which are properly ordered to provide a consistent view to all users of the enterprise applications.

- To balance the deficiency against the need, no **starvation property** is established to ensure the granted resource by not using it simultaneously by multiple processes. As time progresses, the resource is eventually released to grant further access.
- To avoid conflict execution in the system, a third property is established, namely **mutual-exclusion**. This property ensures shared resource accessibility to be leveraged by one process at any point of time.
- To handle resource locking seamlessly, the final property is named **no-deadlock** property. The core purpose of this property is to prevent resource locking mutual progress while competing with each other in the system.

	Forms of Transparency	
#	Type	Objective to hide
1	Access	difference in data representation and how resource is accessed
2	Migration	move a resource to another location
3	Location	where a resource is located
4	Replication	share a resource by several competitive users
5	Relocation	move a resource to another location, while in use
6	Concurrency	share resource by several competitive users
7	Persistance	whether a resource is in memory or on disk
8	Failure	resource's failure and recovery process

With the capability of transparency in the enterprise environment, the distributed system has the ability to deliver the following eight types of transparencies:

- Access
- Migration
- Location
- Replication
- Relocation
- Concurrency
- Persistence
- Failure

Predominantly, this categorization is driven by hiding the system resources of enterprise applications.

Reliability

As described in the first section of this chapter, a distributed system is expected to be more reliable than a centralized system. It seems that the existence of multiple instances increases the level of system reliability. On the flip side, few design challenges on loosely coupled systems have the probability of unreliable characteristics in distributed applications.

Theoretically, reliability is defined as the probability of success. Mathematically, it is represented as *Reliability = 1 - Probability of failure*.

A software reliability curve is pictorially represented as follows:

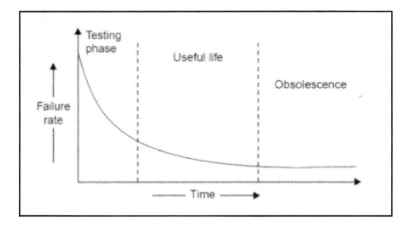

With the inference of the preceding graph, software reliability is defined as the probability of the failure rate in the y axis against the specific time period in the x axis for a particular distributed environment.

By rolling higher reliability in an enterprise application, it is assured that you will be able to avoid/tolerate system faults, tolerate faults, and detect/recover from the identified faults.

Fault tolerance

In an enterprise distributed system, there is a high possibility of error generation due to any mechanical or algorithmic issue. It is defined as a system fault that leads to failure on executing the underlying applications.

In general, faults are classified into three major categories. They are as follows:

- Transient fault
- Intermittent fault
- Permanent fault

Transient faults occur once and then disappear, so it is very difficult to reproduce and resolve the bug. Let me provide a simple example. In a network messaging process, it may be possible to loose data connectivity, and it is pretty hard to reproduce the exact situation. This characteristic is considered the key factor to categorize transient faults.

Intermittent fault repeats multiple times with the characteristics of an occurring fault, and then it disappears for a while, then it reoccurs, and then it disappears, and so on. As a side effect, an intermittent fault is considered the most annoying of component faults in the underlying system. In a similar network example, loose connectivity is the classic use case to illustrate an intermittent fault type.

Permanent fault has a persistent characteristic, so these types of fault continue to exist until the faulty component is repaired or replaced. To continue to our network use case, the physical corruption of network cable is the suitable example. Unless the damaged network cable is fixed or replaced properly, the enterprise application is not suitable to proceed. Further examples of this fault are disk head crashes, software bugs, and burned-out power supplies.

Performance

Performance is quite an interesting field in the IT industry. In simple terms, it is the total number of tasks completed by a computer system. The core objective of the performance factor is to produce the output with a short response time for the given set of tasks.

High throughput will be the goal of performance. There are two factors involved in calculating the value of throughput. This is mathematically noted as follows:

$TH = N / T$

Here, TH - Expected Throughput

N - Number of target tasks

T - Total time require to complete the task(s)

Let me give you a simple example. In a given condition, there are 100 target tasks to be completed in an enterprise application. The total execution time to complete the given 100 tasks may be 20 seconds. So, Threshold (TH) is as follows:

$TH = 100 / 20 = 5$ seconds per task

On comparison with a centralized system, distributed computing is expected to have better performance with high throughput.

To meet the expectation of the preceding characteristics, it is essential to build some performance-oriented aspects in the distributed system.

Decompose

In general, most of the complex large problems are solved in an easy way with the divide and conquer strategy. To illustrate the decomposition strategy, it is better to choose the common network use case. It is possible to transfer the data across the network in large chunks. Instead of transferring the complete large content in one shot, it is much more efficient to process the individual pages.

Similarly, there is another suitable example during the message acknowledgement process. It can showcase better performance by taking advantage of previous messages' acknowledgement with the next message. It is possible to showcase during a series of messages exchange processes.

Caching

In computing theory, some techniques, such as LRU (Least Recently Used), MRU (Most Recently Used), are quite common when it comes to improving performance using the concept of caching. The idea is to temporarily persist the frequently used data at the client site. In turn, the system is not expected to go and retrieve the data on every transaction. Instead, it can refer the cached data in the local layer.

What is the benefit of doing this? Eventually, it improves overall system performance by saving a large amount of computing time and network latency.

Scalability

In computing theory, process is the key component in terms of the execution cycle. In reality, there is always a need to increase the system capability from time to time. With reference to this reality, scalability refers to the adoption capability of any system to align with the work load increments. Scalability is highly integrated with distributed computing by design.

Scale up

In terms of the scaling process, scale up is the traditional model to improve the power of the underlying system. As new resources are added in the same box, it is interpreted as vertical scaling. This is depicted in the following figure:

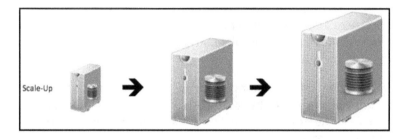

Let me explain this with a simple day-to-day example. On purchasing a personal laptop, the initial hard disk configuration might be 500 GB. After a while, the disk gets full and there is a pressing need to increase the volume of the hard disk. So, the next step might be to increase the volume of the existing hard disk capacity to, say, 1 TB.

Taking advantage of such resources is termed scaling up. This concept is applicable to any type of system resources, such as RAM, processor, disk storage, application, and so on.

Scale out

On similar lines, scale out is another methodology to improve the system performance of an enterprise application. The major difference is in the way of scaling. As demand increases, the additional systems are amended instead of adding the resources to the existing system. So, this design of scaling is termed scaling out or horizontal scaling. It is depicted in the following figure:

Comparing scale up with scale out

In this section, I'm going to address a comparative study between vertical scaling design, that is, scale up and horizontal scaling design, and, scale out technologies used in the industry. Pros and cons to both approaches will help you to decide the suitable design for your need.

Sr.No.	Design factor	Scale up	Scale out
1	Server node	Single server with high power.	Clustered set of server nodes with less power.2
	Computing	Concurrent computing.	Distributed computing.
3	Memory	High powered memory in a single computer.	Less powered memory but collectively simulate high power memory.
4	Processor	Large count of processors in a single computer.	Less processors in a single computer but a cluster of computers is used.
5	Implement challenges	Generally less challenging to implement.	High degree of complexity to implement.
6	Fault tolerance	High possibility of failure.	Easier to run fault tolerance.
7	Utility costs (electricity, cooling)	Low.	High.
8	Network bandwidth	Relatively less due of the single system design.	High degree of network bandwidth for distribution.
9	Vendor lock	Generally severe vendor lock-in due to proprietary	Open source leads to getting away from vendor lock.
10	Total Cost	High.	Relatively low.

Connecting the dots

On connecting the dots of vertical scaling and horizontal scaling, here is the best use case. Generally, disk drives are a good analogy to the scale-up approach, whereas storage virtualization is a good analogy to the scale-out approach.

On observing the recent emerging technology trends of the industry, disk capacity has increased significantly in alignment with processor capabilities, such as multicore technology.

Security

In the computing industry, security is one of the most important principles in an enterprise application. As distributed computing is based on the cluster of the computers, it is highly recommended that you build a stronger security policy here.

Goals

In general, computer security has four goals:

- Privacy
- Secrecy
- Authenticity
- Integrity

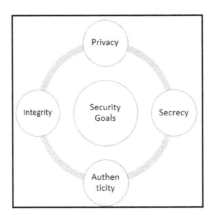

Privacy is considered the information to be used only for the intended purpose, not beyond that. Let's look at a simple example. In the financial industry, there is a term called PII (Personally Identifiable Information). It can be used on its own or with its supplementary information to identify the individual in context. As per the US privacy law and information security, it is mandatory to protect this type of data.

Secrecy is scoped to access only by authorized users, not anyone else. It is pretty simple to explain. In an enterprise application, there might be an administration section to maintain the user base of the system. This section is not supposed to be accessed by anyone in the system. Only some restricted users (such as the administrator) must have the accessibility to this section.

Authenticity is defined as the ability to verify the received request only from the restricted users, not everyone. Let's take an example of private banking by end customers. A bank might maintain the accounts of some n users. The banking application can only be logged into by the registered n customers, not by other people. This is termed authenticity.

Integrity is nothing but maintenance to ensure the accuracy and consistency of the information in an enterprise application. At the same time, the information must be protected from unauthorized access. With system characteristics, it is more integrated into the information reliability factor.

Attack

In computing principles, an attack is any attempt to destroy, disable, or steal unauthorized system access. It violates the security discipline of the proper usage of the underlying system asset.

There are two categories of attacks:

- Passive attack
- Active attack

Passive Attack: With its self-descriptive name, passive attack does not cause any harm to the system with its unauthorized access. As per the shown examples, browsing intrudes an attempt to access other process memories or traverse the message packet in the network. Masquerading is the process of pretending to be an authorized user for unauthorized data or access. Inferencing intrudes the historical records to draw the inferences by running some analysis methods.

Active Attack: This type of attack creates a significant impact on the existing process and so it needs to be addressed thoroughly. The virus program executes the malpractice code from the boot sector of the disk. Worm code impacts the computer network using the security holes. A logic bomb is a piece of code intentionally injected into software to generate a malicious function on a particular condition.

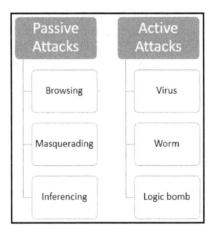

Threats

Threat is a possible security danger in the computing system. It might exploit a vulnerability to breach the security. So, it causes possible harm. There are four categories of threats:

- Interception
- Interruption
- Fabrication
- Modification

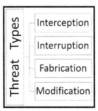

Interception means gaining access to unauthorized service or data in a computer system. Illegal copying is an appropriate example. Interruption makes the system resources unavailable or destroyed, for example, intentional file corruption. Fabrication is related to including the unwanted additional data. Modification alters the original specification of the system to break using unauthorized access.

Summary

In this chapter, you were introduced to the fundamental concepts of distributed computing. Also, it was explained when to use the right way of distributed computation effectively, keeping in mind the scalability and flexibility of enterprise applications. As Microsoft is moving towards an open source strategy, one of Microsoft's .NET solution Message Passing API (MPAPI) is available in CodePlex. MPAPI is an open source framework to enable the programmers without having to use standard thread synchronization techniques like locks, monitors, semaphors, mutexes and volatile memory. In this section, our objective was to learn the fundamental concepts of distributed computing. Microsoft .NET provides a few easy implementation framework with better usage guidelines.

In the next chapter, we will discuss the Software Development Life Cycle (SDLC), which covers various methodologies such as Waterfall, Spiral, Agile, and so on.

4

Software Development Life Cycle

By the end of the previous chapter, it was easy to understand when to use the right way of distributed computation effectively while keeping the scalability and flexibility of an enterprise application. **Software Development Life Cycle (SDLC)** is a term used in systems engineering, information systems, and software engineering as a process. This tutorial elaborates on the various methodologies like Waterfall, Spiral, Agile, and so on. At the end of the chapter, you will understand the fundamental concepts of Enterprise Architecture and its related business needs and benefits.

This chapter will cover the following points:

- What is SDLC?
- The Waterfall model
- The Spiral model
- Agile development
- Microsoft Open Source Strategy to life cycle:
  - Traditional Microsoft model and its origins in MS-DOS
  - Driving factors of the Open Source Model
  - Twin tracks of .NET Framework and .NET Core
  - Current stack of Open Source tools & techniques

This chapter gives an understanding about the SDLC, and how .NET Core and the relevant development processes fit together.

What is SDLC?

SDLC is an industry recognized process with a series of activities or steps to develop a new enterprise application, or to modify the existing software.

Need for a process

In everyone's life, discipline is an important factor in order to be a successful person in their career. Observing disciplined people, it is noticed that they adhere to certain rules and norms at any point of time.

In a similar fashion, software development needs a discipline/process to produce a high-quality enterprise application, which meets or exceeds the expectations of end customers. At the same time, the development effort should be limited to an estimated time and cost.

My job as an Enterprise Architect has cleared this perception, and now I understand the true value of an Enterprise Architect.

Insight of core phases

In general, SDLC has five core phases in any of the models. They are listed and diagrammatically represented as follows:

- Requirement phase
- Design phase
- Implementation phase
- Testing phase
- Production phase

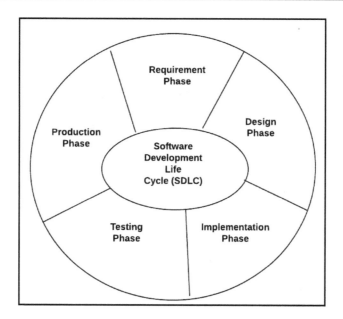

In the requirement phase, the requirements are collected based on the needs of the business stakeholders. The design phase describes the structure and components of the new system as a collection of modules and subsystems. Implementation is the programming phase in which the design is converted into reality. The testing phase is used to certify the functionality of the developed application. Production is the final phase to roll out the system for end customer usage.

SDLC models

The SDLC process has the following few models adopted in the industry:

- The Waterfall model
- The Spiral model
- The Incremental model
- Agile methodology

The Waterfall model

The Waterfall model is developed by dividing the whole process into a few separate phases. Typically, each phase is designed with the simple logic that the outcome of the earlier phase is injected as the input for the next-level phase. By design, each phase of the waterfall mode, is expected to be signed off, before getting into the subsequent phase. It involves the deliverable artifact of each phase like design document, business requirement document, source code, test plan, etc.

Core phases

In a real-life scenario, this model behaves based on our imagination of water falling from top to the bottom, as in a waterfall. It is simply represented in the following diagram. With the similar concept, the Waterfall model is designed as follows with these key phases:

- Business requirement
- System analysis
- System design
- Coding
- Testing
- Maintenance

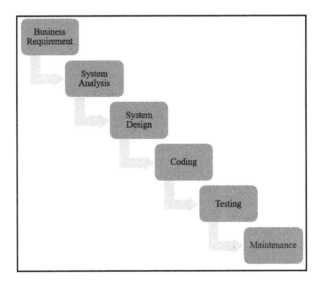

Business requirement

As part of business requirement, all possible specifications and requirements are collected from the business team, and documented as a **Business Requirements Document** (**BRD**). It acts as an evidence of the business agreement. Let us assume a business case study to build a mobile-based application to check the status of the customer support tickets. Then, the BRD will contain the complete functionalities of the mobile application, supported mobile type, the customer credentials, and so on.

System analysis

The given BRD specifications are analyzed in detail from the software system point of view. Based on the analysis, the deliverable document is referred to as a **Functional Specification Document** (**FSD**). FSD is more of a technical response against the given BRD. In our case, let us define one of the FSD entries as, when the end user clicks the sign up button, the application routes to the new user registration form. So, FSD describes the interaction between human and enterprise application, that is, the end user and mobile application.

System Design

System Design Document (**SDD**) is the outcome of the third phase developed by the software design professionals. SDD describes the new system intention or replacement design, with the detailed descriptions of the system architecture and its related components. Some firms develop two levels of SDD, namely, **High Level Design** (**HLD**) and **Low Level Design** (**LLD**) documents. Our use case's SDD is built with the mobile application architecture along with a few internal component designs. Typically, the detail design document covers the input format, database design, processing logic, output layouts, operating environment, interface specifications, and so on.

Coding

In software engineering, the core phase of implementation is coding. In this phase, the software developers build the application using a set of technology tools, languages, and the like. In our use case, the actual mobile application development is part of this phase. Objective C is used for iOS devices, and Java is used for Android devices. The key deliverable of this phase is the source code of the enterprise application.

Testing

Testing is the gateway to validate the functionality, stability, and usability of the developed application. Based on the objectives, there are multiple types of testing in an enterprise. Integration testing covers the connectivity of the components across the application. System testing covers the complete functionality of the application. Performance testing addresses the stability of the product.

Maintenance

Once the certified product is rolled into the production environment, the support team takes control of application maintenance. They monitor the production version continuously, and alert the respective team if anything goes wrong. As the monthly update, the support team is supposed to publish the scorecard of the application in the production environment.

Understanding the Spiral model

The Spiral model is a combination of the iterative development process model and sequential linear development model, that is, the waterfall model, with very high emphasis on risk analysis.

Core phases

The Spiral model is pretty much similar to the incremental model in which more emphasis is placed on **risk analysis** during the course. In the emerging IT industry, risk factor is part and parcel of the process. Instead of avoiding the risk elements, it is advisable to identify the risk and apparently to build the alternative solution. It is referred as risk analysis. The four phases adopted in the Spiral model are explained in the following diagram:

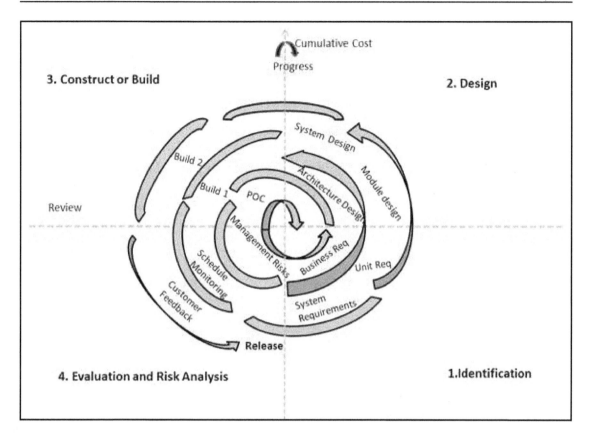

Identification: In the first phase, that is, the Identification phase, it is essential to find out the purpose of the software along with the measures to be taken. It helps to achieve a software to serve all your requirements.

The key coverages in the first phase are listed as follows:

- Studying and gathering requirements
- Detailed study on the feasibility
- Reviews run by a walkthrough to streamline the requirements
- Understanding the requirements document
- Finalizing the list of requirements
- Reviewing the project to take the decision to continue with the next spiral
- If the decision to continue is taken, plans are drafted for the next phase

The core purpose is to identify the business requirements of the system.

Design: This phase calculates all the possible risks with the possibility to encounter; apparently, it is the process to figure out how you would resolve these risks.

The key coverages in the second phase are listed as follows:

- The potential risks are identified based on the drafted requirements and brainstorming sessions
- On identification of the risks, the mitigation strategy is designed and finalized to roll out
- As an artifact, a document is generated to highlight all the risks and its mitigation plans

The core agenda of this phase is to identify the associated risks.

Build: In this phase, the target software is constructed and tested for its core functionality, reliability, and security aspects.

As the core engineering phase, the key coverages in this phase are listed as follows:

- The actual development and testing of the planned software
- Coding of the product
- Execution of the test cases and test results
- Generation of the test summary report and defect report

It focuses on the process of development and testing the target software.

Evaluation: After the current cycle has completed to produce the first prototype, the cycle is re-planned and repeated. The process proceeds to get into the next prototype 2.

As the final step of evaluation, these two key steps are executed:

- Customer evaluates the produced software to provide their feedback for the approval
- Generating the release document to highlight the implemented features

The main purpose of this phase is to plan for the next iteration, if required.

In software development, the aforementioned four phases are repeatedly passed in multiples of iterations named Spirals. In the baseline spiral, the process starts with the planning phase, requirements are gathered, and risk is assessed. Each subsequent spiral builds on the baseline spiral.

Comparing the Waterfall model with the Spiral model

The following table provides a comparison between the Spiral model and the traditional Waterfall model:

Sr.No.	Waterfall	Spiral
1	In the software development life cycle, business requirements are frozen after the initial phase.	In the spiral model, requirements are not frozen by the end of the initial phase. It is kind of executed in a continuous mode.
2	In terms of project execution, there is a high level of risk and uncertainty because of the missing stringent risk management.	By design, the spiral model is modeled to handle better risk management
3	The Waterfall framework type is more of a linear sequential model.	The framework type of the spiral model is based on an iterative process; within each iteration, the linear model is preferred.
4	As the user involvement is only at the beginning of the process, it turns down communication between the customer and developer throughout the development cycle.	User involvement and communication is at a high-degree level between the end user and the engineer.
5	As the model is kind of one-time execution, the reusability factor is least possible here.	During execution of the multiple iterations, the possibility of reusability is quite necessary and developed by nature.

Benefits

In terms of business benefits, spiral development is faster than the traditional model, and so saves cost and effort.

As risk evaluation is well defined in proper method, larger projects are created and handled in a strategic way. Also, it adds control during all the phases of software development.

Spiral model produces the intermediate deliverables at end of each iteration. It gives a great opportunity for the end customers to share their feedback during the early stage. Apparently, this systematic approach means software change management can be implemented faster.

Challenges

As more emphasis is on risk analysis, it is an important phase in the Spiral model, which requires expert associates to execute. Apparently, it increases the overall cost, and so, it is not a good fit for smaller projects.

In the worst cases, Spiral may go on infinitely, which creates wastage on its investment in terms of effort and cost.

As Spiral has a high degree of complexity, and is relatively difficult to follow strictly, documentation is more due to the execution of multiple intermediate phases of the development cycle.

Usage recommendation

Based on the nature of the spiral model, it is highly recommended to use it in large-sized projects where the software needs continuous risk evaluation.

When requirements are a bit complicated and require the continuous clarification, along with the software changes being quite dynamic, the Spiral model is the best fit.

In the same line, when the software development life cycle has sufficient time to get end user feedback for frequent releases, the Spiral model has the highest advantage to roll out.

Agile model

In the legacy Waterfall model, software is developed in the sequential model. On completion of the requirements set, the process moves into design, followed by coding. When we enter the design phase, any change to the requirements is not allowed. As the name suggests, primarily, the water only flows down, you can't make it go up. This is depicted in the following diagram:

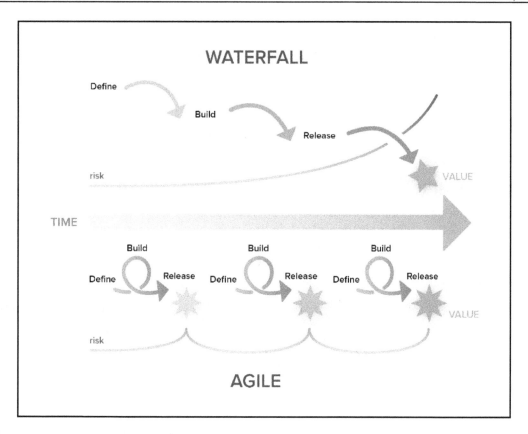

Scrum is the popular term used in the Agile model. Actually, Scrum is one of the software development models in the IT industry to support the emerging industry. Nowadays, IT expects the faster and better deliverables in shorter cycle to support the cost efficiency. In alignment with this strategy, Scrum is designed with a few small teams of intensive, inter-dependent, self-sustaining characteristics. In fact, the deliverables are divided into a small intermediate level, named as Sprint.

Top five reasons to adopt Agile

In the modern IT world, Agile is so popular that everyone is willing to adapt it in their rapid development cycle. Although there are many unfounded reasons, I would like to highlight the top five factors for its industry adoption.

Ambiguous requirements

In the traditional model, assumption leads to confusion in making the end delivery. We assume that the customer will identify all requirements during the initial phase. Though it looks reasonable, the customer is not comfortable to sign off the process officially.

As an outcome, the customer gives a list of known and probable requirements during the initial phase of software development. It is just to avoid missing them in sign-off mode.

Requirement changes

In general, changes are inevitable. The customers don't know what they want in the beginning, and they eventually come back in the later phases. We assume that the cost of change increases during development, and so, a requirements freeze is absolutely required. As a result, we penalize the customer for adding requirement changes later, even though they are valid.

In this emerging highly competitive market, requirements will evolve over a period of time.

Big planning is not practical

We assume that software is so simple that its development can be easily planned from the beginning to the end phase. As all project variables (like scope, size, cost, risk, and the like) can be predicted during the initial phase, we assume that upfront big planning is possible and enough. In fact, planning should also evolve along with the requirements.

To confirm this, the **Standish Group Chaos Report 2015** segments the result of Agile and the Waterfall model based on software projects across sectors between 2011 and 2015. It clearly indicates 39% of Agile success versus 11% of Waterfall against all-sized projects. It comprises of Agile split of 18%, 27% 58% against large, medium, and small projects respectively.

Software review is better than document

In the modern emerging world, customers are happier to review a working software than a bunch of written documents.

In my own experience, the latest customers are asking the question, Demo or Deck ? prior to the review meeting-whether they will be able to see a demonstration of the working software module or not.

Iterative incremental delivery is preferred

In my product development experience, I feel that customers can't wait until the completion of the entire project to get the final product. We assume that the software industry is pretty much similar to the manufacturing industry. As an example, a car manufacturing company produces the final product in a sequential, step-by-step manner. First they produce the chassis, then the engine followed by fitment, and so on.

To impress the customer, the traditional model assumes to deliver the big final product without the intermediate state. But in reality, the customer almost always tends to get a deviation of what they required. It is then too late to rectify it.

To resolve this challenge, the Agile model provides delivery to the customers frequently, in short iterations.

Industry evidence

At XP 2002 conference, Jim Johnson of Standish Group Study reported that the traditional model never used almost half of the features built. The following pie chart shows their survey results:

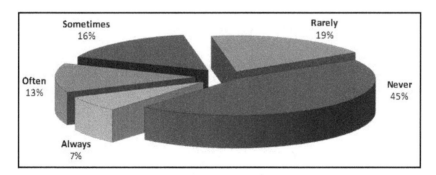

Similarly, the success rate of the Agile model is three times better than the traditional Waterfall model. On conducting various projects between 2002 and 2010, their result speaks for themselves, as shown in the following pie charts:

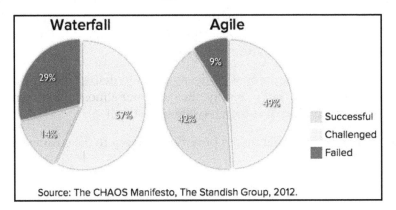

Source: The CHAOS Manifesto, The Standish Group, 2012.

Scaled Agile Framework (SAFe)

These days, **Scaled Agile Framework** (**SAFe**) is quite popular, because it is a freely revealed knowledge base of integrated patterns for enterprise-scale **Lean-Agile** development. It has the bright characteristics of a scalable and modular approach. Apparently, it allows an enterprise to leverage this model that suits their needs.

As a core principle, the SAFe framework synchronizes alignment, collaboration, and delivery for large numbers of agile teams in an enterprise.

SAFe has six core values in its design, which are as follows:

- Code quality
- Program execution
- Business alignment
- Transparency level
- Working model

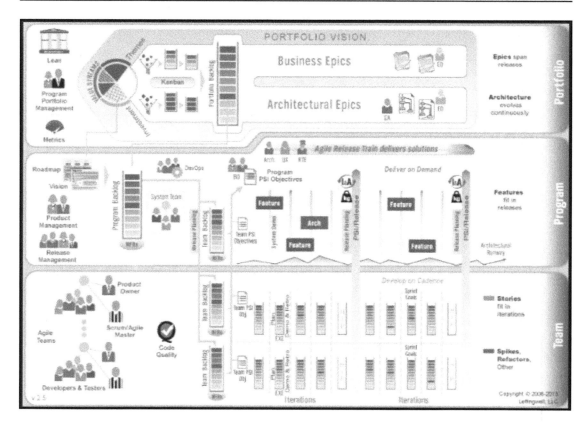

The preceding diagram depicts the design of the SAFe framework.

It operates with common vision, architecture, and UX guidance. The fundamental theme is built around collaboration and adoption of face-to-face planning and retrospectives of the business. As part of the delivery, cross-functional agile teams deliver the working system increments every two weeks.

By implementation, there are two different types of SAFe: 3-Level SAFe and 4-Level SAFe. 3-Level SAFe is for smaller implementations with 100 people or less, or for multiple such programs that do not require significant collaboration. 4-Level SAFe is for solutions that typically require many hundreds of practitioners to develop, deploy, and maintain.

History

The history of SAFe is depicted in the following timeline. The latest version, renamed *SAFe 4.0 for Lean Software and Systems Engineering*, was released in January 2016. Consider the following diagram:

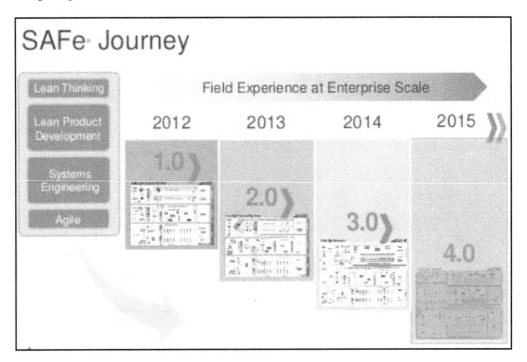

Success Factors

As a matter of fact, SAFe is popular because of its success scorecard measurement, and apparently followed with the improvement process based on the measured score of its development cycle.

As the success factors, the following points are considered as the improvement measures. It helps the management team to arrive at their success metric. Apparently, the management leads to track the investment and its related business values / returns:

- **Cycle time**: measurement of the quickest time taken to get one of the features out
- **Release cycle**: time taken to get a release out
- **Defects**: measured based on the total number and changes in the defects list

- **Productivity**: Calculation of the normalized effort to get a unit of functionality done in the software product
- **Stabilization**: On code completion, a percentage of a release is spent on stabilizing before the release of an enterprise application
- **Customer satisfaction**: Measurement of the end customer's satisfaction level with the rate of change either up or down
- **Employee satisfaction**: Measurement of employee group's satisfaction level either up or down

In reality, most firms execute the patchwork approach to transform into Agile methodology from their traditional software development life cycle models. As a result, a heavy sprint backlog is formed due to extensive dependencies to delivery without impediment. Due to these limitations, SAFe has gained traction as a stage-gated cultural framework in the software development process.

Microsoft open source strategy to life cycle

Open sourcing and crowd sourcing are the latest trends in the software development industry. Though both terms look similar, there is a key difference between open source and crowd source.

Open source is built based on four key pillars, namely, free to use, study, modify, and distribute the software for any purpose. It creates multiple custom software versions. The best well-known example is multiple flavors of the UNIX operating system and Android mobile platform. Open by rule is the theme of the open source culture. Every community member is not allowed to exploit the others.

Crowd sourcing is built based on the marginal interest as well as free time of a large group of people to build an application. This culture benefits the initiator typically without any significant compensation to the participants. In fact, intellectual property and distribution rights are completely owned by the initiator. OpenSignal is the best example of crowd sourcing of the world's wireless network.

Closed source is a complete contradiction to the open source and crowd source culture. It is sometimes referred to as the proprietary model. By design, closed source methodology is owned by an organization with in-house development to generate revenue for their business. Take a look at the following diagram:

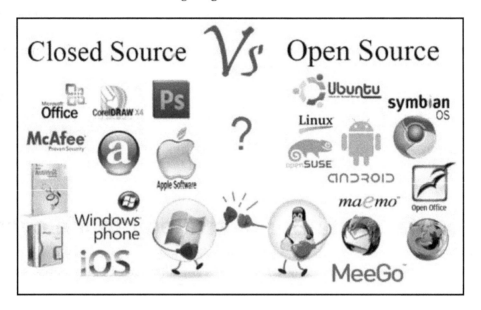

The preceding illustration indicates the list of closed source and open source companies in the IT industry. Microsoft, Apple, and others are the major players among closed source companies, while Linux, Android, and others are prominent among open source companies.

Although Microsoft held an identity as a closed source company, it has switched over to the open source list in recent years. If you take a closer look at the statement made by the CEO of Microsoft, it reflects my words. On June 1, 2001, the ex-CEO of Microsoft, Steve Ballmer, said that Linux is a cancer, which attaches itself, in an intellectual property sense, to everything it touches. It was part of an interview with the Chicago Sun-Times. In October 2014, the current CEO, Satya Nadella, delivered a contradicting note that Microsoft loves Linux, at a San Francisco media conference.

In the coming section, let us analyze the history of closed source and motivation for open source methods deployed in Microsoft.

Traditional Microsoft model and its origin from MS-DOS

Microsoft's Bill Gates's dream was to create a personal computer for every citizen in the world. It might be true now, but his ambition was visionary and very high during the early 1980's.

With his ambition, Microsoft carries a great time line from the MS DOS of 1981 to the Windows 10 operating system of 2015. It was a technologically inspiring path to make his dream come true which is shown in the following timeline diagram:

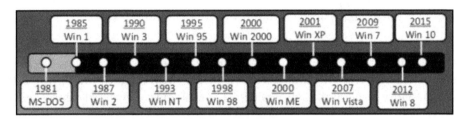

Let us take a look at the smooth journey through Microsoft's major milestones and key deliverables to the industry. Microsoft launched its first operating system named **Microsoft Disk Operating System** (**MS-DOS**) in August, 1981. In terms of user experience, it was not a sophisticated platform; instead, it was just a command-line interface. During this course, Microsoft bought an existing OS from Seattle Computer products for $75K.

Microsoft's first **Graphics User Interface** (**GUI**)-based operating system was launched in the name of Windows 1.0 on November 20, 1985. It was built with a 16-bit multitasking shell on top of an existing MS-DOS installation. Windows 1.0 had the key features of limited multitasking. An interesting fact is that Bill Gates initiated the Windows development program after watching a demonstration of VisiCorp's VisiOn.

Later, Windows 2.0 was released on December 9, 1987, which allows application windows to overlap. Interestingly, it was the first version to integrate the control panel. On the flip side, on March 17, 1988, Apple filed a lawsuit against Microsoft and against HP on March 17, 1988. Apple accused Microsoft and HP of copying the Macintosh System, however, Apple lost the case.

On May 22, 1990, Windows 3.0 was launched with the key deliverable of the protected as well as enhanced mode to run the Windows application with reduced memory. The key improvement was better memory management on the Windows platform. This major contribution came from David Weise and Murray Sargent in 1989.

In the history of Windows OS development, Microsoft released the first major stable version on July 27, 1993-Windows NT. It had an added value of portability to multiple process architectures as well as higher security and stability. As a side note, Bill Gates hired David Cutler from DEC to design Windows NT.

The **Start** button is a revolutionary feature in the Windows platform. Windows 95 was launched on August 24, 1995 with the user methodology and interface to navigate into multitasked 32-bit architectures in addition to the support of 255-character mixed case long files names.

On June 25, 1998, Windows 98 was released with power and network management improvements and USB support. From the end user's point of view, standby and hibernate modes were introduced along with the **windows driver model** (**WDM**) to manage device drivers.

Windows 2000 was released on February 17, 2000 with the addition of **New Technology File System** (**NTFS**), **Microsoft Management Console** (**MMC**), and **Encrypting File System** (**EFS**) active directory along with new assistive technologies to support people with disabilities.

Windows **ME** (**Millennium**) was introduced on September 14, 2000 with the system restore feature and improved digital media and networking tools. The ME version had a tough time in the market, and it was heavily criticized for speed and stability issues. In alignment with this issue, a PC World article dubbed ME as Mistake Edition.

Microsoft came back with another stable OS named Windows XP on October 25, 2001. It had the stable improved task bar and Start menu along with better networking features. XP had a newly improved user interface from the end user's point of view. As the major highlight, XP was the first version of Windows to use product activation in order to reduce software piracy.

After the success of XP, Microsoft was not up to their benchmark by the release of Windows Vista on January 30, 2007. Though Vista was introduced with Windows search, sidebar, shadow copy, and integrated speech recognition, it was bombarded with many criticisms like high system requirements, more restrictive licensing, new digital rights management, and lack of compatibility with some pre-Vista hardware and software.

The world's most dominant (56%) desktop OS, Windows 7, was released on October 22, 2009 with support for virtual hard disks, multi-core processors performance, and an improved touch of handwriting recognition. The main intention was to respond with strong stable deliverables against the criticisms faced by Vista.

Windows 8 was launched on October 26, 2012 with heavier integration of online Microsoft services like SkyDrive and Xbox. In terms of performance, Windows 8 introduced a faster startup through UEFI integration. In terms of user experience, Metro design and a new start screen (no start button) was introduced in the product.

The latest production version of Microsoft Windows, Windows 10, was released on June 29, 2015. As its key features are the return of the Start button, integration with Windows Phone, and a device-dependent interface. In terms of the emerging **Artificial Intelligence (AI)** space, Windows 10 incorporates the Microsoft intelligent personal assistant, Cortana. Take a look at the following diagram:

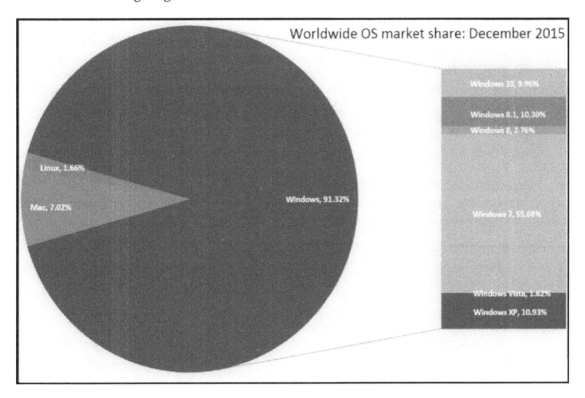

In spite of a long journey of three decades with so many ups and downs, Microsoft still leads the world's desktop OS market share with over 91%. Isn't that amazing?

Driving factors of the open source model

As discussed in the preceding section, three decades of the Windows platform clearly indicates a closed source company. Interestingly, in the mean time, the industry was travelling in the opposite direction with the open source model.

After few years of resistance to the open source model, Microsoft was ready to align with the industry movement. Indeed, Microsoft initiated open sourcing more of its own technologies such as parts of the .NET platform. The Microsoft open-source strategy is focused to help their customers and partners to be successful in today's challenging heterogeneous technology world.

To make a safe landing, Microsoft's open source hosting website named **CodePlex** beta was launched in May 2006, with the official launch in June 2006. After a decade-long journey with CodePlex, Microsoft started moving its bigger open source initiatives into GitHub, because GitHub has become the industry's popular distributed version control and source control management system with a web-based hosting service. As a side note, GitHub's initial product version was released in April 2008.

Microsoft's CodePlex to GitHub strategy move boosted their growth and contribution in the open source space. It made them exhibit a stunning turnaround to the open source world; most importantly, backed up by Microsoft's serious support. You know what?, Now Microsoft is the top organization with the most open source contributors on GitHub. In fact, Microsoft beats Facebook, Docker, Google, Apache, and many other competitors.

Though Microsoft has been working on open sourcing strategy since 2006, a rapid increase has been noticed in recent years. Apparently, it might be because of the change in Microsoft's business strategy and senior leadership changes.

As mentioned in the previous section, it is pretty clear that Microsoft really does love the Linux platform. As a result, Microsoft is going to launch its flagship enterprise database product SQL Server in the Linux platform.

On seeking the last few years' of history of collaboration between Canonical and Microsoft, it is very clear that Ubuntu is one of the first Linux distributions to get an official endorsement to run on Azure. This is possible with a high degree of collaboration on many fronts among the engineering teams of both the firms. As a matter of fact, Azure-managed Big Data stack, HDInsight, is powered by the Ubuntu platform:

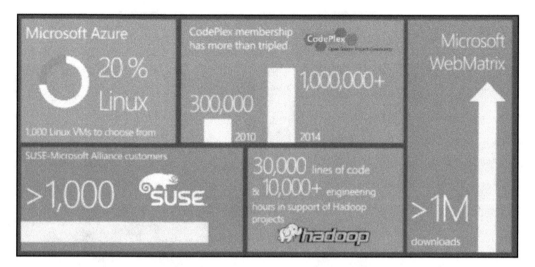

The scorecard seen in the preceding screenshot gives clear facts about Microsoft's Open Source strategy and the related industry contribution. The box in the top-left corner showcases that 20 percent of the operating systems on Azure are based on the Linux platform. With the collaboration effort, the open source operating system is already contributing a lot to Microsoft's bottom line.

Another dimension of metric is the rapid growth of the CodePlex membership. It leads to triple time growth in four years, between 2010 and 2014. This success got reflected in Big Data Hadoop eco system. As the result, there are contribution of 30K LoC (Lines of Code) and the effort of a team of more than 10K engineers.

In essence, Microsoft has so many motivational factors to contribute towards open source projects. It not only adds business value, but is also in alignment with the industry changes.

Twin tracks of .NET Framework and .NET Core

.NET Framework evolved during the early 2000's as a competitive product against the Java platform. On the road map of .NET Framework, it is so interesting to observe the twin tracks of .NET and .NET Core, which is explained in the following screenshot:

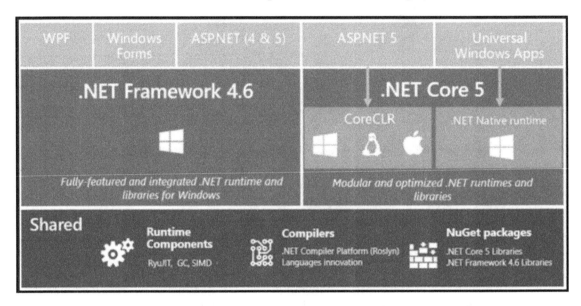

In a nutshell, the .NET framework is marching forward with a closed source strategy, whereas, the .NET Core strategy is towards open source.

Comparing .NET with .NET Core

For better clarity, let me tabularize the various points of difference between these two frameworks

Sr.No.	.NET	.NET Core
1	Complete development environment for Microsoft .NET Application.	As .NET is super set, .NET core will be a subset of the functionalities.
2	Closed source strategy.	Open source strategy.
3	Runs on Windows platform only.	True cross-platform; supports all major OSs like Windows, Linux, Mac, and the like.

4	Proprietary compiler.	Open source compiler, Roslyn.
5	Distributed with Windows.	Distributed with Application.
6	Hosting server IIS, runs only on Windows platform.	Open source hosting server Kestrel, runs across multiple platforms beyond Windows.

As web-based development is so popular in the current industry, it would be wise to follow the timeline of .NET-based web application development methodologies since 1996:

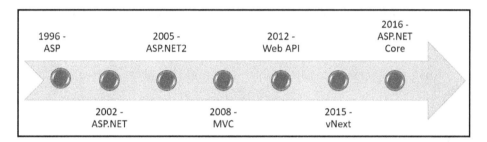

As depicted in the preceding timeline diagram, the Windows OS-based web application started with the **Active Server Pages** (**ASP**) framework in the year 1996. As .NET was stabilized in production during the early 2000's, ASP.NET was released in 2002. From then, there have been multiple flavors of ASP.NET web development, like MVC, Webmail, vNext, and more.

In this great journey, the evolution of .NET Core ignited the evolution of ASP.NET Core, which is a truly cross-platform web application development method in the industry. In fact, ASP.NET reached maturity in 2016.

I'm sure the functionality and features of web app development will migrate from .NET to .NET Core as time progresses.

Current stack of open source tools and techniques

To highlight the adoption of open source tools and techniques by Microsoft, Azure is the best use case to describe here.

Azure clearly has become a multiplatform cloud. Indeed, 25 percent of Azure **virtual machines** (**VM**) are now running Linux. As a top note, Azure now supports five Linux servers as VMs: CoreOS, CentOS, Oracle Linux, SUSE, and Ubuntu. Interestingly, Microsoft is in the process of supporting Docker and Kubernetes container management on Windows and Azure platforms.

Technology experts at Microsoft, Mark Russinovich and Jeffrey Snover, started their contribution towards open source Chef, which was highly visible in ChefConf 2015 by Chef Software Inc.

In terms of the .NET platform, Microsoft's twin track is the clear winner of the .NET open source strategy. In this line, the Microsoft mobile development framework now supports Android emulation as well.

In terms of efforts towards industry collaboration, cooperation, and contribution, Microsoft is actively involved in open source consortiums like AllSeen Alliance, OpenDaylight, and R Consortium. Historically, Apache is quite popular for the open source strategy in the industry. Now, Microsoft supports the Apache Software Foundation to encourage open source growth.

Some of the interesting tools and techniques to observe are .NET Core, TypeScript, R Tools for Visual Studio, Azure's Service Fabric, Visual Studio Code IDE, Team Explorer Everywhere for Eclipse, Computational Network Toolkit for deep learning, AIX tools you can use to build AI in Minecraft, and many more.

The next screenshot shows the current tools and technology stack towards Microsoft Open Source Strategy. It covers the end-to-end solution between the infrastructure and DevOps layers. This stack comprises of popular tools like Grunt, Puppet, Chef, Jodiac, Eclipse, Redis, MySQL, Suse, and so on distributed across the multiple layers of an enterprise application framework:

On observing the strategic direction of Microsoft's recent moves, open sourcing effort comprises of PowerShell, Visual Studio Code, and Microsoft Edge's JavaScript engine. During the release of Windows 10, Microsoft partnered with Canonical to bring Ubuntu in the Windows platform for the first time in history. In the cross-platform mobile development space, Microsoft acquired Xamarin to aid mobile app development. It doesn't stop here. They made an effort to make open sourced Xamarin's SDKs for a broader reach in the industry. SQL Server on the Linux platform is on their roadmap too.

Summary

Now, you are in a position to understand the various types of software development lifecycle processes used in the industry. They includes Waterfall, Spiral, Agile and Scaled Agile framework. Also, you learnt the insight of each model along with the comparison of few instances.

In the next chapter, we will discuss the enterprise practices in software development like maintainability, reusability, testability, and performance optimization in an enterprise application.

5

Enterprise Practices in Software Development

In the previous chapter, we learnt about the **SDLC** (**software development life cycle**), which is a term used in systems engineering, information systems, and software engineering as a process. It elaborates on the various methodologies like Waterfall, Spiral, Agile, etc. As part of the best practices used in Enterprise software development, the essential parts are covered in this chapter. Therefore, this chapter will cover the following points:

- **Application Lifecycle Management** (**ALM**)
- Modern source control repositories such as GIT, TFS, and more.
- Visual Studio Integration with source control component
- Creating custom project templates for .NET Core applications
- Measuring performance using Visual Studio

This chapter will give you an understanding about the enterprise practices in the software development life cycle along with the popular ALM tools and techniques.

What is ALM?

ALM stands for **Application Life Cycle Management**. It is an industry-recognized process with a series of activities or steps used to develop a new enterprise application or modify the existing software.

Core aspects

With the core aspects, ALM can be divided into three distinct areas, namely:

- Governance
- Development
- Operations

Let me illustrate the three core aspects with a simple example, that is, the iPhone's launch by Apple.

Governance encompasses all of the decision-making and project management across the entire firm. In our example, Apple runs the iPhone's business from the conceptual idea to the production roll-out of its multiple versions.

Development is defined as the process of creating the actual application. Practically, the development process reappears several times in an application's lifetime in the majority of enterprise applications. It involves both for upgrades and for wholly new versions. In our context, Apple releases multiple versions of the new iPhone, such as 4, 5, 6, etc. In addition, Apple launches periodic upgrades for existing iPhone devices.

Typically, operation is the work required to run and manage the application. It begins shortly before deployment and then runs continuously. As per our illustration, Apple provides after-sale support to resolve any maintenance issues for the end customers of iPhone products.

ALM vs SDLC

It is common to equate ALM with the SDLC. This is because ALM is constructed around the SDLC's following core phases in an enterprise application development process:

- Requirement phase
- Design phase
- Implementation phase
- Testing phase
- Production phase

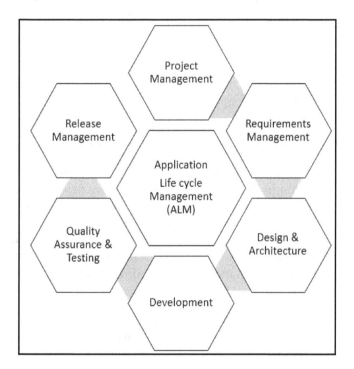

By design, the ALM framework is not developed from scratch; it is built around the SDLC framework. At the same time, ALM is considered more than the SDLC model. However, ALM being more advanced than the SDLC, its simple approach is still considered limiting.

With reference to the previous pictorial representation, the three core aspects are initiated with development as the first part of an application's life cycle. As time progress, the application is updated periodically so that it syncs with the latest features:

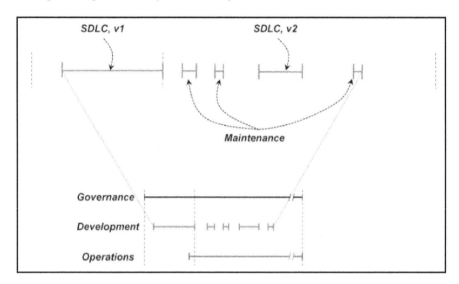

Practically, any software development life cycle is kickstarted only after the business case's approval. With the evolution of the IT industry, the software development methodologies have been changed into various levels. The main shift focuses on shorter and multiple iterations, instead of one huge and complete single cycle. In this context, the image depicts the expansion of SDLC's parts in the development life cycle. As a result, this modern process exhibits software development as a series of iterations. In each sub-process/iteration, it contains its own requirement definition, design, development and quality assurance testing activities.

This solution is not the silver bullet for every problem statement. Nevertheless, this iterative approach is still better than the traditional execution method, which is becoming the norm in many areas.

Let me illustrate with a real world example. As the concept of cross-platforms picked up during the mid 1990s by the Java community, Microsoft started working to release its competitive product, namely, .NET Visual Studio, which was marketed as a .NET developers, **IDE (Interactive Development Environment)** and so it was terms as vision for .NET development tool.

As depicted in the previous image, Visual Studio's product governance kickstarted at the initial time of the product's development, and so the timeline of governance runs from beginning to end in life cycle. This means Visual Studio governance started with Visual Studio 2002 on 13 Feb 2002, and has continued until Visual Studio's latest release on 1 Feb 2017.

In terms of development, each version of Visual Studio runs in an independent SDLC cycle. As per the previous picture, the development cycle is segregated into multiple stages or versions. This is depicted in the middle layer of the previous image.

The operation process actually starts on the eve of the first SDLC process's completion. This is referred to as a Professional Service in the product life cycle. Customer support service is key throughout the operation step. In our example, Microsoft launched Visual Studio's operation with its first release in 2002.

Source Code Control System

The **Source Code Control System** (**SCCS**) is an early version control system. It was developed with the archiving and versioning of program source code and other text files in mind. The original development was in SNOBOL at *Bell Labs* in 1972 by Marc Rochkind for an IBM System/370 computer running OS/360 MVT.

SCCS is primarily used to promote the collaborative development process with seamless effort. It is a software program that supports developers working together while maintaining complete history.

The main purposes of SCCS are listed as follows:

- To allow the development community to work simultaneously
- To avoid the overwriting of each other's work in a collaborative team
- To maintain the complete history of multiple versions

There are a few SCCS available on the market. In this chapter, we are going to deal with two major products, namely, Git and TFS.

As TFS is the leading SCCS product from Microsoft, Git is a free GNU software distributed under General Public License version 2.

Git

Git is a popular open-sourced **Distributed Version Control System (DVCS)**. Here is the design of a Git product for your understanding.

Git consists of three main states in its design. They are:

- Committed
- Modified
- Staged

The committed state refers to data safely stored in the local database. Modified is relates to change in the file/data that have not yet been committed to the database. Staged refers to marking a modified file in its current version to move it into the next commit snapshot.

Git has three core states. These defined states lead into the execution section's three categories, namely:

- Git Directory
- Staging Area
- Working Directory

To start with, the **Git Directory** a storing place for persisted meta data and its related object database for the relevant projects. As it is leveraged to clone a particular repository from one computer to another, it is a highly important component of any Git product.

The **Staging area** is a temporary placeholder, and is usually the file contained in your Git directory. It persists the information about the list of changes to be committed in the next commit cycle. It is often known as an **index**.

The **Working directory** is a placeholder for checking out the version content of a relevant project. Involved with the core process, these files are extracted from the original compressed database in the Git directory. Then, the extracted readable files are placed on the local disk of the end customer. Later, the end user can then use it for their own purpose in this working directory:

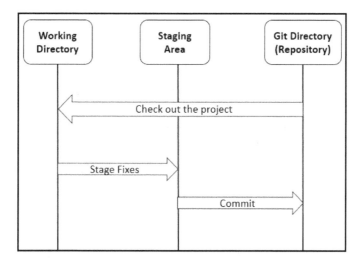

The basic Git workflow is demonstrated in the following diagram:

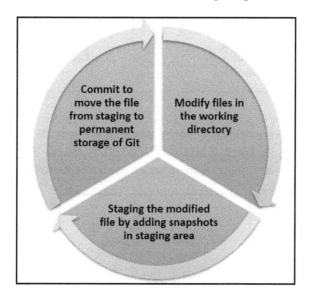

With a good understanding of Git's basic concepts, we can now explore the fundamentals of Microsoft's TFS product.

TFS

In the modern social computing world, collaboration is one of the key factors for success in the business. The **Team Foundation Server** (**TFS**) is a set of tools and technologies designed by Microsoft to enable and promote collaboration within the project's team. TFS coordinates team efforts either to build a product or to complete the project execution:

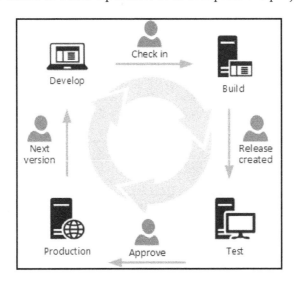

TFS contains a key module to support the version control system. By design, it manages the multiple revisions of source code, documents, work items, and other critical information related to the development project. It increases discipline among the team so as to streamline the version control process. Its features are listed as follows:

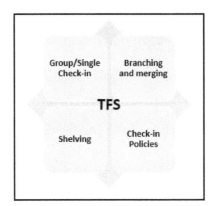

In terms of end customer usage, TFS provides two methodologies to connect with external systems. They are based either in the **GUI** (**Graphical User Interface**) or command line.

In system design, authorization allows user access based on an assigned role. In a similar vein, TFS has two levels of authorization based on the product usage. They are:

- Contributor
- Administrator

Contributor is normal user privilege, where users have access to add, delete, modify, and maintain the records of all changes applied to the underlying file source. It is considered as a normal user mode with the basic functionalities of any version control system.

In contrast, **Administrator** is regarded as a super user of the system. Typically, any administrator manages the version control server by maintaining the integrity of data stored on it. In terms of the TFS product, the administrator has the privilege to manage the workgroups, permissions, setup, and check-in policies.

Git vs TFS

In general, the **Version Control System** (**VCS**) of any development mode is built locally. In an enterprise mode, VCS are broadly categorized into two types, namely, centralized and distributed/decentralized version control systems:

Git and TFS are typical products of two models. After comparing the two models, the functionality differences are presented as follows:

S.No.	Git	TFS
1	Git is a Distributed Version Control System (DVCS). Changes are distributed between users.	TFS is file-system based and not change set-based.
2	By design, creating a branch is extremely quick and cheap, with very little overhead.	Creating branches is very expensive on multiple resources.
3	In terms of cost, Git is an open-source product.	Microsoft's license product.

4	On changing the file content, Git detects the hash difference and marks the file for check-in. During the check-in process, only the changed content goes up. It is more like a snapshot of the data and its difference.	As TFS is based on file-system properties, it is essential to check out a file before it can be committed. If you overwrite that file without checking it out, TFS will not be able to detect a change.
5	If you create 10 branches from a trunk, you are just referencing a snapshot, so the branches take up bytes of data instead of duplicating the data over.	Creating 10 branches from production is essentially copying that folder 10 times.
6	Git supports the concept of **rebasing** or pulling in changes from the trunk or even multiple sources.	TFS simply stores its changes as duplicate files on a server; not rebase.

Visual Studio Integration

After comparing TFS and GIT, any decision should be based on a few key factors, such as the size of a codebase (LoC - Line of Code), team size, and team distribution (by geographic location). On analyzing the previously listed strengths and features, that decision is made easier.

Team Foundation Version Control (TFVC)

TFVC is a centralized version control system. While it works well for small teams with small code bases, TFVC is capable of scaling to support very large codebases (millions of files per branch with server workspaces) and it handles large binary files well. TFVC provides granular permission control, allowing teams to restrict access down to a file level if needed. Since all contributions are checked in to the central server, it is very easy to audit changes and identify exactly which user has committed a given code change.

Git

Git is a distributed version control system where each developer has a copy of the entire source repository. Having a local repository means that Git works well in environments where developers need to work without connectivity. It also offers a simple branching model that enables developers to quickly create local and private branches, enabling flexible workflows. Git also works well in modular codebases where code is distributed across many repositories.

Ultimately, much of the decision about which version control system to use is about preference. However, both systems are equally capable for the majority of teams; it is up to the team to opt for the right choice. Based on the use cases and business scenarios, TFS or Git is selected as the version control system for the enterprise system.

Developing .NET Core project templates for enterprise applications

Software development companies usually develop their own architecture and frameworks for different kinds of projects and in-house products. Depending on the nature of the application, different types of frameworks and architectures are developed. There are Single Page Applications, multi-page applications, Web APIs, Windows services, and so on. These customized frameworks are developed by architects or lead developers to facilitate development efforts and maintain best practices.

We have seen that whenever a new project is started and we want to reuse the existing framework or architecture of some other project, we usually copy files and tweak them to make them usable in the current project. This practice sometimes becomes a cumbersome process for developers when copying files and removing unnecessary code to make it usable. What if we have a ready-made template available in Visual Studio, or some other tooling support that generates the basic boilerplate code and scaffold project?

In the .NET world, we can develop custom templates that can be used to create projects using the same framework code for which the template was created. That customized template then scaffolds the code and creates files and references which were part of the framework, enabling developers or architects to focus on the implementation details rather than configuring and copying the files manually from previous projects.

There are various methods used to create templates for .NET Core projects. We can use VSIX, .NET CLI or Yeoman to create custom templates. The difference between VSIX and .NET CLI is that VSIX is an extension which can be installed as a project template in Visual Studio, where as .NET CLI and Yeoman provide a command line experience for creating projects. In this chapter, we will learn how we can use the .NET CLI to create custom templates.

Creating a custom .NET Core project template using .NET command-line interface tools

Microsoft is working well to make the .NET CLI experience better for developers to create, build, and run projects through the command line interface. You can install the .NET CLI using native installers or use the installation shell script.

Once this is installed, we can go to the command prompt and run commands like `new` to create a new project, `restore` to restore NuGet packages defined in your project, `run` to run the application, `build` to build the application and so on. With this, we don't need the Visual Studio IDE to create, build, or run our project, and we can use Visual Studio Code or any other editor to build our application.

Microsoft has recently introduced and is working on a newer version of .NET CLI, and in the RC3 version a lot of improvements and templates have been made available for you to choose and create projects from. To create custom templates we need to have at least version RC3 or above installed on our machine. To install the latest build, please refer to the following link:
`https://github.com/dotnet/templating`.

The latest build uses the `dotnet new3` command to create projects. Once this is installed, you can type `dotnet new3` on the command prompt and it will show you the number of templates installed.

Creating a template is far easier than creating a new extension. It only requires a `.template.config` folder to be created at the root of the solution or project folder, depending on how many files or folders you want to port, and a `template.json` file that will define some metadata about the template.

Suppose we have an enterprise application architecture ready and we have customized it to bring OWASP security practices, design patterns, and other framework-related code and we need to reuse that project as a template for future projects. We can do that by creating a `.template.config` folder at the root of our solution folder, as follows:

Then, we will create a `template.json` file inside the `.template.config` folder, whose markup will be as follows:

```
{
  "author": "Ovais Mehboob (OvaisMehboob.com)",
  "classifications": [ "Web", "WebAPI" ], // Tags used to
     search for the template.
  "name": "EA Boilerplate ASP.NET Web API",
  "identity": "EA.Boilerplate.WebApp", // A unique ID for
    the project template.
  "shortName": "eawebapi", // You can create the project
   using this short name instead of the one above.
  "tags": {
    "language": "C#" // Specify that this template is in C#.
  },
  "sourceName": "EAWebApplication", // Name of the csproj
    file and namespace that will be replaced.
  "guids": [ // Guids used in the project that will be
    replaced by new ones.
    "8FBE597A-CFF6-4865-B97A-FCE69005F098",
  ]
}
```

Next, we can use the following command to install this template in the .NET CLI tool:

```
dotnet -i "Path of your project"
```

We can then create a new project by executing the following command:

```
dotnet new3 eawebapi
```

Performance measuring for .NET applications

In this section, we will learn what factors we should consider while measuring performance for .NET applications. We will learn what the performance metrics are and how we can utilize different tools in Visual Studio to measure them. We will discuss UI responsiveness, CPU and memory performance metrics, and how to analyze memory leaks.

When any application faces performance bottlenecks, the first thing to identify is the root cause of the area which is causing that bottleneck. Usually, when anything happens on the performance side, developers or architects immediately jump into rectifying that issue by optimizing different ends. However, in doing that, the bottleneck remains still exist. Measuring performance is essential before undertaking any steps for optimization. We should spend time on identifying the root cause before optimizing the application code or other areas.

CPU utilization

Applications that do a lot of CPU work are known as CPU-bound applications. Applications that involve a lot of I/O, object locking, threading, image processing, or any other task that involves CPU utilization are termed as CPU-bound applications. To monitor the performance of CPU-bound applications we can use tools like Sampling and Instrumentation.

Sampling is done by running some flow of an application then aggregating them with multiple users to know the percentage measure of application performance and CPU utilization whereas Instrumentation is monitoring the exact chunk of code being executed followed with the time taken during execution. This is more detailed level but to carry out this operation we need to modify or change application's code to capture this information which is always not possible for applications hosted on production servers.

Using the Sampling method in Visual Studio to collect performance statistics

When you start sampling on your application, it collects information about the methods that are executing in the application flow and provides a summary as a result. Methods that are heavily executed during the execution cycle become part of the active function call tree known as **Hot Path**. Once the test is completed, it generates the timeline graph that you can use to look for the bottleneck.

In Visual Studio 2015 or greater, we can start the sampling process by going to the **Analyze > Performance Profiler...** menu. Make sure the configuration is set to release mode.

Once you run your application, it starts recording your application flow and identifies the Hot Path. You can perform operations on your app that can produce performance issues and then stop your application and profiler:

To get the sampling profiling result, choose the CPU sampling and finish. This will run the profiler in the background and open up an application where you can perform any action and execute any scenario. Once you close your application, a profiling report will be generated.

Profiling report shows three sections that are Sample Profiling report, Hot Path, and Functions, which do most of the individual work. Sample profiling report displays the graph shows the CPU usage in a percentage at a particular time. Hot Path tells you which code path in your application is responsible for most of the CPU execution. Hot Path displays the Inclusive and Exclusive samples. Inclusive samples are collected during the execution of the target function and contain the samples of the child functions that are executed, whereas exclusive functions do not contain the child function execution and contain the direct execution of the instructions executed by the target function. We can also click on any of the functions being executed to see the code that has taken that time.

Here is Hot Path showing that 100% execution time was done on `GetData` method:

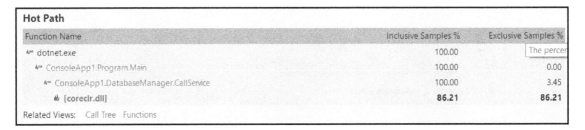

Hot Path		
Function Name	Inclusive Samples %	Exclusive Samples %
⊿ dotnet.exe	100.00	The percer
⊿ ConsoleApp1.Program.Main	100.00	0.00
⊿ ConsoleApp1.DatabaseManager.CallService	100.00	3.45
⚭ [coreclr.dll]	86.21	86.21
Related Views: Call Tree Functions		

We can click on **GetData** to see the complete function call and the code being executed:

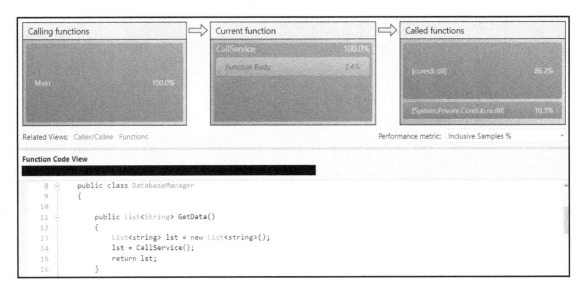

```
 8     public class DatabaseManager
 9     {
10
11         public List<String> GetData()
12         {
13             List<string> lst = new List<string>();
14             lst = CallService();
15             return lst;
16         }
```

Measuring UI responsiveness

User Interfaces are the core essence of any business application. Business application could be a desktop-based application, web-based, or a native application that runs on mobile. Measuring UI responsiveness is an essential practice in an enterprise world to make an application more responsive by emending UI-related issues and providing users a better experience. Desktop applications or native mobile applications have one UI thread that locks user access until the current request is processed. It could be a huge database call or any other backend processing like image or file that locks the UI thread. Thus, give bad experience to user.

To measure UI responsiveness, we can use the Concurrency Visualizer extension of Visual Studio that can be added in Visual Studio IDE from extensions and updates. This is not supported for web projects but provides tabular, graphical, and textual data to represent the relationship between your application threads and the system where application is running on.

To run Concurrency Visualizer you can click on the **Analyze** > **ConcurrencyVisualizer** option in Visual Studio, where you can start a new process, attach an existing one, and so on.
The Concurrency Visualizer extension for Visual Studio can be installed from the Visual Studio market place (http://marketplace.visualstudio.com).

Once it runs, it starts analysing your system UI and provide detailed results like utilization, threads and cross-core thread migration, delays in synchronization, overlapped I/O operations, and much more. Here is the sample screenshot of the report it generates after running an analysis on a particular application:

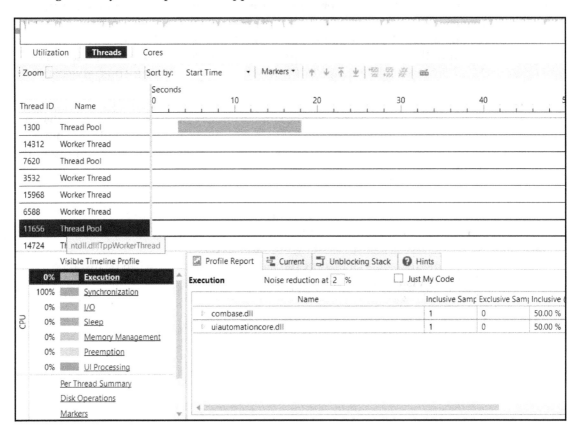

Analysing memory leaks

Sometimes bad design and pitching something on production without prior testing or code reviews embrace quality issues. Memory leak is one of the most common factors in software that increases the memory, where often, restarting or killing the process is the only possible solution.

Memory leak is a type of resource leak in which the application does not manage the memory property and does not deallocate or dispose the objects from **heap** storage.

In the managed world of .NET, **GC** (**garbage collection**) is done automatically by the CLR from time to time and developers don't follow the practice of disposing objects and often rely on the GC to free up memory. However, this is not always a good practice with enterprise-level applications or that involve a lot of Disk I/O, Database, and other related operations.

Memory leaks for managed .NET application is a lot more complex to identify, but there are certain tools that help to diagnose the memory leaks in an application.

When we run the managed .NET application, four types of heaps memory are created to store the objects as follows:

Type of Heap	Description
Code heap	Stores the actual native code instructions when the JIT is done
Small object heap	Stores objects that are less than 85K in size
Large object heap	Stores objects that are greater than 85K in size
Process heap	Process wise heap starts for 1MB and expands

.NET maintains a complete data structure on Stack, where all the primitive data types are stored and the addresses of the objects stored on heap. This is used by the .NET to determine the program execution. Internally, when a method is called, .NET creates a container that contains all the information related to the method parameters, variables, and lines of code that will be executed for that method. If that method is calling another method, a new container is created and stacked on top of it. On the other hand, when the method completes, the container is removed from the top of the stack and so on.

When the GC runs, it checks for the objects allocated on heap storage but not referenced by any other object of program execution. Other than in the stack, there are more references where GC checks for the objects are Static or Global object references, Object finalization, interop references, and CPU registers. These references are known as GC Roots. Garbage collectors traverse the GC Roots tree and check each of the objects being used and if there are no references freed up from memory.

Identifying memory leaks

There are various tools like JetBrains dotMemory, PerfView, and others to analyse or identity memory leaks for performance. dotMemory is a very good tool but requires a license for commercial use. In this section, we will use Perf View and see how memory leaks can be identified.

To install PerfView, you can go to Microsoft download centre site, `https://www.microsoft`
`.com/en-us/download/details.aspx?id=28567`, and download.

It's a simple `.exe` file and you don't need to install it. PerfView is highly suitable for
production use. It is quite easy to use and takes snapshots while your application is running
without affecting or freezing the application performance.

Another important tool is the VMMap, which shows complete information, such as size,
committed, private, and other information related to storage for a particular process. After
running VMMap you can select the process for which you want to know the GC Roots
storage information as follows:

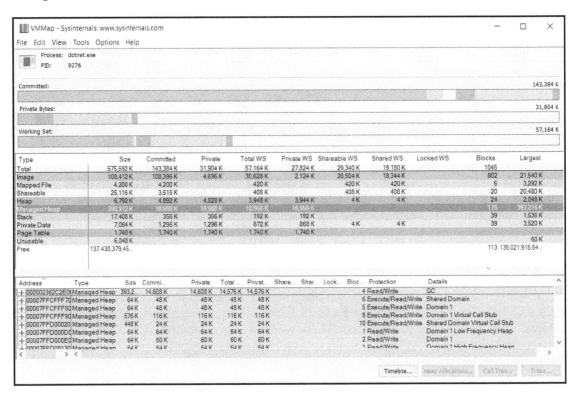

This tool is good to get the glance view storage allocation, but to rectify the exact area where the problem persists we will use PerfView.

To take a snapshot from PerfView, run the PerfView and click on **Memory** > **Take Head Snapshot** option:

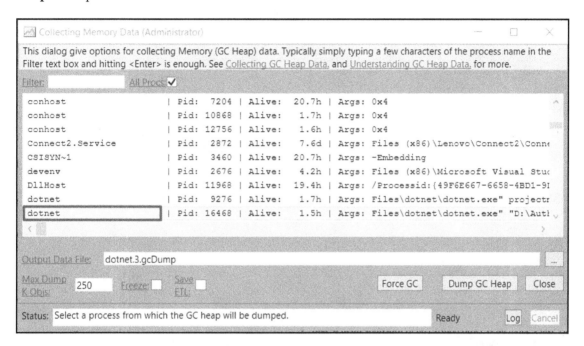

Max. Dump K Objs is the total size of the objects snapshot will be taken. If the size is big, PerView automatiaclly performs Heap Sampling and extracts the maximum of 250 K.

Force GC is an option from where we can explicity run GC to perform garbage collection.

Dump GC Heap takes the snapshot and stores it your PerfView for further analysis. You can take multiple snapshots and compare the differences:

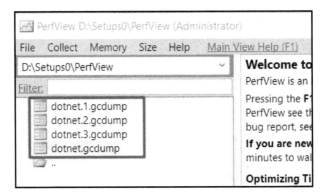

You can open a dump file, and it opens up the GC Heap viewer that provides a list of aggregate stacks encountered during sampling. It includes the methods frames that were captured during sampling:

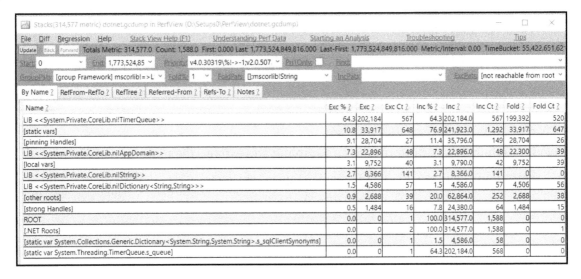

The important columns to note are **Exc%**, **Exc**, **Inc%**, and **Inc**. Exclusive represents the time spent on a particular method, whereas Inclusive represents the exclusive time plus the time x in the methods. We can also drill down each object and see the child objects in the tree.

This is a great tool to identify memory leaks, and to learn more you can refer to the *Channel 9* video at the following link:

```
https://channel9.msdn.com/Series/PerfView-Tutorial.
```

Summary

Now, you will have learnt the important aspects and best practices of application life cycle management, popular ALM tools, custom templates for .NET Core applications, and how to measure the performance of .NET applications using Visual Studio in an enterprise software development process.

In the next chapter, we will discuss how to implement layered architecture using ASP.NET Core and client-side frameworks.

6
Layered Approach to Solution Architecture

There are various approaches when developing a solution architecture, and it is important to note that complexity should only be added in the architecture when it is required. Adding complexity to the architecture is not a bad practice and is acceptable if it solves a particular need or reduces the development effort for developers during the development life cycle. In a **layered architecture**, the application consists of various layers, namely, presentation, service, business, and data access layers, and every layer is responsible for serving specific tasks.

The layered approach is one of the widely used approaches in developing enterprise applications. In this chapter, we will study some of the core concepts of layered architecture and also develop an architecture using .NET Core to discuss this topic.

In this chapter, we will focus on the following topics:

- Discuss the following layers in layered architecture:
  - Presentation layer
  - Service layer
  - Business layer
  - Data access layer

- Implement a practical implementation of each layer using .NET Core, ASP.NET Core, Entity Framework, and Angular

Layers in layered architecture

An enterprise application consists of various layers. Each layer is independent and fewer dependencies on the other layer that makes it more pluggable and easy to maintain. Communication with other layers can be made through interfaces that encapsulate the logic or implementation details from the calling layer. Normally, business applications are n-tiered and logically divided into the presentation layer, service layer, business layer, and data access layer. The benefits of layered architecture are as follows:

- It is a loosely coupled system
- Teams can work on different layers, in parallel, with minimal dependencies on other teams
- Changes to any layer in terms of technology or business logic have little impact on the other layers
- Testing can be done easily

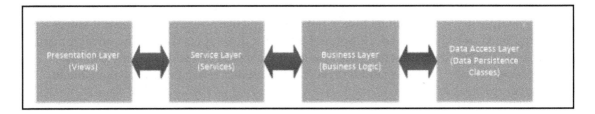

Presentation layer

This layer contains all the user interfaces of an application. In terms of ASP.NET Core, it contains MVC controllers, views, static files (images, HTML pages), JavaScript files, and other client-side frameworks like Angular, Knockout, and others. This is the frontend layer with which the user interacts. Keeping this layer separate facilitates upgrading the existing interfaces or design without making any changes to the backend layers.

There are some architectural principles which should be followed when designing the presentation layer. A good presentation layer design can be achieved by following these three principles:

- First of all, our data should be separated from view and use patterns like MVC, MVVM, or MVP to address separation of concerns.
- Separate teams should work on the UI and business layer simultaneously.

- Minimize the application logic separate from the presentation layer -- the presentation layer should only contains forms, fields, validation, and related checks. All server-side logic should reside on the business layer.

Service layer

The service layer is the main layer, which connects the presentation layer to the business layer. It exposes some methods through class libraries, Web APIs, or web services used by the presentation layer to perform certain operations and access data. Moreover, it also encapsulates the business logic, and exposes POST, GET , and other HTTP methods to perform certain functionality. There are few advantages of keeping it web-based instead of making it a shared library project.

The following table shows the advantages of both a web-based and a shared library:

Advantages	
Web service (Web API, WCF, Web Services)	**Shared library (POCOs)**
Technology agnostic – any consumer can access	No Internet connection is required
Code cannot be decompiled	No serialization overhead
Easy upgrades or bug fixes	No risk of forgery
Scalable	Higher performance as native code is called
Centralized deployments	There is no downtime of service impacting the consumer

The service layer can also contain methods that do not call the business layer, but are helper methods or common methods, which are used by the presentation layer and other consuming parties to the achieve desired functionality. For example, the service layer can contain a method that takes a list of strings as a parameter and returns a **CSV (comma separated value)** string where this operation does not require any backend database operation.

Securing services is highly recommended when building enterprise applications; keeping the endpoints open leads to counterfeiting of the data from unauthorized access. With ASP.NET, this can easily be achieved by authenticating the user using the ASP.NET security mechanism, protecting resources imperatively through the Authorize attribute or custom policies. The service layer is the primary layer that exposes data to third-party sources. Therefore, logging and transactions should be properly addressed.

There are various approaches to implement the Service layer using the .NET stack. We can use Web API, Service Stack, WCF, and POCOs to create the service layer. However, with .NET Core, we can develop services using Web API, Service Stack, and the POCOs libraries. Whereas WCF can be developed on .NET 4.5 or earlier versions of the .NET framework, proxies can be created using WCF Connected Services.

Business layer

The business layer is the core layer in the layered architecture. It contains the actual logic of the application and manages the events that trigger from the presentation layer. There are different approaches when building the business layer and every approach is dependent on the scope and timeline of the project.

Let's discuss a few patterns that are highly used when designing or architecting the business layer:

Transaction Script pattern

With this approach, the business layer provides simple public methods to perform a particular functionality. This is a procedural approach, where each method represents the corresponding operation taken on the presentation layer. For example, the SubmitVendor action may have a corresponding method in the business layer such as CreateVendor and so on.

Table Module pattern

In this approach, each class represents one entity, used to perform **CRUD (create, read, update,** and **delete)** operations on the table. Considering the .NET stack, we mostly used the DataSet and DataTable objects, that is bound to the particular table in the backend database.

Active Record pattern

With the Active Record pattern, each instance of the class represents a database row. So, if we have an instance of the class that is representing a particular row, we can use that instance to perform CRUD operation on that row and this can be implemented using Entity Framework or other **ORM (Object Relational Mapper)** tools.

If you have noticed in the Entity Framework, every class is bound to a consequent table, and contains properties that are tightly bound to the table columns. With this pattern, each POCO class represents a database row and contains a key and other properties to represent that row.

Domain Driven Design (DDD) pattern

Domain Driven Design is a complex pattern, but not tightly coupled with the backend database. In this approach, classes are structured in such a way as to represent the entity of the domain and not the table. For example, if we are going with the DDD pattern, we may have three tables--User, Address, and Profile, which represent the company's employee as a domain entity. This is a good approach, however, it takes sufficient time to understand and structure the domain entities. It represents the business language and hides the logical details from the presentation layer.

Data access layer

The **DAL (data access layer)** is the core layer that interacts with the backend database. There are certain core classes we develop, which communicates with the database, manage connections and execute the CRUD operations. Certain patterns can be implemented to minimize the redundant effort of opening and closing connections and applying transactions that can be encapsulated through a simple interface and used by the business layer to perform CRUD operations. The most widely used pattern for this layer is the **Repository** pattern, which we will explore later in this chapter.

Objectives of layered architecture

The objective of layered architecture is to provide separation between each layer. Each layer should be designed in such a way that it has very little, or no impact on the other layers. There are different techniques to achieve decoupling between layers and interfaces are one of the techniques that are primarily used. Instead of using the concrete implementers, we use interfaces to communicate with the other layers and the changes do not impact on others. For example, there are cases where we may want to change the database engine in the DAL and instead of using SQL Server we can choose Oracle. Or, in the case of the UI, we may want to change the Web Forms framework for an MVC framework. Good architecture always provide this decoupling and reduces dependencies.

Practical implementation of layered architecture in .NET Core

So far, we have learnt the core concept of layered architecture and the usage of each layer. To elaborate and study more about the best practices and design patterns used to implement layered architecture using .NET Core, we will develop an enterprise application architecture and take a simple **tenant** website.

Scope

We will take a scenario where customer is a tenant and is already registered. The customer uses the **TMS (Tenant Management System)** to lodge service requests. In this chapter, we will implement the basic Service Request form and primarily focus on the architecture. You can try and complete the rest of the implementation from the code provided with this book.

Logical architecture

Logically, our solution is divided into five projects. The following is the architecture diagram showing how each project is lined up and represents each layer of the layered architecture:

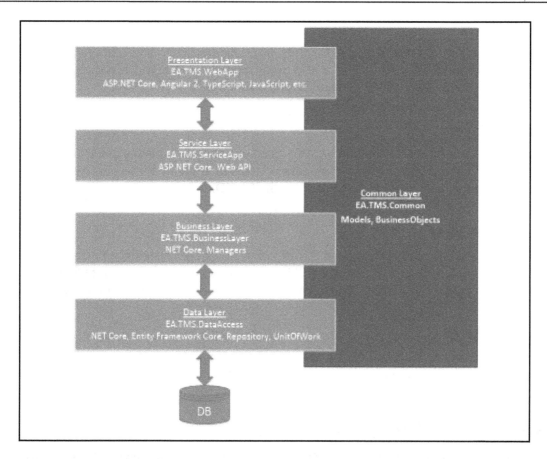

Following is a description of each layer in our project:

Presentation layer

Web application project is named as EA.TMS.WebApp. This is an ASP.NET Core project and contains views, Angular components, and TypeScript files to interact with the service layer to perform HTTP operations. It also provides user authentication using the **CAS** (**centralized authentication system**) system, developed in Chapter 10, *Security Practices with .NET Core*, to authenticate users and provide authorized access.

Service layer

The service layer project is named as `EA.TMS.ServiceApp`. This is an ASP.NET Core project and contains Web APIs. This is also protected using CAS. This service layer interacts with the **BL** (**business layer**) to perform business functionality.

Business layer

The business layer project is named `EA.TMS.BusinessLayer`. This is a .NET Core class library project and contains business manager classes to implement business requirements. This will call the data access layer to perform the CRUD operations.

Data access layer

The data access layer project is named `EA.TMS.DataAccess`. This will be the .NET Core class library project. In this project, we will implement Repository and Unit of Work patterns and define our custom Data Context class to use with Entity Framework Core.

Common layer

The common layer project is a .NET Core class library project and we have named it `EA.TMS.Common`. This is shared between all the layers.

Setting up the environment

To set up our development environment, here are the list of pre-requisite setups that we need to run on our machines:

1. Install Visual Studio 2015 or 2017 from `http://www.visualstudio.com`.

   Visual Studio is also available for Mac now and you can download it from the same link as mentioned above.

2. If using Visual Studio 2015, make sure Update 3 is installed. This is needed to work smoothly with Angular, which is based on TypeScript 2.0.
3. Install the latest .NET Core version from `https://www.microsoft.com/net/core`.
4. Install TypeScript 2.0 for Visual Studio 2015 or a later version.
5. Install Node 4 or later. You can check the version by running the command `node -v` at the command prompt.

6. As we will be developing an **SPA** (**Single Page Application**) and using Angular as the frontend client-side framework, we have the option to either configure it on our own, or install a Visual Studio extension for Angular, which makes the basic boilerplate configuration simple. In this chapter, we will develop a web application project from scratch without using ready-made extension.

7. Another way to create projects is using the .NET CLI tools. The new .NET CLI tooling provides certain templates that you can use to create projects by running simple commands through a command-line interface. The main benefit of using these tools is cross-platform. We can use these tools in Linux, Mac, and Windows operating systems to create projects and use Visual Studio Code, or any other editor, to write code.

Creating the solution

Once our development environment is setup, we will start creating the layers as follows.

Creating the common layer

We will start by creating the common layer first. This layer is the common layer and is referenced by all the other layers. It contains some core classes and helper functions which will be used by each layer. The data access layer will create a database from the entities defined in the common layer. The business layer will use the entities and business objects defined in the common layer to perform data manipulations and the presentation layer will use it to bind the models with the views.

To start with, create a new **Class Library (.NET Core)** project. Once it is created, we will add a few entities specific to the **Tenant Management System**:

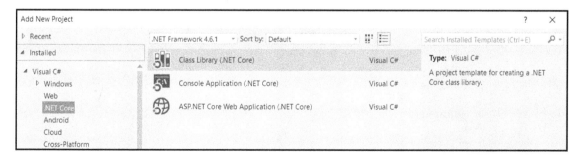

The following entity will hold user profile information and is derived from the `IdentityUser` class provided in the ASP.NET Core Identity Framework. We will use ASP.NET Identity Core and Identity Server to perform user authentication and authorization. To learn more about Identity Core and how to configure it in an ASP.NET application, please refer to Chapter 10, *Security Practices with .NET Core*.

Here is the code of the `ApplicationUser` class:

```
public class ApplicationUser : IdentityUser
{
}
```

Normally, when designing the entity models, all the generic properties should reside under the base entity. So, we will create a `BaseEntity` class, which will be inherited by all child entities.

Here is the code for the `BaseEntity` class:

```
public abstract class BaseEntity
{

    public BaseEntity()
    {
        this.CreatedOn = DateTime.Now;
        this.UpdatedOn = DateTime.Now;
        this.State = (int)EntityState.New;
    }
    public string CreatedBy { get; set; }
    public DateTime CreatedOn { get; set; }
    public string UpdatedBy { get; set; }
    public DateTime UpdatedOn { get; set; }

    [NotMapped]
    public int State { get; set; }

    public enum EntityState
    {
        New=1,
        Update=2,
        Delete =3,
        Ignore=4
    }

}
```

In our `BaseEntity` class, we have four transactional properties--`CreatedBy`, `CreatedOn`, `UpdatedOn`, and `UpdatedBy`, which are common for every entity derived from it. These fields are good to store the user information and the transaction date time. `EntityState` is used to manage the state of each object and helps the developer to set states when manipulating a grid or a collection.

Entities mapped to database tables

The following is the `ServiceRequest` class that will be used to submit the service requests of the tenant:

```
[Description("To store Service Requests submitted by Tenants")]
[Table("ServiceRequest")]
public class ServiceRequest : BaseEntity
{
    [Key]
    public long ID { get; set; }

    public long TenantID { get; set; }
    [ForeignKey("TenantID")]
    public virtual Tenant Tenant { get; set; }

    [MaxLength(1000)]
    public string Description { get; set; }

    [MaxLength(300)]
    public string EmployeeComments { get; set; }

    public int StatusID { get; set; }
    [ForeignKey("StatusID")]
    public virtual Status Status { get; set; }

}
```

Please refer to the code provided with this book to define more entities.

Business objects

We will create a separate folder for `BusinessObjects` inside the common layer. `BusinessObjects` are classes that are composite entities or business models and contain properties to carry data for a specific business model. The following is a sample `TenantServiceRequest` business object:

```
public class TenantServiceRequest : BaseEntity
{
```

```
        public string Description { get; set; }
        public string EmployeeComments { get; set; }
        public string Status { get; set; }

        public long TenantID { get; set; }
        public string TenantName { get; set; }
        public string Email { get; set; }
        public string Phone { get; set; }
    }
```

Logging events

Logging events contain some constant numbers, which are used while logging information. When developing an enterprise application, it is a recommended approach to provide a specific action number, irrespective of whether it's an error, information, warning, and so on.

This helps the developer to trace out the exact action which was executed on that piece of code when the message was logged. And, in the event of an error, it immediately gives at a glance meaning about the error type, making it easy for the developer or support team to identity the root cause and resolve it.

Here are a few of the sample logging events we have defined in our project, which will be used through the layers where logging will be implemented:

```
    public static class LoggingEvents
    {
        public const int GET_ITEM = 1001;
        public const int GET_ITEMS = 1002;
        public const int CREATE_ITEM = 1003;
        public const int UPDATE_ITEM = 1004;
        public const int DELETE_ITEM = 1005;
        public const int DATABASE_ERROR = 2000;
        public const int SERVICE_ERROR = 2001;
        public const int ERROR = 2002;
        public const int ACCESS_METHOD = 3000;
    }
```

Logging helper

`LoggingHelper` is a helper class, which will be used throughout the project to log the exception and read the complete stack trace about the exception:

```
    public static class LoggerHelper
    {
        public static string GetExceptionDetails(Exception ex)
```

```
    {
        StringBuilder errorString = new StringBuilder();
        errorString.AppendLine("An error occured. ");
        Exception inner = ex;
        while (inner != null)
        {
            errorString.Append("Error Message:");
            errorString.AppendLine(ex.Message);
            errorString.Append("Stack Trace:");
            errorString.AppendLine(ex.StackTrace);
            inner = inner.InnerException;
        }
        return errorString.ToString();
    }
}
```

More helper methods and classes can be added in the common layer, which can be used throughout the application layers.

Here is the final structure of our common layer:

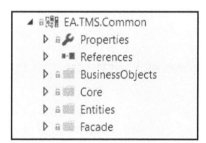

Data access layer

All the repositories and database persistence classes reside under the data access layer (**DAL**). This layer is used by the business layer to perform database operations. For database persistence, we will use Entity Framework Core - Code first model. Entity Framework is an **object relational-mapper (ORM)**, which enables developers to work with relational data using domain specific object and allows the use of LINQ or Lambda expressions to search or filter data.

Let's start by creating a new **Console Application (.NET Core)** project. The reason why we create the .NET Core console application is because we will run the .NET CLI commands to run database migrations and it will not work with the class library project as per the present configurations:

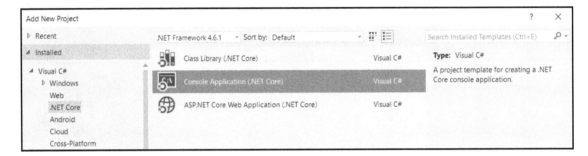

In our DAL, we will implement a Repository, Unit of work pattern, and Factory patterns.

Creating Data Context

When working with the code first model of Entity Framework, we need to define our custom context class, which should be derived from the DbContext class. Any class that inherits from the DbContext class is used to perform the database manipulation on the entities. In our case, we will use IdentityDbContext, which is a wrapper on the DbContext class and takes the IdentityUser object. IdentityDbContext is a generic base class, which can be customized with entity types that extend from the IdentityUser types.

Given next is the DataContext class, which contains the DbSet property for each entity. DbSet represents the entity set that is used to create, update, delete, and read records from a particular table to which the entity is mapped. If DbSet is defined for a particular entity, then the table will be created on running the database migration and the relationship and other constraints will be added based on the configuration defined. Entities that are not defined through the DbSet property will not be affected by migration and their corresponding tables will not be generated.

Here is our DataContext class containing a few DbSet properties and derived from IdentityDbContext class:

```
public class DataContext : IdentityDbContext<ApplicationUser>
{
    public DataContext()
    {
    }
```

```
protected override void OnConfiguring(
DbContextOptionsBuilder optionsBuilder)
{
    base.OnConfiguring(optionsBuilder);
    optionsBuilder.UseSqlServer("Data Source=.;
    Initial Catalog=TMS;
    Integrated Security=False;
    User Id={your_db_userid};
    Password={your_db_password};");
}

protected override void OnModelCreating(ModelBuilder builder)
{
    base.OnModelCreating(builder);
}
+
public virtual void Save()
{
    base.SaveChanges();
}

#region Entities representing Database Objects
public DbSet<Employee> Employee { get; set; }
public DbSet<Job> Job { get; set; }
public DbSet<JobTask> JobTask { get; set; }
public DbSet<JobWorker> JobWorker { get; set; }
public DbSet<Property> Property { get; set; }
public DbSet<ServiceRequest> ServiceRequest { get; set; }
public DbSet<Status> Status { get; set; }
public DbSet<Tenant> Tenant { get; set; }
#endregion
}
```

Creating DbFactory

In an enterprise application, we may have multiple databases from where we need to perform database operations. So, rather than injecting DataContext directly into the Repository, we will create a DbFactory class and inject our DataContext through dependency injection. For example, if we have multiple data context classes pointing to different databases, we can inject them all through the parameterized constructor in DbFactory and expose properties to return their instance.

It is always better to expose interfaces, as it encapsulates the actual implementation. We will create the `IDbFactory` interface and then implement it using the `DbFactory` class.

Here is the code of the `IDbFactory` interface:

```
public interface IDbFactory
{
    DataContext GetDataContext { get; }
}
```

The following is the code of the `DbFactory` class:

```
public class DbFactory : IDbFactory, IDisposable
{

    private DataContext _dataContext;
    public DbFactory(DataContext dataContext)
    {
        _dataContext = dataContext;
    }

    public DataContext GetDataContext
    {
        get
        {
            return _dataContext;
        }
    }

    #region Disposing

    private bool isDisposed;
    public void Dispose()
    {
        Dispose(true);
        GC.SuppressFinalize(this);
    }

    public void Dispose(bool disposing)
    {
        if (!isDisposed && disposing)
        {
            if (_dataContext != null)
            {
                _dataContext.Dispose();
            }
        }
        isDisposed = true;
```

```
        }

    #endregion
}
```

Repository pattern

The Repository pattern is widely used in an enterprise application and decouples the DAL with the managers defined in BL through interfaces. It abstracts the underlying technology and architecture of DAL and makes it easy for an architect or developer to change it easily without affecting the BL managers or the objects that are consuming it. For example, we use a repository to separate the implementation of retrieving the data from the business logic and keep it agnostic to the type of data that comprises the data access layer. In this way, our data source could be a database, web service, or any flat file, or the like and changing the data source would not affect the business layer by using the Repository.

In our case, we will implement a generic repository so that any model can use that interface to perform CRUD operations. To implement the Repository pattern, we will create an interface as follows:

```
public interface IRepository
{
    IQueryable<T> All<T>() where T : class;
    void Create<T>(T TObject) where T : class;
    void Delete<T>(T TObject) where T : class;
    void Delete<T>(Expression<Func<T, bool>> predicate)
        where T : class;
    void Update<T>(T TObject) where T : class;
    void ExecuteProcedure(string procedureCommand,
        params SqlParameter[] sqlParams);
    IEnumerable<T> Filter<T>(Expression<Func<T, bool>> predicate)
        where T : class;
    IEnumerable<T> Filter<T>(Expression<Func<T, bool>> filter,
    out int total, int index = 0, int size = 50)
        where T : class;
    T Find<T>(Expression<Func<T, bool>> predicate)
        where T : class;
    T Single<T>(Expression<Func<T, bool>> expression)
        where T : class;
    bool Contains<T>(Expression<Func<T, bool>> predicate)
        where T : class;
}
```

The preceding `IRepository` interface has generic methods, which can be implemented by the Repository class to perform transaction handling, saving or updating records in the database and searching the records based on different filtering criteria.

Given next is the `Repository` class that implements the `IRepository` interface:

```
public class Repository : IRepository
{
    DataContext _context;

    public Repository(IDbFactory dbFactory)
    {
        _context = dbFactory.GetDataContext;
    }

    public T Single<T>(Expression<Func<T, bool>> expression)
        where T : class
    {
        return All<T>().FirstOrDefault(expression);
    }

    public IQueryable<T> All<T>() where T : class
    {
        return _context.Set<T>().AsQueryable();
    }

    public virtual IEnumerable<T> Filter<T>(
    Expression<Func<T, bool>> predicate) where T : class
    {
        return _context.Set<T>().Where<T>
          (predicate).AsQueryable<T>();
    }

    public virtual IEnumerable<T> Filter<T>
      (Expression<Func<T, bool>>
    filter, out int total, int index = 0, int size = 50)
      where T : class
    {
        int skipCount = index * size;
        var _resetSet = filter != null ? _context.Set<T>
          ().Where<T>
        (filter).AsQueryable() : _context.Set<T>().AsQueryable();
        _resetSet = skipCount == 0 ? _resetSet.Take(size) :
        _resetSet.Skip(skipCount).Take(size);
        total = _resetSet.Count();
        return _resetSet.AsQueryable();
    }

    public virtual void Create<T>(T TObject) where T : class
    {
        var newEntry = _context.Set<T>().Add(TObject);
    }
```

```
public virtual void Delete<T>(T TObject) where T : class
{
    _context.Set<T>().Remove(TObject);
}

public virtual void Update<T>(T TObject) where T : class
{
    try
    {
        var entry = _context.Entry(TObject);
        _context.Set<T>().Attach(TObject);
        entry.State = EntityState.Modified;
    }
    catch (Exception ex)
    {
        throw ex;
    }
}
public virtual void Delete<T>(Expression
  <Func<T, bool>> predicate) where T : class
{
    var objects = Filter<T>(predicate);
    foreach (var obj in objects)
        _context.Set<T>().Remove(obj);
}
public bool Contains<T>(Expression<Func<T, bool>> predicate)
  where T : class
{
    return _context.Set<T>().Count<T>(predicate) > 0;
}
public virtual T Find<T>(Expression<Func<T, bool>> predicate)
  where T : class
{
    return _context.Set<T>().FirstOrDefault<T>(predicate);
}
public virtual void ExecuteProcedure(String procedureCommand,
  params SqlParameter[] sqlParams)
{
    _context.Database.ExecuteSqlCommand(procedureCommand,
        sqlParams);
}

}
```

Unit of Work pattern

We implement the **Unit of Work (UOW)** pattern to avoid multiple calls to the database server on each object change. With Repository, we store the object state on any particular transaction and submit the changes once through the UOW pattern.

The following is the interface of Unit of Work that exposes four methods to begin and end transactions and to save changes:

```
public interface IUnitOfWork
{
    void BeginTransaction();

    void RollbackTransaction();

    void CommitTransaction();

    void SaveChanges();
}
```

The next item is the implementation of Unit of Work, which takes the `DbFactory` instance, and allow methods to begin and end transactions and call the `SaveChanges` method to push the changes in one call to the database. This way, a single call is made to the database server and any operation performed on the Repository will be done in-memory, within the database context:

```
public class UnitOfWork : IUnitOfWork
{
    private IDbFactory _dbFactory;

    public UnitOfWork(IDbFactory dbFactory)
    {
        _dbFactory = dbFactory;
    }


    public void BeginTransaction()
    {
        _dbFactory.GetDataContext.Database.BeginTransaction();
    }

    public void RollbackTransaction()
    {
        _dbFactory.GetDataContext.Database.RollbackTransaction();
    }

    public void CommitTransaction()
```

```
    {
        _dbFactory.GetDataContext.Database.CommitTransaction();
    }

    public void SaveChanges()
    {
        _dbFactory.GetDataContext.Save();
    }
}
```

Running migration

Running .NET CLI commands is straightforward. There are various commands that helps you with adding migration, removing migration, updating the database, dropping the database, and so on.

Let's start by creating the initial migration first. To create the initial migration, you have to go to the root folder path of your data access layer project and run the following:

`dotnet ef migrations add Initial`

In the preceding command, `Initial` is the name of the migration. When the command is executed, it actually searches for the class derived from the `DbContext` base class, and creates the database and tables for the connection string defined. Otherwise, the local DB store will be used.

On running, a new `Migrations` folder is created containing the file suffix `Initial.cs`, as shown in the following image:

Each migration class has two methods, namely, `Up` and `Down`, which are used to apply or revoke changes.

To create a database or to apply changes on the existing database, we have to run the following command:

`dotnet ef database update --verbose`

In the last command, `-verbose` is the switch used when you want to know the details of the operation being executed.

Now, once this command is executed successfully, our database and tables will be created, as shown in the following screenshot:

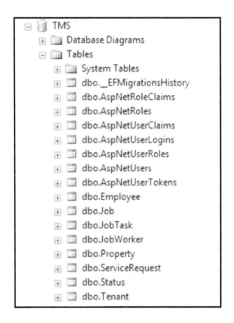

If you notice, in the last screenshot, there are some `AspNet*` tables, which are not defined in our `DataContext` class, but created automatically. The reason is the `IdentityDbContext` class, which takes the `IdentityUser` type. To study more about `IdentityUser` and `IdentityDbContext`, please refer to `Chapter 10`, *Security Practices with .NET Core*. Another important thing to note is the `_EFMigrationsHistory` table. This is the default table created after running the Entity Framework migrations and contains the entry of each migration. When running the migrations from .NET CLI command, Entity Framework actually checks the last migration entry in this table, and executes the corresponding migrations accordingly. To learn more about migrations, please refer to this link: `https://docs.microsoft.com/en-us/aspnet/core/data/ef-mvc/migrations`.

The next screenshot shows the final structure of the data access layer:

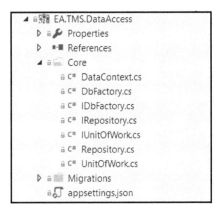

Business layer

The Business layer contains the actual logic of the application. It exposes interfaces and defines business managers to perform business operations. To start with, we will create a **Class Library (.NET Core)** project and reference data access and common layer projects:

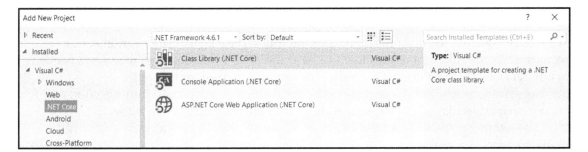

Develop core classes

We will start by creating a `Core` folder and defining a few classes, which will be common for all the managers and referenced by all business managers.

`IActionManager` is the interface that exposes four common methods to perform the CRUD operations. Any manager implementing this interface has to define the implementation for CRUD operations:

```
public interface IActionManager
{
    void Create(BaseEntity entity);
    void Update(BaseEntity entity);
    void Delete(BaseEntity entity);
    IEnumerable<BaseEntity> GetAll();
    IUnitOfWork UnitOfWork { get; }
    void SaveChanges();
}
```

`BaseEntity` is our base entity class from which every entity in the common layer is derived.

Next, we will add the abstract `BusinessManager` class, which will be inherited by all the concrete classes. Currently, this does not have any method defined, but in future, if any abstract methods need to be added, methods can be defined and all the business managers can use them:

```
public abstract class BusinessManager
{
}
```

We will be injecting the business managers into the service layer. However, in certain scenarios, there could be a requirement to have multiple or all, business managers needed in any service controller class. To handle this scenario, we will develop the `BusinessManagerFactory` class, inject the instances through constructor injection and expose properties that return the scoped objects to the controller. Here is the `BusinessManagerFactory` added in our `BusinessLayer` to provide access to any manager needed at any time:

```
public class BusinessManagerFactory
{
    IServiceRequestManager _serviceRequestManager;
    ITenantManager _tenantManager;
    public BusinessManagerFactory(IServiceRequestManager
    serviceRequestManager=null, ITenantManager tenantManager=null)
    {
        _serviceRequestManager = serviceRequestManager;
        _tenantManager = tenantManager;
    }

    public IServiceRequestManager GetServiceRequestManager()
```

```
    {
        return _serviceRequestManager;
    }

    public ITenantManager GetTenantManager()
    {
        return _tenantManager;
    }


}
```

Developing business managers

Now we can start developing our business managers, which can be used by the service controllers in service layers. When designing enterprise application architecture, it's always a better choice to expose interfaces rather than classes. This is recommended to encapsulate the actual implementation and to ensure that unnecessary methods or properties are not known by the consumer object.

Add the Managers folder and keep the interface and its implementation in its domain-specific folder.

The following is the IServiceRequestManager that exposes one method to return the list of service requests lodged by tenants:

```
public interface IServiceRequestManager : IActionManager
{
    IEnumerable<TenantServiceRequest>
        GetAllTenantServiceRequests();
}
```

We have derived this interface from the IActionManager interface, so the implementer class can provide implementation for the CRUD methods as well.

Now we will add the ServiceRequestManager class that implements the IServiceRequestManager interface as follows:

```
public class ServiceRequestManager : BusinessManager,
IServiceRequestManager
{
    IRepository _repository;
    ILogger<ServiceRequestManager> _logger;
    IUnitOfWork _unitOfWork;

    public IUnitOfWork UnitOfWork
    {
```

```
        get
        {
            return _unitOfWork;
        }
    }

    public ServiceRequestManager(IRepository repository,
    ILogger<ServiceRequestManager> logger,
    IUnitOfWork unitOfWork) : base()
    {
        _repository = repository;
        _logger = logger;
        _unitOfWork = unitOfWork;
    }

    public void Create(BaseEntity entity)
    {
        ServiceRequest serviceRequest = (ServiceRequest)entity;
        _logger.LogInformation("Creating record for {0}",
          this.GetType());
        _repository.Create<ServiceRequest>(serviceRequest);
        _logger.LogInformation("Record saved for {0}",
          this.GetType());
    }

    public void Delete(BaseEntity entity)
    {
    }

    public IEnumerable<BaseEntity> GetAll()
    {
        throw new NotImplementedException();
    }

    public void Update(BaseEntity entity)
    {
        throw new NotImplementedException();
    }

    public IEnumerable<TenantServiceRequest>
      GetAllTenantServiceRequests()
    {

        var query = from tenants in _repository.All<Tenant>()
        join serviceReqs in _repository.All<ServiceRequest>()
          on tenants.ID equals serviceReqs.TenantID
          join status in _repository.All<Status>()
          on serviceReqs.StatusID equals status.ID
```

```
        select new TenantServiceRequest()
        {
            TenantID = tenants.ID,
            Description = serviceReqs.Description,
            Email = tenants.Email,
            EmployeeComments = serviceReqs.EmployeeComments,
            Phone = tenants.Phone,
            Status = status.Description,
            TenantName = tenants.Name
        };
    return query.ToList<TenantServiceRequest>();
}

public void SaveChanges()
{
    _unitOfWork.SaveChanges();
}
}
```

If you have noticed, we have injected Repository, Logger, and UnitOfWork. Both Repository and UnitOfWork objects will be scoped per request, whereas the Logger object will be a singleton object. We will register them through the .NET Core built-in dependency injector in the service layer Startup class.

Similar to ServiceRequestManager, we will add another manager under Managers > TenantManagement to provide tenant management. Here is the code for the ITenantManager interface:

```
public interface ITenantManager : IActionManager
{
    Tenant GetTenant(long tenantID);
}
```

The implementation for the TenantManager class is as follows:

```
public class TenantManager : BusinessManager , ITenantManager
{
    IRepository _repository;
    ILogger<TenantManager> _logger;
    IUnitOfWork _unitOfWork;
    IServiceRequestManager _serviceRequestManager;


    public IUnitOfWork UnitOfWork
    {
        get
        {
```

```
            return _unitOfWork;
        }
    }

    public TenantManager(IRepository repository,
    ILogger<TenantManager> logger,   IUnitOfWork unitOfWork,
    IServiceRequestManager serviceRequestManager) : base()
    {
        _repository = repository;
        _logger = logger;
        _unitOfWork = unitOfWork;
        _serviceRequestManager = serviceRequestManager;
    }

    public virtual Tenant GetTenant(long tenantID)
    {
        try
        {
            _logger.LogInformation(LoggingEvents.GET_ITEM,
            "The tenant Id is " + tenantID);
            return _repository.All<Tenant>().Where(i => i.ID ==
            tenantID).FirstOrDefault();
        }catch(Exception ex)
        {
            throw ex;
        }

    }

    public void Create(BaseEntity entity)
    {
        Tenant tenant= (Tenant)entity;
        _logger.LogInformation("Creating record for {0}",
         this.GetType());
        _repository.Create<Tenant>(tenant);
        SaveChanges();
        _logger.LogInformation("Record saved for {0}",
        this.GetType());
    }

    public void Update(BaseEntity entity)
    {
        Tenant tenant = (Tenant)entity;
        _logger.LogInformation("Updating record for {0}",
          this.GetType());
         _repository.Update<Tenant>(tenant);
        SaveChanges();
        _logger.LogInformation("Record saved for {0}",
```

```
            this.GetType());
    }

    public void Delete(BaseEntity entity)
    {
        Tenant tenant = (Tenant)entity;
        _logger.LogInformation("Updating record for {0}",
         this.GetType());
        _repository.Delete<Tenant>(tenant);
        SaveChanges();
        _logger.LogInformation("Record deleted for {0}",
        this.GetType());
    }

    IEnumerable<BaseEntity> IActionManager.GetAll()
    {
        return _repository.All<Tenant>().ToList<Tenant>();
    }

    public void SaveChanges()
    {
        _unitOfWork.SaveChanges();
    }

}
```

SaveChanges() actually uses the UnitOfWork instance and this will be called either by the service controller (part of our Web API project) or from the manager itself. It depends on the requirement and is open for the developer to use it as per need.

Logging in .NET Core

Logging is a built-in module in .NET Core. Logging can simply be enabled by requesting the ILoggerFactory or ILogger<T> through dependency injection. When using ILoggerFactory, the category name has to be defined, whereas, with ILogger<T>, the class type name will be used as the category name.

The default provider is AddConsole, which logs the message on the console application. However, new providers can also be implemented and added by calling the AddProvider method of ILoggerFactory.

This screenshot shows the final structure of the business layer:

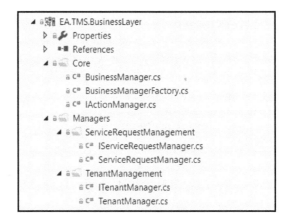

Creating the service layer

Service layer is the middle layer between the presentation and business layers. It abstracts the actual logic implemented on the business layer from the presentation layer and exposes services that can be consumed by the presentation layer. This layer should be secure enough to allow only authorized access to the resources.

We will develop the service layer using the ASP.NET Core Web application and use Web API to expose services. This layer will reference the business and common layers defined previously.

Let's create a new **ASP.NET Core Web Application (.NET Core)** project and name it `EA.TMS.ServiceApp`:

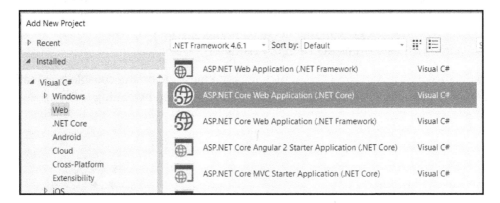

Creating base controller

We will define our own `BaseController` to define the `ActionManager` and `Logger` instances, which can be used by the Action filters (we will discuss these later in this chapter). The benefit of this approach is that you can put common methods and properties in `BaseController` and derive Web API controller from it. This is the code of `BaseController`:

```
public class BaseController : Controller
{
    private IActionManager _manager;
    private ILogger _logger;
    public BaseController(IActionManager manager, ILogger logger)
    {
        _manager = manager;
        _logger = logger;
    }
    public IActionManager ActionManager { get { return _manager; }
}
    public ILogger Logger { get { return _logger; } }
    public HttpResponseException LogException(Exception ex)
    {
        string errorMessage =
          LoggerHelper.GetExceptionDetails(ex);
        _logger.LogError(LoggingEvents.SERVICE_ERROR, ex,
          errorMessage);
        HttpResponseMessage message = new HttpResponseMessage();
        message.Content = new StringContent(errorMessage);
        message.StatusCode =
          System.Net.HttpStatusCode.ExpectationFailed;
        throw new HttpResponseException(message);
    }
}
```

Adding Custom Action Filters

In ASP.NET Core, filters allow the running of code before or after the execution of a particular resource in the pipeline. It can be configured on method, controller, or globally. They run within the MVC Action Invocation pipeline known as **Filter pipeline** when a particular action is selected by MVC based on the routing:

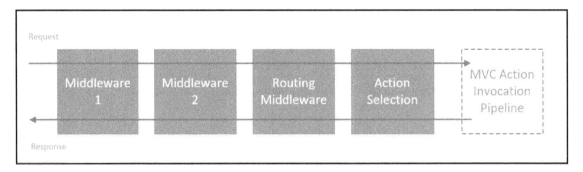

ASP.NET Core provides various filters, such as Authorization filters to decide whether the user accessing the resource is authorized or not. Resource filters are used to filter incoming requests in the pipeline and are mostly used for caching. Exception filters are used to apply policies that run globally to handle unhandled exceptions. Action filters help wrap calls to individual action methods and Result filters to wrap the execution of independent action results.

An Action filter is an attribute that can be applied on controller and action method levels.

In this chapter, we will develop these two action filters:

- LoggingActionFilter
- TransactionActionFilter

Logging Action Filter

We will create a custom LoggingActionFilter filter to log an exception when any method is executed. This way, we can log the information for every controller which has this attribute annotated:

```
public class LoggingActionFilter : ActionFilterAttribute
{
    public override void OnActionExecuting(
      ActionExecutingContext context)
    {
        Log("OnActionExecuting", context.RouteData,
          context.Controller);
```

```
    }

    public override void OnActionExecuted(
      ActionExecutedContext context)
    {
        Log("OnActionExecuted", context.RouteData,
          context.Controller);
    }

    public override void OnResultExecuted(
      ResultExecutedContext context)
    {
        Log("OnResultExecuted", context.RouteData,
          context.Controller);
    }

    public override void OnResultExecuting(
      ResultExecutingContext context)
    {
        Log("OnResultExecuting", context.RouteData,
          context.Controller);
    }

    private void Log(string methodName, RouteData routeData,
    Object controller)
    {
        var controllerName = routeData.Values["controller"];
        var actionName = routeData.Values["action"];
        var message = String.Format("{0} controller:{1}
        action:{2}", methodName, controllerName, actionName);
        BaseController baseController =
          ((BaseController)controller);
        baseController.Logger.LogInformation(
          LoggingEvents.ACCESS_METHOD, message);
    }
}
```

In the preceding code, the `Log` method is the helper method, which takes the method name, `RouteData` and `Controller`, and logs the information in the `Logger` instance injected through DI.

Transaction Action Filter

To handle transactions, we will develop a custom `TransactionActionFilter`, which can be used to begin and end transactions and to commit or rollback in case any error occur.

Here is the code for `TransactionActionFilter`:

```
public class TransactionActionFilter : ActionFilterAttribute
{
    IDbContextTransaction transaction;
    public override void OnActionExecuting(
      ActionExecutingContext context)
    {
      ((BaseController)context.Controller).ActionManager
        .UnitOfWork.BeginTransaction();
    }

    public override void OnActionExecuted(
      ActionExecutedContext context)
    {
        if (context.Exception != null)
        {
          ((BaseController)context.Controller).ActionManager
            .UnitOfWork.RollbackTransaction();
        }
        else
        {
            ((BaseController)context.Controller).ActionManager
              .UnitOfWork.CommitTransaction();
        }
    }
}
```

Add controllers

Next, we will add a controller, which will derive from our custom `BaseController` class.

The following is the code of `ServiceRequestController`, which contains an HTTP POST method to save the service requests of the tenant:

```
[LoggingActionFilter]
[Route("api/[controller]")]
public class ServiceRequestController : BaseController
{

    IServiceRequestManager _manager;
    ILogger<ServiceRequestController> _logger;

    public ServiceRequestController(IServiceRequestManager
    manager, ILogger<ServiceRequestController> logger) :
      base(manager, logger)
    {
```

```
            _manager = manager;
            _logger = logger;
        }
        [HttpGet]
        public IEnumerable<TenantServiceRequest> GetTenantsRequests()
        {
            return _manager.GetAllTenantServiceRequests();
        }

        [TransactionActionFilter()]
        [HttpPost]
        public void Post(ServiceRequest serviceRequest)
        {
            try
            {
                _manager.Create(serviceRequest);
            }
            catch (Exception ex)
            {
                throw LogException(ex);
            }


        }
    }
```

Given next is our `Startup` class, which registers all the dependencies in the
`ConfigureServices` method:

```
    public void ConfigureServices(IServiceCollection services)
    {

        services.AddScoped<IUnitOfWork, UnitOfWork>();
        services.AddScoped<IDbFactory, DbFactory>();
        services.AddScoped<DataContext>();
        services.AddScoped<IRepository, Repository>();
        services.AddScoped<IServiceRequestManager,
           ServiceRequestManager>();
        services.AddScoped<ITenantManager, TenantManager>();
        services.AddScoped<BusinessManagerFactory>();
        // Add framework services.
        services.AddMvc();

    }
```

And here is the `Configure` method:

```
    public void Configure(IApplicationBuilder app,
       IHostingEnvironment env, ILoggerFactory loggerFactory)
```

```
{
    loggerFactory.AddConsole(LogLevel.Information);
    loggerFactory.AddDebug();

    app.UseMvc();

}
```

Creating the presentation layer

The presentation layer is the frontend of any application. It contains views, view models, tag helpers, and static files, like images, CSS, and JavaScript. With the recent changes in web development and client side frameworks, companies are now choosing SPA (Single Page Applications) for web frontend. SPA applications are more responsive in nature and provide better user experience in terms of response time and performance.

Single Page Applications

The SPAs are web applications that have a single web page and all views render inside it dynamically when the user interacts with the application. SPAs use AJAX to call backend data through services and most of the work is done on the client side:

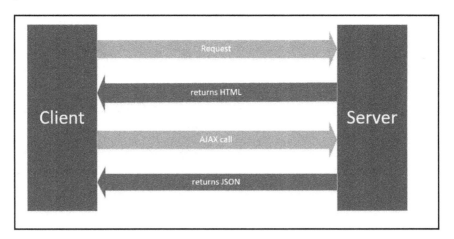

Benefits of a SPA

Following are few benefits of SPAs:

- SPAs are responsive in nature, as most of the resources, including CSS, JavaScript, and Images, are only loaded once throughout the application lifespan

- A SPA reduces the size of response by making AJAX requests to the server and receives a JSON response
- SPAs make it easy to scale and cache resources

Developing the presentation layer using ASP.NET Core and Angular

In this chapter, we will use ASP.NET Core and Angular on the presentation layer. We will use ASP.NET Core MVC (Model View Controller) to define views and load them through the routing module dynamically into the main single page container.

There are many benefits of using ASP.NET MVC view with Angular routing. Some of them are as follows:

- We can use `ViewBag` to define additional properties at runtime
- It provides a secure Action method through `AuthorizeAttribute`
- We can implement logging using custom Action filters or by injecting `ILogger<T>` at the controller level

To start with, open Visual Studio 2015 and select the **ASP.NET Core Web Application (.NET Core)** project template to create a new project and name it `EA.TMS.WebApp`:

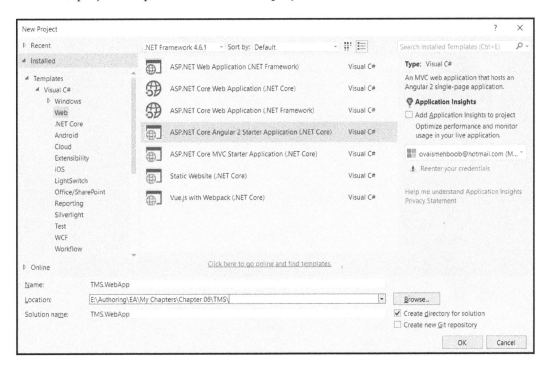

When you build your project, it will start restoring the packages.

Setting up frontend packages

To develop the frontend with Angular, we need some tools, such as TypeScript, Gulp, and **NPM (Node Package Manager)**. Angular code can be written using TypeScript, JavaScript, and Dart. There are certain benefits of using TypeScript, for example, it shows errors at compile time, and provides static types. Secondly, it follows the **ES6 (CMAScript6)** standard, which helps to define classes, interfaces, and inheritance, and allows architects to design the frontend following OOPS principles.

The ASP.NET Core architecture is different than what we have seen in the previous versions. All the static files should reside in the wwwroot folder. Keeping any static file outside wwwroot will make it inaccessible. When working with TypeScript, we create (.ts) files outside the wwwroot folder and with a little configuration, it places the files under a folder in the wwwroot folder. However, there are certain other files used by the project, which will be needed by the frontend pages and we will use Gulp to copy them to the wwwroot folder. Gulp is a JavaScript task runner, which is used to automate tasks and has complete support in Visual Studio.

NPM, on the other hand, is the package manager to manage node modules. In ASP.NET Core, we can add a file called package.json and define node modules. On saving, it automatically downloads the dependencies defined in this file from Node and restores them in the node_modules folder.

Let's add the package.json file and define the following modules:

```
{
  "name": "angular-quickstart",
  "version": "1.0.0",
  "private": true,
  "scripts": {
    "typings": "typings",
    "postinstall": "typings install"
  },
    "dependencies": {
      "@angular/common": "~2.2.0",
      "@angular/compiler": "~2.2.0",
      "@angular/core": "~2.2.0",
      "@angular/forms": "~2.2.0",
      "@angular/http": "~2.2.0",
      "@angular/platform-browser": "~2.2.0",
      "@angular/platform-browser-dynamic": "~2.2.0",
      "@angular/router": "~3.2.0",
```

```
            "@angular/upgrade": "~2.2.0",
            "angular-in-memory-web-api": "~0.1.15",
            "core-js": "^2.4.1",
            "reflect-metadata": "^0.1.8",
            "rxjs": "5.0.0-beta.12",
            "systemjs": "0.19.39",
            "zone.js": "^0.6.25"
        },
        "devDependencies": {
        "typings": "2.0.0"
        }
    }
```

All the @angular packages are angular dependencies, where typings is a development dependency, which facilitates by providing intellisense when we write TypeScript code.

Next, we will add the Typing.json file and add the following global dependency:

```
    {
      "globalDependencies": {
        "core-js": "registry:dt/core-js#0.0.0+20160602141332"
      }
    }
```

We will create all the TypeScript files under the app folder at the root of the project. But before creating TypeScript files, let's add the TypeScript configuration file known as tsconfig.json and add the following JSON:

```
    {
      "compilerOptions": {
        "target": "es5",
        "module": "commonjs",
        "moduleResolution": "node",
        "sourceMap": true,
        "emitDecoratorMetadata": true,
        "experimentalDecorators": true,
        "removeComments": false,
        "noImplicitAny": false,
        "rootDir": "app",
        "outDir": "wwwroot/app"
      },
      "compileOnSave": true,
      "exclude": [
        "node_modules"
      ]
    }
```

Some of the important attributes have been listed in the following table:

Attribute	Meaning
target root	ECMAScript standard to which the TypeScript file will be transpiled. TypeScripts folder (in our case, the app folder) where our TypeScript file resides.
outDir	The Output directory where the generated JavaScript files will reside
sourceMap	Good for debugging purpose. Setting this to true generates a mapping file known as *.js.map, which contains mapping information between TypeScript and the generated JavaScript file.

Finally, we will add the Gulp.js file and add the following script to copy the necessary packages to the lib folder in wwwroot:

```
var gulp = require('gulp');

var libs = './wwwroot/lib/';

gulp.task('restore:core-js', function () {
  gulp.src([
    'node_modules/core-js/client/*.js'
  ]).pipe(gulp.dest(libs + 'core-js'));
});
gulp.task('restore:zone.js', function () {
  gulp.src([
    'node_modules/zone.js/dist/*.js'
  ]).pipe(gulp.dest(libs + 'zone.js'));
});
gulp.task('restore:reflect-metadata', function () {
  gulp.src([
    'node_modules/reflect-metadata/reflect.js'
  ]).pipe(gulp.dest(libs + 'reflect-metadata'));
});
gulp.task('restore:systemjs', function () {
  gulp.src([
    'node_modules/systemjs/dist/*.js'
  ]).pipe(gulp.dest(libs + 'systemjs'));
});
gulp.task('restore:rxjs', function () {
  gulp.src([
    'node_modules/rxjs/**/*.js'
  ]).pipe(gulp.dest(libs + 'rxjs'));
});
gulp.task('restore:angular-in-memory-web-api', function () {
  gulp.src([
```

```
      'node_modules/angular-in-memory-web-api/**/*.js'
    ]).pipe(gulp.dest(libs + 'angular-in-memory-web-api'));
});

gulp.task('restore:angular', function () {
  gulp.src([
    'node_modules/@angular/**/*.js'
  ]).pipe(gulp.dest(libs + '@angular'));
});

gulp.task('restore:bootstrap', function () {
  gulp.src([
    'node_modules/bootstrap/dist/**/*.*'
  ]).pipe(gulp.dest(libs + 'bootstrap'));
});

gulp.task('restore', [
  'restore:core-js',
  'restore:zone.js',
  'restore:reflect-metadata',
  'restore:systemjs',
  'restore:rxjs',
  'restore:angular-in-memory-web-api',
  'restore:angular',
  'restore:bootstrap'
]);
```

Configuring the ASP.NET Core pipeline

So far, we have configured our client-side packages. In ASP.NET Core, we can add static files, security and MVC middleware. To implement security in an ASP.NET Core project, please refer to Chapter 10, *Security Practices with .NET Core*.

When developing an SPA application, we use the client-side framework heavily for routing modules and template rendering. Many client-side frameworks, such as Angular, provide their own routing modules to render pages in the main parent container. To enable those routing, we need to add the following spa-fallback entry followed by our MVC entry as shown next:

```
app.UseMvc(routes =>
  {
    routes.MapRoute("default", "{controller=Home}/
    {action=Index}/{id?}");
    routes.MapRoute("spa-fallback", "{*anything}",
      new { controller = "Home", action = "Index" });
  });
```

Moreover, static files middleware should be added so all the static files, such as images, JavaScript, and CSS, can be loaded:

```
app.UseStaticFiles();
```

> Static files middleware should be added before the MVC middleware in the pipeline.

Adding the Angular components

In this section, we will create custom components using TypeScript and create a root `app` folder inside our Web App project.

Under `app` folder, we will create another folder known as `shared` and this is where we will create some common components which will be used throughout the application:

Creating a Message component

This component will be used to show messages on the screen when the user performs any action. These messages will be success, error or warning messages displayed in the browser.

First, we create `MessageModel`, which takes the `type` and `msg` parameters in a parameterized constructor and can be passed to `MessageService` to push messages in an array.

Create a file, `message.service.ts`, in the `app > shared > message` folder, and place the following code:

```
export class MessageModel {

    type: string;
    msg: string;

    constructor(type: string, message: string) {
        if (type == 'E')
            type = 'danger';
        else if (type == 'S')
            type = 'success';

        this.type = type;
        this.msg = message;
    }
}
```

Creating HTTP client component

This component is a wrapper of the Angular http module and can be used to send RESTful messages to our service layer.

Add `http-client.service.ts` under the `app` > `shared` > `httpclient` folder, and add the following code:

```
import {Injectable, Inject} from '@angular/core';
import {Http, Headers, RequestOptions, Response} from
  '@angular/http';
import { Observable }      from 'rxjs/Observable';
import { APP_CONFIG, AppConfig }    from '../../app.config';

@Injectable()
export class HttpClient {
    options;
    headers;
    apiEndpoint: string;

    constructor(private http: Http,
        @Inject(APP_CONFIG) config: AppConfig) {
        this.apiEndpoint = config.apiEndpoint;
    }
    get(url) {
       this.headers = new Headers({ 'Content-Type':
         'application/json'
       });

        this.options = new RequestOptions({ headers:
          this.headers });
        return this.http.get(this.apiEndpoint + url);
    }

    post(url, data) {
        this.headers = new Headers({ 'Content-Type':
          'application/json' });
        this.options = new RequestOptions({ headers:
          this.headers });
        let options = new RequestOptions({ headers:
          this.headers, });
        return this.http.post(this.apiEndpoint + url,
          data, options);
    }
}
```

Adding service request View Model

Next, we will add our View Model, to which the form controls will bind. Add the `data-models.interface.ts` file in `app` > `shared` > `models`, and add the following code:

```
export class ServiceRequest {
  id: number;
  tenantID: number;
  description: string;
  employeeComments: string;
  statusId: number;
}
```

We can add as many models as required under this file.

Adding a shared module

In Angular, you can define modules; this helps to keep components, providers, and other resources under one module. We can refer other modules using imports, as shown next, and export components, using the exports key. Here, we create a shared module to keep our `MessageComponent` and our custom HTTP client service in one place and then we refer this module in other modules to leverage these features:

```
import { NgModule }        from '@angular/core';
import { CommonModule }    from '@angular/common';
import { MessageComponent } from './message/message.component';
import { HttpClient } from './httpclient/http-client.service';
import { MessageService } from './message/message.service';
import { Http, HttpModule } from '@angular/http';

@NgModule({
  imports: [
    CommonModule,
    HttpModule
  ],
  exports: [
    MessageComponent
  ],
  declarations: [
    MessageComponent
  ],
  providers: [
    MessageService,
    HttpClient
  ]
})
```

```
export class SharedModule {
}
```

Adding configuration settings

In our application, we will be making RESTful calls to our service layer and specifying the base service URL, authentication server (CAS) URL, or other attributes, in one place. So, let's add the `app.config.ts` file in the `app` folder and specify the following code:

```
import { OpaqueToken } from '@angular/core';

export let APP_CONFIG = new OpaqueToken('app.config');

export interface AppConfig {
  apiEndpoint: string;
  title: string;
  casEndPoint: string;
  appEndPoint: string;
}

export const TMS_DI_CONFIG: AppConfig = {
  apiEndpoint: 'http://localhost:5001/api/',
  title: 'TMS System',
  casEndPoint: 'http://localhost:5001',
  appEndPoint: 'http://localhost:5050'
};
```

Adding Application module

This is our main Application module, which contains the `ServiceRequest` component. We can create domain-specific modules depending on the application size. Here, we also refer the `SharedModule`, which we created earlier, so that we can access our custom HTTP client service and `MessageComponent`:

```
import { NgModule }      from '@angular/core';
import { BrowserModule } from '@angular/platform-browser';
import { APP_BASE_HREF } from '@angular/common';
import { AppComponent }  from './app.component';
import {MenuComponent} from './menu.component';
import { routing } from './app.routes';
import { ServiceRequestComponent } from './components/
 tenant/service-request.component';
import { SharedModule } from './shared/shared.module';
import { APP_CONFIG, TMS_DI_CONFIG } from './app.config';
import {FormsModule} from '@angular/forms';
import {ServiceRequestService} from './components/tenant/
  service-request.service';
```

```
@NgModule({
  imports: [
    BrowserModule,
    routing,
    SharedModule,
    FormsModule
  ],
  declarations: [
    AppComponent,
    ServiceRequestComponent,
    MenuComponent
  ],
  bootstrap: [AppComponent],
    providers: [
      { provide: APP_BASE_HREF, useValue: '/' },
      { provide: APP_CONFIG, useValue: TMS_DI_CONFIG },
      ServiceRequestService
  ]
})
export class AppModule { }
```

Configuring Angular Routes

To configure routing, we will create `app.routes.ts` under the `app` folder and add the following code:

```
import { ModuleWithProviders }  from '@angular/core';
import { Routes, RouterModule } from '@angular/router';
import { ServiceRequestComponent } from './components/
tenant/service-request.component'
import { MenuComponent } from './menu.component'

//Routes Configuration
export const routes: Routes = [
  { path: 'createServiceRequest', component:
    ServiceRequestComponent },
  { path: 'menu', component: MenuComponent },
  {
    path: '',
    redirectTo: '/menu',
    pathMatch: 'full'
  },
];

export const routing: ModuleWithProviders =
  RouterModule.forRoot(routes);
```

Adding App component

App component is the main component, which hooks up with the main Angular app. Here, `tenant-mgmt` is the main selector, which loads the `Feature/Index` page. This selector will be added in the Home/Index page.

```
import { Component } from '@angular/core';

@Component({
  selector: 'tenant-mgmt',
  templateUrl: 'Feature/Index'
})
export class AppComponent {
}
```

Adding Menu component

To load menus, we have to create a separate file, `menu.component.ts`, in the `app` folder and load the `Feature/Menu`, page as follows:

```
import { Component, AfterViewInit } from '@angular/core';
import { Router } from '@angular/router';
@Component({
  selector: 'menu',
    templateUrl: 'Feature/Menu'
})
export class MenuComponent {

}
```

Adding Main module

The `Main.ts` bootstraps the Main Application module; the code is given as follows:

```
import { platformBrowserDynamic } from
  '@angular/platform-browser-dynamic';
import { AppModule } from './app.module';
const platform = platformBrowserDynamic();
platform.bootstrapModule(AppModule);
```

Adding domain-specific components

For each business domain, we will create a service class and a component class. The service class will be responsible for making all the HTTP calls to the service layer, whereas the component class will be responsible for model binding and using the service class to submit or receive data.

Here is the implementation of the service class as discussed:

```
import 'rxjs/add/operator/map';
import 'rxjs/add/operator/catch';
import { Injectable, Inject }     from '@angular/core';
import { Observable }     from 'rxjs/Observable';
import { HttpClient } from  '../../shared/httpclient/
  http-client.service';
import {Response} from '@angular/http';
import { ServiceRequest } from '../../shared/models/
  data-models.interface';

@Injectable()
export class ServiceRequestService {

  constructor(private httpClient: HttpClient) { }

  getServiceRequest(id: any): Observable<ServiceRequest> {
    return this.httpClient.get('serviceRequest?id=' + id)
        .map(this.extractData)
        .catch(this.handleError);
  }

  getAllServiceRequests(): Observable<ServiceRequest[]> {
    return this.httpClient.get('serviceRequest')
        .map(this.extractData)
        .catch(this.handleError);
  }

  postServiceRequest(serviceRequest: any):
    Observable<ServiceRequest> {
    let body = JSON.stringify(ServiceRequest);
    return this.httpClient.post('serviceRequest/post',  body)
        .map(this.extractData)
        .catch(this.handleError);
  }

  private extractData(res: Response) {
    let body = res.json();
    return body || {};
  }
  private handleError(error: any) {
    let errMsg = (error.message) ? error.message :
        error.status ? `${error.status} -
        ${error.statusText}` :'Server error';
    console.error(errMsg); // log to console instead
    return Observable.throw(errMsg);
  }
```

```
    }
```

Following is the implementation of the `ServiceRequest` component, which calls the service class as discussed earlier:

```
import { Component } from '@angular/core';
import { ServiceRequest } from '../../shared/models/
  data-models.interface';
import { MessageService, MessageModel } from '../../shared/
  message/message.service';
import { ServiceRequestService } from './service-request.service';

@Component
({
  selector: 'createServiceRequest',
  templateUrl: 'Tenant/Create'
})

export class ServiceRequestComponent {

  serviceRequest: ServiceRequest;
  disable = false;
  serviceRequestService: ServiceRequestService;
  message: MessageService;

  constructor(messageService: MessageService,
    serviceRequestService: ServiceRequestService
  ) {
      this.message = messageService;
      this.serviceRequestService = serviceRequestService;
      messageService.clearMessages();
      this.serviceRequest = new ServiceRequest();
    }

  onSubmit() {
    this.serviceRequestService.postServiceRequest(
      this.serviceRequest)
      .subscribe(() => {
        serviceReq =>
          this.message.pushMessage(new MessageModel('success',
          'Service Request Submitted Successfully'));
      },
      error => {
          this.message.pushMessage(new MessageModel(
            'danger', 'Failed to submit ' + error));
      });
    }
}
```

Adding SystemJS config file to Bootstrap Angular

We will now add a custom `systemjs.config.js` file in the `wwwroot/app` folder, which tells our System loader to load the `Main.js` file (generated from `Main.ts`):

```
(function (global) {
  System.config({
    paths: {
        // paths serve as alias
        'npm:': './lib/'
    },
    // map tells the System loader where to look for things
    map: {
        // our app is within the app folder
        app: 'app',
        // angular bundles
        '@angular/core': 'npm:@angular/core/bundles/core.umd.js',
        '@angular/common': 'npm:@angular/common/bundles
         /common.umd.js',
        '@angular/compiler': 'npm:@angular/compiler/bundles
           /compiler.umd.js',
        '@angular/platform-browser': 'npm:@angular/
          platform-browser/bundles/platform-browser.umd.js',
        '@angular/platform-browser-dynamic': 'npm:@angular/
          platform-browser-dynamic/bundles/
          platform-browser-dynamic.umd.js',
        '@angular/http': 'npm:@angular/http/bundles/http.umd.js',
        '@angular/router': 'npm:@angular/router/bundles
           /router.umd.js',
        '@angular/router/upgrade': 'npm:@angular/router/
          bundles/router-upgrade.umd.js',
        '@angular/forms': 'npm:@angular/forms/bundles
           /forms.umd.js',
        '@angular/upgrade': 'npm:@angular/upgrade/
          bundles/upgrade.umd.js',
        '@angular/upgrade/static': 'npm:@angular/upgrade/
          bundles/upgrade-static.umd.js',
        // other libraries
        'rxjs': 'npm:rxjs',
        'angular-in-memory-web-api': 'npm:angular-in-memory-
          web-api/bundles/in-memory-web-api.umd.js'
    },
    // packages tells the System loader how to load when no
    filename and/or no extension
    packages: {
        app: {
            main: './main.js',
            defaultExtension: 'js'
```

```
        },
        rxjs: {
            defaultExtension: 'js'
        }
    }
  });
}) (this);
```

Next, we create another `importer.js` file under the `wwwroot/app` folder and call `System.import` to load our Main module.

```
System.import('app/main').catch(function (err) {
    console.error(err);
});
```

Lastly, we will just add the following script references in our `_Layout.cshtml` file residing in the `Views/Shared` folder:

```
<script src="~/lib/core-js/shim.min.js"></script>
<script src="~/lib/zone.js/zone.js"></script>
<script src="~/lib/reflect-metadata/Reflect.js"></script>
<script src="~/lib/systemjs/system.src.js"></script>
<script src="~/lib/rxjs/bundles/Rx.js"></script>
<script src="~/app/systemjs.config.js"></script>
<script src="~/app/importer.js"></script>
```

So, when our application starts, our Layout page loads the `systemjs.config.js` and `importer.js`. This `importer.js` loads the `Main.js` file and bootstraps our main `AppModule`, which we created earlier. This `AppModule` bootstraps our `AppComponent`, which is our main application component and displays the Feature/Index page, where the `tenant-mgmt` selector is defined.

Creating MVC Controllers and Views

So far, we have configured Angular and developed few components that are shared and related to the service request. We will have three controllers to show the home page, user features, and service request.

Add the MVC `HomeController` in the `Controllers` folder and add a default Index action method, as follows:

```
public class HomeController : Controller
{
    // GET: /<controller>/
    public IActionResult Index()
    {
        return View();
    }
}
```

In our `Startup` class, our default routing will be set to the home controller. Therefore, this is the main landing page for displaying single-page templates.

Then, in the `Index.cshtml` page, we will add our `tenant-mgmt` selector, as shown next:

```
<tenant-mgmt><img src="~/images/loading.gif" /></tenant-mgmt>
```

This selector will render our `Feature/Index` partial view, which we will define next.

Add a `FeatureController` under the `Controllers` folder and add following action methods:

```
public class FeatureController : Controller
{
    public IActionResult Index()
    {
        return PartialView();
    }

    public IActionResult Menu()
    {
        return PartialView();
    }

}
```

The following is index view snippet of the `FeatureController` contains the `message` selector and `router-outlet` to render the template:

```
<div class="row">
  <div style="padding:10px 0px 0px 30px" >
    <messages></messages>
    <router-outlet></router-outlet>
  </div>
</div>
```

Here is the Menu view of `FeatureController`, which shows tiles when the home page is accessed:

```
<div class="row">
  <div class="col-md-7 col-sm-10 center-block floatnone">
    <div class="col-sm-3 categoryBox">
        <a [routerLink]="['/createServiceRequest']"
          class="CreateServiceRequest">
            <span class="icon">
                <i class='fa fa-CreateServiceRequest'></i>
            </span>
            <span class="name">Create ServiceRequest</span>
        </a>
    </div>
    <div class="col-sm-3 categoryBox">
        <a href='#' class="ViewServiceRequest">
            <span class="icon">
                <i class='fa fa-ViewServiceRequest'></i>
            </span>
            <span class="name">View ServiceRequests</span>
        </a>
    </div>
    <div class="col-sm-3 categoryBox">
        <a href='#' class="AssignWorker">
            <span class="icon">
                <i class='fa fa-AssignWorker'></i>
            </span>
            <span class="name">Assign Worker</span>
        </a>
    </div>
    <div class="col-sm-3 categoryBox">
        <a href='#' class="WorkersManagement">
            <span class="icon">
                <i class='fa fa-WorkersManagement'></i>
            </span>
            <span class="name">Workers Management</span>
        </a>
    </div>

  </div>
</div>
```

Next, we will develop a `Create ServiceRequest` page and add `TenantController`.

The following is the code of `TenantController`:

```
public class TenantController : Controller
{
    public IActionResult Create()
    {
        return PartialView();
    }


}
```

Create `.cshtml` of `TenantController` as shown next:

```
<div class="row">
  <div style="padding:5px 0px 0px 30px"
    class="col-lg-12 col-md-12 col-sm-12">
      <div class="form-group">
        <h3>Enter Service Request:</h3>
      </div>
      <form (ngSubmit)="onSubmit(serviceForm)"
        #serviceForm="ngForm">
        <div class="form-group">
          <label for="name1">Enter Complaint:</label>
          <textarea rows="8" cols="800" maxlength="200"
            class="form-control" id="description"
            name="description" ngModel></textarea>
            @*<div *ngIf="formErrors.description"
              class="smallthin">
              {{ formErrors.description }}
            </div>*@
        </div>
        <div class="form-group">
          <button type="submit" style="float:left;"
          class="btn btn-success" [disabled]="disable">
          <i class="fa fa-check"></i>
          Send Request</button>
        </div>
      </form>
  </div>
</div>
```

When we click on the **Create ServiceRequest** tile, the following page will be displayed and will show a simple textbox to enter the complaint:

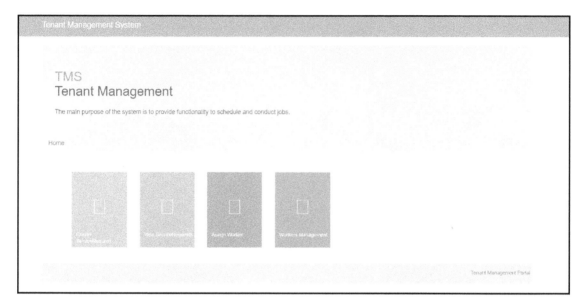

Summary

In this chapter, you have learnt some best practices when designing an n-tier architecture. We explored some patterns, such as Repository, Unit of Work, and Factory in the data access layer, which provide many advantages for decoupling the dependencies, and how to use them in the business layer for database manipulation. We explored the benefits of keeping entities and other helper classes in the common layer so that they can be used throughout the layers. In the service layer, we developed a few controllers to show how the business managers can be injected and how logging and exception handling can be done. And finally, in the presentation layer, we configured Angular and designed a frontend framework to invoke HTTP services, display messages, and view models to carry data. In the next chapter, we will learn about implementing a Service Oriented Architecture using .NET Core.

7
SOA Implementation with .NET Core

In this chapter, we will draw heavily from the skills and knowledge that we have gained in the previous chapters of this book. The matter in this chapter is dense and focuses on the architectural perspective, therefore it demands good attention. Once we understand the core SOA architecture principles, then coding SOA services becomes a piece of cake.

The topics that will be covered in this chapter are as follows:

- SOA definition
- SOA modeling
- SOA pivotal components
- Types of SOA services
- Sample SOA implementation

SOA definition

Shrinking the concepts learned in the first chapter on enterprise architecture, we can segment them into four perspectives:

- Business perspective
- Application perspective
- Information perspective
- Technology/Infrastructure perspective

For this chapter, our core focus is on the application perspective, where we'll talk about implementation of **Service-Oriented Architecture** (**SOA**) into our enterprise using the .NET Core as the primary software technology. By saying this, we take heavy presumptions that our business architectures have been created, our data models are ready, our infrastructure is either already there or coming into place based on our enterprise's technology architecture, and now we are moving forward to our agreed-upon application architecture (which we will talk about as our SOA definition and theory) to look for solutions with .NET Core as a primary enabler.

What is SOA?

SOA is an architectural style that primarily promotes service orientation.

Service orientation implies loosely-coupled systems that are fundamentally focused on satisfying the business functions. In SOA, you think in terms of services that fulfill business processes in a self-contained manner.

It is easier to look at SOA as the solution to interfaces and integration problems, but it provides much more. SOA is more than just an integration framework. It defines the vision and approach to enterprise architecture that builds upon software services representing heterogeneous business functions. SOA promotes an overall approach by scoping the main business landscape, identifying the business units and relevant stakeholders, then defining or improving the business processes, and exposing the interfaces and solutions in terms of reusable, self-contained, interoperable, flexible software services.

SOA also mandates setting up operational cycles for running healthy systems as well as for maintenance and upgrade cycles. It not only enables the registry and discovery framework for services, but also provides the platform for the governance of software services that ultimately monitors, reports, and governs the business functions for the relevant business units in an enterprise.

SOA modeling

There are a number of SOA models and frameworks that exist in the market, but we will consider those which are the most referenced ones.

SOA Reference Model

A **reference model** is an abstract framework to understand and describe the significant entities and relationships among them for some environments. It is used or referred to for development of consistent standards or specifications supporting the environment of the enterprise.

The OASIS **SOA Reference Model (SOA-RM)** is an abstract framework that provides the fundamental concept of SOA to understand the entities and relationships between them, and for the development of SOA standards within an organization.

In the dictionary, service is defined as *An act or a variety of work done by one for another*. OASIS SOA-RM defines service in this one line: In SOA, services are the mechanism by which needs and capabilities are brought together.

The following reference model defines the principal concepts of SOA:

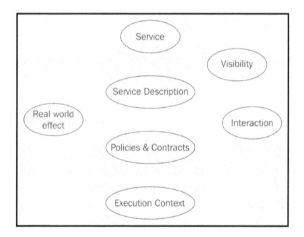

SOA principal concepts from OASIS SOA-RM

The explanation for each concept is as follows:

- **Service**: A mechanism to enable access to one or more capabilities
- **Visibility**: A service provider and the service consumer need to see each other
- **Interaction with services**: Performing actions against a service such as sending/receiving messages
- **Real world effect**: The intent and result of interacting with a service
- **Service description**: The information required information in order to interact with a service

- **Policies and contracts**: Policies are constraints to use a service, and contracts are an agreement between two or more parties
- **Execution context**: A set of infrastructure elements, process entities, policy assertions and agreements, which are identified as a part of service interaction between the service provider and service consumer

The following diagram is for the Oasis SOA-RM reference model describing the services:

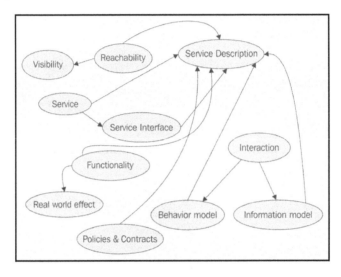

OASIS SOA Reference model diagram for service description

OASIS SOA-RM is a top-reference point for SOA concepts, and provides foundational knowledge for SOA architecture. It not only provides the SOA knowledge, but it can also be used to measure the sanity and validation check for SOA architectures, frameworks, and implementations.

Reference model and reference architecture relationship

The relationship between a reference model and reference architecture has been defined very nicely by the OASIS SOA model; therefore, their diagram is as follows:

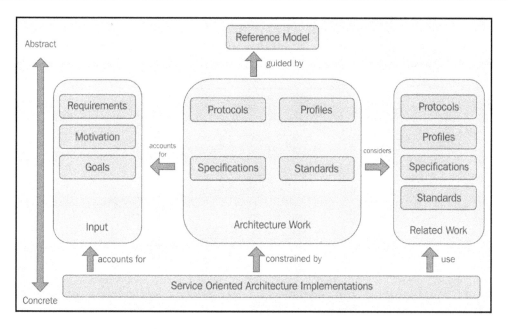

Reference model relationship to reference architecture work (OASIS)

From this preceding diagram, we can see that reference models work as the fundamental guiding principles for a given domain, and are more abstract building blocks of the architecture models.

SOA Reference Architecture

A reference architecture is an architectural design pattern that indicates how an abstract set of entities and relationships realizes a predetermined set of requirements, fundamental concepts, and relationships (that is, reference model) in the domain of interest.

The purpose of reference architecture is to give a realization, which is a high-level solution artifact, and to architects, a standard model from which to architect specific solutions for their respective business domain.

According to TOGAF, and in general, we have the following **reference architecture continuum** from abstract to concrete by influencing and refining further. For each of these categories of architecture, we have a reference architecture:

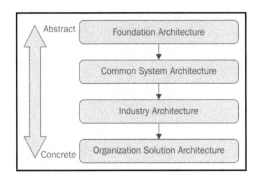

Reference architecture continuum

The diagram means that an SOA reference architecture is categorized as a common systems architecture. It's a generalized reference architecture for SOA, independent of any specific industry and implementation.

The following diagram shows the standard and widely adopted SOA reference architecture as provided by **The Open Group (TOG)**. This reference architecture is focused on solution and **application architecture** as per the **The Open Group Architecture Framework (TOGAF)**. Generally, all SOA implementations eventually satisfy the elements in this model:

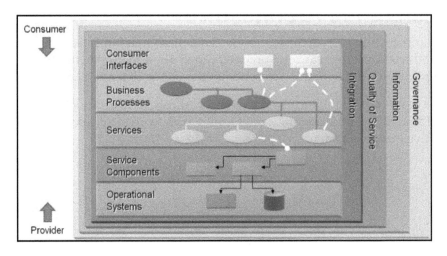

SOA Reference Architecture (TOG)

We will now see a simple description of these high-level layers, as mentioned in the preceding SOA reference architecture:

- **Operational Systems layer**: This contains the operational system components of an enterprise. It primarily includes the infrastructure to support SOA implementation.
- **Service Components layer**: This includes the software components, which provide implementation for the service.
- **Services layer**: This includes services with description, contracts, policies, and containers with service components.
- **Business Processes layer**: It's a collection of the business processes of an enterprise.
- **Consumer Interfaces layer**: This includes the software components, which enable users to interact and use the services.
- **Integration layer**: This is probably the most critical layer for an SOA platform. It provides the integration building blocks, including messaging, message transformation, message hub, event processing, service composition, and service registry discovery discovery.
- **Quality of Service layer**: This layer basically monitors, reports (and manages) the quality of service of the SOA implementation, including its errors, performance, reliability, availability, and security.
- **Information layer**: This logically includes data, meta-data, analysis, interpretation, and transformation of data.
- **Governance layer**: This layer contains the governance rules and regulations, and their application on the services and operations.

Common reference information architecture

Information architecture basically shows the information flow in the SOA implementation environment, and the interactions between different tiers, systems, and processes. The following diagram shows the widely adopted IBM SOA Foundation reference information architecture:

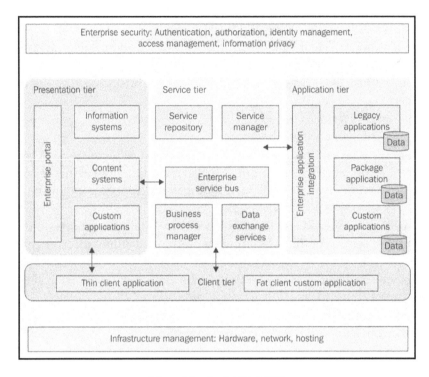

Reference Information Architecture (IBM)

Common reference Infrastructure architecture

The Infrastructure architecture depicts the fundamental infrastructure services required to set up, build, deploy, and maintain the SOA platform components.

This helps in identifying the existing infrastructure, which could be affected by the SOA implementation. It is also useful when making platform, technology, and vendor choices for the SOA platform.

The following figure depicts the widely adopted IBM SOA Foundation reference Infrastructure architecture:

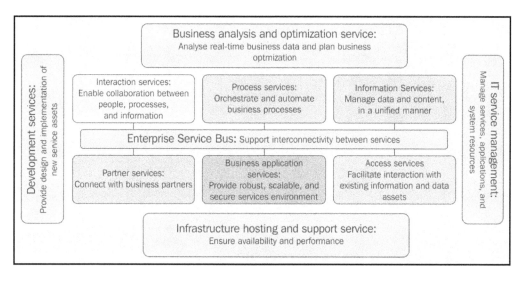

Reference Infrastructure Architecture (IBM)

SOA features and components

Here, the SOA components that we will discuss are just to give you an idea about the meta-technical architecture level concepts. These are not the de-facto standards, but they provide a strong basis to build your organization's SOA architecture. Therefore, we take a summarized look at one of the most common industry standard architecture.

Service Component Architecture

Service Component Architecture (**SCA**) is one of the most popular standards, dating from 2005. It defines the architectural components of an SOA platform in a technical manner. It is standardized by the OASIS, mainly in collaboration with IBM, Oracle, and TIBCO.

It provides a model to compose applications that follow the SOA principles:

In a nutshell, SCA has the following key elements:

- Assembly model:
    - Defines the structure of composite applications by having series of artifacts defined by elements contained in XML files
- Composite:
    - Is a basic artifact, which is the unit of deployment for SCA
    - Contains one or more components
    - Eventually, it holds remotely accessible services
- Component:
    - Contains business functions
    - Functions are exposed as services, which can either be used internally or by other components made available through entry points
    - When a component depends on services provided by other components, these dependencies are called **References**
- Services:
    - Remotely accessible web services, primarily based on XML

- Implementations:
  - These are present in components
  - They are configurable by the component statically or dynamically
  - SCA provides the implementation and binding specifications
- Policy Framework:
  - Specifies how to add constraints, security, transactions, QoS, and messaging policies
- **Enterprise service bus (ESB)**:
  - SCA specifies inclusion and usage of the ESB
- **Service Data Objects (SDO)**:
  - Service Data Objects to access the data sources

With further sections, we will see the software implementation perspectives of the SOA platform and finally look at some indicative sample code with .NET Core.

Service types

Services are the most important aspect of the SOA. In an SOA platform, you have many services, and it is important to categorize them so that it is easy for service development and service management.

By achieving business processes in terms of service, it increases the modularity, business understanding, improved and trackable information flow, and better organization of the business functionality; it also promotes reusability by exposing service interfaces to other services and systems.

The following table describes the categories of services. Note that it's not required to categorize your SOA services in this particular way, but use this as a guidance in the right direction:

Service categories	Short description
Interaction services	Primarily related to the presentation layer, it supports interaction between applications and users. Usually a part of the MVC pattern.
Process services	Also called composite services, they provide the composition logic, especially business flows. Could be part of the MVC pattern.

Information services	Expose the data logic of the enterprise design. Provide access to the data storage. Could be part of the MVC pattern as well. These services could be sub-divided, and can have their own sub architecture with respect to the enterprise data architecture.
Access or adapter services	Provide access to legacy data or application. Provide access to a resource or expose the resources as a service.
Mediation services	They normally bind one service (usually, a producer) to more than one service (data consumers). They provide routing logic of data and services, data enrichment, and filtering. Some also call it a distributor service.
Business services	Provide encapsulated business functionality to internal and external consumers.
Security services	Enable application and enforcement of security attributes to other SOA services. Provide interactive and non-interactive layers of services as well as hookable services.
Registry services	Enable service discovery and service registry as well as policies by providing managed access to various SOA artifacts.
Infrastructure services	Provide measurement and monitoring of infrastructure ensuring the integrity of the SOA operational environment.
Management services	Provide metrics, measurements, reporting services regarding other SOA services. Include outages, severe error detections and alerts, enforcing administrative policies towards achieving and maintaining the service level.
Development services	These are, generally, an entire suite of services related to tooling like modeling, development, testing, logging, debugging, instrumentation, error reporting, and alerting used in an SOA solution.
Strategy services	Mostly related to business intelligence services for improving business outcomes. Also may include the services that process the strategies of business to create an implementation roadmap covering both business and IT.

Service composition

Service composition is the combination of existing services to create a new service, or to achieve a newer functionality.

Since services are essentially business functions or processes in SOA, it describes the capabilities of business. SOA enhances the visibility and capabilities of a business by allowing them to create new functions or capabilities by combining the existing ones into a well-formed composition.

There are two primary styles of service composition on a theoretical level, which are as follows:

Service orchestration

According to the dictionary (www.merriam-webster.com), orchestration is defined as *The arrangement of a musical composition for performance by an orchestra. Orchestration is a composition of services in which one of the services is a master service, which controls, schedules, and directs all of the other services.*

Service choreography

The dictionary (www.merriam-webster.com) defines choreography as follows:

- *The art of symbolically representing dancing*
- *The composition and arrangement of dances especially for ballet*

Basically, services can be compared to a set of dancers, and a business process to choreography, a direction, or a business process. Each dancer, or a group of dancers, or each service is autonomous in how they all carry out the direction.

So, in service choreography, the composed services interact and cooperate with each other without the presence of a master, director, or controller service composing or combining them.

An easy example of this would be the execution of a combination of cross-departmental or cross-organizational services, where there is no single service controlling the flow.

In the Microsoft world, we achieve service orchestration through the Windows workflow foundation, and orchestration and choreography through the BizTalk server, which also supports **Business Process Execution Language** (BPEL).

Common technology standards

Besides many other technology standards, these are the most common ones that are agreeably associated with the SOA platform:

- **Hypertext Transfer Protocol (HTTP)** Hypertext Transfer Protocol)
- XML Schema (XSD, DTD, or similar)
- XML (For data representation, transfer, and/or storage)
- SOAP (Messaging standard protocol)
- **Web Services Description Language (WSDL)**
- JSON (JavaScript Object Notation has lately become more popular than XML)
- XPath, XQuery, and XSL Transformation
- **BPEL (Business Process Execution Language** (XML- based construct for services orchestration)
- **UDDI (Universal Description, Discovery, and Integration (UDDI))**

Service discovery

One may hardcode the URL of a service in the service consumer configurations, or one can use the dynamic mechanism to fetch the URL at program execution (initialization) time. This fetching of the actual URL is part of service discovery. UDDI is one of the ways to register services and their URLs, and also to retrieve them by their respective consumers. Service discovery mechanism can also be custom-built by an organization in combination with the configuration management system. Most of the SOA solutions provide service discovery as part of the solution.

This feature of SOA does not necessarily enforce the policy framework, while some of the service discovery solutions offer lifecycle management as well.

Message broker

A message broker in an enterprise is basically a message-oriented middleware, which is used for sending messages between two or more clients. In a simple mechanism, it's basically an implementation support for the producer and consumer pattern. In general, they provide one-to-one communication (point-to-point/queues) and one-to-many communication (publish-subscribe/topics) as well.

Message broker promotes loose coupling, and enables asynchronous communication within distributed applications.

Some implementations use TCP as the underlying data transfer protocol, while others also give provisions for UDP, Multicasts, and hybrids. Data types for payload that are commonly available include string, binary, XML, and JSON along with the options to enable compression.

There are some brokerless messaging approaches, but those are not found commonly in SOA platforms.

Some of the message brokers in the market include IBM's WebSphere MQ, Microsoft's MSMQ, Oracle's Service Bus, and TIBCO's EMS besides many others. As an example, let's look at some of the highs and lows of MSMQ. Note that these points are just for demonstration, and in no way give an exhaustive product evaluation.

The highs for MSMQ are as follows:

- Built-in Microsoft Windows (infrastructure)
- No need to pay extra if you have a Windows server license (cost)
- Active Directory Integration (security)
- Libraries already present with .NET Framework (not with .NET Core as of now)
- Transaction support (integrity)

The lows for MSMQ are as follows:

- Not so popular in bigger enterprises (popularity here might be related to reliability, and the number of use cases supported)
- Limitations on the size of message and queue (limitations for big-sized message flow)
- Not a cross-platform product
- A newer product, Azure Service Bus, is now a better alternative

Enterprise Service Bus (ESB)

Enterprise service bus or ESB is a collection of features, functionality, and tooling, and has become almost an essential component, rather a backbone, for any SOA implementation.

ESB Segments

At a higher level, ESB can be said to have these six main segments:

- Storage resources (in memory, persistent, transfer)
- Gateway services (protocols, security)
- Message broker (as explained previously)
- Solution designer (IDE)
- Service adapters (data and services connectors to various resources including third parties)
- Management Interface (administration, installation of components, management, and monitoring)

The following diagram shows the main segments in ESB:

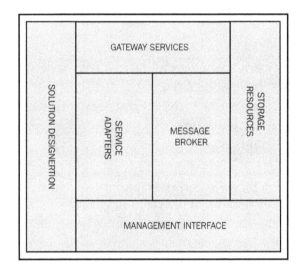

Main Segments of ESB

ESB features

There are a number of features which are commonly found in various ESB solutions. Let's have a quick look at them, as they can be helpful to understand its offerings, technical capabilities, and to compare and evaluate it.

The following is an unordered and non-exhaustive list, but contains the elements that can be considered essential for an ESB solution:

- Location transparency (producer and consumers are unaware of the endpoints)
- Messaging
- VETRO
    - Validation (format and data validation)
    - Enrichment (addition of attributes)
    - Transformation (conversion from one format to another, for example, one XML schema to another using XSLT)
    - Routing (for example, message dispatching based on filters)
- Process and message monitoring
- Message security
- Protocol conversion (for example, HTTP to JMS)
- Monitoring, Administration, and Tracking

Some of the market-leading ESB solutions include IBM's WebSphere ESB, Oracle's Service Bus, and the TIBCO BusinessWorks ESB.

Data

Data modeling, including business and data architecture, is part of SOA architecture, which is a big topic by itself. We would just mention here some of the essential things with reference to the data modeling for SOA implementation.

Master Data Management (MDM)

MDM includes information, processes (creation and maintenance), policies, standards, governance, and tools common across the enterprise.

It holds these two main types of data:

- Reference data (data referenced across the organizational system)
- Analytical data:
    - Identification and verification of entities and their relationships

- Analytics on master data, for example, number of total customers increased in a month
- Analytical information (for example, in terms of metrics) fed from data warehouse(s)

Common data model

This is also a part of data architecture, which, basically, describes the data model to be used across the span of SOA-wide services. The common data model is defined and synchronized between persistent storage (database) and the message schemas travelling throughout the SOA services.

Common data model also includes transformations to and from various other data models depending on the outward and inward interfaces from systems outside SOA or legacy systems. Transformations can be dynamic at runtime, ETL scheduled, or could be offline, triggered by external processes in a batch conversion manner.

Live business metrics

This kind of data is a runtime aggregation of the tracking, logging, and error data coming from all of the SOA services. This is a summarized data model to provide a live snapshot of a system information flow before it is processed by business intelligence and data warehouse services.

Services gateway

SOA platforms usually (but not necessarily) have a services gateway. These gateways are meant to have most of the web services registered inside them for controlling access, throttling, statistical measurements, QoS, and service mappings besides other functionalities.

Some of the main and common features of any services gateway include the following:

- HTTP and JMS-based service producers and consumers
- Security (authentication, authorization, certificates, encryption, and so on)
- Validation (for example, WSDL, SOAP Requests, and more)
- Throttling
- Routing (web services routing)
- Service Proxy

- Transformation (for example, from one service to another)
- Caching
- Central logging and reporting (real time and non-real time)
- Mediation (becoming common across gateways)

Note that, with the advent of the REST-based Microservices architecture, API Gateways are becoming more common than the SOA services gateways. We will take a look at the API Gateway in the next chapter.

SOA services library

SOA services library is not an essential component of an SOA platform, but these kind of libraries are common to SOA implementations. It is an enterprise library, generally used within implementation technologies such as .NET, Java, and various others.

The purpose of this library is to encapsulate the implementations of the most common concepts such as logging, which are used across (almost) all of the implementations of SOA services.

These concepts can, in general, be called system services or SOA APIs. These can be implemented and exposed either within the execution context of a business service, or as a remotely callable service.

The concepts and functionalities encapsulated in the SOA services library, provided to all SOA services may include, but not be limited to the following:

- Common implementation technology framework libraries
- Context (SOA service meta business context)
- Logging
- Error handling mechanism
- Common services structure
    - Constants
    - Common schemas, XML, JSON, and Strings
    - Service or system states
    - Common SOA internal service references (static and dynamic)
- Information to enable caching mechanism

Tracking, logging, and error handling in SOA

Tracking mechanism enables tracking of input message and message processing at various stages, which often span across multiple services.

Logging mechanism is a general logging feature of any SOA service implementation, which is unified so that all services log in a given SOA standard.

Error handling mechanism deals with error logging, related severity, priority, and handling of error in terms of reporting or retrying/correction. Error reporting may include monitoring and alerting services.

Some of the attributes that help facilitate these mechanisms may include the following:

- Log Levels (uniform log levels for all implementations)
- Timestamp (includes time zones for global enterprise)
- RequestID (GUID generated by the Sender/Client application to track the transactional flow)
- TrackingID (GUID generated to keep track of message flow)
- BusinessUnits (inserted by the Application)
- DomainID, ApplicationID, ModuleName (these are pre-defined values, perhaps in SOA services library)
- ServiceStep (used by Mediation / Orchestration)
- BusinessKey (context sensitive info for a message or a set of related messages)
- RetryCount (retries indicator if error retry/correction is activated)
- MessageType (Pre-defined values to identify the type of a business message)
- Message (could be short message and a full message)
- Description (useful for logging)

Notes

The points listed here can be considered as an advisory note:

- Enterprise tracking and locking mechanisms are deployed as a centrally accessible service, which does not have to be implemented as a central logger, but mainly as a distributed logger and message tracker.
- Logging is usually implemented asynchronously. This means that all the business SOA services perform the logging part by invoking log-related services asynchronously, and usually, via the SOA services library.

- Tracking, logging, and error logging mechanisms are often implemented as a combination using the same network traffic.
- Since the traffic which has the highest frequency in the whole SOA platform is the tracking and logging traffic, it has to be implemented with the utmost care with every minute detail. It is also the most critical of all other types of services in the SOA platform.
- It is not necessary to implement all logging via the same mechanism or same set of services. For example, we can have a central logger for certain log levels, and perhaps, logstasher components (per machine) with **ElasticSearch** database for another set of log levels.

Sample SOA implementation

The word sample is defined as *A small part of something intended as representative of the whole* in the dictionary (`https://www.vocabulary.com/dictionary/sample`).

So, in this section, we will implement a few types of services, which represent the most commonly implemented SOA service patterns. And we will be using .NET Core for all of the stuff. Therefore, it's a limited SOA sample implementation.

Introduction

Since the book is focused on enterprise architecture implementation instead of pure architectural knowledge or theory, therefore, we have tried to cover (or touch upon) all fundamental parts of an SOA architecture in just one chapter instead of the whole book as this topic deserves in the architectural sense.

For our sample implementation, we will directly see the implementation in C# .NET Core for some of the common types of SOA services, assuming that all the reference architectures, organizational standards, business and data models, and SOA solution architecture are in place.

Sample enterprise

We will take as an example for our sample enterprise, for which we are implementing an SOA platform.

Let's say the name of our organization is **H.I.J.K,** which may have `hijk.com`, just a random letters sequence I came up with. HIJK is a medium-to-large enterprise with more than a thousand employees. It has various departments that are supporting the company to run its business. They have software applications supporting their main business products or services, and each of their departments also have other types of software applications, which are supporting the structure of an organization for its sustainability and growth.

Departments of a sample enterprise

The departments of the organization in focus for our sample implementations are as shown in following figure:

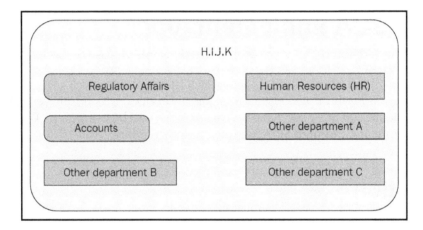

Sample organization with some of its departments

Sample data models for departments

Let's consider a very cut-down version of data models for the departments we consider for our sample SOA services. These data models typically come out as a result of business and data architecture.

 Note that all of this sample implementation is just for demonstration purpose, and are quite far from reality; so do not consider this as any real-world production level architecture, design, or code, but only for demonstration purposes to make things easy to understand under the given time and resources.

The following diagrammatic representation shows a sample data model:

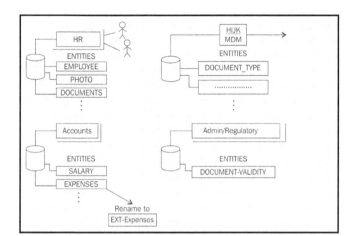

Sample data model (trimmed)

Sample business processes for departments

We will now consider a few business processes or business functions which are normally identified, created, and maintained by business analysts, and primarily, provide knowledge and support to business architects and project managers.

The following diagram displays the list of business processes use cases for the HR and Accounts department, for which we will create tiny SOA services with .NET Core:

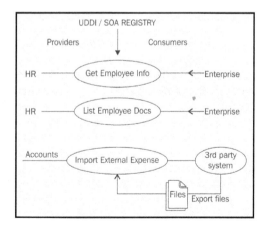

Sample HR and Accounts business use cases

The following is a list of business functions primarily related or owned by the Regulatory Affairs department of our sample organization, H.I.J.K:

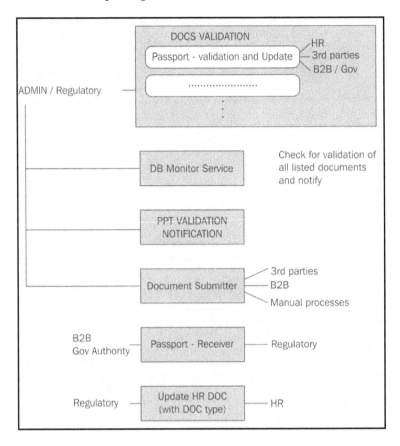

Sample Business Services for Regulatory Affairs department

In case you have not noticed, these are business services which are more closely mapping to the implemented SOA services in the SOA platform; or say, which are more technically oriented.

Sample database models for departments

The next diagram shows an extremely cropped version of any database ERD. Basically, it is just to give an idea of a database model to show the various departments that an enterprise may have. Note that each department may have implemented their own applications, or are using some vendor applications or hybrid, and can also have a variety of storage layers in an inconsistent or incompatible manner. Hence the need for a service- based standardized communication model, so as to enable them to talk together in a unified manner, across the organization:

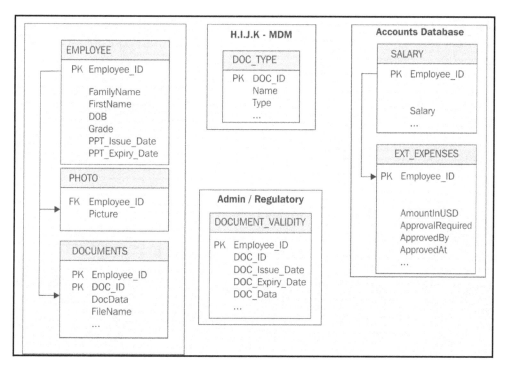

Sample Databases for departments

Bounded contexts

You may have noticed that we did not actually talk about the actual business domain of our sample enterprise, but only considered its departments, which communicate with each other on a particular sub-domain. Consider that the HR department has its own people, processes, tools, and applications, which constitute its particular bounded context. Similarly, the Accounts and Regulatory departments have their own bounded contexts.

Here, in our sample scenario, the primary business processes are related to employee's documents in the HR department, which are validated and facilitated by the department of Regulatory Affairs. What we are looking at is a couple of bounded contexts talking or merging to achieve some business process; for such an interaction, we need context maps for the domain modeling, according to the **Domain Driven Design (DDD)** methodology.

Bounded context focuses on a single primary business domain, which gives all team members (business, IT, customers, and so on) shared and agreed understanding in a consistent manner. Thus, bounded context implementations become autonomous components. These components do not have dependencies on anything outside the bounded context, and they are capable of running together in isolation. Naturally, these are candidates encouraged to utilize the concepts of containerization. Fortunately, we will visit containerization in the later chapters of this book.

Context maps provide the relationship between bounded contexts, both in terms of business as well as technical implementation. These provide useful documentation to view and realize the integration between the different bounded contexts. Our sample business processes above can be considered as part of context maps if we are doing domain modeling using DDD.

Services implementation

Now that we are well aware of our sample enterprise, and we know what business functionality we are targeting to implement as SOA services, let's talk code.

 Note that the main idea of this chapter is to understand the architecture and design for the implementation of SOA services using the .NET Core technology. Therefore, the sample code here is just indicative, and only for demonstration purposes.

Solution structure

In this section, we will briefly view the high-level code organization for our sample SOA services. Doing this will not only make it easier for you to follow the sample code, but also give you an idea of the steps taken to reach the level of SOA services implementation. Sample services here are just an example and are incomplete, and in some places, left to be inconsistent to exhibit the real-world style; however, they follow the step-by-step structural pattern, which is fundamental to the implementation of an SOA platform.

Note that the organization of SOA services, conventions, versioning, and change of management are part of implementation of any SOA platform, which should be part of the platform definition process.

The following screenshot is an eagle-eye view of the structure of the solution for SOA services in the given context:

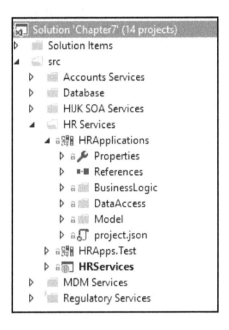

Indicative solution structure for department wise SOA services

In the preceding screenshot, you can see how all services are organized in their own distinct location, and, more or less, they all follow the same conventions of the project hierarchy and layers. In real life, all SOA services need not, and would not, present as part of the same single solution- it would be an overkill.

We have chosen to leave the implementation of services in proper layers, for example, segregating Model/Entities, the Business Logic Layer, and the Data Access Layer, but in real implementation, they should be well taken care of as per organizational standards. A good detailed overview of the layered architecture has already been presented to you in a previous chapter of this book, which should be a starting point.

Each SOA service, for any department, has at least these modules:

- Service Interface layer:
    - This can be either based on SOAP/XML (exposing WSDL).
    - Or this can be either based on RestEST services with JSON, or XML, or both.
    - In our examples, we have chosen to go with REST-based HTTP web services, because they are modern, lightweight, a bit faster, and more popular with JSON-based usage. Additionally, **Windows Communication Foundation** (**WCF**) currently supports only web services client functionality on the .NET Core cross-platform framework.
- Business Logic layer
- Data Access layer
- Model or Entities layer
- Testing layer

Sample database

The database chosen for our SOA services is **SQLite**, which is a very simplistic file-based relational and cross-platform database. SQLite is supported directly by .NET Core instead of using third- party providers. SQLite is not an enterprise-grade database, and it has a lot of limitations, but we have used it here for ease of use and simplicity.

While, realistically, every department of an enterprise may have their own separate databases (along with specific security) as well as shared storage, in this example, we have just used the same database with different tables. Also, note that it is quite possible that the IT teams, for their respective departments in the same company, might have implemented database accessing functionalities in different ways. For example, some departments may be able to use ADO.NET, while others may use Entity Framework Core or another ORM layer. .NET Core directly supports both ADO.NET and EF Core for SQLite databases, and in our sample code, we have used both for different departments.

Sample development and system services

SOA Services library is the fundamental component of each SOA service in the platform. Services offered by this library can be regarded as System services or Development services.

We have created a dummy template of the SOA services library, and it is enough to give you a good start. The primary interfacing part of this library starts with the SOA context. As the name suggests, it provides the context to an implementing service in the given SOA platform. The context enables tracing and tracking for the SOA service as well as the standard logging provider.

The following are the minimum number of classes and services provided by the SOA services library:

Classes in SOA services library

The most important and the vital class, which is used by all SOA web services, is SOAContext. Also, it's the first class for which we view the code, so we will view it completely to have an idea of how we are going to structure the whole class, including the comments:

```
// <copyright file="SOAContext.cs" company="HIJK">
// Copyright (c) HIJK Ltd. All rights reserved.
// </copyright>
// <summary>
// <project>HIJK SOA Services</project>
// <description>
// HIJK SOA wide basic services across the whole platform
// </description>
// </summary>

namespace HIJK.SOA.SOAServices
{
    /// <summary>
    /// This object provides the basic SOA context to
    all the SOA services in the HIJK's SOA Platform
    /// </summary>
    public class SOAContext
    {
```

```csharp
      public SOALogger soaLogger;
      //SOATracker soaTracker;

      private SOAServiceStructure soaServiceStructure;

      public SOAContext()
      {
        //Basic SOA Services, libraries,
        configuration initialization
        soaLogger = new SOALogger();
      }

      /// <summary>
      /// Initialize the SOA context
      /// </summary>
      public void Initialize()
      {
        //Initialize soaLogger & soaTracker
        //Read configuration or other meta-information
        mechanism to discover the SOA Service
        (which is using it) under the context
        //Create SOAServiceStructure: SOAMetaInfo & SOAPayload
        //Debug, SOA, Verbose logs
      }


      /// <summary>
      /// Close the SOA context successfully
      /// </summary>
      public void Close()
      {
        //Close the context
        //SOALogger.Log
        //SOATracker.Finish
      }

      /// <summary>
      /// Close the SOA context with error
      /// </summary>
      /// <param name="soaError"></param>
      public void Close(SOAError soaError)
      {
        //Close the context
        //SOALogger.LogError
        //SOATracker.Finish
      }
    }
  }
```

The web services will always use `SOAContext.Initialize()` at the start of their web service method, and `Close()` before the end of the method to open and close the context, and being part of the services in the SOA platform.

`SOA context` can be initializing some configuration, keeping the payload types and meta-information regarding the service, setting the service bus channel so that all this information will be automatically used in case of tracking, logging, and error handling when required behind the scenes.

 Note that the log levels can either be mentioned in the static or dynamic configuration as per the platform level configuration mechanism.

All services are implemented using ASP.NET Core REST Web API with MVC; therefore, all the services expose the functionality through Controllers. For example, the Employee service is `EmployeeController`.

Sample information service

These types of SOA services primarily expose the data logic of the enterprise. In our sample, we have Employee information service and the employee's document listing service. Let's see the code for the Employee information service:

Employee information SOA service

The following is a sample code for employee service to give an idea as a reference implementation for a REST-based web service:

```
/// <summary>
/// This class exposes the APIs related to Employee in HR Database
/// </summary>
[Route("api/[controller]")]
public class EmployeeController : Controller
{
  private SOAContext soaContext;
  private IEmployeeManager _manager;

    public EmployeeController(IEmployeeManager employeeManager)
    {
      _manager = employeeManager;
    }
```

```
/// <summary>
/// Gets the list of all Employees
/// Usage: GET api/employee
/// </summary>
/// <returns></returns>
[HttpGet]
public IEnumerable<Employee> Get()
{
  soaContext = new SOAContext();
  soaContext.Initialize();

  var retVal = _manager.GetListofAllEmployees();
  soaContext.Close();
  return retVal;
}
```

If your environment is configured to use `localhost:5000` for testing, then the URL to test this REST-based SOA service shall be `http://localhost:5000/api/employee`, which will then give you the list of all employees.

We can configure our solution setup to return the data in the JSON or XML format or both of them based on the client's request.

From the preceding code, we see how this employee SOA information service uses the context and closes it, which is provided by the SOA services library.

We do not need to go into the details of implementation for the underlying business layers, data access layers, and other stuff in general for understanding the SOA services design. But since it's the first web service code that we're looking at, we will take a look at all the steps of the code up to the database level.

You can also see the full source code provided in the form of projects for each chapter, which is shared with you along with the book.

Employee Information business logic layer

The interface for the Employee Manager class looks like this:

```
namespace Applications.BusinessLogic.Managers
{
    public interface IEmployeeManager : IBusinessManager
    {
      int GetTotalNumberOfEmployees();


      /// <summary>
```

```
/// Adds the new employee into the DB
/// </summary>
/// <returns></returns>
Employee AddNewEmployee(Employee newEmployee);

void RemoveAnEmployee(Employee newEmployee);

 /// <summary>
/// Gets the List of All Employees eventually
from data source
/// </summary>
/// <returns></returns>
IEnumerable<Employee> GetListofAllEmployees();

Employee GetAnEmployee(int employeeId);
    }
  }
```

Let's look at the implementation code, which is as written as follows:

```
public class EmployeeManager : IEmployeeManager
{
    private IRepository _employeeRepository;
    protected readonly Employee DEFAULT_EMPLOYEE;

    public EmployeeManager(IRepository
    employeeRepository) : base()
    {
        _employeeRepository = employeeRepository;
        DEFAULT_EMPLOYEE = new Employee { FirstName =
        "Not found", FamilyName = "Not found", Employee_ID = 0 };
    }

    public int GetTotalNumberOfEmployees()
    {
        return _employeeRepository.GetRecordsCount<Employee>();
    }

    public Employee AddNewEmployee(Employee newEmployee)
    {
        _employeeRepository.Create(newEmployee);
        return newEmployee;
    }

    public IEnumerable<Employee> GetListofAllEmployees()
    {
        return _employeeRepository.GetAll<Employee>();
    }
```

```
public void RemoveAnEmployee(Employee newEmployee)
{
    _employeeRepository.Delete(newEmployee);
}

public Employee GetAnEmployee(int employeeId)
{
    var employee = _employeeRepository.GetEntity<Employee>
    (employeeId);
    if (employee == null) return DEFAULT_EMPLOYEE;
    return employee;
}
}
```

Repositories in the data access layer

From this preceding code for the business layer project, we can see that we access the data source via the repository pattern. This enterprise application pattern has been already briefed upon in the previous chapter. Our repositories are present in the data access layer. Although we have a data access layer with repositories present in almost every service for each department, let's just take a look at one of the repositories, which is for the HR department:

```
/// <summary>
/// This repository class takes care of
disposing underlying dbcon/context objects
/// </summary>
public interface IRepository
{
   TEntity GetEntity<TEntity>(int id) where TEntity : class;
   IEnumerable<TEntity> GetAll<TEntity>() where TEntity : class;
   void Create<TEntity>(TEntity entity) where TEntity : class;
   void Update<TEntity>(TEntity entity) where TEntity : class;
   void Delete<TEntity>(TEntity entity) where TEntity : class;
   int GetRecordsCount<TEntity>() where TEntity : class;
}
```

Now, let's look at the implementation of a generic repository; we have removed some of the trivial code:

```
/// <summary>
/// Generic implementation of IRepository
interface for HR business apps.
/// The class takes will take care of disposing
underlying dbcon/context objects.
/// </summary>
public class GenericRepository : IRepository
```

```
{
  protected IDataContextCreator _dataContextCreator;
  public GenericRepository(IDataContextCreator dataContextCreator)
  {
    _dataContextCreator = dataContextCreator;
  }

  public void Create<TEntity>(TEntity entity)
  where TEntity : class
  {
    using (var context = _dataContextCreator.GetDataContext())
    {
      context.Set<TEntity>().Add(entity);
      context.SaveChanges();
    }
  }

  public IEnumerable<TEntity> GetAll<TEntity>()
    where TEntity : class
  {
    using (var context = _dataContextCreator.GetDataContext())
    return context.Set<TEntity>().ToList();
  }

  public int GetRecordsCount<TEntity>() where TEntity : class
  {
    using (var context = _dataContextCreator.GetDataContext())
    return context.Set<TEntity>().Count();
  }
}
```

Employee information core data access layer

The data access layer of this service uses the DataContext (DbContext) in the Entity Framework for the underlying SQLite database for storage. Let's view the sample code here:

 Note that in some services, we used the ADO.NET code, while in others, we use Entity Framework Core for the data access layers. This is done just to get a realistic feeling of some practical inconsistencies that could happen, however, but still on the SOA service interface layer, all the standards should be uniform.

```
public class DataContext : DbContext
{
  #region Entities representing Database Objects
  public DbSet<Employee> EMPLOYEE { get; set; }
  public DbSet<Photo> PHOTO { get; set; }
  public DbSet<Document> DOCUMENTS { get; set; }
```

```
#endregion

protected override void OnConfiguring(
  DbContextOptionsBuilder optionsBuilder)
{
  base.OnConfiguring(optionsBuilder);
  optionsBuilder.UseSqlite(@"Filename=C:\SOA_Sample.db");
}
}
```

For SQLite in the previous code, here we are using a fixed path just for demonstration purposes, and there are no special configurations that we set for using the SQLite database.

Entity in an employee information model

Now, let's just see the code for the Employee entity. Remember, we have already seen the tables for our sample SOA services scenario.

An extremely simple Employee class can be written as follows:

```
public class Employee
{
  [Key]
  public int Employee_ID { get; set; }
  public string FamilyName { get; set; }
  public string FirstName { get; set; }
  public DateTime DOB { get; set; }
  public string Grade { get; set; }
  public DateTime PPT_Issue_Date { get; set; }
  public DateTime PPT_Expiry_Date { get; set; }
}
```

Sample adapter service

Access or adapter services enable access to certain data. In our sample scene, we have at least one adapter or access service. We have a business process in the accounts department, which gets a list of external expenses from a third-party system through files in some format (let's say, XML or CSV). So, a web service is required, which receives the files one by one, parses the files, and saves them in the database.

Since we are discussing the SOA architecture, and not coding the web services, from now on, we will only see the example pattern, and have a suggestive skeleton service.

Our sample indicative implementation for a file receiving adapter service would look like the following:

```
/// <summary>
/// Receives the external expenses file and save it to
Accounting database.
/// Case when file comes from another web service
/// Type: Adapter Service
/// </summary>
[HttpPost]
public void Post()
{
  if (Request.HasFormContentType)
  {
    var form = Request.Form;
    foreach (var formFile in form.Files)
    {
      var filePath = Path.GetTempFileName();
      using (var fileStream = new FileStream(
        filePath, FileMode.Create))
      {
        formFile.CopyTo(fileStream);
      }
      //1. Parse the uploaded files
      //2. Save the data into database using data access layer
      //3. Delete the temp files
    }
  }
}
```

In the *Sample Business Processes for Departments* section given earlier, we have the following examples of access service:

- The first example is the one that is able to communicate with third-party B2B services able to receive the Passport document after its renewal from government authorities to the Regulatory Affairs department.
- The second is the one in which the received document is sent from the Regulatory Affairs department to the HR department.

Sample background service

Background services in SOA are continuously running services, which may or may not expose some service-callable interface. A background service is usually considered as a technical category of service, and is usually categorized depending on the function of a service. Our sample service could be categorized as an interaction or a data access service, which is a background running service acting as a DB Monitor, which periodically checks the database for a document's validity. Upon detecting the expiry documents, it calls another service to notify the change. We will see the sample code of the notification service (DocumentValidity) called by the background service in the next session.

This kind of service needs to be hosted in a process depending on the operating system. If it's Windows, the service can be a console app, an app without UI scheduled by Windows schedule, or an always running Windows service. If it's Linux, it would probably be configured as a service, or as an executable in Init.d or as a cron job. The skeleton code of our background service, which is hosted in a .NET Core console app, would look like the following piece of code:

```
public class DBMonitor : IDisposable
{
  private SOAContext soaContext;
  public DBMonitor()
  {
    soaContext = new SOAContext();
  }

  public void Initialize()
  {
    //Does the initialization, configuration, schedules,
    database, check ups..
    soaContext.Initialize();
  }

  public void Work()
  {
    //Perform all the mandated tasks as per schedule
    //Periodically watch DB tables for documents validity
    //Detect the change
    //Notify the change in respective document that it is
    expiring soon -- calls DocumentValidity notification service
  }

  //IDisposable Interface
}
```

The simple code in the host process would be something like this:

```
public static void Main(string[] args)
{
  var monitor = new DBMonitor();
  monitor.Initialize();
  monitor.Work();
}
```

 Note that we can use the same code and host it, for example, in the windows service as it is.

Sample interaction (notification) service

Interaction services provide interaction between applications or users. In our sample scenario, we have our service that provides interaction between two applications without the need of a third software in between. For this purpose, we have a DocumentValidity service, and we call it a notification service, which receives the notification from one service and processes it to another within the same Regulatory Affairs context (department):

```
Let's view the simple code for our sample notification service:
/// <summary>
/// This API gets the notifications from the DB Documents
 Validation Notification service.
/// Usage: - GET api/DocumentValidity/notify?employeeId=2&docid=1
/// Type: Interaction Service
/// </summary>
/// <param name="employeeId"></param>
/// <param name="docId"></param>
/// <returns></returns>
[HttpGet("Notify")]
public IActionResult Notify(int employeeId, int docId)
{
  soaContext = new SOAContext();
  soaContext.Initialize();

  //Start document validation/expiry process by
  invoking DocumentSubmitter to Authorities depending
  on the type of the document
  DocumentSubmitterProxy.ProcessDocumentSubmission(
    employeeId, docId);

  soaContext.Close();
  return new OkResult();
```

```
}
```

Note that our notification service gets called by another SOA service (the preceding code), and this service, after receiving the notification, calls another service creating a service composition as a service choreography.

Sample mediation service

Mediation services get the data from one service and distribute it amongst more than one target service. These services receive the data, may normalize data or transform data with respect to a common data model, enrich the data by adding new fields or filling up the empty fields in the transformed data, and perform filtration based on some attributes before forwarding the data to a set of target services or not, and then ultimately calling the sets of target services.

For our sample scenario, we have one **mediation service**, which is **Document Submitter**. This service receives the data, and is supposed to call various other target services like other authorities through B2B and third-party channel services, or may send e-mails to trigger the manual processes. In calling the target endpoints, it might need to transform the data into the target format, enrich the data with some more fields like license keys, registry information, and authority-specific authentication mechanism, and filter the payload so as not to send the data all the time to all services, but only to limited desired targets:

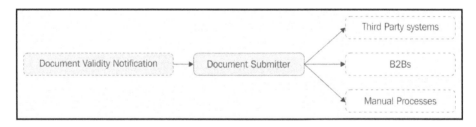

Sample Mediation Service

As you can see, this service is very specific to the actual requirements, so we cannot give the sample code, but understanding this scenario, one can imagine how the code would look like. There is no sample code for Document Submitter. As you can see in the preceding the diagram, an experienced engineer can realize that the implementation of a Document Submitter mediation service is very specific to the actual requirements in which target services it will be calling eventually.

Sample scenario of a service choreography

In our sample scene, we have a business process in the Regulatory Affairs department, which is about the documents validation process. This process is actually a service composition in the form of service choreography. Remember, in choreography, there is no director or controller for the execution of all the services, but they are executed sequentially in a set order to achieve a business process.

Our sample process starts from the **DB Monitor** background service, which sends one message or one service call for each expiring document in its validation process. It sends out the notification through our service **Document Validity Notify**, which then calls the **Document Submitter** service to pass on the documents for their renewals (for example), and after some time (required to process the renewal request forms), we get the renewed document back via one of the B2B services **Passport Receiver** (for example, to receive the specific document, that is, Passport). The **Passport Receiver** service will then call the **Update HR Document** (UploadSingleFile) service to pass on the new document to the HR department to save a copy in their database:

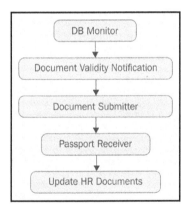

Sample Service Choreography

This concludes our service composition as a choreography. Since it's not a workflow, we do not need to explicitly close the status of the business process and there is no need to update the process starter.

Summary

In this chapter, our primary focus was to understand and build the SOA software implementation architecture. We took a top-down approach from how to define architecture to SOA-specific architectural concepts using the right aspects and attributes to consider while modeling the SOA platform.

We then took a closer look at the essential artifacts required for developing a general SOA architecture and gradually moved towards the technical perspective of the implementation architecture.

Finally, we did a skeleton implementation for some of the SOA services in our sample scenario. We used .NET Core with C#, realizing how easy it is to write the code with rich framework support, especially for REST-based web services. As an additional perk, our code is already cross-platform; we can even write the code in one platform and deploy it to other platforms.

8

Cloud-Based Architecture and Integration with .NET Core

Cloud architecture has evolved at a rapid pace in recent years, and offers highly reliable and scalable solutions. This has drawn the attention of enterprise companies, who are now adopting cloud services, and either migrating their existing systems or creating new systems on the cloud. Another advantage of the cloud is the cost. Previously, mid-or-small-sized companies had to invest a lot into building their infrastructure, and had to buy highly-priced servers to host applications. Apart from this, they also needed a support contract, or had to hire a local team to support the application, depending on its complexity. On the other hand, with the cloud, companies can use the pay-as-you-go model or purchase a subscription, and host their applications without needing to purchase any hardware or hire a team to maintain the infrastructure. In this chapter, we will use the cloud platform of Microsoft, known as Microsoft Azure, and develop and host applications built using .NET Core.

We will cover the following topics in this chapter:

- Discuss the three computing models of Cloud, namely IaaS, PaaS and SaaS
- Focus on Microsoft Azure as a Cloud provider and discuss the difference between Virtual machines, Cloud services, and App services
- Explore how we can develop .NET Core applications using Azure App Services, which not only provides a Rapid Application Development model, but also facilitates deploying and maintaining an application on the cloud
- Explore how we can develop background services and event handling on the cloud using WebJobs and Azure Functions
- Discuss scalability and performance options in Azure App Services
- Explore logging and monitoring options for .NET Core application using Azure

Cloud Computing Models

Generally, every cloud platform, especially Azure, provides these three kinds of models:

- Infrastructure as a Service
- Platform as a Service
- Software as a Service

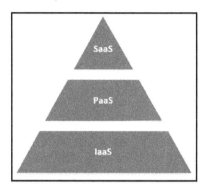

Infrastructure as a Service (IaaS)

IaaS is a form of cloud computing that provides virtualized resources, such as virtual machines, containers, networking services such as firewalls, and other computing resources. Companies or individuals can use these services via the Internet and setup their whole infrastructure over the cloud. This benefits small, mid-sized, and even large companies, as they can avoid hardware costs and pay for only the services they use. The IaaS platform provides high availability and scalability, and can be managed through the cloud portal. For example, to create a **virtual machine** (**VM**), you can log in with your cloud account, choose an option to create a new VM by selecting an operating system (for example, Windows or Linux), and then choose any of the pre-built images for the version you want to install. Within minutes, the VM becomes ready, and you can use that VM to install any of the tools and host your applications. The premier IaaS providers are Microsoft Azure, Amazon Web Services, Google Compute Engine, IBM SmartCloud Enterprise, and Rackspace Open Cloud. Some examples of the IaaS model are VM, Storage, and networks.

Platform as a Service (PaaS)

PaaS offers platform services, such as Web Apps, and cloud services such as SQL Server Services, Azure App Services, and so on. Whereas IaaS is all about containers and virtual machines, and anything installed inside that VM has to be managed manually by the user, PaaS offers cloud services where all the services are managed by the cloud provider. For example, if we need to host our database server on the cloud, one option is to take a VM and install the SQL Server on that VM itself. Using this model, the management of the SQL Server or the setting up of load balancing and failover has to be done by the user. But if we go with the SQL Server cloud service, which is platform as a service, it does all the load balancing, failover is done automatically, and we just need to care about our application databases and SQL objects. There are some constraints when working with the PaaS model, as it only supports a minimal set of versions of the tools or platforms services, and it totally depends on the business requirement, where the architect can decide to choose between IaaS and PaaS. Some examples of PaaS in Azure are App Services and SQL Azure.

Software as a Service (SaaS)

SaaS is a cloud service where the consumer can access software applications running on the cloud via the Internet. Applications such as Twitter, Office 365, and Flickr are all examples of SaaS. Consumers are charged monthly, weekly, or on an on-demand basis, as per the agreement. With traditional software applications, companies purchase the software at a one-time cost, and install it in their own environment. Unlike on-premise installation, SaaS runs on the cloud, and offers an on-rent model, where customers can register for a service to use software and pay as they use. A good example of SaaS is Office 365.

Azure compute

When Microsoft first introduced Azure, they started with Platform-as-a-Service where they have **Web Role** and **Worker Role**. But, gradually, they started the Infrastructure services and defined the **VM Role**. Since April 2015, they have replaced all these roles, and given a new look to the Azure computing model, which is classified into these four components:

- Virtual machines
- Cloud service
- App Service
- Service Fabric

Virtual machines

A virtual machines is a part of IaaS and allows the user to provision any machine running on the cloud; the user can remotely connect to that machine and do whatever they want. With virtual machines, you can also manage resources such as CPU, memory, and disks (HDD or SSD), and all are quite easy to set up using the cloud portal. Similar to virtual machines, Microsoft has also introduced the concept of containers. Containers are light-weight application hosts, which refers to virtualized resources such as filesystem, windows registry, and others. Containers run on top of virtual machines to sandbox any application running inside it. We can set up a Linux virtual machine and set up a container, which runs ASP.NET Core, on top of it. Containers are now only supported on the Linux platform but Microsoft is working on it being supported on Windows as well. Moreover, containers are cheaper than virtual machines in terms of cost.

Cloud services

Cloud services is a PaaS (Platform as a Service) and is designed to support applications that need auto-management of scalability and reliability by Azure. Cloud services run internally on VMs and provide an abstraction layer on top. It has two types of roles, which are as follows:

- Worker Role
- Web Role

Worker Role

This role is used to run any application which does not require IIS. This role is mainly used to run background services.

Web Role

Web Role is primarily used to run web applications, such as ASP.NET, PHP, Web API, WCF, and others, which runs on IIS.

Cloud service can be deployed as a package and, during deployment, you can specify the roles that you need, choose the target operating system, and scale your service accordingly. Cloud service is managed by Azure Service Fabric, and it controls the environment and the virtual machines that your service is hosted on. So, for example, if you have selected two instances to be running and once instance fails, Azure Service Fabric detects that failure and uses some other rack in the same data center to bring up that instance. It uses the shared storage between multiple VMs, and makes it easy to switch between different VMs in case of any failure.

App Services

With App Services, there is another layer of abstraction which hides the underlying cloud services. With App Service, we don't need to choose the Worker Role or Web Role that our application will be running on. Instead, we can simply choose any app model from Web App, API App, Logic App, and Mobile App, and deploy the application with easy and simple steps. In the next section, we will discuss App Services in detail, and see how firm it is to develop applications for different app models.

Azure Service Fabric

Azure Service Fabric is the distributed system platform used to develop applications on microservices architecture. It provides an easy way to package and deploy microservices, and to manage their scalability through the Azure portal. It is the new middleware platform for building enterprise-class cloud applications.

Azure Service Fabric provides a runtime to build distributed, stateless, and stateful microservices, and powers various services, such as Azure SQL database, Microsoft Power BI, Azure IoT Hub, and others. To learn more about Service Fabric and microservices architecture, please refer to Chapter 9, *Microservices Architecture*.

Features comparison between virtual machines, cloud services, Azure App Services, and Service Fabric

The following table compares the main features of virtual machines, cloud services, Azure App Services, and Service Fabric:

Features	Virtual machines	Cloud services	Azure App Services	Service Fabric
Azure managed OS		✓	✓	✓
Quick deployment			✓	✓
Shared storage, which enables easy scaling			✓	✓
Deployment slots to keep multiple environments		✓	✓	✓
Operating system and patches updated by Azure		✓	✓	✓
Deploy code from Git	✓		✓	
Deploy code from TFS	✓	✓		✓
Access to Azure storage services	✓	✓	✓	✓
Support for different languages like ASP.NET, Node.js, PHP, and Python	✓	✓	✓	✓
SSL support	✓	✓	✓	✓
Remote Access to servers	✓	✓		✓
Integrated Monitoring support	✓	✓	✓	

Rapid application development using Azure App Services

Microsoft Azure provides a complete RAD (Rapid Application Development) platform to develop applications that are websites, Web APIs, logic applications, and Mobile Apps under one umbrella known as Azure App Services. In this section, we will explore all the app models provided in Azure App Services, and understand the unique capability of each and when to use what to achieve a particular scenario.

Azure App Services contains four types of application models, which are as follows:

- **Web Apps**
- **API Apps**
- **Mobile Apps**
- **Logic Apps**

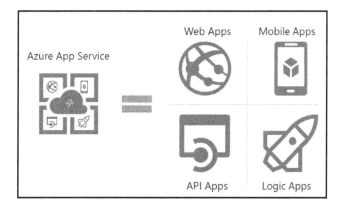

The benefit of Azure App Services is that you just need to focus on your application business requirement rather than going into the low-level details of plumbing servers, defining worker roles or web roles, and so on. You can choose the app model that fits your requirement and develop your application on the fly.

Azure provides App Services using App Service Fabric, which abstracts the server and the underlying resources through App Service Fabric. App Services provides certain capabilities which make creating applications simpler. These capabilities include authentication and authorization, scaling, a hybrid model that enables connecting to on-premise resources like the database running in your own organization, continuous integration to deploy applications from different source controls such as Git or TFS on every check-in, and support for troubleshooting. Consider the following figure:

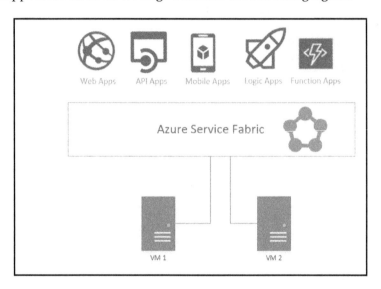

Web Apps

Traditionally, with web application hosting, we need a separate server or a machine where we set up our web server. With .NET Core, we can develop a web application that can be hosted on IIS if we have the Windows operating system installed on our server, or Apache or Nginx web server if we have the Linux operating system. Setting the machine and web server requires the sufficient amount of time and effort. We need to make sure that the .NET Core runtime has been installed, set up the application pool during deployment, and if our web application is a public website, then we need some DevOps support to make it publicly accessible. We also need to make sure that it is secure and has the latest service packs installed.

With Azure Web Apps, hosting a web application is simple. With a few basic steps, we can deploy any web application on the cloud, which is accessible over the Internet and provides capabilities for doing authentication and the authorization of users, scalability such as load balancing servers, and connecting to the on-premise database servers. The developer or architect hosting the web application on the cloud does not need to get into other details such as setting up a web server, configuration application pool, and so on.

With Web Apps, we can host any web application that is developed on .NET, Node.js, Python, Java, and PHP. When we register a web application in Azure Web App, it creates a public URL, which can be accessed from the Internet. The default URL is {name_of_webapp}.azurewebsites.net, but we can attach custom domains to it as well. We can also use deployment slots with our Web Apps, which enables us to set up different environments such as development, staging and production. Moreover, we can also set up continuous integration, which enables us to configure the source repository where our code resides, like Git or TFS; automatic deployment is done once we check-in or push our changes to that repository.

Hosting an ASP.NET Core application on Azure

Deploying an ASP.NET Web Application on Azure is simple. You can either create an application through the Azure portal, or create a web application from Visual Studio and publish it to Azure using Visual Studio or .NET CLI (command-line interface).

Suppose we have an ASP.NET Core application in place and we want to deploy that application on Azure. To do so, we will just right-click on the web application project from Visual Studio, and choose **Publish**. A dialog will open, and ask you to select the target to be published, as shown in the following screenshot:

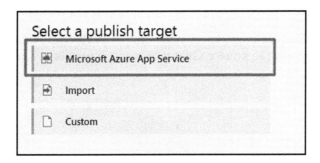

Once you select **Microsoft Azure App Services**, it will give options to select your Azure subscription, and choose any of the existing running App Services. As this is a new web application, we will choose **New**, as shown in this screenshot:

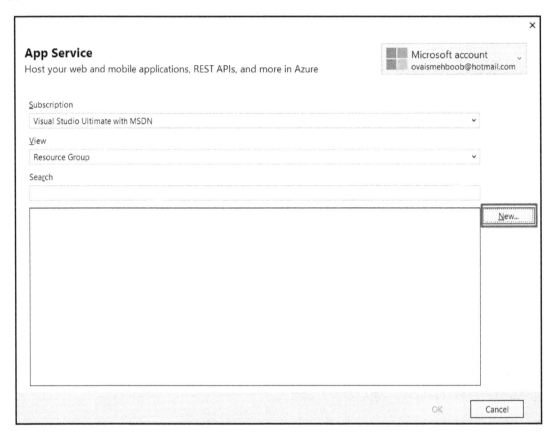

From the **Create App Service** page, specify the unique **Web App Name**, select **Subscription**, select existing **Resource Group** or create a new one, and finally, select **App Service Plan**:

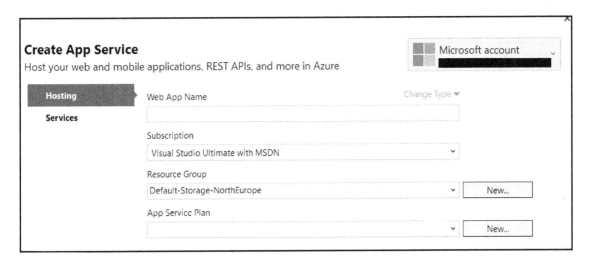

App Service Plan gives an option to select the **Location** where the application will be deployed and the **Size** of the machine that shows the number of processor core(s) and RAM:

Finally, it shows up a dialog containing the server name, **Destination URL**, and other details, as shown in the following screenshot:

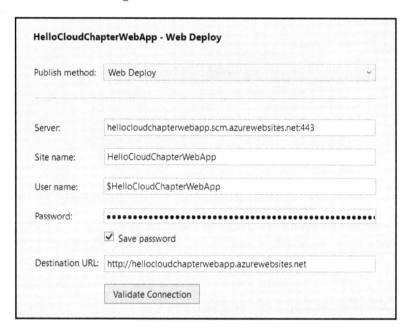

Azure has also introduced a template for Web App on Linux, which can create and deploy your ASP.NET Core application on Linux running in a Docker container. While creating, you can specify the **App name**, **Subscription**, **Resource Group**, and container, and select the .NET Core runtime stack to create an ASP.NET Core application:

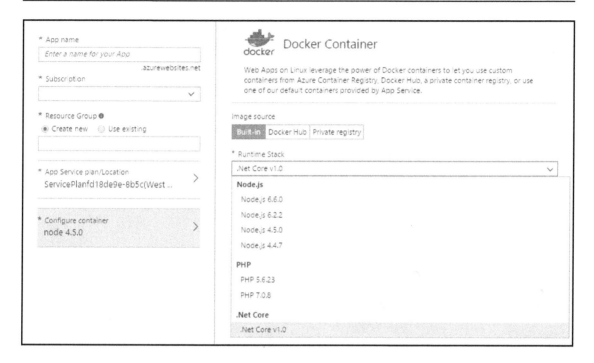

Deployment slots

Enterprise applications usually have different environments, such as development, staging, and production. These environments help developers to develop on the development environment, test on staging, and when everything is tested, move towards production. In Azure App Services, we can specify the deployment slot while deploying the application, and even configure the percentage of the web traffic to a particular environment to test a real-time scenario. For example, suppose we have a web application running as vms.azurewebsites.com, and we have another deployment where another upgraded version having the URL vms.staging.azurewebsites.net is running. We can test the real-time scenario by sending a percentage of the traffic to the staging web application, and once we are satisfied with the upgraded version, we can swap the production from staging. This swapping can be done without any downtime. Internally, when the swapping process starts, Azure swaps the virtual IP address assigned to the slots, and makes sure that the source slot is warmed up, so that it responds immediately when someone accesses it. Swapping can be done in both directions, that is, from staging to production and vice versa. Deployment slot is a full web application, but scaling is only possible for the deployment that has been marked as production.

Deployment slots can be configured from the Azure portal by navigating to the web application and selecting the **Deployment slots** option, as shown in the following screenshot:

To check configuring the deployment slot, please refer to `https://docs.microsoft.com/en-us/azure/app-service-web/web-sites-staged-publishing`.

API Apps

API Apps allows you to host Web APIs on Azure App Services. We can expose existing Web APIs, or develop a new Web API project, either from Visual Studio, or from the Azure portal with a few clicks.

It provides the following features:

- APIs that can be hosted on Azure App Services should be developed either on .NET, Java, PHP, Node.js, or Python.
- API Apps provides authentication and authorization out-of-the-box, and provides different connectors to authenticate using Facebook, Google, Microsoft accounts, Azure AD, as so on.
- It has built-in Swagger to see API metadata and consume through web. Swagger is a powerful open source framework, which provides certain tools that help to design, build, document, and consume RESTful APIs.

- It provides the Client SDK so that the party consuming that API can easily generate the client code through Visual Studio or command prompt, and this is supported for clients developed on .NET, Java, Node.js, and JavaScript.
- It supports **CORS** (**Cross Origin Resource Sharing**), which allows calling Web APIs from cross domains.
- It can be used in integration with Logic Apps, and Logic Apps can use orchestration to delegate calls to our Web APIs.
- We can easily do monitoring, scaling, setting up of deployment slots, and many other things through the Azure API Management interface.

Configuring Swagger in ASP.NET Core Web API and deploying on Azure

Swagger is an open source framework, which helps to design, build, document, and consume RESTful APIs. There are many benefits of using swagger in an enterprise web application, which include the following:

- It generates good documentation based on the XML comments specified in your .NET code
- It supports Client SDK generation and discoverability

Swagger is configured out-of-the-box when we create an API App from the Azure portal, but when deploying APIs which are already created, we may not have this framework configured. We will see how to configure Swagger in an existing Web API developed on .NET Core, and deploy it as an API App on Azure in the next section.

Generating swagger documents in ASP.NET Core can be achieved using `Swashbuckle`, a .NET Core implementation. It has the following two components:

- `Swashbuckle.SwaggerGen`: Generates JSON-based documentation of .NET Core Web API.
- `Swashbuckle.SwaggerUI`: Generates UI-based documentation of .NET Core Web API.

We can start by adding a NuGet package, `Swashbuckle`. Make sure to select the prerelease option if the package is not available. Once this package is added, we have to add the Swagger service in the `ConfigureServices` method of the `Startup` class.

Add the following entry in the `ConfigureServices` method of the `Startup` class:

```
services.AddSwaggerGen(options =>
{
  options.SingleApiVersion(new Info
  {
      Version = "v1",
      Title = "Hello World Swagger API",
      Description = "API to Configure Swagger",
      TermsOfService = "None"
    });
});
```

Finally, enable Swagger middleware in the `Configure` method of the `Startup` class as follows:

```
app.UseSwagger();
app.UseSwaggerUi();
```

Now, when we run the application or host it on Azure, we can access Swagger JSON by calling this URL: `http://{websiteaddress}:{port}/swagger/v1/swagger.json`.

Swagger UI can be accessed by calling the following URL: `http://{websiteaddress}:{portno}/swagger/ui`.

Creating proxy classes using AutoRest in .NET Core

Usually, with SOAP-based web services, we can easily generate client proxy classes by adding a service reference through Visual Studio. Whereas, with Web APIs, we use `HttpClient` class to do GET, POST, or any other operation on Web API, and write a few lines of code to set the request header, request body, other parameters, and serialize the response received from the server.

On the other hand, if our Web APIs are Swagger-enabled, we can easily generate client proxy classes using some third-party tools and libraries, where `AutoRest` is one of them. With `AutoRest`, we can generate client proxy classes by executing one single command through a command-line interface.

To start with, add a NuGet package, `AutoRest`, in your application which is going to access a Web API. Once the NuGet package is added, we can go to the user's directory and run `autorest`:

```
C:\Users\{username}\.nuget\packages\AutoRest\0.17.3\tools
```

To generate the client code, we can run the following command:

```
C:\Users\{username}\.nuget\packages\AutoRest\0.17.3\tools\autorest -Input
http://{webapiname}.azurewebsites.net/swagger/v1/swagger.json -
OutputDirectory Api
```

In the above command, `Api` is the output folder where the proxy classes will be generated, and it can be further used to consume Web API. Here is the sample snapshot of the folder generated:

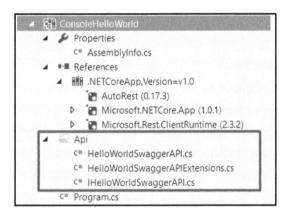

This is the sample code to access Web API:

```
public static void Main(string[] args)
{
    HelloWorldSwaggerAPI api = new HelloWorldSwaggerAPI();
    api.ApiValuesByIdGet(1);
}
```

Enable CORS

When accessing Web API from client applications, it restricts access to web resources unless they are being used from the same domain where the application is running. In the ASP.NET project, we can enable **CORS (Cross Origin Resource Sharing)**, which allows a restricted resource to be accessible by any other domain where the client application is running. CORS in the ASP.NET project can be configured in several ways, and can specify Origin, Header, and Method, which we need to be allowed from external sources.

To enable CORS in ASP.NET MVC 6, we have to add a NuGet package, as follows:
`Microsoft.AspNetCore.Cors`

We can configure CORS at the Controller, Action, or Middleware levels. To enable CORS, we have to first define the policies, and this can be done either in the `ConfigureServices` method or `Configure` method of the `Startup` class.

Here is an example of setting up CORS in the `ConfigureServices` method:

```
services.AddCors(options => {
  options.AddPolicy("AllowLimited", builder =>
    builder.WithHeaders("Content-Type", "Accept")
    .WithMethods("GET", "POST").AllowAnyOrigin();
});
```

The preceding policy will allow only `GET` and `POST` requests, and each request should have a request header as `Content-Type` and `Accept` to accept requests from any domain as specified in `origin`.

To enable CORS at the Controller or Action level, we can specify the `EnableCors` attribute in the `Controller` class or `Action` method, and specify the policy as defined in the `ConfigureServices` method:

```
[EnableCors("AllowLimited")]
public class PersonController : Controller
{
}
```

And here is the example of adding `EnableCors` on the method level:

```
[EnableCors("AllowLimited")]
[HttpGet]
public IEnumerable<string> Get()
{
  return lst;
}
```

To use CORS at the middleware level, we can call the `UseCors` method and specify the policy, as defined earlier.

```
public void Configure(IApplicationBuilder app,
  IHostingEnvironment env, ILoggerFactory loggerFactory)
{
  app.UseCors("AllowLimited");
}
```

Mobile Apps

Mobile Apps in Azure App Services gives a provision to develop any platform app from Android, Windows, and iOS, which can use Azure backend services such as calling a web service, authentication, offline syncing capability, and push notifications:

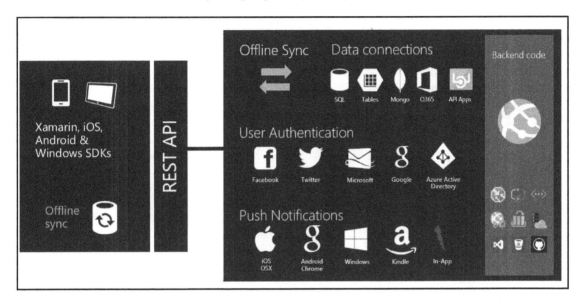

We can develop Mobile Apps through the Azure portal on the fly by choosing a **Web + Mobile** option from the marketplace and creating an application.

Mobile Apps consists of these two projects:

- A backend project, which runs on .NET or Node.js
- A client project, which can target any platform from Android, Windows, iOS (Swift, Objective-C), Xamarin (Android, iOS, Forms), and Cordova

When you choose **Mobile App** from the Azure portal, it gives two options, as shown in the following screenshot:

The **Mobile App** option can be used if we want to customize a backend Web API project associated with our **Mobile App**. On the other hand, the **Mobile Apps Quickstart** option only allows you to download the client project for any platform, as mentioned earlier. Once the project is downloaded, it contains all the boilerplate code written to connect to the backend API and to enable offline syncing.

Offline sync

Offline sync can be enabled to use mobile application data when it is offline and not connected to the Internet. It can be achieved with a combination of the Mobile App SDK on the client and the backend API on the server. This is helpful for devices that are not always connected to the Internet and need to store some data locally while they are offline. A good example is the Courier service app, which takes the user's signature on the device and stores the signature in the local database. When workers are connected to the Internet, that information is pushed to the backend.

To enable the local data store in Mobile App, Mobile App comes with out-of-the-box boilerplate code, which uses SQLLite for local storage of data. But you can change it if you want to use some other technology for local database storage.

For example, if we create a Xamarin (Android) application from the Azure portal, we can download the code and enable offline syncing by just enabling the defined directive, OFFLINE_SYNC_ENABLED.

After enabling the offline sync, the first sync is done when the client's application is first started and the local database is set up. The Mobile App retrieves the data from the server, and stores it in the local store. Any changes or database operations performed on the app will store it first to the local storage, and then sync to the server. This way, the app behaves seamlessly without showing any delay or error. Syncing data is done through the Mobile App SDK, and can be used to detect conflicts and to resolve those conflicts.

Push notifications

Push notifications is a mechanism to send notifications to the client devices on any event. In Azure, this can be done by setting up a centralized **Notification Hubs**. Notification Hubs is a service from Azure which provides the capability to send notifications to different platforms on a large scale:

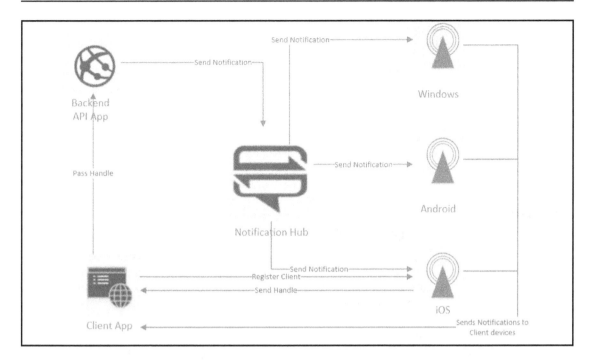

The process starts by registering each platform application with the **Notification Service**. Notification Service is a system that notifies the client's device on any event. When the device is registered on the Notification service, it sends the handle that the **Client App** can send to the **Backend API App**, which sends it to the **Notification Hub**. When the backend sends the notification, it sends it to the **Notification Hub** first, and then the **Notification Hub** sends that notification to the specific Notification Service, which finally delivers the notification to that particular **Client App**.

 To learn more about Mobile Apps, please refer to following link:
https://azure.microsoft.com/en-us/documentation/learning-paths/a
ppservice-mobileapps/.

Logic Apps

In any enterprise, workflows are very important to run the business. Workflows are developed so that the system can send notifications to different users for a specific workflow level as assignment, and also persist the state of each workflow instance that can be used for further processing. With Azure App Services in Microsoft Azure, we can use Logic Apps to create workflows by orchestrating Software as a Service components.

With Logic Apps, we can compose a workflow that runs in Azure and the Azure Service Fabric takes cares of all the underlying controlling of the workflow.

Logic Apps consist of the following three components, which can run in Azure or on-premise:

- Connectors
- Triggers
- Actions

Connectors

To start configuring the workflow, we have to first set up a connector. A connector can be a push connector or a poll connector. Push connectors are those in which Logic App is notified by the connector when the event is fired, whereas poll connectors are those in which the connector is notified by Logic App when the event is fired. Connectors are classified into the following categories:

- API Apps, Logic Apps, and Azure Functions.
- **Microsoft Managed APIs**: There are managed by Microsoft and contain some third-party and Microsoft-built APIs. These type of connectors include GitHub, Facebook, Dropbox, Azure Blog, SQL Azure, CRM online, SharePoint online, and others.
- **Marketplace**: These are also third-party and Microsoft-built APIs, but are managed by Microsoft. Marketplace has a large number of connectors available, and they are mostly hybrid connectors such as SAP Connector, IBM DB2, Oracle, BizTalk API Apps, and others.

Trigger

A trigger is the event that runs automatically based on a schedule or on an on-demand basis, and can be configured on the connectors. For example, we can set up a trigger to run Logic App on the Web API App if somebody accesses a particular GET or POST request on that API.

Actions

Action is the process that runs on trigger. Actions can be connectors that can be used to trigger any action. For example, we can set up any trigger on a Web API if someone accesses the GET or POST method, and once that trigger happens, we can use the Oracle connector to insert an entry in some table.

Creating Logic App in Azure

Logic App can be created by selecting the **Web + Mobile** option in the search pane and by then selecting the **Logic App** option.

You can select the **Pin to dashboard** option while creating any app on Azure so that it can be added to the main dashboard panel and is easily accessible.

Once you open Logic App, you can see the **Logic App Designer**, pane as shown in this screenshot:

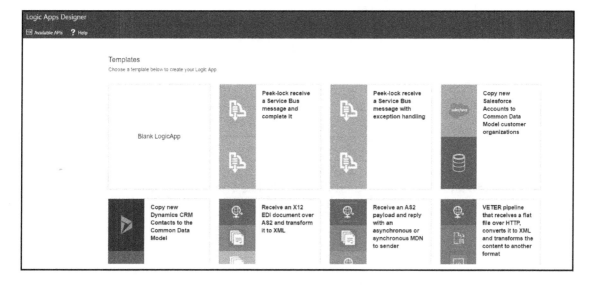

You can select any predefined templates, or create a blank app. Predefined templates provide a quick way to create a Logic App to provide a certain functionality, and with a few simple wizard steps, the app becomes ready. These templates include sending an e-mail when the SharePoint list item is modified, delivering an e-mail on new tweets added to your Twitter account, and so on.

With the **Blank LogicApp** option, we have a choice to select the connector from the available connectors, such as using Managed Microsoft API, or APIs from App Services in the same region, or using API Management available in the user's subscriptions. We can compose Logic App using designer and edit the workflow through code view using the Logic App definition language. Let's take the example of a simple workflow that posts a tweet on a configured Twitter account whenever new blogpost is published on WordPress. To achieve this scenario, we first select the WordPress (when a post is created) activity from Microsoft Managed API, and provide the WordPress credentials. We can also set the interval at which Logic Apps should check for any new post published on a WordPress site:

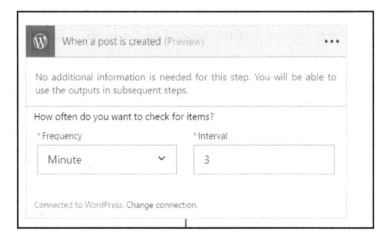

Next, we can add an action or loop activity, and choose Twitter connector to post a tweet on the configured account:

When adding a new step, you can choose from adding an action, a condition, a for loop, do until loop, or scope:

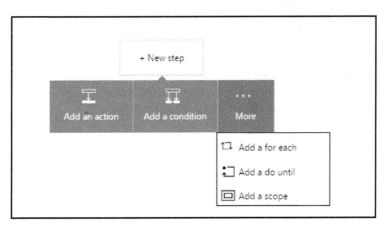

So with Logic Apps, you can quickly create workflows that run under Azure App Service on the Azure portal, and are easily configurable with a provision of a number of available connectors to choose from.

Scaling Azure App Services

Scaling is a technique to scale web applications in conditions when there is a higher load or a lesser load, and to keep the performance or the user response time consistent.

With Azure Web Apps, Mobile Apps, API Apps, and Logic apps, scaling can be done in four ways, which are as follows:

- **Scale up**: To increase the resources such as CPU, memory, and other attributes based on the pricing tier of the underlying VM
- **Scale down**: To decrease the resources such as CPU, memory, and other attributes based on the pricing tier of the underlying VM
- **Scale out**: To balance the load by diverting the traffic of incoming requests to multiple VMs
- **Scale in**: To reduce the number of VMs if the load weighs down

Scaling can be done manually or scheduled, or can be done based on the usage of CPU, memory, or disk space. Scaling can be done easily by opening the Web App blade in the Azure portal and selecting the scale up and scale out options.

Background services and event handling in cloud

In Microsoft Azure, we can develop background services known as **WebJobs**, and these WebJobs can be hooked up by other applications using **WebHooks**. In this section, we will study WebJobs in detail, learn to develop long-running background services, and use WebHook to invoke their methods from external applications.

WebJobs

WebJobs are background services that can be run by triggering from outside sources, on-demand, or continuous. They run under the same Web App and are managed by Azure Service Fabric. These are a good choice when we have to run an application as a background process for a longer run. One Web App can have a multiple number of WebJobs, and they can all share the same memory, CPU usage, and storage. As WebJobs and Web Apps share the same resources, any of the high-intensity jobs can affect the performance of other WebJobs or Web Apps, and vice versa. WebJobs can listen for events from Queue, blobs, and WebHooks, and can be triggered manually or scheduled to run at a certain time.

WebJobs are highly recommended for scenarios where heavy plumbing is needed. For example, let's consider a correspondence system that generates documents for different vendors as selected on the form, and each vendor gets the document containing information specific to that vendor. In this scenario, if the vendor list is big, the user may get a request timeout, as a document will be generated and e-mailed for each vendor. To design this scenario, we can use Azure Storage Queue, which keeps the messages needed to be processed. This queue will trigger our Web Job to process that message by generating a document, and send that as an attachment to the corresponding vendor:

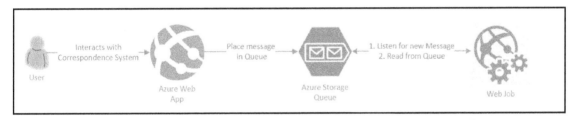

There are many other scenarios, like image processing, file maintenance, and other long running tasks that take a substantial amount of time and may experience the server response timeout scenarios.

WebJobs can be triggered in three different ways, as follows:

WebJobs Type	Description
On-Demand	This is generally triggered from the Azure portal, or if listening to some storage queues, tables, Service bus, and blobs using Azure, the WebJobs SDK can trigger automatically when any new message is created.
Scheduled	WebJobs can be scheduled and triggered at a specified time.
Continuous	Runs continuously, but explicit code needs to be written to keep it alive.

WebJobs can be deployed by placing the files in a particular filesystem, and can be any of the following types:

- `.exe` (executable file)
- `.bat` (batch file)
- `.sh` (Bash file)
- `.php` (PHP file)
- `.py` (Python file)
- `.js` (JavaScript file)

Developing WebJob using .NET Core

To create a Web Job, we can create a .NET class library project, or, if Azure SDK for Visual Studio 2015 is installed, we can select the project **Azure WebJob** template from the **Cloud** section, which generates the basic boilerplate code to kick-start the project. However, with .NET Core, there is no tooling support currently provided in Visual Studio 2015 and some manual work is needed. Moreover, Azure WebJobs SDK is also not supported with .NET Core. However, if you want to run your .NET Core console application as a WebJob, it can be done with a few simple steps, as shown next.

For example, if you have a .NET Console application, and you want to run that as a WebJob in the Azure portal, the following steps can be taken:

1. Create a batch (`.bat`) file under your console application's `netcoreapp` folder, and add the following script:

   ```
   ECHO OFF
   dotnet YourConsoleApp.dll
   ```

2. Develop a zip package of the `netcoreapp` folder, and upload it on Azure, as shown in the following screenshot:

3. Specify the name of the WebJob.
4. Upload the Zip file created.
5. Select **Type**: either **Triggered** or **Continuous**.
6. Select the type of the **Triggers**: either **Manual** or **Schedule** (Schedule triggers need a CRON expression to be set).

> The CRON expression includes six fields, which are as follows:
>
> {second} {minute} {hour} {day} {month} {day of the week}
>
> For Example: 30 */5 * * * *
>
> This means: At 30 seconds past the minute, every 5 minutes.

To use Azure Storage Queues, Service Bus, or other Azure components, we need Azure WebJobs SDK, which is not supported in .NET Core. But we can use .NET Framework 4.5.2 or greater to leverage a particular requirement.

Developing WebJobs using WebJobs SDK and .NET Framework 4.5

In the previous section, we saw how easily we can deploy any .NET Core console application as WebJobs on Azure. However, there is a limitation of WebJobs SDK, that is, it cannot run with .NET Core, hence, we have to stick with .NET framework 4.5.

WebJobs SDK provides built-in features that simplify complex plumbing and make it easy for developers to use and build them in less time. For example, to enable WebJobs SDK to listen to a queue or a service bus for the creation of any new items, we can just add any method in the functions class and specify the trigger attributes on a parameter that passes the object as JSON or XML (as configured) being inserted in the Azure queue.

To start with, install the Azure SDK, which installs some templates specific to Azure, and provides a new Azure WebJobs template to create the basic WebJob on the fly:

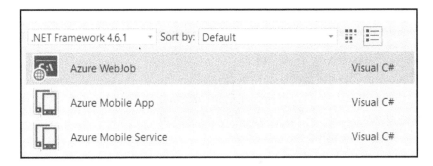

On selecting the **Azure WebJob** project template, it creates a `Function` class and initializes a `JobHost` to run the WebJob:

```
var host = new JobHost();
host.RunAndBlock();
```

JobHost is the entry point of Azure WebJobs SDK and its primary purpose is to perform indexing, monitoring, and scheduling the functions defined using the WebJobs artifacts.

In the `Function` class, we can define static methods and define the storage, WebHook, and other trigger attributes that run whenever any change is made.

The following is an example that triggers this method whenever any queue item is added in the `MessageQueue`, where `MessageQueue` is the name of the queue created on Azure. We can achieve the complete event-based trigger by just adding the `QueueTrigger` attribute on the message parameter:

```
public static void ProcessQueueMessage([QueueTrigger(
"testqueue")] String message, TextWriter log)
{
   log.WriteLine(message);
}
```

Moreover, WebJobs are also smart in serializing the JSON response to the object if specified as a parameter. In the preceding code snippet, we have used the `String` parameter. However, this can be changed to an object if we needed some object to be serialized based on the JSON response. So, for example, if the JSON text receiving has an ID and Name, then we can define a POCO class in .NET, which can contain properties like `ID` and `Name`, and the signature will be as follows:

```
public static void ProcessQueueMessage([QueueTrigger(
"testqueue")] Message message, TextWriter log)
{
   log.WriteLine(message.Name);
}
```

There are many other triggers, such as `FileTriggerAttribute`, `ErrorTrigger`, and others, which you can check out in the WebJobs SDK documentation.

Azure WebJobs versus Azure WorkerRoles

Azure WorkerRoles were introduced in the early stages of the Azure platform and it enables developers and architects to deploy background services on the cloud which run independently on a dedicated virtual machine. This is also a PaaS solution, but needs manual work to handle triggering, scaling, and other configuration. The following table gives a comparison of both WorkerRole and WebJob:

	WebJob	WorkerRole
Hosting	Hosted inside WebApp	Hosted independently on VM
Scalability	Scalable with WebApps	Scaled independently
Remote Access	Remoting WebJob is not supported	Can be remoted, as deployed on VM
Deployment	Easy deployment	Complicated deployment

Triggers	Automatic Triggering support provided out of the box	Manual coding work is required
Logging	Supports logging out of the box	Manual coding work is required
Debugging	Can be easily debugged through Visual Studio	Debugging is not easy
Pricing	Cheap price	Expensive as compared to WebJob
Tenancy	Multi-tenant deployment supported	Only single tenant supported

Using WebHooks for event-based scenarios

WebHooks are HTTP callbacks and work on a Publisher/Subscriber model. We register a WebHook which is a URL of our Web API on any notification service, such as VSTS, DropBox, GitHub, PayPal, Salesforce, Slack, Trello, Wordpress, and many more. Once an event occurs as per the configuration, it will make an HTTP POST request to our Web API (URL specified during the WebHook registration), and send us the data. On the other hand, we can also use the WebHook pattern in our Web API project to push the HTTP POST callback to the subscribers registered on our application.

Any WebJob hosted on Azure provides a WebHook link, which can be used by any third-party application to trigger.

Using WebHook of WebJob from VSTS

Many services such as Git, VSTS, Dropbox, PayPal, and others provide a provision to subscribe to WebHooks. Every WebJob is exposed with a WebHook, and the URL and credentials are accessible from the Properties page of WebJobs.

To use WebHooks with WebJobs, we have to add a NuGet package, `Microsoft.Azure.WebJobs.Extensions.WebHooks`, and then use WebHooks in the `Main` method, as follows:

```
class Program
{
    static void Main()
    {
        var config = new JobHostConfiguration();

        if (config.IsDevelopment)
        {
            config.UseDevelopmentSettings();
        }
```

```
            config.UseWebHooks();
            var host = new JobHost(config);
            host.RunAndBlock();
        }
    }
```

We will modify our WebJob and add another method, which will be hooked up when the WebHook is triggered from VSTS. To invoke our method on the triggering of WebHook, we have to annotate our method parameter with the `WebHookTrigger` attribute. So, let's add the `ProcessWebHookMessage` method, which takes the message `string` parameter annotated with `WebHook` and a `TextWriter` to write the log in WebJobs logs.

Here is the method signatures which we will add in the `Functions` class:

```
public static void ProcessWebHookMessage(
  [WebHookTrigger] string message, TextWriter log)
{
    log.WriteLine("Webhook has been invoked and the
    message received is {0}", message);
}
```

Now build and publish your WebApp on Azure.

With VSTS, we can register a WebHook by selecting a project and proceeding towards the **Service Hooks** link, as shown in this screenshot:

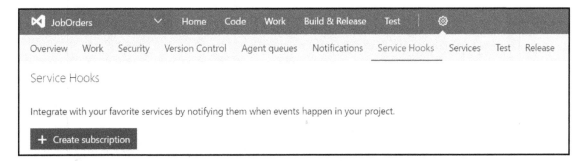

To register a WebHook, we have to click on the **Create Subscription** button, which opens up a pop-up window where you can select the target service that exposes the callback URL. In this case, we will select **Web Hooks** and proceed with the **Next** button:

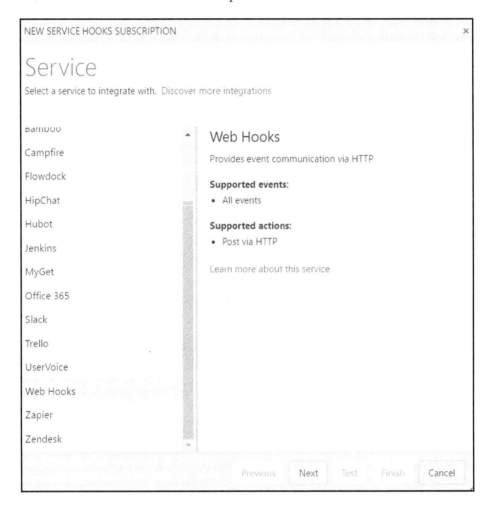

The next screen has some wizard steps where you can select the Trigger event, define filters, and specify the URL and credentials. The next screen will be the trigger window, where we can select the **Build completed** event:

And, finally, we can define the URL, username, and password, which can be retrieved from the Azure portal properties page.

The WebJob URL provided in the properties page is a generic one, and you have to tweak that based on your class and the method name which contains the `WebHookTrigger` attribute annotated for the input parameter.

The default URL format is as follows:

```
https://{WebAppName}.azurewebsites.net/api/continuouswebjobs/{WebJobNam
e}/passthrough/{ClassName}/{MethodName}
```

In our case, `ClassName` will be `Functions`, and `MethodName` will be `ProcessWebHookMessage`, which has the `WebHookTrigger` attribute defined for the message parameter.

After setting this up, you can test it by hitting the **Test** button, and if the configuration is fine, you will get a success message, as shown in the following screenshot:

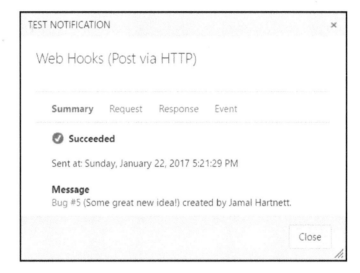

Finish the wizard, and once the project is built, the WebHook will be triggered and log the message in Azure logs.

Azure Functions

Azure Functions are autonomous functions that run on the cloud. Compared to WebJobs, where you can define multiple functions in the Functions class and hook them up on any event, Azure Functions are quite easy to set up and represent the independent chunk of code that runs to achieve the desired functionality on the cloud. They are easy to set up, can be configured directly on the cloud, and even the code can be written through the editor on the Azure portal itself.

Azure Functions can be developed using C#, Node.js, F#, Python, and PHP languages.

The benefits of Azure Functions include the following:

- **Pay as per use model**: You pay only for the time used to run your code
- **Triggering support**: Like WebJobs, we can use triggers to handle events
- **Integrated security**: You can protect functions using OAuth and other social accounts such as Facebook, Google, Microsoft Account, and Twitter
- **Integration support**: It easily integrates with Azure App Services and SaaS (Software as a Service) offerings
- **Open source**: The Azure Functions runtime is open source, and is available on GitHub

Creating a basic Azure Function to listen for Queue events

Let's create a simple Azure Function to learn how easily it can be developed to read the events from the Storage Queue in Azure.

To start with, we will log in to the Azure portal, and go to the marketplace, and search for `Function Apps`. The creation of Function App is the first step before creating an Azure Function, and more than one Azure Function can run under a single Function App:

Click to create the Function App, and provide values like **AppName**, **Subscription**, **Resource Group**, **Hosting Plan**, and so on. Once the Function App is created, we can start adding functions.

Azure Function App provides various function templates, which we can choose from. Choosing any of these templates generates a basic boilerplate code, which you can customize based on your needs. For example, the QueueTrigger-CSharp template can be used to listen for Queue events and add the basic code of reading it from queue, and so on.

Let's choose the **QueueTrigger-CSharp** template, and create a new function:

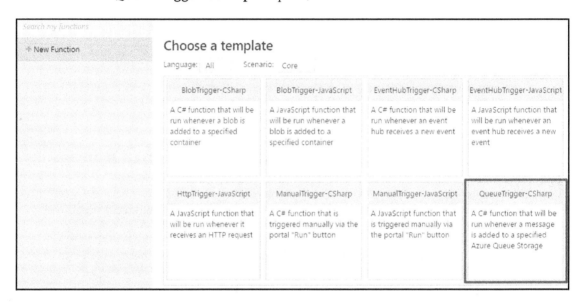

Once the function is created, we can use the online code editor to write C# code if C# was selected as the language for that particular template:

```
Code (run.csx)         Save         Run

1  using System;
2
3  public static void Run(string myQueueItem, TraceWriter log)
4  {
5      log.Info($"C# Queue trigger function processed: {myQueueItem}");
6  }
```

We can modify the function, and specify the Trigger events as we did in the WebJobs section. We can also pass JSON content as the Queue messsage, and if the parameter accepts object, it will automatically be serialized and injected to that function. It also provides complete monitoring in terms of logs and the count of functions being accessed with complete information about the function parameter values. To learn more about Azure Functions, please refer to the following link:

```
https://docs.microsoft.com/en-us/azure/azure-functions/.
```

Scalability and performance options in Azure App Services

When designing the architecture of any web application, remember the following components of performance efficient and scalable web applications:

Increasing storage performance

Every business application uses a relational database as a backend persistence for data. When we talk about relational databases, we cannot exclude database servers such as Microsoft SQL Server, Oracle, IBM Derby, and so on, used to create the databases, tables, stored procedures, and other useful objects. Relational databases also exhibit properties known as the acronym **ACID** (**Atomicity**, **Consistency**, **Isolation**, and **Durability**):

- **Atomicity**: Multiple operations can be done on a database as a unified transaction which can either succeed or fail. On failure, all the operations will be rolled back to the previous state.
- **Consistent**: Avoid inconsistencies in results, like keeping the atomicity and avoiding partial changes to the database
- **Isolation**: Concurrent transactions cannot read each other's data. This means that if two transactions are being executed, and if some transaction has to read the data, then it has to wait until the other transaction commits its changes.
- **Durability**: Once the transaction is committed, the changes are saved in the database and can be retrieved later.

An ACID transaction is the true essence of any enterprise application that involves lots of database operations. However, the consistency and isolation attributes highly affect scalability, as we know that consistency does not allow partial updates and Isolation avoids any other concurrent transaction to wait until the first one is completed. Hence, if the number of concurrent transactions are higher because of scaling out our databases, the number of transactions increases as well, and affects the overall performance of the application.

We will discuss the solution to this problem in the following sections.

Command-Query Responsibility Segregation (CQRS) pattern

This pattern actually splits the read operations from the write operations by segregating commands from queries. Commands are objects that encapsulate the data in the write model, whereas queries are just a read operation on the read model. Practically, this can be achieved by replicating the database in two, for example, DatabaseA and DatabaseB, which are synchronized through replication techniques. All updates or command operations are done on DatabaseA and read operations on DatabaseB. Thus, reading data from DatabaseB will not affect the performance of write operations, as it points to DatabaseA.

With the Read model (database), we can also apply non-cluster indexes, which are good when searching data. Unnecessary indexing reduces the performance of write operations, as the index tables need to get updated on each write operation. But, with this pattern, performance will not be affected, as they are two separate models.

Denormalization

Normalization is the process of defining database tables and relationships in a way that maintains integrity and avoids redundancy. In enterprise applications, we have some reports or views that use heavy SQL Joins to bring data in one table view. These joins are quite heavy operations on the database, and highly affect performance.

Denormalization is a technique in which data can be saved in a single flat table, and the retrieval of data is considerably faster than making SQL Joins or Sub queries. If a business application is complex in nature, we cannot definitely convert its database into a Non-Relational schema. But we can implement the CQR pattern, and modify our READ model to store the values in flat tables, and use some replication techniques to store the data from the write model to the READ model using **DTS** (**Data transformation services**), and so on.

On the other hand, if the database is not complex, we can use non-relational (NoSQL) databases, thus reducing query execution time and increasing the responsiveness of the application.

Non-relational databases do not ensure data consistency. They keep that data in key/value formats and do not check the value of the key if it's being replicated within the database.

In Azure, we have two options to use non-relational databases, which are as follows:

- Azure SQL storage
- MongoDB

Azure Table storage

Azure Table storage is a non-relational database. It's a key-value table, where each record is identified by `PartitionKey` and `RowKey`. `PartitionKey` is used by Azure if the database is partitioned, and to know which partition this data belongs to. Partitioning is normally done if the database size is huge and indexes slower the performance when creating, updating or deleting records. On the other hand, `RowKey` is the primary key within a partition.

Azure Table storage stores the value in any format and uses JSON to serialize the data. We can also use OData queries on Azure SQL storage and obtain fast results. They allow easy scalability and provide replication out-of-the-box, which brings higher availability.

To learn more about Azure Table storage, please refer to the following link:

```
https://docs.microsoft.com/en-us/azure/storage/storage-dotnet-how-to-use-
tables.
```

MongoDB

MongoDB is a NoSQL database and is provided with Azure as a PaaS or IaaS model. It is a scalable, high-performance NoSQL database, which can be installed either on a virtual machine on Linux or Windows, or by using Azure Worker Role on Windows. To learn more about MongoDB, please refer to www.mongodb.com.

Caching

Caching is another technique to reduce the load on a server by reading the data from the cache. There are two types of cache, namely, local cache and distributed cache.

Local cache

Local cache is local to each single instance of an application. For each instance, there will be a separate cache store, and the content is saved for each instance's cache. Although there might be inconsistencies in data between the different cache stores for each instance, this is fast and mostly good in cases where the data does not change often. For example, configuration data or setup tables, which are not updated frequently, can use this cache. A good example would be a list of all the countries or cities. Azure provides a local cache mechanism using In-Role Cache, whereas, in .NET Core, we can use `IMemoryCache` to implement local caching.

Shared cache

Shared cache is also known as distributed cache, and it is used for data which is dynamic in nature and changes a lot. The best example is transactional data, which is updated by many instances of an application simultaneously. With shared cache mechanism, the data is stored at a central location, and is relatively slower than local cache.

To implement the local or shared cache mechanisms, Azure provides three types of cache, which are described in the following table:

Cache	Description
In-Role Cache	In-Role Cache is mostly used for the distributed caching mechanism, but we also have an option to enable the local cache. We can host this cache in Azure Web App or Worker Role and exclusively dedicate roles to caching or share a role with another application.
Managed Cache	This is just like storage services and is easily redundant and scalable.
Redis Cache	It's an in-memory data store used as cache and stores values in strings, hashes, lists, sets, and sorted sets.

Using Redis Cache in Azure

Redis stands for Remote Dictionary Server. It is an open source in-memory distributed database. It is a highly performant cache and provides rich data types, which can store data in the key-value format. Azure provides a managed service for Redis, so we don't have to install on run manually. We can just use this service to cache our data, and it is recommended as the best caching mechanism in store.

To use Redis, we can install a NuGet package (`stackexchange.redis`), which is a client API of Redis to use on Azure. The main benefit of using Redis over other caching mechanisms is the data types. It provides various data types other than strings only. Cache types mostly allow data to be saved as string only, but with Redis, we can store data as strings, sets, lists, sorted sets, and hashes.

Creating the Redis Cache

In order to proceed with configuring Redis in your ASP.NET Core web application running as Azure Web App, we first create the Redis Cache in Azure. Redis Cache can be created by going to the marketplace on the Azure portal and finding the Redis Cache template to create.

To create the Redis Cache, we have to input **DNS name**, **Subscription**, **Resource group**, and more, as shown in the next screenshot:

The DNS format of the Redis Cache is
`{RedisCacheDNSName}.redis.cache.windows.net`.

Configuring the .NET Core app to use Redis Cache on Azure

Once the cache is created, we can configure our .NET Core client application, probably an ASP.NET Core one, by adding a NuGet package as `StackExchange.redis`. Once the package is downloaded, we can use the Redis client API to use the Redis Cache that we have created on Azure.

To connect to the Redis Cache, we can add a namespace `StackExchange`, Redis, and create a connection class using `ConnectionMultiplexer`, as follows:

```
ConnectionMultiplexer connection =
ConnectionMultiplexer.Connect(
  "myrediscache.redis.cache.windows.net:6380,
   password=VOBP7q7Msw8bSy6+u0=,ssl=True,abortConnect=False");
```

`ConnectionMultiplexer` takes the `connection` string, which can be obtained from the Redis Cache on Azure by accessing the **Access Keys** option under **Settings**. The key benefit of `ConnectionMultiplexer` is that it recreates the connection automatically if connectivity is lost due to a network issue and is then resolved.

Once the connection is made, we can read the Redis Cache by calling the `GetDatabase` method of the `connection` object:

```
IDatabase cache= connection.GetDatabase();
```

Finally, the values can be set or retrieved through the `Set` and `Get` methods from the `cache` object created earlier.

```
cache.StringSet("UserName", "John");
cache.StringGet("UserName");
```

.NET objects can also be set to the cache, but they should have the serializable attribute annotated at the class level. For example, we can simply serialize the person object into the JSON format, and save it in the cache as follows:

```
cache.StringSet("PersonObject",
JsonConvert.SerializeObject(personObj);
```

Queuing

Queuing is another technique that can be used to resolve long-running processes by splitting them into queues and processing them asynchronously. A good example is image processing or document generation, which could become a cumbersome process if executed in a synchronous manner. With the help of Azure Queues, Blobs, and other options, we can split these tasks by creating queue items when the client request is initiated, and processing those items in the background using background services. We have already discussed WebJobs and Azure Queues, which are the best approaches for this kind of processing, earlier in this chapter.

Logging and monitoring in Azure

In this section, we will talk about the logging and monitoring options in Azure.

Logging

The .NET Core app models, such as ASP.NET Core, support logging out-of-the-box. Logging can be enabled by injecting the `ILoggerFactory` instance through the `Configure` method of the `Startup` class, and then using that to add providers. There are a few built-in providers available in the `Microsoft.Extensions.Logging` namespace. For example, to log information at the Console level, we can call the `AddConsole` method on the instance of `LoggerFactory` or `AddDebug` to log information in the **Debug** window when the application is running under the debug mode.

Following is the list of logging provider's shipped with ASP.NET Core:

- Console
- Debug
- EventSource
- EventLog
- TraceSource
- Azure App Service

This is the sample code snippet to inject the logger factory instance on the `Configure` method in the ASP.NET Core application:

```
public void Configure(IApplicationBuilder app,
    IHostingEnvironment env, ILoggerFactory loggerFactory)
```

```
    {
        loggerFactory.AddConsole(Configuration.GetSection("Logging"));
        loggerFactory.AddDebug();
    }
```

Once the logger factory is injected, we have to inject the `ILogger` instance at the Controller level; we can use methods such as `LogInformation`, `LogWarning`, and others to log for different severity levels:

```
public class HomeController : Controller
{
    ILogger _logger;

    public HomeController(ILogger logger)
    {
        this._logger = logger;
    }
}
```

In this section, we will not go into the details of how logging can be done. To check that, please refer to `Chapter 6`, *Layered Approach to Solution Architecture*.

ASP.NET Core logging in Azure

As you learnt in the previous section, ASP.NET Core applications can be hosted on Azure using Azure Web App or Azure API App. In ASP.NET Core applications, we can enable logging in our application hosted on Azure that writes logs in a text file or Blob storage.

Azure provides different types of logging, which are categorized into two categories, as follows:

Web server diagnostics

This is used to capture and log information about the web server. It is further classified into the following three types:

Web server logging

This logging logs information about HTTP transactions using the W3C extended log format. This can be enabled when we need to determine site metrics such as total number of requests being made, or from which IP a request is made, and so on.

Failed request tracing

This logging logs detailed information when the application fails. It contains the complete trace of the web server components used to process the request, and so on.

Detailed error logging

Contains information about the HTTP status codes that indicate a failure. This can be used to determine why the server returned an error code.

Application diagnostics

This type of logging is used to write application-level logging. It is classified into the following two types of logs:

Application logging (Filesystem)

This is used to log application-level logging on a text file. While configuring, we can set the logging severity level and it logs the error into a text file.

Application logging (Blob)

To log application-level logging on Blob storage, we can set the minimum severity level.

Azure application-level logging can be enabled in ASP.NET Core by adding a package, `Microsoft.Extensions.Logging.AzureAppServices`, through NuGet, and then calling the `AddAzureWebAppDiagnostics` method from `loggerFactory`, as follows:

```
public void Configure(IApplicationBuilder app,
IHostingEnvironment env, ILoggerFactory loggerFactory)
{
    loggerFactory.AddConsole(Configuration.GetSection("Logging"));
    loggerFactory.AddDebug();
    loggerFactory.AddAzureWebAppDiagnostics();
}
```

`AddAzureWebAppDiagnostics` also has an overloaded method, which allows you to pass the `AzureAppServicesDiagnosticSettings` object. This object can be used to override default settings such as the template of logging output, file size, and Blob name. Once this is enabled on the `Startup` class, we can use the same `ILogger` object injected in our MVC controllers and log the information. The logs will be generated based on the number of logger providers added.

When we deploy our application on Azure App Service, we can enable Azure logging (text file and Blob) through the diagnostic section. To do that, we will first go to our Azure App, and then search for diagnostic logs.

We can enable text file logging by selecting the **On** button of **Application Logging (Filesystem),** as shown in the following screenshot:

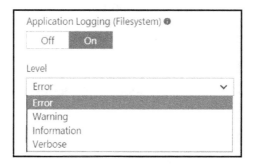

Level denotes the minimum severity level for which the logging will be done. Setting this to **Verbose** logs everything like **Verbose**, **Information**, **Warning**, and **Error**. However, if the severity is set to **Error**, it will only log an error, as there is no severity level that exists after error.

The default values of a text file are as follows:

Path	/LogFiles/Application folder
File name format	diagnostics-yyyymmdd.txt
File size limit	10 MB
Max. number of files retained on Azure	2

Blob table logging can be enabled by selecting the **On** of **Application Logging (Blob)** as shown in this screenshot:

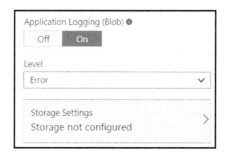

In the case of Blob, we can specify the level and configure the **Storage Settings**. In **Storage Settings**, we can either select the existing Blob, or create a new one. While creating a new Blob storage you will be prompted for **Name**, **Performance**, and **Replication**, as shown in the following screenshot:

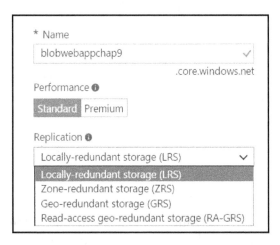

The default values of Blob storage are as follows:

Blob name	`{appname}{timestamp}/yyyy/mm/dd/hh/{guid}-applicationLog.txt`

 Azure App Services does not generate any file or Blob entries when the application is running locally and not on Azure.

Accessing logs

Logs created on the filesystem can be accessed to download logs using an FTP client tool, Azure Power shell, or by Azure **CLI** (**Command-Line Interface**).

Accessing logs via FTP

To access the logs using FTP, you can go to the **Diagnostic and Logs** option of your Azure Web App, and then use the FTP URL and the FTP/deployment username to connect.

Accessing Logs via Azure PowerShell

To download logs using Azure PowerShell, we first have to install Azure PowerShell from the PowerShell gallery. Run PowerShell from your machine using administrative rights.

Run the following command, which will install the Azure Resource Manager modules from the PowerShell gallery:

```
Install-Module AzureRM
```

Then run another command that installs the Azure Service Management module from the PowerShell gallery, as follows:

```
Install-Module Azure
```

Once these modules are installed, you can connect to your Azure account by executing the following command:

```
Add-AzureAccount
```

This command asks you to provide your credentials and, once added, you have to set your subscription to where your website is running. Subscription can be set by running the following command:

```
Select-AzureSubscription '{subscription-name}'
```

Now, to stream the logs of your web application on the console itself, you can run the following command:

```
Get-AzureWebsiteLog -Name '{name_of_webapplication}'
```

To save the logs in a folder, you can run the following command:

```
Save-AzureWebsiteLog -Output 'C:\users\logs\logs.zip' -Name '{name_of_webapplication}'
```

Monitoring

Enterprise applications consist of several layers, that is, the data access layer, business layer, service layer, and presentation layer. Each layer is connected in a way that can be easily pluggable without affecting the other layers. Almost all applications deployed on Azure provide basic monitoring, which covers CPU usage, disk read/write, data in/out bandwidth, and so on.

The Azure portal provides some monitoring tiles out-of-the-box, which we can add on the dashboard to give us an overview, at a glance, of our running applications, VMs, and so on. This service is known as Azure Monitor and Diagnostic service.

We can also read the monitoring information from the code running on Azure by using the Azure Management API. This API provides easy access to insights into our applications. It provides real-time analytics reports and identifies trends that can be helpful for our business.

SCOM (System Center Operations Manager)

Another option for getting insights into the services running on Azure is by using SCOM. This is software used by Operations teams to manage and monitor the network. For Azure, we can add the Azure Management Pack for Operations, which helps to get a complete insight into the services running on Azure. This is helpful when we don't have access to the actual VM that our app is running on, and we cannot install anything on the VM to monitor performance, logs, and so on. For example, with Azure App Services, we can run our Web Applications on the cloud, but the actual VMs where our Web Application is running is behind the Service Fabric, and direct access to the VM is not possible. In this scenario, we can install the SCOM and Azure Management Pack for Operations to serve our purpose of monitoring.

Application Insights

Application Insights is an **Application Resource Management** (APM) service. It is used by developers to monitor an application's performance by using analytical tools on Azure, which provide real-time analysis on how the user interacts with your application. No matter whether our application runs on the cloud or on-premise, we can monitor its performance using Application Insights, which supports any web application built on .NET, Java, and Node.js.

Application Insights can be integrated with web applications in the following scenarios:

Application hosted on Azure

With this option we don't need to write custom code to integrate Application Insights with our application. We can configure from the Azure portal itself. However, in certain scenarios we can tweak our application a bit and write custom code to send more telemetry information to the Application Insights resource running on Azure.

Application hosted on-premise

With this option, if our ASP.NET Core application is hosted on IIS, we can install the **Application Insights Status Monitor** application and associate our web application with the Application Insights resource running on Azure.

Use Application Insights API

With this option we can write custom code and use Application Insights API in our ASP.NET Core application to send telemetry information to Azure. Traditionally, this is the most recommended approach and, this way, we can send more telemetry information on the Application Insights resource running on Azure and configure things as per our need.

Setting up Application Insights in ASP.NET Core Application

To set up Application Insights, we first have to log in to the Azure portal and add a new item, **Application Insights**, as follows:

Select **Application Insights** and click on **create**. Once this is done, we have to copy the **INSTRUMENTATION KEY**, which we can provide in our ASP.NET Core application. You can copy the **INSTRUMENTATION KEY** by clicking on **Essentials in Application Insight** on the Azure portal.

Next, we will add the Application Insights instrumentation package in our ASP.NET Core package, which actually monitors our app, and send its report to the Azure portal, where Application Insights is configured.

Add the following package from NuGet package manager:

```
Microsoft.ApplicationInsights.AspNetCore
```

Now we have to specify the instrumentation key in our ASP.NET Core `appsettings.json` file. To do this, create a file, `appsettings.json`, in the root folder of your web application, and then write the following code snippet, which holds your `InstrumentationKey`. The configuration snippet of `appsettings.json` is as follows:

```
{
  {
    "ApplicationInsights": {
```

```
        "InstrumentationKey": "a79a8184-a86e-4d8b-b694-8497436a5ebe"
    }
  }
}
```

To read `appsettings.json`, we have to write some code to build the configuration system that will read the settings from different sources (in our case `appsettings.json`), and give us the `Configuration` object that can be used to retrieve the settings from key/value pairs. To do this, we will add following two packages from NuGet package manager:

```
Microsoft.Extensions.Configuration.Abstractions
Microsoft.Extensions.Configuration.Json
```

Next, we will add the following code snippet in our `Startup` class:

```
var builder = new ConfigurationBuilder()
            .SetBasePath(env.ContentRootPath)
            .AddJsonFile("appsettings.json", optional: true,
              reloadOnChange: true)
            .AddJsonFile($"appsettings.
            {env.EnvironmentName}.json", optional: true)
            .AddEnvironmentVariables();
            Configuration = builder.Build();
```

In the preceding code, we read the JSON file and environment variables on the Windows machine, and build a configuration. Configuration is the `IConfigurationRoot` property defined in our `Startup` class, as shown next:

```
public IConfigurationRoot Configuration { get; }
```

Now, to use the `ApplicationInsights` service, we have to add `ApplicationInsightsTelemetry` in our `ConfigureServices` method of the `Startup` class, as follows:

```
services.AddApplicationInsightsTelemetry(Configuration);
```

Finally, we can add this as middleware in our `Configure` method, as shown next. It's recommended to add the this middleware as the very first item in the pipeline, otherwise proper reporting will not be done:

```
app.UseApplicationInsightsRequestTelemetry();
app.UseApplicationInsightsExceptionTelemetry();
```

`UseApplicationInsightsRequestTelemetry` is used to monitor and get the telemetry information of all the requests being processed, whereas `UseApplicationInsightsExceptionTelemetry` can be used to monitor exceptions.

Now you can run your application and monitor the performance on Application Insights:

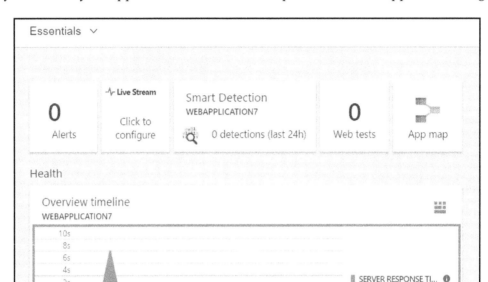

Application Insights provides different options to view telemetry information. There is a search explorer, which can be used to diagnose actual requests, traces, and exceptions. Metrics explorer can be used to diagnose response times, user counts, and page views. Analytics is used to write queries to fetch information related to telemetry, and through set alerts, you can specify alerts that send notifications on special conditions based on your criteria.

Summary

In this chapter, you learnt the basics of cloud computing, and how Microsoft Azure plays a role in providing IaaS, PaaS, and SaaS models. We primarily focused on Azure App Services, and explored ways to develop and deploy a .NET application on Azure. Scalability is an essential key, and you learnt how easy it is to scale out or scale up our applications running on Azure by using different techniques to increase the performance of our application. Last, but not least, we discussed the logging and monitoring options in Azure, and saw how we can use Application Insights with web applications running on the cloud to monitor application request/response times and other metrics. The next chapter is all about security, where you will learn about the different security models available to secure the .NET Core applications.

Microservices Architecture 9

Microservices are a hot topic these days, both in the architectural community as well as in the development community. It is a continuously evolving space, where there are no fixed patterns regarding the technology and technique to be applied in order to successfully achieve the microservices implementation. However, the architectural concepts and patterns remain the same.

We have learnt enterprise architectural concepts in the SOA chapter and have seen various cloud-based architectural offerings in the Chapter 8, *Cloud-Based Architecture and Integration with .NET Core*. In this chapter, we move further on these concepts and features and look carefully towards the modern microservices-based architecture. We will first cover the architectural aspects related to microservices, and then the development aspects of the microservices implementation. Once again, we will draw heavily from the skills and knowledge that we have gained in the previous chapters, especially the Chapter 7, *SOA Implementation with .NET Core*.

We will cover the following topics in this chapter:

- Microservices definition
- Distinction from SOA and monolith applications
- Architectural elements
- Architectural motivations
- Example architecture

Microservices architecture definition

In the previous chapter, you learned what is a service, what is business and information modeling, and what is services modeling. All of these concepts and practices apply to microservices architecture as well.

What is microservices architecture?

Microservices architecture is a collection of microservices. A microservice can be defined as follows:

- The smallest service that does only one thing, that is, **Single Responsibility Principle (SRP)**
- It's an independent piece of code and independently manageable without dangling dependencies
- It's the owner of its own data; no sharing except via services

It is an architectural approach to develop an application (or a system) as a set of small services, where each service works independently in its own process space and communicates using lightweight mechanisms. The services are naturally built around business capabilities just like in SOA, and are independently deployable components as described by bounded contexts in **DDD (Domain Driven Design)**. There is a minimal aspect of centralized management of these services as opposed to traditional SOA architecture

Microservices and SOA

The advent of microservices has disrupted the existence and architecting for SOA. Although microservices and SOA are similar things, as both are service oriented, there are some subtle technical differences in architecture and their implementation. With the high usage of cloud-based applications, DevOps processes, and agile methodologies, it's becoming more common, and rather natural, to follow the microservices approach.

Certainly, many of the techniques used in microservices come from the experiences of the development community in SOA and DDD. According to some pundits, microservices architecture is a form of SOA, and it is also referred to as SOA done right. Microservices has principles and patterns of service orientation around business capabilities, independent and autonomous, bounded-context, event-driven and more, all of these have roots in SOA and DDD.

In SOA, all organizations tend to follow a certain theme, standards, and programming languages with conventions uniformly all across pieces of code. On the other hand, in microservices, each microservice package is independent--it can use its own programming language, its own configuration, and data (SQL, NoSQL), which is common only across its team. Two microservices packages can be implemented entirely differently using different implementation technologies while having a common way of exposing and consuming the service interfaces.

In SOA, heavy focus is on centralization, and therefore, inclusion of a certain **Enterprise Service Bus** (**ESB**) is inevitable. A specific ESB brings its own set of ontologies and conventions. In microservices, the focus is on decentralization in the form of completely independent components designed for failure situations independently. Microservices are sometimes even referred to as an ESB anti-pattern.

In SOA, centralized governance often inhibits change, while in microservices, each service package is its own owner, that is, completely autonomous.

Microservices and monolithic applications

Monolithic applications are applications that are deployed as a single executable unit or a package (for example, deployment archive). Enterprise applications are often built in three main parts, which are as follows:

- frontend
- middle-tier / server-side-code
- backend (database)

The server-side code (internally designed as a layered architecture but) is a single logical executable unit, and often, a single process. Any change to the application needs to build and deploy the whole server-side part to the production server.

Monolithic applications can scale horizontally by replicating the whole server-side application instance into multiple servers or VMs. Therefore, scaling requires scaling of the entire application instead of the part of application that needs extra resources.

Microservices architecture divides applications into a number of autonomous microservices. Each microservice is a self-contained package of all code along with its data without unmanaged external dependencies. Microservices scales out by deploying them independently, and replicating them across servers, VMs, or containers:

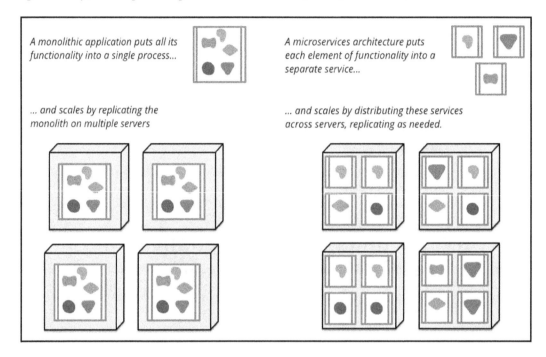

Monoliths and microservices (Courtesy of James Lewis and Martin Fowler)

Web API and web services

Microservice is often referred to as a remotely callable API, but it is much more than the older network-callable API or remote process execution standards such as **Remote Method Invocation (RMI)**, **Common Object Request Broker Architecture (CORBA)**, or **Distributed Component Object Model (DCOM)** - callable API standards.

Web API is, however, most common in the Microsoft world, where Web APIs (server-side) are REST-based services that use HTTP verbs to define actions on the business resources (data). This kind of service typically uses JSON or XML (or sometimes in binary) as the request and response format.

Web services are services which are traditionally **SOAP (simple object access protocol)** based services whose request and responses are in XML, or sometimes, in binary. A web service is typically exposed by a standard **WSDL (web services description language)** as an interface definition language, which is used to create the proxies at the web service caller end.

Characteristics of a microservices architecture

Microservices architecture is more of a concept than a defined architecture with a specific set of requirements. It's a better way to achieve the software, which is built to scale reliably and responsively.

James Lewis and Martin Fowler laid out the following characteristics which typically come with microservices:

- **Componentization via services**: A component is a unit of software that is independently replaceable and upgradeable. The advantage of using services as components (rather than libraries) in a whole system, is that services are independently deployable.

- **Organized around business capabilities**: Services directly reflect the business capabilities, and achieve the related business processes in the respective business domains and bounded-contexts.

- **Products not Projects**: It is a notion that the development team should own the product for its lifetime. The product-based mentality makes closer ties to business capabilities. It brings the developer nearer to the business users or consumers, and helps him/her see how the software behaves in production.

 Note that the model naturally favors the agile-based methodologies and the microservices architecture's natural inclination towards cloud-based infrastructure and DevOps processes.

- **Smart endpoints and dumb pipes**: Microservices are to be decoupled and cohesive as much as possible. The purpose here is to minimize the intelligence in your infrastructure. Microservices use simple and dumb HTTP communication protocol without any extra smartness built on top of it, and that promotes lightweight messaging between various services urging event-based communication patterns.

Note that it tends to suggest microservices as an ESB anti-pattern.

- **Decentralized governance**: Microservices architecture puts developers directly in charge of their code. They decide the technology, environment, deployment, monitoring, and support. Each microservice has its own developer who can decide on their own about all the aspects of the service life cycle. Centralized governance, on the other hand, as seen with SOA, focuses on centralizing the tools and technologies as well as monitoring, whereas, microservices emphasizes that not all problems can be solved by the same technology and toolings.

- **Decentralized Data Management**: Following the bounded-context concept from DDD, the data for each microservice resides in a different space--either different instances of the same database technology, or entirely different database systems depending on the specific needs. It also allows for the right technology for the right problem. So, the data is decentralized and managed by only within the owner microservice.

- **Infrastructure automation**: With microservices, the automation of infrastructure-related tasks becomes natural. This includes continuous integration and continuous deployment to development, test, performance, and in some cases, even to production environments with the obvious necessity of extensive automated testing.

- **Design for failure**: Compared to monolithic applications, microservices divide the application into a number of autonomous services, and therefore, increase the instances of failures. Since failure with a microservice can happen anytime, especially with communication, it is imperative to detect failure quickly and take an even quicker action. Microservices are architected for automated monitoring, and in many cases, automated recovery and restore.

- **Evolutionary design**: Microservices itself is an evolutionary design with roots in SOA and DDD. This architecture must support Plug and Play of services where you add some service for a period and then remove or discard it, such as a promotional event in your business domain. Since a microservice is self-contained and autonomous, changing and improving its internal design and technology is encouraged to be done without affecting the whole business and by only upgrading of a business capability (due to technical or business in nature).

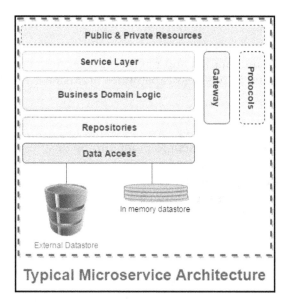

Architecture of a single microservice

Best for microservices architecture

Microservices architecture is still not very common and mature in terms of implementation. And the architecture does not enforce uniform application of it; rather, it promotes variety in terms of using specialized tools and techniques for specific use cases. Therefore, it is essential to follow some of the best practices for designing your microservices as curated from the industry.

The following is a list of some of the most common and important practices for designing the microservices.

Documentation

It is extremely important to have documentation at all levels with microservices architecture.

The documentation should be easily accessible and enough to get an understanding of the use cases as well as usability.

It should have documentation for all levels. For example:

Business capabilities

Since services in the microservices architecture are built around business capabilities, it is imperative to have the documentation and references present in both the microservice technical documentation and in business capabilities or business functions documentation.

Business processes

Unified documentation should be present to point out the business process or business processes implemented by this microservice, or if this service is part of some business process orchestration. This is particularly helpful for identifying business and technical dependencies both for the business community as well as the developer community in the given organization.

Microservice interfaces

Adequate documentation should be available to show inputs and outputs of the service interface. It is beneficial to also include a sample code to see the client calls in working.

Microservice code

This should not only include the comments for automated documentation generation, but also comments on the significant level of code. Microservices are heavily owned and the responsibility of the core team overall. If the addition of a team member is required, or for example, merging of two microservices is required, it is very important to have a very good technical level of understanding to achieve the task smoothly.

Microservice data store

Adequate documentation should be present on your data storage layers of the microservices in order to identify which microservice and business capability it belongs to. For example, if the organization is using same database server but different database instances for each microservice.

Logging and monitoring

Build your microservices with the logging as part of your microservices architecture before you begin.

The same is applicable to monitoring principles, strategies, and toolings.

Logging and monitoring is equipped to enable troubleshooting and alerting services to highlight the issue as soon as possible, and that the recovery mechanisms kick-in even faster in the form of both automated recovery and manual recovery according to the devised strategy based on the nature of the incident.

Immutable Infrastructure

Immutable Infrastructure is defined as follows:

> *"A pattern or strategy for managing services in which infrastructure is divided into "Data" and "Everything else". "Everything else" components are replaced at every deployment, with changes made only by modifying a versioned definition, rather than being updated in-place."*

In layman terms, you can reset the phone to factory settings in your smartphone while keeping all the user data intact; and you may keep doing that.

For microservices, when you need to upgrade, you replace the whole service as a fresh one; you do not upgrade or make changes in place in your infrastructure. The data it uses or maintains or builds up remains (mostly) the same. This ensures the application stability and maturity of the microservice.

Containerization

The implementation mechanism of microservices emphasizes the emphasis of microservices that you keep the deployment separation and the none-to-minimal dependencies on other external resources outside this microservice boundary. A microservice is cohesive within itself, and because it's autonomous, it's best to deploy each microservice in its own separate container. This makes it easy to deploy and easy for the tools to manage deployment.

Each container creates its own boundary around the microservice, and this enables a number of microservices to coexist, and to serve the business without affecting each other beyond their boundaries.

For simplicity, a container can be considered as a tiny VM running a stripped-down version of OS.

Deploying a microservice in the container also enables a simpler and flexible way to enable the scaling for your microservice. (Note that we will cover more on containerization in the last chapter.)

Stateless

Keep your microservices as stateless as possible.

This enables automatic failover, simpler load balancing, and auto scaling up or down for your microservice.

When it's stateless, the main concern is that there are enough instances of service to service the clients, and you can simply use automated scaling.

Architectural elements

In this section, we will review some of the architectural concepts and elements which are related and often utilized when implementing microservices-based architecture.

For microservices, and in general, these are useful concepts and enterprise patterns which can be applied when designing and implementing any kind of software product or service.

Bounded Context in Domain Driven Design

We will introduce here the concept of Bounded Context, which is the main pattern in the DDD) as coined by Eric Evans in his book in 2003. We are going through this pattern, because it's one of most essential concepts when designing microservices architecture.

DDD (Domain Driven Design)

DDD is a software development approach to complex enterprise applications, which involves connecting the technical implementation to the evolving problem/business domain model of the given enterprise.

Paul Rayner from `DomainLanguage.com` summarizes DDD nicely as follows:

> DDD advocates pragmatic, holistic and continuous software design: collaborating with domain experts to embed rich domain models in the software--models that help solve important, complex business problems.

Guiding principles

The following are the core guiding principles that set the direction for the DDD:

- To have the primary focus of the project on the main business domain and the business domain logic of the given enterprise.
- To design the software based on the model of the business domain
- Close and iterative collaboration between domain and technical experts to build the conceptual model of the particular business domain

(Note that the third guiding principle is also a core focus of the **Agile software development**.)

Foundational concepts

The DDD has its basis on the following foundational concepts:

- **Context**: The settings applied to word(s) or sentence(s), which determine its meanings. Context specification dictates the domain object's behavior and interaction as well as other factors like what business rules to apply. This means that the same domain object under a different context would have to process different business rules.
- **Domain**: Domain is the body of knowledge (the ontology), influence, or the business activity. The particular environment, which a software solution addresses, is the domain of the software.
- **Model**: A model is an abstract representation, which describes the aspects of the domain, and it can be used to define the solution to the problems related to that domain. The model helps in communication between the domain experts and technical experts. It becomes the conceptual foundation for the software design. In order for the model to be effective, it has to have zero contradictions, ambiguities, and inconsistencies.

- **Ubiquitous language**: Ubiquitous language is the usage language in DDD between domain experts, technical experts, developers, and users of the system. The language is based on the defined model, and should be rigorous, leaving no ambiguity; otherwise, the defined software solution would not be perfect for the domain.

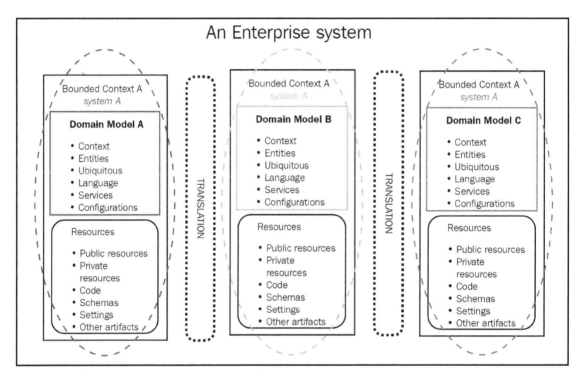

Bounded Contexts (DDD) in a sample enterprise application

Bounded context

DDD is applied to large and complex business domains instead of simpler ones; it helps by dividing the domain into different bounded contexts, and specifying their interrelationships. The basic idea behind the bounded context is the **separation of concerns** principle.

Take, for example, a domain of an organization which has departments like HR, Accounts, Regulatory Affairs, and so on. Each has its own responsibility, vocabulary, and different roles, but work together in the principal business domain for a particular industrial vertical. Then these departments can have their own bounded context defined in the DDD model.

Bounded context creates an explicit boundary, and encapsulates or contains a particular model. This model has its own ubiquitous language, which is understood by the domain and technical experts for this model. It is very well possible that the language and vocabulary used in this bounded context has a different meaning in other bounded contexts. For example, a customer in a marketing sub domain might be referred to as a payer in an accounting subdomain.

In DDD, there is a core domain, supporting domains, and generic domains. Core domain is the revenue generation of the enterprise. Supporting domains are to support your core business, like the HR sub-domain. Generic domains are the ones that you need, but you do not worry too much about them. For example, a timesheeting software for a company is a generic domain and is a likely candidate that is bought as an off-the-shelf component.

A bounded context may represent a single sub-domain, while it is also possible that two bounded contexts are implementing a single sub-domain. It is less likely that one bounded context is encapsulating more than one sub-domain; however, it is not a restriction.

There are scenarios where you need communication between two or more bounded contexts. A bounded context does not keep reference of any other bounded context, as it would violate the boundaries principle, and as well as it may also collide the ubiquitous languages between them. The communication between two bounded contexts is normally carried out via domain events; these are event messages (usually asynchronous) that carry only information in the format or language, which is valid in the whole domain. As messages contain the data and not the model, they do not violate the boundaries of the bounded contexts. When one bounded context needs info from another bounded context, it subscribes to its domain events.

Communication can be carried out by one microservice calling another microservice to gather or pass on the information. Another communication case is a service orchestration implementing a certain business process, and which needs to invoke services in several bounded contexts; such activity is carried out by a special process called the process manager, which is not necessarily a business process manager tool. Process managers are not part of any bounded context; they usually carry out the business process across the bounded contexts, because such process managers have are valid at the domain level, which is usually above the subdomains.

The Bounded Context concept is very important for the definition, maintainability, and life cycle of a microservice. It allows us to deal with the relevant model in the protected boundary, which provides both logical and technical limits to the microservice process. This boundary is essential for a microservice for it to be autonomous and self-contained.

Microservices come in systems

It is extremely rare that we see a software having only one microservice entirely. This perhaps might happen in case of certain **POC (Proof of Concept)** or prototype applications. Microservices always come in systems, meaning, we always have sets of microservices working together in a systemic manner to achieve the organizational goals. Microservices architecture does not mandate the use of particular technological artifacts, so it becomes a challenge to integrate if communication patterns and protocols are not implemented with certain agreed standards. Once we have common interface languages agreed upon, for example, JSON as data format, REST for HTTP-based service calls, and AMQP for messaging, we are ready to generate orchestrations.

Sometimes, we need to integrate with non-standard or unconventional communication patterns, sometimes we need to expose our APIs or microservices to a wide variety of clients, and sometimes, we need extra control and reports of how our microservices are consumed, and how they perform.

Let's see some of the patterns which are essential for integration of microservices for a number of use cases.

A great place to discover microservices patterns and their implementation for a world-class level of services, with billions of clients served, is
`http://netflix.github.io`
Yes, it is the Netflix architectural artifacts, open-sourced and available to use by the community.

Service discovery

When working together, microservices need to communicate with each other, and since microservices typically run in virtualized or containerized environments, the number of instances running and their locations are unknown. These addresses are dynamic, and are constantly changing depending on the scaling applied, subject to load.

In the following sections, we will look at the two patterns of service discovery that help the microservices consumer or other services to locate and consume them.

Client-side service discovery

In client-side discovery, a service consumer, before making a request, first gets the location of a service instance by querying a **service registry**, which knows the locations of all the active service instances for the particular microservice requested.

One of the famous open-source implementations of a service registry pattern is Eureka, which was developed by Netflix.

Server-side service discovery

In server-side discovery, when a service consumer makes a request, it makes it via a router or a load balancer running on a fixed or known location. This sort of router would then require a service registry (which could be built in the router) and forwards the request to an available service instance.

AWS **Elastic Load Balancer** (**ELB**) provides such an implementation. Kubernetes provides a proxy service which implements server-side discovery router.

 Kubernetes is an open-source system for automating deployment, scaling, and management of containerized applications. It is also used extensively to orchestrate Docker containers.

Service registry

Service consumers either use client-side discovery or the server-side discovery to locate the actual running microservice instance. They eventually get the location of a service from the service registry.

Service registry is a datastore of microservices that records their instances and locations.

An instance of a microservice is responsible for registering itself with the service registry. It registers itself with the service registry on startup, and makes itself available for discovery. On shutdown, the service instance unregisters itself from the service registry. There is a mechanism that enables the service instance to keep updating the registry at periodic intervals in order to validate its existence.

API gateway

When having a lot of microservices, discovery, location, integration, security, and analytics become a challenge. Then comes the need for the software service called API gateway. An API gateway addresses a number of concerns within the microservices architecture, and provides certain features which are useful in the implementation of the architecture.

Features commonly provided by an API gateway include the following, and are to be sought when deciding which API gateway to use in the implementation of your microservices architecture:

API Security: The API gateway controls the access to services for partners, customers, and employees (developers, DevOps, and so on). Some API gateways also provide features of API key management, payload inspection, and validation.

- **Quality of service**: API gateways provide features like throttling, restrictions, and routing on services as well as network level QoS monitoring.
- **Unified services environment**: Such features include addressing, mediation, and orchestration of microservices as well as translation of data formats and protocols. API gateways also expose the right API according to the right client trying to consume the API based on its own platform. For example, mobile, iOS, Android, web, and others.
- **Policy management**: API gateways enable policies to easily configure the API gateway and settings to control and protect deployed API services, and to provide segregated access to development, test, and production environments.
- **Analytics**: API gateways also provide API analytics of various kinds, which are able to generate reports and charts based on usage metrics for all services and also for the API gateway itself.

Architectural motivations

In recent years, software technology, software development life cycle, and development methodology has seen many new faces and modes. The software community has continuously been shaping itself towards betterment. One such phenomenal improvement is agile software development, which impacts not only the development but also design and architecture of the software we build today.

Agile Manifesto

Let's see what is Agile Manifesto in its original form, and that can make us realize how microservices has to eventually hatch up.

Agile software development also meant to bring back software development control to the developer community from the project management and quality standards communities. The Agile Manifesto includes the following guidelines:

- Individuals and interactions over processes and tools
- Working software over comprehensive documentation
- Customer collaboration over contract negotiation
- Responding to change over following a plan

That is, while there is value in the items on the right, we value the items on the left more.

These are clear motivations reflected here, and are also the differentiating points for SOA-enterprise-standards-based architecture's transition to microservices architecture.

Agile Manifesto is based on twelve principles. For example, one of the principles is *Continuous attention to technical excellence and good design enhances agility*. Since these are pretty generic development motivational principles, we leave them to the source. Please visit http://agilemanifesto.org to see all of the principles.

Reactive Manifesto

Similarly, the modern design and architecture motivation is Reactive programming. Reactive Manifesto was published in September 2014. We will summarize the key points from the Reactive Manifesto, and you can realize how important they are, and how they affect our design and development of microservices.

Please visit http://www.reactivemanifesto.org to read the actual manifesto. You may also sign the manifesto on the site.

Software today involves massive processing, storage, and communication needs. According to IBM, 2.5 exabytes that is 2.5 billion gigabytes (GB) of data was generated every day in 2012. Eric Schmidt (Executive Chairman, Alphabet) said,
Every 2 days we create as much information as we did from dawn of a man up to 2003.
90% of the world's data today has been created in the last two years alone (according to a report from 2015).

Even the software strategies and architectures that are 10 years old are outdated. Today's demands cannot be simply met by yesterday's software architectures.

Today's demands are better met by Reactive Systems, and these systems are

- Responsive
- Resilient
- Elastic, and
- Message driven

Systems that are built as Reactive Systems are designed to be more flexible, loosely-coupled, and easily scalable. This way, they are easier to maintain, more tolerant of failure, and when failure occurs, they handle it with a proper response rather than disaster.

Reactive systems

Let us take a look at the features of reactive systems:

- **Responsiveness**: Reactive systems respond in a timely manner. Such systems are meant to detect the problems quickly, and to deal with them efficiently. Reactive systems focus on rapid responses, and they usually set up an upper bound so as to provide the users with quick and consistent quality of service.
- **Resilience**: The systems are responsive in the event of a failure. The resiliency is achieved by replication, containment, isolation, and delegation. Failure of one system does not affect or impact the replicated system. The client either does not notice failure, or does not have to handle the failure as it is handled automatically.
- **Elasticity**: Primarily, the system stays responsive under different loads. A reactive system can scale up or scale down based on less load or more load. This also means that the system should have no bottlenecks. Scaling up or down can either be predictive or reactive based on the configuration with the combination of statistics by the reactive system.

- **Message-driven**: This property is perhaps the primary enabler to maintain the other properties of the reactive systems. A reactive system depends on asynchronous message communication. It ensures loose-coupling, location transparency, and clear isolation between message sender(s) and message receiver(s) / processor(s). Having explicit message-passing enables simpler load management, easier elasticity, and flow control based on message queuing mechanisms. Asynchronous non-blocking communication means that the recipient processors only consume resources while they are active, thus creating less system overhead.

Reactive microservices architecture

Reactive principles are not something new. They have been tried and tested over a number of decades, and now the community has embraced them with the reactive manifesto, making them more common and popular than ever.

Microservices is an architecture which has learned from the successes and failures of SOA. It has used all the good methodologies and rearchitected them from ground up, primarily using reactive principles and modern infrastructure. Microservices are one of the best examples of the implementation of the reactive manifesto.

One of the principles of the microservices architecture is to divide and conquer, where you decompose the larger system into isolated subsystems based on microservices using bounded context-based decomposition. Microservices are more than just a list of principles and technologies. They are the way to approach the building of a complex system design.

Key aspects of Reactive Microservices

There are some key aspects of the reactive principles applied to microservices. Although these should be part of microservices in general, but they are more highlighted in the context of reactive microservices to do away with the prior pitfalls we had with SOA frameworks and technologies.

- **Isolation**: Isolation between microservices is to limit them as if each is running in its own sandbox process. These microservices should be isolated not just between various microservices, but also between the multiple instances of the same microservice as well. The isolation should be failure protective in the sense that failure in one service should not affect the processing of another instance or other running microservices, and should be easily replaceable by other instances.

- **Autonomous**: A reactive microservice should be autonomous as much as possible, which means that it should expose its interface and behavior and fulfill it without external factors. The microservice should have support for a self-healing mechanism internally, or as a standard in the microservices-based architecture. Autonomous services enable flexibility for service orchestration and collaboration as well as scalability, availability, and runtime manageability.

- **Single responsibility principle** (**SRP**): A component should have only one reason to change. This, in other words, also means that a component should do one thing and do it well. When a microservice has a single reason to fulfill, it simplifies both the business process and the technical implementation associated with it, which allows it to be autonomous as well.

- **Statelessness**: The best reactive microservices are stateless as much as possible. There are certain circumstances that require the state to be shared amongst microservices; it should be limited where applicable. The data should be segregated between different microservices, and this can be split using DDD's bounded context technique as described previously. An effective and quick way, which could be applied to certain types of data persistence for the state of microservices, is known as **Event Sourcing**. With this, we capture the state change of an object as a new row of an event to be stored in the Event Log. It is a way of persisting the application's state by storing the history, which ultimately determines the current state of your application.

- **Asynchronous messaging**: Asynchronous communication enables non-blocking execution of the code, which results in efficient use of computing, storage, and communication resources. Asynchronous messaging and event-based models for a service allow the services to be dynamic and easily scalable by adding the number of instances consuming the events coming up at a rate over a message queue. Having a message queue allows multiple consumers or multiple instances of the same microservices to process in parallel--this not only uses the resources efficiently, but also responds quickly enabling better usability experience. Reactive microservices architecture is not in favor of REST-based HTTP services, as these usually imply synchronous communication, and do not ensure loose coupling between producers and consumers. It is recommended to use the usual REST communication only where there are only a couple of microservices communicating together in a tight (business and technical) coupling scenario.

- **Mobility**: When microservices are isolated and autonomous with a single responsibility, they are also better as mobile as possible. This means you can shift services from one physical location to another or add more instances of services, but the client is not affected and gets a consistent response in a timely manner. This is also called location transparency. Here, reactive microservices should not only be location transparent, but should be virtually addressable so that each microservice is reachable and replaceable effectively. Mobility of services is achievable rather easily once the asynchronous messaging patterns are in place.

Serverless architecture

Serverless architectures are cloud-based systems and offerings, where the applications do not use the usual server processes, hosting application server, and the physical server resources. They rely on the remotely hosted and invocable micro APIs (FaaS), frontend with client-side logic, and the combination of third-party services (with some BaaS). Consider the following diagram:

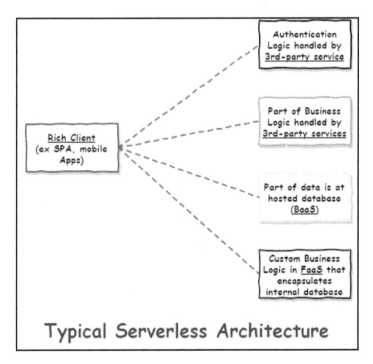

Backend as a Service (BaaS)

With cloud computing and the advent of microservices, BaaS started to gain momentum as well. BaaS systems are those that provide infrastructure software services, and these include storage as a service, database as a service, messaging, and notifications as a service. With serverless architecture, applications usually use a combination of BaaS services, which are often provided by the vendor cloud echo system such as Google's Firebase and Amazon DynamoDB. Other third-party BaaS services may include authentication services (like Auth0, AWS Cognito, and Azure Active Directory).

There are different strategies where some organizations decide to use a rich frontend app talking directly to the database as a service, for example (which some also call stored procedure as a service), and other organizations still prefer to have a thin version of middle-tier API backend services in the middle of the frontend and the BaaS.

Function as a Service (FaaS)

In the most common and latest definition of serverless architectures, FaaS stands at the heart of this design.

In this type of serverless architecture, the server-side logic is written as functions, which are, primarily, invocable/triggered-over events that reside in some sort of tiny light-weight containers that may live on a per call / per request / per event basis, and are hosted and fully managed by the cloud infrastructure provider. These functions utilize other server-side resources as provided by the cloud infrastructure providers that are part of its ecosystem.

Popular examples of FaaS include **AWS Lambda** and **Azure Functions**. There could also be a single service that attempts to provide a complete set of capabilities (for example, data stores, messaging servers, and so on) around FaaS, which is inclusive of number of BaaS services. Examples of such a service provider include **Parse backend** or **Firebase**.

We have covered some more information on Azure Functions in a previous chapter of cloud architecture, so you may look that up for reference.

Key aspects of serverless architecture

The most important architectural aspect of serverless architecture is the **event-driven programming** model. And by virtue of the provided industrial architectural models for serverless architecture, the biggest advantage, and thus the perspective, is the cost-saving model. Another advantage is that the developers get freedom from almost all of the admin tasks.

In modern programming models, typically, **rich client apps** having tight client-side control flow and dynamic content generation replace (if not reduce) the server-side controllers. Such rich JavaScript applications, mobile apps, and loads of IoT apps, which coordinate the interaction between the various third-party services (information providers and BaaS) by making API calls and using FaaS with events for business logic, are the plausible use cases for serverless architecture.

Type of code

With various FaaS providers supporting multiple programming languages as well as containerization, you can virtually run any type of code in almost any programming language with the support of container-based execution.

Stateless

All the functions which are used as FaaS are stateless. This means that if you need to maintain the state across various function calls of the same function, or while coordination between various functions, then you need a separate datastore--be it any type of a database, storage, or cross servers accessible in memory cache, such as **Redis**.

Short-lived

FaaS are contained in tiny light-weight containers. These functions are short-lived code components with a life cycle usually matching the timeline of a single HTTP request/response cycle.

Note that since the containers have a shorter life cycle, they live and die out completely, usually on a per-request basis. Therefore, they are stateless, could take more time to launch (couple of milliseconds) due to the container being spun up, and could be terminated by the FaaS provider after the given maximum time. This means that you are not supposed to have always running functions; that is also against the design of serverless architecture.

Containers do not have to be Docker containers, but now, some providers have started to support Docker-container-based function deployments.

Almost zero administration

With various FaaS providers, you just need to deploy your code simply (in most cases, a zip file), and all the infrastructure and admin is taken care of by the provider, for example, AWS Lambda or Azure Functions.

Automatic scaling

These FaaS providers let your functions scale up and down automatically, and thus, provide very effective use of computer resources. They are also extremely cost effective with zero amount of headache for developers, who do not even have to think about the factors of scaling. Developers will have to write the code with parallel programming in mind.

Event-driven

Functions are event driven by nature, and thus provide an unlimited amount of vertical scaling, otherwise max bounded by the FaaS providers. It makes high availability of your backend FaaS services a breeze.

AWS, Azure, and a number of others provide a set of triggers, which let you invoke your functions. Additionally, now providers also support possible invoking of your functions from the API gateways, whereby your rich client app can invoke a service on the API gateway, and that triggers the execution of your functions. However, this does entail a heavy reliance on the API gateway when it ultimately mimics to act as a microservice, which is mostly not considered as a good practice. Additionally, the chances of vendor lock-in are also increased.

For message-oriented communication to functions and between different functions, a message queuing system as a service is facilitated by the vendor, for example, SNS by AWS and Queue Storage by Azure. The following is the serverless architecture transitions (an Indicative view) diagram:

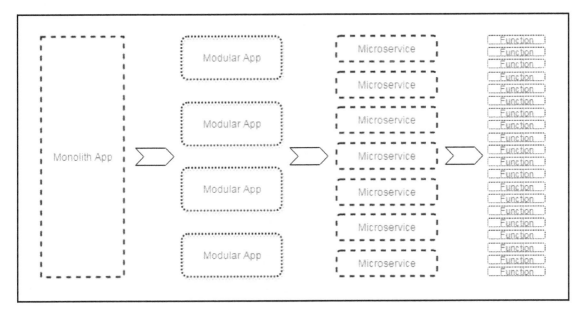

Indicative transitions to the serverless architecture

Let's wrap it up

We can see that serverless architectures have a heavy influence on the event-driven reactive programming model, and it frees up the developers from infrastructure admin hassles, reducing a lot of DevOps as well. Serverless architecture, at least as of now, is completely not for high performance applications due to the response time, but is an excellent piece of software design to facilitate rapid deployment and shorter time-to-market apps, and for ideas to reach quickly to your customer's satisfaction.

Azure for microservices

Cloud computing readily comes to mind when thinking about implementation of microservices architecture. These days, there are loads of reliable cloud services providers, especially after the advent of **OpenStack**, an open source cloud software.

> OpenStack is an open source software for creating private and public clouds.

There are also some globally leading cloud services providers such as Amazon Web Services, Microsoft Azure, IBM Bluemix, RedHat OpenShift (PaaS), and Heroku (PaaS).In this section, we will see our options for microservices with the Microsoft Azure cloud computing services provider.

To implement the microservices architecture with Azure, we have, at least, the following three possibilities:

- Azure Functions
- Azure Service Fabric
- Azure Container Service

All of them have their own unique advantages and features, which lets you choose one or the other, or even a combination of them, depending on the needs of your particular microservice according to its domain and technology model. Although you could use the API App from Azure App Services to host your microservices, and have a separate API App for each microservice, API apps do not specialize in satisfying all the characteristics of microservices architecture.

Azure Functions

Azure Functions are the simplest and easiest way to develop, host, and manage microservices. They can be developed and hosted locally as well.

 As of today, February 2017, Azure Functions can be hosted locally using the Azure Functions CLI, and local development and tooling will also be released soon allowing development and debugging on DEV machines.

Azure Functions support development in various languages including C# and NodeJS, and you can write the code while staying within the Azure portal on your browser.

Azure Functions are basically meant to be event based, which means that they execute only when the desired event occurs; they get charged for up to milliseconds of the executable time, so you pay only when your function is executed, and not for any idle time. They scale automatically based on the load, and you do not need to configure the scaling limits or scaling factors at all. You do not need to manage any hosting environment either, thus reducing the DevOps to almost none.

Since Azure Functions are event based and promote the reactive microservices architecture, they provide an excellent number of input and output bindings for integration with various other systems to get events from. These bindings include Azure BLOB storage, table, Event Hub, queue storage, Azure service bus, HTTP, Azure notification hub, Twilio (SMS service), and more.

One Azure Function App is composed of one or more individual functions. All of the functions in a single function app share the same pricing plan, continuous deployment, and runtime version. You can write the functions in multiple programming languages, and they can all share the same function app.

With Azure Functions, you can develop and ship faster, with shortest development-to-deployment cycles, focusing only on the business logic, ideal for quick testing multiple versions with least worries about the cost, deployment, and maintenance.

 Kudu: It's a troubleshooting and analysis tool for use with Microsoft Azure. It is also useful for development within the Azure Portal. With this, you can browse through your App Service folder hierarchy. It is extremely useful when digging around Azure Functions. Visit here for more information: `https://github.com/projectkudu/kudu/wiki`

Azure Service Fabric

Azure Service Fabric is less open then having your VMs in the cloud, but much more flexible with control than Azure app services. Service fabric is a system that can run on your development machines, on Azure cloud, on-premises datacenter, and also on other clouds. Many of Microsoft's own services run on Azure Service Fabric as do those of many big enterprises such as BMW.

Azure Service Fabric is great for web applications, ASP.NET Core, Owin, guest process executions, and containers. The service fabric proposes to develop microservices with reliable services or actor models. With service fabric, you are provided with the following features:

- Life cycle management
- Always on services / VMs behind the scene
- Programming models (ex-reliable actors, reliable services)
- Orchestration
- Health and monitoring of resources
- Dev and Ops tooling
- Auto scaling

Service fabric is great for hyper-scale web, including availability and reliability, hyper-scale, and state management within clusters with continuous delivery and containerization support. These features make it an excellent choice for mass-scaled games, IoT at scale, and microservices-architecture-based implementations.

Azure Container Service

Modern enterprise applications use containers. Containerization is at the heart of microservices implementation ensuring proper technical bounded context to the organizational business services.

Azure fully supports Docker-based containers, and containers can be deployed in well-segregated DEV, TEST, and production environments of an enterprise in the Azure cloud. With a lot of containers for your microservices, the integrity of containers becomes complex, and the Azure container service eases it by automating the management of high density containers with reliability and performance using open source orchestrators like Mesos DC/OS, Docker swarm, and Kubernetes. It provides control on containers cluster management.

Bringing it together

If an application has various parts distinctively separated into multiple containers, and each container microservice has different scaling and business variation needs, the **Azure Container Service** (ACS) might be a choice for this scenario. Also, if you are not yet there, but planning to implement the architecture with various containers of varying needs, again ACS is a good choice.

If an application architecture is strongly based on Docker Linux containers, ACS seems to be good choice, better than ASF.

If an application or system has a number of long running, high available stateful processes, the **Azure Service Fabric** (ASF) is a good choice. ASF supports the gateway pattern--so, many services are behind the gateway and transparent to the client, smoothly implementing high availability, load balancing, and scalability to a massive scale on ASF clusters.

ASF directly supports the Actor model, which is ideal for IoT applications where millions of devices are sending messages to services on ASF with a seamless integration into the Azure notification hub and Azure event hub.

If you have a serverless architecture at hand, and all the communication is event based, you want a worry free infrastructure with minimal DevOps processes, and your microservices cut down to an extremely granular level with seamless support for automatic scalability, Azure Functions are the one you should be looking for. This comes with the added advantage of cost savings on the infrastructure, admin tasks, and scalability areas.

Implementation samples

Up to now, we have covered pretty much all of the important aspects, comparisons, and technicalities of the microservices architecture and the number of related concepts. We will now consider building the design and the technical architecture of a sample application, which would enable us to see in motion some aspects of the microservices architecture that we have learnt so far.

We encourage you to view an excellent working example of a complete IoT implementation using the Azure IoT set of services called *MyDriving - An Azure IOT and Mobile application* at
`https://azure.microsoft.com/en-us/blog/mydriving-an-azure-iot-an d-mobile-sample-application`

We will design the architecture of an enterprise based on the microservices principle; we will also do another example for a sample application, whose design will be based on serverless architecture, keeping reactive microservices principles intact and utilizing the FaaS facilities provided by the Azure cloud.

Microservices architecture for our sample enterprise

In this example, we will build the microservices-based architecture for our sample enterprise. For this first example design, our sample enterprise can have a business domain of the digital production industry, or an industry selling specific types of products, for example, tires or batteries that could be used in vehicles. The domain industry could be different to some extent for our sample architecture, but they will have the similar problem domains in order to achieve their business goals. We will list down the departments or teams that will be working for this company so that you will understand how this breakup can work for more than one industry. We will design in a way to satisfy all the teams to achieve their tasks in a healthy and efficient manner as well as for the business to achieve its targets for current demand as well as future growth.

Problem domains

Let's say our sample company has to publish some content on its website for the audience to make them well aware about their products; they sell their products to various customers, and they try to attract more customers by networking various events in the world. Therefore, it depends heavily on how they market themselves using the technology and right tools to not just be profitable to run the business successfully today, but also be able to grow without significant costs and resource limitations in terms of hardware, software, and manpower.

Given this as a background, we decide on the following teams, which are working for the enterprise to achieve its goals.

Publishing team

This team is responsible for publishing content regarding the features and benefits about the products offered by the company. Given the various usual functions performed by such type of teams, this team has decided that they need some software capability allowing them to publish the contents and manage them in some sort of manner.

This team needs a simple, task-focused publishing application.

Marketing team

A marketing team is required with the obvious goal to market the company's products and increase the popularity, ultimately leading to a growth in demand for the products.

This team also has the responsibility to utilize digital advertisements as well as social media and SEO aspects--everything to increase the visibility of the company and its products.

They need to maintain certain documentation records. They also need some kind of integration between the social media platforms and the company's own system / website for showcasing.

Sales team

Tasked to increase the sales and revenue stream, this team needs to know all information about the products, marketing, production/manufacturing, potential customer leads, and work flows for customer tracking leading to successful deals.

This team needs the industry leading CRM with integration features.

Platform administration team

This team would have a broader scope of tasks to perform. They manage the controls and features on the company's website or the whole platform. They have to deal with the content layout on the featured website, integration aspects of various applications, and to come up with grouped plans for display of information on the website, requiring coordination between various teams.

This team needs an effective administration platform for the whole system to be developed for the enterprise. The team will hold a good amount of business domain information as well as the technical solution domain to achieve and to help other teams achieve their tasks effectively.

Other teams

There would be a number of other teams helping the enterprise achieve its goals. These teams could include, for example, a manufacturing management team, a facilities team, perhaps a separate HR team, and more. However, for the sake of simplicity of the demonstration of the architecture, we will limit our sample problem domains only to these teams listed so far.

Contexts for the respective teams

Now that we have identified the teams, and also sort of identified their focused and main set of requirements to let them work on their objects, let's narrow it down to the technical design of the individual team level.

Naturally, we followed the DDD methodology, or at least some stripped version of the DDD sets of processes, and there we have identified our contextual teams and processes. Let's assume that our teams, as identified previously, fit the single bounded context per team on the basis of the business and technical domains having their own special needs, and therefore, could have their own segregated IT systems and databases.

Since we are building the Microservices-based architecture at this stage, and for the sake of coverage in the book, we won't go into the granular business requirements and into details of insider implementation of each microservice and the number of interfaces it could contain.

We consider this as a microservices-based architecture, and not the design and architecture for the internal components and service interfaces of each microservice and their implementation details. Note that microservices-based architecture gives full independence to the teams, both technical and business, to come up with their own strategy, design, technology and implementation of their bounded contexts inside a container, but only having agreed on the exposed microservices interfaces and standard communication patterns and mechanisms.

So we have decided to develop and deploy at least one container per context as per our architecture, and at least two containers for each team's context (for UI and for system interfaces). Since implementation inside each container is technologically independent, and each microservice from the given view is technology agnostic, every team is free to implement their container in the technologies that they prefer fit. For example, the sales team could use the **LAMP** stack inside their container, while the marketing team used the **MEAN** stack, and the publishing team the .NET Core-based stack for technical implementation.

Let's assume that after some discussions, we have decided to use an industry leading **CRM** (**Customer Relationship Management**) system, and to integrate it with our set of interfaces. The CRM system would be primarily used by the sales team. We also assume that since it's a market leading CRM, it exposes a set of APIs that allow us to integrate our custom code to this CRM both for read and write operations. If, for any reason, our chosen CRM system does not expose APIs or web services, we will have to wrap those components and convert them as callable APIs over HTTP and/or over Message Queue. This newly exposed API project could either be developed as a Web API inside the Azure cloud, or, depending on our architecture, it could be developed as a separate microservice inside its own unique container.

Customer Relationship Management system

Let's assume that after some discussions we decide to use an industry-leading CRM system, and integrate it with our set of interfaces. The CRM system would be primarily used by the sales team, and hence, integration of interfaces would be required with the sales microservices. Consider the following diagram:

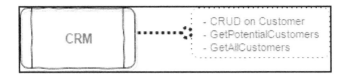

Customer Relationship Management system used within the sample enterprise

Document Management System

We also decide to use a certain Document Management System to save, retrieve, link, and manage various types of documents.

Just as a reminder, document storage and linking could be achieved, for example, via Google Drive for enterprise, SharePoint, Documentum, or even particular Azure Storage or Blobs. In any case, the underlying **Document Management System** (**DMS**) will expose certain APIs to link and deal with various actions to the various types of documents. This actually depends on the use cases and feature requirements by the various departments of the company; however, we have just decided here to use the same DMS across various teams and their systems:

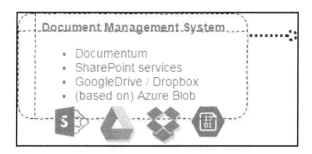

Indicative Document Management System (DMS)

We will now design the high-level microservices architecture for each team of our sample enterprise based on the bounded context that are presumably coming out of our enterprise DDD practice carried out earlier at some hypothetical date.

Understanding the Microservices Bounded Team Contexts

Before we do the breakup and high-level design of microservices with respect to the teams, let's develop and understand the conventions that we will keep in our design, as sort of agreed between our team of architects for building this new system.

All the respective boxes below in context diagrams showing the systematic context for each team are the high-level microservice designs based directly on the bounded contexts determined by the respective responsible teams.

We have decided that all of the user interface components for all the contexts will be treated as a separate microservice. Meaning, they will be packaged and deployed separately as an independent process other than its respective system interfaces microservice. Both are isolated but sort of dependent, but they can be available on the same machine or a VM.

The user interface microservice basically does not expose any service, and is, primarily, a services consumer. UI components usually consume the services from its own bounded contexts. As per convention, we will try that all external (outside the bounded context) service interfaces are linked to our system interfaces, and not to user interface, wherever possible.

Most of the user interface services can be made as SPA. Our user interface app for the platform administration team is not necessarily an SPA, but it's a special app interface which basically combines all other teams' interfaces under one umbrella. So we will design our user interfaces, technically, in a way that they are embeddable UIs without losing the **user experience** (**UX**). Rather, they should somehow enrich the main portal, which is represented as a software under the platform admin team.

All the service-callable interfaces that represent APIs or some functionality are exposed by the system interfaces microservice. So we will basically have a number of system interfaces microservices from various team contexts talking to each other.

The big boxes on the right of each context which basically represent an external system, which is being utilized as a separate interface integrated into our services context. In a way, it depicts our business case as well as the technical scenario in an easy and simple format. It does not exactly show the services that are being exposed by the respective systems, but in real life, it will show all the essential connection points.

Similarly, we have only shown very few basic and only high-level services exposed by our microservice's system interfaces for each team's context. This is only for demonstration purpose.

General service information flow

The general mechanism for information flow of our microservices is quite simple and straightforward. It should always be kept in mind when implementing any microservice for our sample enterprise. Meaning, we should agree on the enterprise architecture level to keep some of the fundamental mechanisms and modes of implementations across all of the microservices as uniform. The internal implementation and technologies, or even the development languages, could be different.

Note that this is a generic microservice implementation mechanism, which we use just for our sample enterprise here. It's not a generic way just for any type of microservice though it is quite a common one. We keep it simple for the purpose of understanding and learning the core concepts.

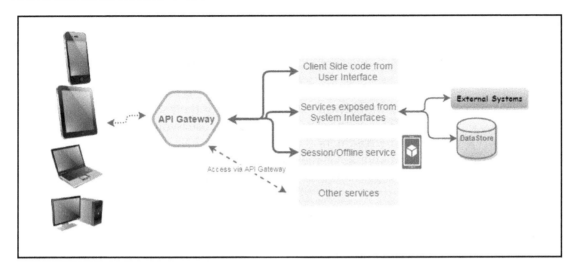

Generic microservice information flow

Sales Team Context

Based on the high level requirements listed earlier, we come up with a certain solution design for the system, which will eventually be used by the sales team. Note that this team uses an external system for CRM like Salesforce and DMS, such as Documentum:

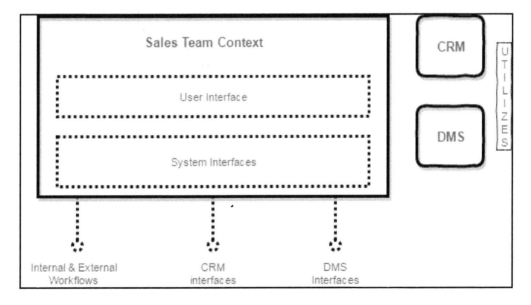

High level microservice design for simplified sales team's bounded context

Marketing Team Context

Our sample marketing team has two top-level functions. One is social media marketing and the other involves advertising, which could be both digital as well as in the form of physical banners.

The social media wing uses some software like **hootsuite** for their social media campaigns, publishes the contents, and extracts the stats out of it to expose to other channels of the enterprise, while the other advertisement wing can perform their duty in various ways. Let's assume that their documentation is maintained in the particular location and structure inside the DMS. The DMS is capable of exposing the information and the data stored inside it based on the API-level interfaces.

Since the social media wing publishes contents on say Facebook or YouTube, those contents are to be exposed on the main enterprise's portal based on the most liked or most viewed category. We will see the main portal / site further in the platform administration context:

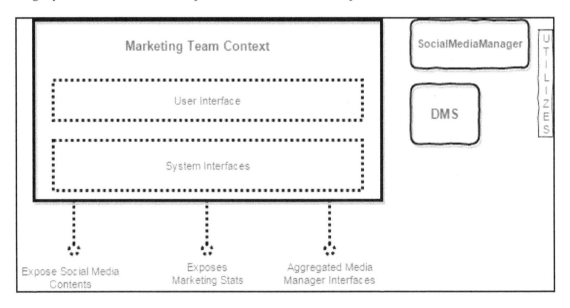

High level microservice design for simplified marketing team's bounded context

Publishing Team Context

In our sample enterprise, we have a publishing team who needs to publish the contents about the company's products, their features, benefits, and the related information on the web. Basically, it's a content publishing team, and therefore, they need a capability for something like a content management system. There is an option to use either a full-fledged content management system and then integrate its contents to our main enterprise portal, or we use our existing capabilities of DMS and build a cut-down version of a CMS with features that just fit our needs. For the purpose of this high-level microservice architecture, we abstract out this specific technical implementation point:

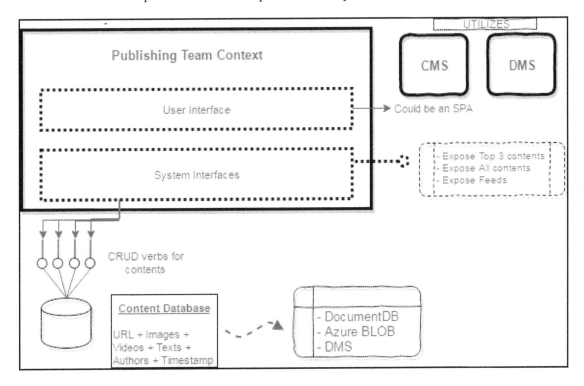

High level microservice design for simplified publishing team's bounded context

From the preceding design diagram, you can see that the essential attributes of the content include URL, images, text, and videos. Now some of these could be saved in our DMS and linked to the main content, and some of the new media can be directly uploaded as part of the content being posted. In either case, it can be uploaded to our DMS or to CMS if we are using a dedicated one. Here, if we simplify the business process, it does not look too big to implement our own core-focused CMS along with the combination of DMS.

The contents or the media of the contents could be stored in the Azure cloud as well as the selected DMS alongside the selected CMS if any. Wherever the data is stored, the important thing is its accessibility, and when we are dealing with microservices, the accessibility should be consistent in terms of the desired interface exposed, no matter which underlying content storage technology is used.

The sample microservice design diagram shows three of the required services, which would be ultimately utilized by the enterprise's portal in its front page or otherwise.

Platform Administration Team Context

This is the team that seems to have, by far, the most responsibilities as compared to other departments. Although it may not be occupied on a day-to-day basis like other teams, but in the beginning, it will be the most critical and busy team in the whole company.

Perhaps, the name given to this team is not so suitable, but anyway, we can list down the responsibilities performed by this team in our sample enterprise as follows:

- Maintain the enterprise portal configuration
- Keep the website healthy (administration tasks)
- Link other teams and their interfaces to the main enterprise portal
- Set up all the various artefacts from various teams within a well-defined theme of the portal
- Fetch and display all the agreed upon and required data in a proper format by calling the respective microservices-based APIs exposed by the systems of other teams
- Decide on the layout and agree on the variation on a timely basis so that the other service providers evolve their microservices-based interfaces accordingly.
- Allow various departments to log in to the main portal, and provide them accessibility to their system as much as possible--it's not necessary that they achieve all of their respective tasks from within the main portal
- The team should have the capability to browse through the DMS as it is a vital component of all the teams
- This team basically has the visibility and responsibility of the whole portal as a platform

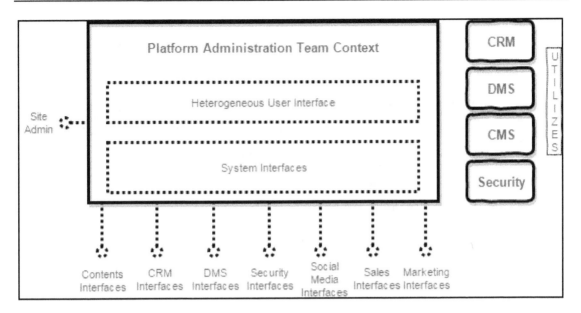

High level microservice design for simplified platform admin team's bounded context

The platform administration team has technical and business relationship and interfaces with the maximum number of systems that would be present in our sample enterprise. Note that it also links to all the external systems as well. Meaning, it has the maximum amount of communication going on, so network security, traffic, user experience, and optimization is of utmost importance for this platform and the team.

Enterprise portal mockup

The main idea of our sample enterprise application is a central enterprise portal for the public and the company's own employees with respect to the teams. We decided to build our architecture based on microservices, and have thus given full independence to the other teams to develop their IT systems according to their needs and standards while just keeping the core communication patterns. The existence of a dedicated platform administration team is mainly due to the fact that we channelize all the information from various systems coming into the main portal properly.

Let's say we have created the final and agreed mockup after various meetings with business users, teams, management, architects, and developers. We involved supposed UX experts to come up with the design, which should be able to gather all the information we need to present in a consistent, pleasing, and complete manner:

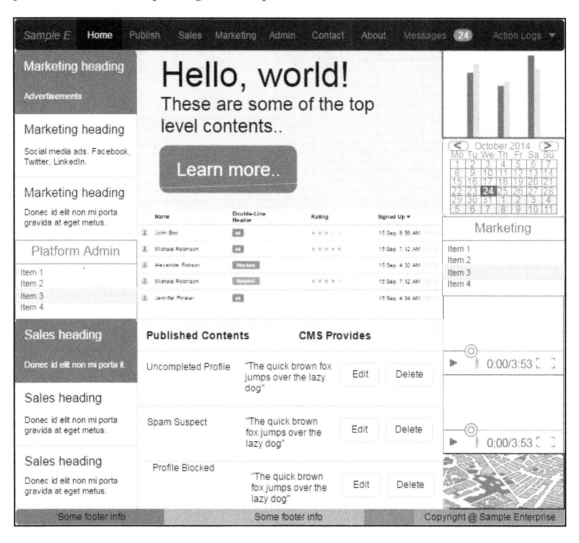

A mockup designer view of the sample enterprise portal

The information in the portal is pretty organized, and comes from various channels utilizing the APIs exposed by the various systems or applications. I think it would be nicer and easier to grasp if we see a layout regarding our enterprise portal in a grid form:

Mockup design grid layout for sample enterprise portal

We may comprehend the design better with the layout view. This is the enterprise portal platform where the main platform is an aggregator of information and displays it in a consistent and useful manner.

The main portal has a **Top Highlights** area, which could be either manually inserted information or a combination of manual plus gathered information, but this is completely managed by the platform administration team.

Information displayed in the middle of the portal is basically from our publishing team, and comes straight out of their CMS system. This platform portal basically fetches some of the information using the provided microservices from the publishing team's and embeds the focused and trimmed UI of their system directly inside this portal.

Information in the left and right bars is fully dynamic, and is managed by the platform admin team in terms of its arrangements and first-time configuration and development. These bars basically display the information gathered from the systems of the sales and marketing teams. The information is only gathered by calling the respective relevant microservices APIs. For example, as shown in the preceding microservice design diagram of the publishing team, the system exposes an API to give the top three (configured) items, and those items are displayed by the portal. Similar APIs are also exposed by the systems from the sales and marketing teams, although not shown in the preceding figures.

Note that as mentioned earlier, all the service calling is achieved via a load balancing API gateway so that our scaling factor remains transparent to the client caller of those microservices.

Overall microservices architecture

All of our step-by-step design exercises given previously, and the building and merging of individual microservices architecture have finally led us to arrive at the point where we have one big and summarized picture of the overall microservices-based architecture for our sample enterprise, which is depicted as follows:

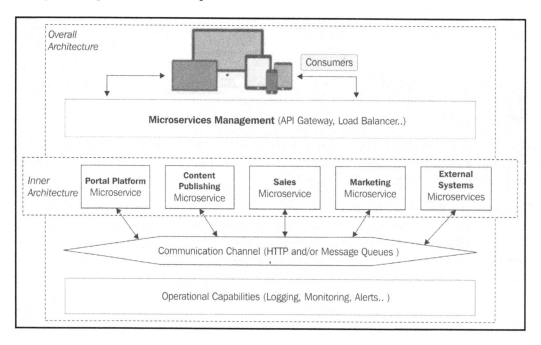

Microservices based architecture for sample enterprise

The core microservices application is what as shown in this preceding picture inside the inner architecture, and this is what we have architected as individual contexts. All the access points to the microservices are maintained and accessed via the API gateway.

All the services feature logging, tracking, and monitoring mechanisms on each service call level. It can be implemented as a cross-cutting concern of aspect-oriented programming, and by calling a dedicated logger service just the way we talked about in the SOA chapter. The only difference would be that the logger service itself will be packaged as a unique microservice. It is possible that logger service might either listen on HTTP or be message-oriented or both; it can avoid being listed on the API gateway, and could possibly be invoked directly to avoid an extra network hop.

We have not talked about the communication methods for our microservices architecture yet, but we will briefly see what is available.

Common communication mechanismsin microservices

Communication as well as the overall microservices architecture is supposed to be simplified. Though we have not proposed the mechanism that we will use, it can be either synchronous or asynchronous. We can say for our architecture that all the communication between the user interface services and system interface services will be synchronous over HTTP, and all the communication between system services interfaces will be asynchronous using a message broker.

Synchronous communication

For synchronous communication, the preferred communication mode is by using REST APIs with JSON-based objects over the HTTP protocols. When we talk about synchronous communication with HTTP with scale, it always flows through an API gateway, which acts here more like a proxy though it has its full-feature set as we covered in the previous section. The API gateway enables our services to be location transparent, load balanced, and simply allows them to scale silently without affecting the consumer of the services.

Asynchronous communication

When asynchronous communication is required, it mostly flows through a centralized component called a message bus or a message broker, which provides us at least with message queues. With message queues, the communication pattern is more like a consumer/producer scenario (and less like request/response, which is preferred as a synchronous pattern), where the consumer and producers could be one or many. The only thing that the services consumers need to know is the service queue name, where they could put their message, and they receive an answer asynchronously on the response queue which was provided as part of the metadata of the request message.

For asynchronous messaging, your message bus can be a PaaS like Azure Service Bus or Amazon SQS (Simple Queue Service), or it can reside in a bare metal server, a VM, or as a separate container. Examples of those include TIBCO EMS, Rabbit MQ, IBM WebSphere MQ, IronMQ, Apache Active MQ, Apache Kafka, and more.

There is a bit different and lightweight performance-oriented messaging engine called ZeroMq. ZeroMQ is an asynchronous messaging library specialized for concurrent applications. It provides a message queue, but unlike message-oriented middleware (MOM), a ZeroMQ-based system can work without a dedicated message broker.

Serverless architecture for a sample application

Microservices architecture, when broken down into many functions serving in a FaaS manner to fulfill the same, is sometimes referred to as a Nanoservices architecture. For our part, we will focus on and follow our new example as a sample for creating a simple serverless architecture.

Our sample application - Home automation

We want to develop a home automation application and want to begin with the simplest one. We will have some smart electricity bulbs, which are not just energy efficient but would also be remotely controllable and send status updates.

For having some control on non-smart devices, we have, let's say, developed a smart extension cord which has smart switches where you can plug any accessory, while the smart switch can give us the status as on or off.

We could have another device such as an energy monitor having some energy-consumption-specific sensors, or say, a monitor camera to read the electricity meter and transfer the readings to us periodically so as to measure consumption. For the simplicity of our design, let's skip this device for our sample architecture.

Along with these other devices, say we have a master device which we'll call **Home Hub** (**HH**). This device basically captures from and transfers the data to other smart devices over, say, Bluetooth. Our smart devices talk over Bluetooth to transmit their status as on or off (to the least) to the home hub. The HH device is able to configure and connect to the home Wi-Fi, or plug in to your home router. It is this HH device which gathers information from the local smart devices, and transmits information to our server application.

This application basically is as an IoT application, and the gathered data can be applied to perform analytics (both real-time and batch), and provide feedbacks on efficiency back to the home users. Machine learning can also be applied to deduce interesting results. However, for now, we are not looking to apply analytics or intelligence.

High-level application design

Let's assume that after hours of discussions and a range of factors (geologically disperse, high number of devices hitting with light-weight data quite frequently, and more) we have decided to go with a cloud-based solution, and selected Azure cloud services as our provider.

Based on our requirements, the high-level design we come up with is as shown in the following diagram:

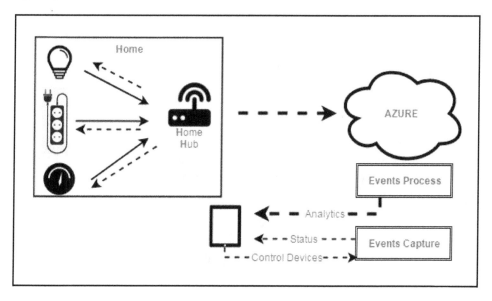

High level design

The preceding diagram clarifies our understanding of how the home hub gets inputs from the devices, and transfers them over to the event processor in the cloud. The consumer's smartphone running our app can receive the status remotely about his electrical appliances at home; he will also be able to control them to a certain extent, for example, for switching them on or off.

Serverless architecture in Azure

It is decided to implement our application as a serverless architecture using FaaS by Azure following the event-based cloud programming model. We will leverage the Azure Functions to build our processing logic.

We will use some of the Azure products in our architecture, so let's just quickly see their definitions before we draw the architecture diagram.

Azure Functions: They process events with a serverless code, and are fully scalable on demand, automatically. In this architecture, we will use them to execute some logic based on certain events. Note that the IoT Hub to Azure Function functionality is still newly released, otherwise, we connect from IoT Hub –> Event Hub –> Azure Function.

> For more information on the topic of Azure Function and IoT Hub, please browse through the following site:
> `https://azure.microsoft.com/en-us/blog/azure-iot-gateway-sdk-int`
> `egrates-support-for-azure-functions`

Event Hubs: These can (only) receive millions of events per second, and are fully scalable. They enable you to ingress massive amounts of telemetry into the cloud. In this architecture, we will use Event Hubs to receive messages from smart devices based on the iOS, Android, and Windows operating systems.

Notification Hub: It's a cloud-scale push notification engine to send (only) push notifications (millions of messages) to any platform. Here we will use it to send messages from Azure Function in the cloud to smart devices based on the iOS, Android, and Windows operating system.

> Note that (as of now) to allow Azure Function to send messages to the IoT Hub, we need to include the NuGet package `Microsoft.Azure.Devices` in the `Project.json` file. Currently, it supports .NET 4.6

IoT Hub: It allows us to connect, monitor, and manage billions of IoT devices. It enables us to have reliable, bi-directional, real-time communication. It supports a broad set of operating systems and protocols, which is why we are using it here. We use it in our architecture to talk to our Home Hub, which runs some micro-operating system, let's say a tiny-sized Linux box which is able to communicate via the C language.

DocumentDB: It's a NoSQL-document-oriented database-as-a-service (BaaS). It's a super-fast, planet-scale NoSQL DB, which you can query using the familiar SQL and JavaScript syntax over document and key-value data without dealing with schema. Here we are using it to store quickly millions of messages in a schema-less database to be processed at later stage, say, for example, Big Data.

Stream Analytics: It enables real-time stream processing of the events received from such as Event Hubs. It allows performing of real-time analytics for your IoT solutions. Here we use it just to demonstrate the idea that with Azure IoT solutions, we can perform real-time analysis on a stream of data ingress, and push back the notifications to our customers.

Blob storage: It's a cloud-scale object storage for unstructured data (images, videos, audio, documents, and so on). In our design, it is required to receive data from Stream Analytics, which will later trigger our respective Azure Function.

Finally, this image depicts our serverless architecture ready for implementation:

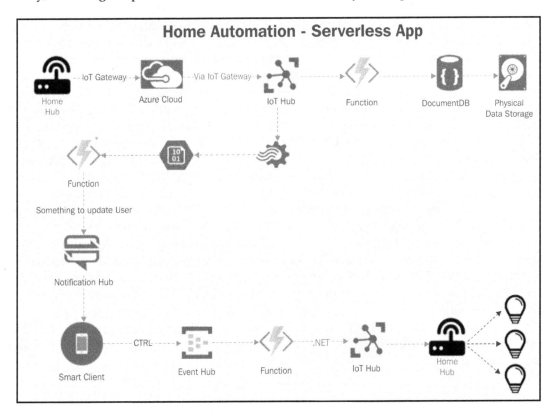

Serverless architecture for a sample IoT Home Automation app

Let's wrap it up

In the second example implementation, we presented the problem, drew a high-level design, and directly proposed the solution unlike the way we drilled the first implementation. One reason for this is that this problem is simpler than the previous one; the other reason is that by now, we have already learnt a lot about the underlying architectural principles.

Let's just have a quick end-to-end roundup of this Azure-based serverless implementation architecture.

We have a home hub device connected to the Internet, equipped with some microchip based OS, most likely a Linux distro, running our engine written in C language, and talking to us over an Azure cloud. This HH device acts as a gateway allowing the consumer to control other home smart electrical devices. It uses the Azure IoT gateway, SDK, allowing it to communicate with the IoT Hub in both directions. From the IoT hub, we trigger an Azure Function, which saves data to a NoSQL PaaS database: DocumentDB. Data stored here can be used for various purposes at a later stage, but is not part of our problem now. Real-time stream data also flows from the IoT hub to Azure stream analytics, doing some calculations, like warning users that all of their light bulbs have been switched on for the last 12 hours; these results are stored in the Azure blob. Saving it auto triggers our event-based function, which then sends the calculated warning over to the user on his smartphone to alert them using the Azure notification hub (which is capable of sending notifications on Android, iOS, and Windows). The user can see the alert information on his smartphone, and can take an action like sending a control message to switch on or off the smart device appliances. It does so by sending an event to an Event Hub which is capable of receiving messages from smartphones. Note that, here, we could have also used IoT Hub instead of Event Hub. After receiving a control message on Event Hub, another Azure function is automatically triggered, which passes on the notification to an IoT Hub, which then passes on the control message to the devices' gateway, that is, Home Hub. HH is able to switch on or off the individual devices, as it's connected to them over low-energy Bluetooth. We could have also let our smartphone directly connect to the home hub by implementing another interface dedicated for smartphones, and then, after getting the control message and acting on it, the device gateway could send this update to the Azure cloud. But then we could not have controlled the smart devices at home when we are outside the home, and we would've needed to make our HH even more complex. These trade-offs let us decide which option is more viable for us to take, and then we go in that direction given all the practical limitations and possibilities.

Summary

In this chapter, we first took a theoretical dive, and from concepts, we moved towards the more technical aspects of microservices-based architecture. You learned the core microservices principles, its differences from other standard architectures, and best practices. You also understood the core architectural elements as well as motivational practical manifestations. We noted some key differences between Azure Functions, service fabric, and container service. On the way, we touched base on some theory of DDD and reactive programming, and understood the core principles of serverless architecture as well.

Finally, we designed two example architectures--one based on microservices, and the other with serverless paradigms using Azure cloud offerings. We hope that you learned quite a lot in this chapter, and enjoyed it as well.

In the coming chapters we will learn various security aspects and features available from .NET Core environment after that we will look at DevOps processes with detailed information on containerization and will implement a simple multi-containers microservices application using the docker on the Azure container service.

10
Security Practices with .NET Core

Security is the core component in any enterprise application. With proper implementation, we can not only protect sensitive information from unauthorized user access but also maintain the integrity of the data. Security can be implemented using different techniques, where authentication and authorization are the two main principles. In this chapter, we will discuss the different approaches of implementing security in an ASP.NET Core web application and cover the following topics:

- Authenticating websites using cookie middleware, external authentication, ASP.NET Identity and two-factor authentication
- Exploring different options for authorizing user access
- Discussing the core concepts and flows of OAuth and OpenID Connect
- Implementing a Central Authentication System (CAS) using IdentityServer4
- Exploring safe storage to store sensitive information

ASP.NET Core comes with a wide range of **Open Web Interface for .NET (OWIN)** middleware that facilitates developers and architects to authenticate applications using identity, open authentication, social authentication such as Facebook, Google, and Microsoft, and two-factor authentication. Moreover, custom middleware can also be implemented to implement a specific security model. For authorization, ASP.NET Core Identity system provides a rich security model for defining roles, claims, and policies, which we will cover later in this chapter.

OWIN defines a standard interface between .NET web servers and web applications. The goal of the OWIN interface is to decouple servers and applications, encourage the development of simple modules for .NET web development, and, by being an open standard, stimulate the open source ecosystem of .NET web development tools.

Authentication and authorization modes

Authentication and authorization are the two core components for securing applications. Authentication is the process of verifying a user's identity by obtaining credentials and using those credentials to verify their identity, whereas authorization is done after a successful authentication and it validates if the authenticated user has sufficient rights to access a particular resource of an application. A typical example is the shopping cart application, where a user can sign in to choose products, check out, and make payments; whereas some information is still hidden from registered users, and features such as manipulating items, managing user access, and other administrative permissions are only given to admin users.

Securing applications with ASP.NET Core Identity

ASP.NET Core Identity is the new powerful, pluggable, and extensible security system developed on .NET and it can be used with ASP.NET Core applications. It provides greater control over database schema, linking with an existing application's database, and provides APIs to perform user management, role management, and signing in/signing out options.

By default, it is configured with SQL Server, but as it supports Entity Framework on the backend, other database servers can also be used that are supported by the Entity Framework. For example, you can use Oracle, SQLite, or Postgres and also attach other non-relational data providers such as MongoDB and NoSQL as well.

As far as the authentication models are concerned, it provides various built-in OWIN based middleware that can be simply added into the middleware pipeline to support social authentication, OAuth authentication, and so on.

Here are a few of the benefits of using the ASP.NET Core Identity framework in an enterprise application:

- **One ASP.NET Identity system**: One ASP.NET Identity system that can be used with all the application frameworks of ASP.NET, starting from ASP.NET Core MVC 6, web forms, web pages, web API, and SignalR.
- **Schema modification**: The default security database schema can easily be modified using the Entity Framework Code First model. Extensions of existing tables or the creation of new tables can easily be done by defining POCO classes and making a DbSet entry in the Context class.
- **Providers**: Various providers that can be added as a middleware component and offer easy integration with any application.
- **Easy enablement of user restriction**: User access can easily be restricted by defining roles, claims, and policies, and it can be linked with any MVC controller class or action method.
- **OWIN Integration**: Based on OWIN middleware and it can be used with any OWIN based host. It uses OWIN Authentication for login/logout scenarios.
- **NuGet package**: Can easily be used and added into your project as a NuGet package.

Security architecture in ASP.NET Core

In ASP.NET Core, the authentication is implemented as middleware. With previous versions of ASP.NET Security, there was only a FormsAuthentication cookie, but with the new ASP.NET Core Identity system, multiple cookies can be defined. Different authentication providers are provided and, instead of only authenticating users from the local identity data store, we can also authenticate users from external providers such as Microsoft account, Google, Facebook, and Twitter.

Everything in the new Identity system is based on claims. That means all properties on the user's identity object are now defined through claims. Properties such as name, e-mail, department, role, designation, and many others, are a few examples of the common properties associated with the user's identity and we can use these properties to authorize user permissions. ClaimsPrincipal is the main class through which claims can be defined. However, implementing custom claims through the IPrincipal interface is now deprecated.

Encoding sensitive information is often needed in many web applications. Through new cryptographic protection APIs, developers can easily encrypt information, and they provide support key management and rotation. The core of the ASP.NET data protection stack is the replacement for the `<machineKey>` element that we used to have in previous versions of ASP.NET.

Cross Origin Request Sharing (CORS) prevents a web page from making AJAX requests from client-side scripting languages such as JavaScript. With ASP.NET Core, enabling CORS and allowing request and response headers, HTTP methods, and origin is much easier and simpler than before.

Another core component is logging, which is included by default with ASP.NET Core. You can start logging by simply creating a logger instance using `LoggerFactory` and also develop and implement custom loggers to log information in the database or any other medium.

One of the most common types of attack on websites is referred to as **cross-site request forgery** (known as **CSFR** or **XSFR**). This happens when a user accesses some malicious website or opens up some malicious e-mail that contains some script and submits harmful requests on a site where the users are authenticated. This way, the malicious site forges requests, as they appear to come from a legitimate user. The forged request then attempts to impersonate authenticated users and performs an activity. To prevent these attacks, we can add anti-forgery middleware in the application pipeline and it does all the plumbing to verify whether the request is coming from the same user as it should be.

Now, let's discuss some of the core API's of the Identity system.

Getting to know the core APIs of the Identity system

Here are the two core classes of the ASP.NET Core Identity system.

HttpContext and AuthenticationManager

The `HttpContext` class is the core of ASP.NET Core. `HttpContext` is the object that gives information about current requests and responses, for example, you can get information about the current request headers, query strings, request body, content type, and much more. This class is improvised in ASP.NET Core, and a few more methods have been introduced.

In terms of security, they have introduced a new property known as authentication that returns the `AuthenticationManager` object. `AuthenticationManager` provides some methods to check whether the user is authenticated and it performs user sign-in and sign-out operations.

 You can check out the latest `AuthenticationManager` class on GitHub at https://github.com/aspnet/HttpAbstractions/blob/dev/src/Microsoft.AspNetCore.Http.Abstractions/Authentication/AuthenticationManager.cs.

Understanding the authentication and authorization process

ASP.NET Identity Core makes a vital shift in the way that authentication works with the previous versions. In earlier versions, current users of the request are of the `IPrincipal` type that can be retrieved through the `HttpContext` object, whereas with ASP.NET Core Identity, the user is of the `ClaimsPrincipal` type that implements `IPrincipal`. In previous versions, authorization was typically role-based, whereas now it's completely claims-based and known as `ClaimsIdentity`. The `ClaimsIdentity` object contains a list of claims that the user has, for example, first name, last name, e-mail address, bank account, and phone number are some of the popular claims, but there are many more. A claim is nothing but a key value pair that can be defined using the `Claim` object. Claims are used to represent the properties of the user that can be used further for authorization purposes.

The ASP.NET Core Identity system is integrated with the ASP.NET platform. You can add the `Authorize` attribute on any controller or action method and secure that based on the user, user's role, user claims, or through custom policies. This `Authorize` attribute is responsible to validate if the user is authorized to execute that controller or action method. When the user is authenticated, a cookie is set on the browser that contains the list of claims that the user has, and it can be retrieved by calling the `User.Claims` method.

Authentication

In this section, we will learn about ASP.NET Core Identity and IdentityServer4, and learn the core concepts that can be used to implement authentication in the ASP.NET Core web application.

Implementing authentication using ASP.NET Core Identity and customizing the Identity data store

In this section, we will implement ASP.NET Core Identity in an ASP.NET Core MVC application. This section will cover all the details on configuring the Identity and adding functionality to register, log in and log out, and modify the default data store to save some other information of the user and implement authorization in a simple web application that does not have a service layer in terms of a Web API.

The ASP.NET Core application can be created either through Visual Studio 2015 or a greater version, or it can also be created using the .NET CLI or Yeoman command-line tools. When creating an ASP.NET Core web application, you have a choice to select the specific service accounts:

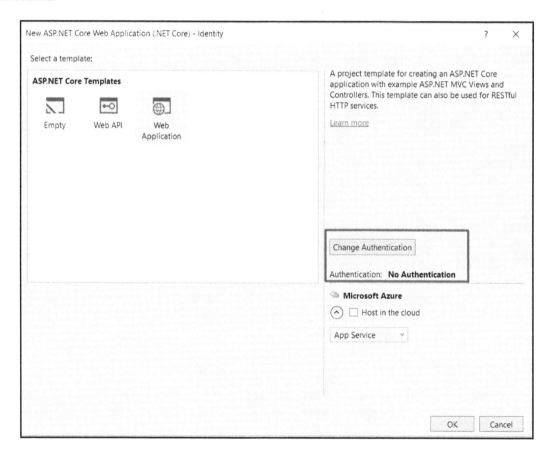

When you click on the **Change Authentication** dialog, it opens up the dialog to select the type of authentication you want to use and configure your web application, shown as follows:

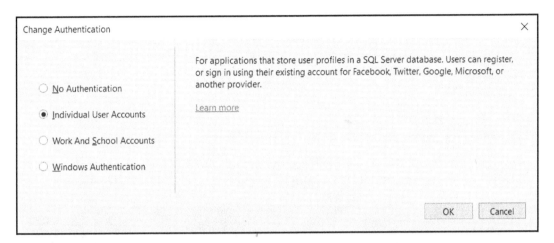

The following table shows the details of each authentication type:

Authentication Type	Description
No Authentication	If no authentication is required
Individual User Accounts	To store the user profile in a database and bring authentication to the user store and external authentication providers
Work and School Accounts	To authenticate users with Active Directory, Microsoft Azure, Active Directory, or Office 365
Windows Authentication	For intranet applications

When you select the Web Application option as a project type and select any of the preceding authentication types from individual accounts, work and school accounts, or windows authentication, Visual Studio adds some boilerplate code into your project that has all the basic configuration, as per the selected authentication type. `AccountController` is created to perform user registration, log in or log off users, and `ManageController` is created to manage logins, add phone numbers, and more.

By default, the Web application project is configured to use the `localdb` store to save user information and other information into the database, but this can be modified and the corresponding database connection string can be specified from the `appsettings.json` file, as shown in the following screenshot:

```
{
    "ConnectionStrings": {
        "DefaultConnection": "Server=(localdb)\\mssqllocaldb;Database=aspnet-Identity-5e118a64-89bb-47a4-ab69-4c9e872c4205;Trusted_Connection=True;MultipleActiveResultSets=true"
    },
    "Logging": {
        "IncludeScopes": false,
        "LogLevel": {
            "Default": "Debug",
            "System": "Information",
            "Microsoft": "Information"
        }
    }
}
```

After running your application, you will see the default website loaded and it should contain options to register and log in as a user:

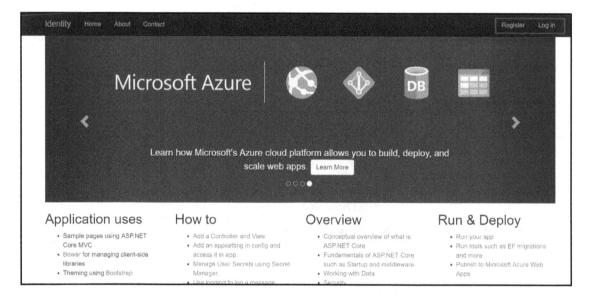

Configuring authentication using Identity in an empty web application project

To clarify our understanding, we will walk through an empty project template and learn how security can be implemented in an ASP.NET Core web application step by step.

To start with, let's create an ASP.NET Core MVC web application project. With the empty project, there is no option to select the authentication type. We will start by configuring the Entity Framework to configure data persistence, then configure ASP.NET Core Identity, and finally create controllers to perform user registration, log in, and log out.

Configuring Entity Framework Core

Let's add Entity Framework Core by adding NuGet packages. Add the following packages through the NuGet package manager console:

```
Microsoft.AspNetCore.Identity.EntityFrameworkCore
Microsoft.EntityFrameworkCore.SqlServer
Microsoft.EntityFrameworkCore.SqlServer.Design
Microsoft.EntityFrameworkCore.Design
Microsoft.EntityFrameworkCore.Tools
```

Defining data context and user classes

Once these packages are downloaded, we can create our custom `DataContext` class that will be derived from the `IdentityDbContext` class. Usually, with Entity Framework Code First model, we inherit our custom data context class from the `DbContext` class and then define `DbSet` properties of entities to create tables. With ASP.NET Core Identity, we have to inherit our custom data context class from the `IdentityDbContext` class and specify a class that inherits from `IdentityUser`. `IdentityDbContext` is the main base class provided by the ASP.NET Core Identity framework that derives from all the necessary classes required to manage roles, claims, users, tokens, and more.

Here is a screenshot of the `IdentityDbContext` class:

```
namespace Microsoft.AspNetCore.Identity.EntityFrameworkCore
{
    public abstract class IdentityDbContext<TUser, TRole, TKey, TUserClaim, TUserRole, TUserLogin, TRoleClaim, TUserToken> : DbContext
        where TUser : IdentityUser<TKey, TUserClaim, TUserRole, TUserLogin>
        where TRole : IdentityRole<TKey, TUserRole, TRoleClaim>
        where TKey : IEquatable<TKey>
        where TUserClaim : IdentityUserClaim<TKey>
        where TUserRole : IdentityUserRole<TKey>
        where TUserLogin : IdentityUserLogin<TKey>
        where TRoleClaim : IdentityRoleClaim<TKey>
        where TUserToken : IdentityUserToken<TKey>
    {
        public IdentityDbContext(DbContextOptions options);
        protected IdentityDbContext();

        public DbSet<TRoleClaim> RoleClaims { get; set; }
        public DbSet<TRole> Roles { get; set; }
        public DbSet<TUserClaim> UserClaims { get; set; }
        public DbSet<TUserLogin> UserLogins { get; set; }
        public DbSet<TUserRole> UserRoles { get; set; }
        public DbSet<TUser> Users { get; set; }
        public DbSet<TUserToken> UserTokens { get; set; }

        protected override void OnModelCreating(ModelBuilder builder);
    }
}
```

`IdentityUser` is the wrapper of the `DbContext` class that is needed by all the custom data context class to define entities. With the `IdentityDbContext` class, we can still define our custom entities and also get the Identity specific models such as `IdentityUser`, `IdentityRole`, and more, and extend them by making relationships using the Fluid API or through attributes amongst entities. We will look at extending entities later in this chapter.

Here is the code of our custom `ApplicationDbContext` class that derives from the `IdentityDbContext` base class:

```
public class ApplicationDbContext :
IdentityDbContext<ApplicationUser>
{
  public ApplicationDbContext(DbContextOptions
    <ApplicationDbContext> options) : base(options)
  {

  }
  protected override void OnModelCreating(ModelBuilder builder)
  {
      base.OnModelCreating(builder);
  }
}
```

If you notice, we are passing the `ApplicationUser` class when deriving from the `IdentityDbContext` class. This is because the `IdentityDbContext` class is specific to the `IdentityUser` class provided by the ASP.NET Core Identity framework. However, it's always better to define your custom class, which can be derived from `IdentityUser`. This way, you can customize your custom user class and add other properties as well to the default user entity. For now, we will just derive it from `IdentityUser` and specify it in the `ApplicationDbContext` class defined previously:

```
public class ApplicationUser : IdentityUser
{
    public string TwitterHandler { get; set; }
    public string LinkedInProfileLink { get; set; }

    public string SkypeAccount { get; set; }
}
```

Configuring database connection and application configuration settings

To define connection strings, add the Application Configuration file known as `appsettings.json` and specify the SQL server connection string, as follows:

```
{
  "ConnectionStrings": {
    "DefaultConnection": "Data Source=.;
    Initial Catalog=ERPDB; Integrated Security=True;"
  }
}
```

Any database server's connection can be defined if it is supported by Entity Framework.

In the `Startup` class, we can now add this `appsettings.json` file to read all the key values defined and build a dictionary object that can be used to refer the connection string. Add the following code snippet in the `Startup` constructor:

```
public Startup(IHostingEnvironment env)
{
    var builder = new ConfigurationBuilder()
        .SetBasePath(env.ContentRootPath)
        .AddJsonFile("appsettings.json",
        optional: true, reloadOnChange: true);
}
```

To resolve the `SetBasePath` and `AddJsonFile` methods, you have to add NuGet packages such as `Microsoft.Extensions.Configuration.FileExtensions` and `Microsoft.Extensions.Configuration.Json`.

The preceding code will only initialize and set the builder object to load the `appsettings.json` file. In order to access the keys, we have to call the `builder.build` method that returns `IConfigurationRoot`, which is a unified dictionary object and it can be used throughout the application to read configuration values. If multiple sources are specified in the `ConfigurationBuilder` object, all those sources, keys, and values will be combined into one dictionary object, known as `IConfigurationRoot`.

So, add this entry in the `Startup` constructor, as follows:

```
Configuration = builder.Build();
```

And add the property in the `Startup.cs`, as follows:

```
public IConfigurationRoot Configuration { get; }
```

`IHostingEnvironment` will be a dependency injected in the `Startup` constructor by the ASP.NET Core framework and it can also be used in scenarios such as if you have separate connection strings for development, staging, and production environments and you want to use the specific connection string based on the environment that your application is running on.

Configuring Entity Framework and Identity services

We can add the Entity Framework and Identity as middleware. `ConfigureServices` is the entry point where all services are added and called by runtime.

Add the following code snippet in the `ConfigureServices` method to add Entity Framework:

```
services.AddDbContext<ApplicationDbContext>(options =>
    options.UseSqlServer(Configuration.GetConnectionString(
        "DefaultConnection")));
```

Next, we can add Identity, as follows:

```
services.AddEntityFrameworkSqlServer()
    .AddDbContext<ApplicationDbContext>(options =>
        options.UseSqlServer(
        Configuration.GetConnectionString("DefaultConnection")));
    .AddDefaultTokenProviders();
```

To add the SQL Server support, we have to call the `AddEntityFrameworkSqlServer` method and then we specify the `DbContext`, which is `ApplicationDbContext`, by calling the `AddDbContext` method.

The following code will add the Identity framework into your application:

```
services.AddIdentity<ApplicationUser, IdentityRole>()
        .AddEntityFrameworkStores<ApplicationDbContext>()
        .AddDefaultTokenProviders();
```

`AddIdentity` also takes options to configure identity options. There are two built-in options provided, known as `AllowedUserNameCharacters` and `RequireUniqueEmail`.

- `AllowedUserNameCharacters`: To accept characters in a username
- `RequireUniqueEmail`: E-mail should be unique

Enabling authentication using Identity

Authentication can be enabled by calling `UseIdentity` in the pipeline through the Configure method of the `Startup` class, as follows:

```
public void Configure(IApplicationBuilder app,
IHostingEnvironment env, ILoggerFactory loggerFactory)
{
    loggerFactory.AddConsole();

    if (env.IsDevelopment())
    {
        app.UseDeveloperExceptionPage();
    }

    app.UseIdentity();

    app.Run(async (context) =>
    {
        await context.Response.WriteAsync("Hello World!");
    });
}
```

The app.UseIdentity method adds cookie-based authentication in the pipeline, which means that when the user is authenticated a cookie will be added in the browser and later used for authentication purposes. The App.UseIdentity method internally uses app.UseCookieAuthentication and sets the cookie named as Identity.Application, whereas, through the AuthenticationOptions, this can be customized. We can also use app.UseCookieAuthentication in case we need to specify all the configurations explicitly.

By now, our application will only display the Hello World! message. In an empty web application project, everything has to be configured manually, whereas with the ASP.NET Core web application project, all the boiler-plate code is added out-of-the-box to register users, authenticate users, and to perform log in and log out operations.

Creating an identity data store in SQL server

Now we can run migration through the Entity Framework command-line tooling support.

Go to the Command Prompt and navigate to the application's folder where your project file resides.

First, execute this command which creates the migration:

```
dotnet ef migrations add Initital
```

Initial is the name of the migration and once you run this command, it will create a Migrations folders and a file whose name will be ended with Initial.

 The naming of migration files is date and time followed by _ and the name of the migration.

Here is a screenshot of the **Migrations** folder created:

If you open the `*_Initial.cs` file, you will notice that it contains the Up and Down methods used to create or remove changes to and from a database.

To update the database, we will execute the following command shown in the following snippet that creates the ASP.NET Core Identity tables:

```
dotnet ef database update
```

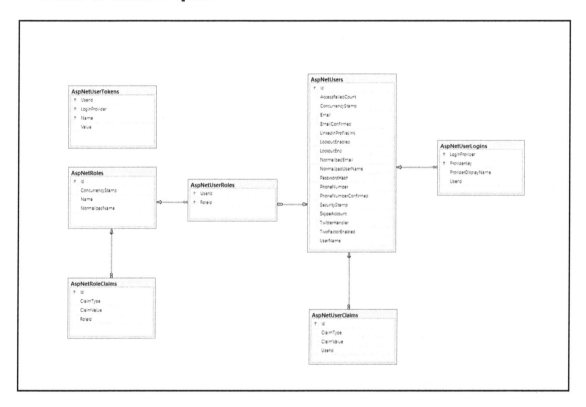

This is an out-of-the-box model provided with ASP.NET Core Identity. With this configuration, we can register users and perform login and logout operations. In a later section, we will see how to restrict access to website resources based on roles, claims, and policies.

Customizing existing Identity data store and adding new entities

ASP.NET Core Identity model uses Entity Framework Core Code First model and, because of this extension, it is quite simple. We can add new classes that represent tables and provide relationships with existing Identity tables. We can also derive new classes from existing Identity entities and add more properties, such as a LinkedIn profile, Twitter, and so on.

Here, in this section, we will add a table known as User Profile, which contains information related to an employee's designation, and add some properties, such as a Twitter and LinkedIn profile in the Identity user entity itself.

The following is the updated ApplicationUser class, which inherits from IdentityUser and contains new properties such as a Twitter handle, LinkedIn profile, and a Skype account:

```
public class ApplicationUser : IdentityUser
{
    public string TwitterHandler { get; set; }
    public string LinkedInProfileLink { get; set; }
    public string SkypeAccount { get; set; }
}
```

And here are a few more entities for designation, organization, and user profile:

```
public class UserProfile
{
    [Key]
    public long UserProfileID { get; set; }
    public bool IsActive { get; set; }
    public int DesignationID { get; set; }
    public Designation Designation { get; set; }
    public int OrganizationID { get; set; }
    public Organization Organization { get; set; }
    public DateTime EffectiveDate { get; set; }
    public int ApplicationUserId { get; set; }
    public ApplicationUser User { get; set; }
}

public class Designation
{
    [Key]
    public int DesignationID { get; set;}
    public string DesgName { get; set; }
    public string Description { get; set; }
```

```
        public bool IsActive { get; set; }
    }

    public class Organization
    {
        [Key]
        public int OrganizationID { get; set; }
        public string OrganizationName { get; set; }
        public string Address { get; set; }
        public string City { get; set; }
        public string State { get; set; }
        public string Country { get; set; }
        public string PoBoxNo { get; set; }
        public string Website { get; set; }
        public bool IsActive { get; set; }
        public List<Designation> Designations { get; set; }
    }
```

 To learn about Entity Framework Code First model, please refer to this link `http://ef.readthedocs.io/en/latest/intro.html`.

After creating these entities, we have to add the `DbSet` entries to create tables. Add this code snippet in `ApplicationDbContext`, as follows:

```
        public DbSet<Organization> Organizations { get; set; }
        public DbSet<Designation> Designations { get; set; }
        public DbSet<UserProfile> UserProfiles { get; set; }
```

Now we will add the Entity Framework migration, as done before, and that will create another `.cs` file that contains code to create tables. After running that migration, it will create the following tables:

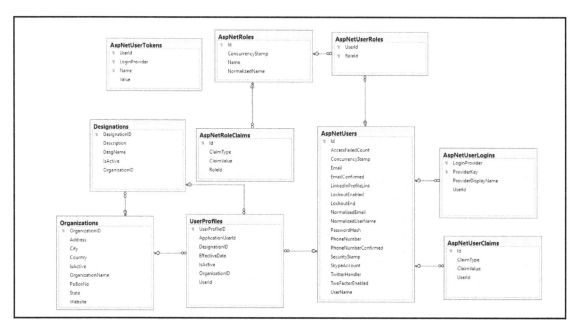

This is how we can extend the Identity tables and configure Identity.

Creating and Signing-in/Signing-out users

ASP.NET Core Identity provides two core classes, namely `UserManager` and `SignInManager`, that can be used to register users and enable user sign-in and sign-out operations. We can add an Account controller and specify them in the constructor, which then is automatically dependency injected into the controller through the parameterize controller constructor and it can be used to perform these operations.

`UserManager` and `SignInManager` both are generic types and they take the type of the class that derives from `IdentityUser` (in our case, ApplicationUser). `SignInManager` internally uses `AuthenticationManager` and wraps most of the complex parts of the authentication.

Here is the `AccountController` class, having a constructor taking two parameters:

```
using Microsoft.AspNetCore.Identity;

public class AccountController : Controller
{
    SignInManager<ApplicationUser> _signInManager;
    UserManager<ApplicationUser> _userManager;


    public AccountController(SignInManager<ApplicationUser>
    signInManager, UserManager<ApplicationUser> userManager)
    {
        _signInManager = signInManager;
        _userManager = userManager;
    }
}
```

To register a new user, we can define some methods, such as `Register`, in our `AccountController` class and call the `SignInAsync` method as follows:

```
[HttpPost]
[AllowAnonymous]
[ValidateAntiForgeryToken]
public async Task<IActionResult>
  Register(UserViewModel model)
{
  if (ModelState.IsValid)
  {
    var user = new ApplicationUser { UserName = model.Email,
      Email = model.Email,
      TwitterHandle = model.TwitterHandle,
      LinkedInProfileLink = model.LinkedInProfileLink,
      SkypeAccount= model.SkypeAccount };
    var result = await _userManager.CreateAsync(user,
    model.Password);
    if (result.Succeeded)
    {
      await _signInManager.SignInAsync(user,
        isPersistent: false);
      return RedirectToAction(
      nameof(HomeController.Index), "Home");
    }
  }
  return View(model);
}
```

In the preceding code, we have defined a `Register` method that takes `UserViewModel` as a parameter. `UserViewModel` contains all the properties needed to register a user. A user can be created by calling the `CreateAsync` method that takes the user object and password as parameters. If the user is created, we can sign-in the user by calling the `SignInManager` object that actually signs in the user and sets the authenticated cookie in the browser that can be used for authorization.

`CreateAsync` contains two overloaded signatures. One that takes a user object and a password as parameters, and another that only takes the user object as a parameter. The difference is that the one that takes the password also stores the password at the time of creation, and the other creates the user with an empty password:

```
Task<IdentityResult> CreateAsync(ApplicationUser user);

Task<IdentityResult> CreateAsync(ApplicationUser user,
    string password);
The SignInAsync method also has two overloaded methods:
Task SignInAsync(ApplicationUser user, bool isPersistent,
[string authenticationMethod = null]);

Task SignInAsync(ApplicationUser user,
Microsoft.AspNetCore.HTTP.Authentication
.AuthenticationProperties authenticationproperties ,
[string authenticationMethod = null]);
```

The following table shows description of each parameter:

Parameter	Description
`ApplicationUser`	User object that derives from `IdentityUser`
`isPersistent`	Gets or sets whether the authentication session is persisted across multiple requests
`authenticationMethod`	Name of the method used to authenticate the user
`AuthenticationProperties`	Properties applied to the login and authentication cookie

If the user is already registered, we can call the alternative method known as `PasswordSignInAsync`, as follows:

```
var result = await _signInManager.PasswordSignInAsync(
    model.Email,    model.Password,
    model.RememberMe, lockoutOnFailure: false);
```

The `PasswordSignInAsync` method also has two overloaded methods:

```
Task PasswordSignInAsync(ApplicationUser user,
    string password, bool isPersistent, bool lockoutOnFailure);
Task PasswordSignInAsync(string user,
    string password, bool isPersistent, bool lockoutOnFailture);
```

The difference between these two is obvious. One takes a user object as a first parameter and the other takes a username as a string in the first parameter.

The following table shows a description of each parameter:

Parameter	Description
`ApplicationUser`	User object that derives from `IdentityUser`
`User`	Username
`isPersistent`	Gets or sets whether the authentication session is persisted across multiple requests
`lockoutOnFailure`	To set the lockout failure value that locks the account after a specified count of retries

The `Signout` operation can be done by calling the `SignOutAsync` method of the `SignInManager` object. This clears the cookie from the browser.

Adding claims in ASP.NET Identity membership

When using Identity middleware, adding claims is not as simple as with cookie middleware. We need to create a custom claims factory class that derives from the `UserClaimsPrincipalFactory` class and overrides the `CreateAsync` method that injects the user object. When the user is signed in, these claims will automatically be added in the cookie.

To create the claims factory class, add the following code:

```
public class AppClaimsPrincipalFactory :
UserClaimsPrincipalFactory<ApplicationUser, IdentityRole>
{
    public AppClaimsPrincipalFactory(
    UserManager<ApplicationUser> userManager,
    RoleManager<IdentityRole> roleManager,
    IOptions<IdentityOptions> optionsAccessor) : base(
    userManager, roleManager, optionsAccessor)
    {
```

```
        }
    }
    public async override Task<ClaimsPrincipal>
    CreateAsync(ApplicationUser user)
    {
        var principal = await base.CreateAsync(user);
        ((ClaimsIdentity)principal.Identity).AddClaims(new[]
        {
            new Claim(ClaimTypes.GivenName,"Jason"),
            new Claim(ClaimTypes.Surname,"Scott"),
            new Claim(ClaimTypes.Role,"Manager"),
            new Claim(ClaimTypes.Role,  "Supervisor")
        });
        return principal;
    }
```

In the preceding code snippet, we have overridden the `CreateAsync` method and added four claims, such as given name, surname, and two roles. When the user is signed in, the claims will be added in the cookie.

Finally, we have to inject the claims factory instance as a scoped object through **Dependency Injection** (**DI**) in the `ConfigureServices` method of the `Startup` class. This way, when the user is signing in, it will inject our custom claims factory class, `AppClaimsPrincipalFactory`, in the Identity system and use its `CreateAsync` method to add claims:

```
services.AddScoped<IUserClaimsPrincipalFactory<ApplicationUser>,
AppClaimsPrincipalFactory>();
```

How authorization works

Authorization is done after authentication and it used to protect resources from the user that are not permissible. In ASP.NET Core, we can check and protect the user for accessing any resource by calling the `User.Identity.IsAuthentication` property that returns a Boolean value. `True` indicates that the user is authenticated.

By writing the following code in our `ManageUsers` action method in the MVC controller it will check if the user is already authenticated, otherwise returns the `ChallengeResult`, that redirects the user to the access denied page as configured in the authentication middleware:

```
public IActionResult ManageUsers()
{
    if (User.Identity.IsAuthenticated == false)
```

```
    {
      return new ChallengeResult();
    }
    return View();
  }
```

We can replace the preceding code by just adding the `Authorize` attribute as follows:

```
[Authorize]
public IActionResult ManageUsers()
{
  return View();
}
```

The Authorize attribute can be applied either at a Controller level or action method level and it also takes claims, roles, and policies to filter requests. Authorization techniques are covered later in the chapter.

Using cookie middleware without ASP.NET Core Identity

If you want to use your own data store and login controls to authenticate a user, Cookie middleware is the best choice. Cookie middleware serializes the user principal into an encrypted cookie and it uses that cookie to validate users on every request. The user principal can be retrieved by calling the `HttpContext.User` property.

Cookie middleware can be used by adding a NuGet package named `Microsoft.AspNetCore.Authentication.Cookies` and the following code snippet in the `Configure` method in the `Startup` class:

```
CookieAuthenticationOptions options = new
  CookieAuthenticationOptions();
options.AuthenticationScheme = "CookiesMiddlewareAuth";
options.LoginPath = "/Account/Login";
options.AccessDeniedPath = "/Account/AccessDenied";
options.AutomaticAuthenticate = true;
options.AutomaticChallenge = true;
app.UseCookieAuthentication(options);
```

The following table shows a description of few properties that
`CookieAuthenticationOptions` provides:

Property	Description
`AuthenticationScheme`	Name of the middleware or by which the middleware is known.
`LoginPath`	Relative path to the login page, to which the request will be redirected when an unauthenticated user accesses it.
`AccessDeniedPath`	Relative path to the page that shows that the user does not have access rights to a particular resource or page.
`AutomaticAuthenticate`	This flag indicates that on every request middleware should run and validate the request. It also reconstructs the principal it created earlier.
`AutomaticChallenge`	This flag indicates that the application should redirect the user to the login page or access denied page if the user is not authenticated.
`CookieDomain`	Determines the domain used to create the cookie.
`CookieHttpOnly`	Determines if the browser should allow the cookie to be accessed by JavaScript.
`CookiePath`	Determines the path used to create the cookie. Default value is '/' for the highest browser compatibility.
`CookieSecure`	Determines if the cookie is only allowed to be transmitted on HTTPS requests. The default setting is that, if the page using the calling sign in process is using HTTPS, it will default to HTTPS and this bit can be used in the scenario if a sign-in page, or the portions of a page, is using HTTP.
`ExpireTimeSpan`	Expiry time to which the cookie will remain valid.
`SlidingExpiration`	This can be set to `True` to instruct the middleware to issue the new cookie with a new expiry time when it reaches half way through the expiration window.

Cookies can be created by calling the `SignInAsync` method of `AuthenticationManager`.
The following is the Login (HTTP POST) method that can be called when the user logs in
through the Web application:

```
[HttpPost]
[AllowAnonymous]
[ValidateAntiForgeryToken]
public IActionResult Login(LoginViewModel model,
string returnUrl = null)
{
    var claim = new Claim[]
    {
        new Claim("sub","123456789"),
        new Claim("name","ovaismehboob"),
        new Claim("email","ovaismehboob@yahoo.com"),
        new Claim("twitter","ovaismehboob"),
        new Claim("role", "Admin"),
        new Claim("role", "User")
    };
    ClaimsIdentity claimIdentity = new ClaimsIdentity(
      claim, "CookiesAuth");
    HttpContext.Authentication.SignInAsync("CookiesAuth",
      new System.Security.Claims.ClaimsPrincipal(claimIdentity));
    return Redirect(returnUrl);
}

HttpContext.Authentication.SignInAsync(
  "CookiesMiddlewareAuth", new
  System.Security.Claims.ClaimsPrincipal(claimIdentity));
```

The first parameter takes the authentication scheme that uses the cookie middleware setup
on the `Configure` method and it uses that for authentication. Claims can be defined by
initializing a new `Claim` instance and specifying the key values pair, which can be added to
the claim array as shown previously.

`SignInAsync` uses the claims passed through the claims identity and sets the cookie.
Claims can be retrieved by calling `User.Claims`, as follows:

```
<dl>
    @foreach (var claim in User.Claims)
    {
        <dt>@claim.Type</dt>
        <dt>@claim.v</dt>
    }
</dl>
```

A sign-out operation, on the other hand, can remove the cookie from the browser and sign out the user. A signing-out operation can be done by writing the following code:

```
HttpContext.Authentication.SignOutAsync("CookiesMiddlewareAuth");
```

This method also takes the authentication scheme. So, if multiple middleware are set up, you can sign out the user for a specific authentication scheme, which clears up the cookie from the browser.

Claims transformation

Every cookie has an expiry time and the default cookie expiration time in ASP.NET Identity Core is 30 minutes, which is configurable. Claims transformation is a valuable feature that allows developers to add or update claims on every request. For example, if at a particular time we don't want a user to access a resource. We can add a piece of information through claims transformation and validate it through the `Authorize` attribute in our MVC or Web API controller or action level.

Let's go through an example in which we will add the `AllowSecure` claim that will be validated when the user accesses the `AdminController`. The claims transformation has to be added in the HTTP pipeline in the `Startup` class. Add the following code in the Configure method of the `Startup` class:

```
bool isAllowed = GetUserAllowedBit();
if (isAllowed)
{
    app.UseClaimsTransformation(user =>
    {
        user.Context.User.Identities.First().AddClaim(new
        Claim("AllowSecure", System.DateTime.Now.ToString()));
        return Task.FromResult(user.Principal);
    });
}else
{
    app.UseClaimsTransformation(user =>
    {
        if (user.Context.User.Identities.First()
        .FindFirst("AllowSecure") != null)
        {
            user.Context.User.Identities.First()
            .RemoveClaim(new Claim("AllowSecure",
                System.DateTime.Now.ToString()));
        }
        return Task.FromResult(user.Principal);
```

```
        });
    }
```

In the preceding code, we have called our custom `GetUserAllowedBit` method that returns the Boolean value if the user is allowed or not. If the user is allowed, the claim will be added through the claims transformation; otherwise it will be removed from the user's claims.

Before annotating our Controller with the `Authorize` attribute, we will set up the policy and specify `AllowSecure` claim to be required for any user accessing that resource which is protected with this policy.

To understand the policy, please refer to the following authorization techniques. The following code will register the policy in the pipeline:

```
services.AddAuthorization(options =>
{
    options.AddPolicy("SecureAccess", policy =>
        policy.RequireClaim("AllowSecure"));
});
```

Our `AdminController` can be protected by just adding the `Authorize` attribute and reading this claim, as follows:

```
[Authorize(Policy ="SecureAccess")]
public class AdminController : Controller
{
}
```

Cookie middleware events

Cookie middleware provides various events that can be overridden by defining the method name through `CookieAuthenticationOptions`. This is beneficial in terms if you need to add your own logic of setting up a browser cookie or clearing up a browser cookie, validating a cookie, and more.

The following are the events provided in the `CookieAuthenticationOptions`:

Event	Description
`RedirectToAccessDenied`	When an access denied causes a redirect in the cookie middleware.
`RedirectToLoginIn`	When a sign in causes a redirect in the cookie middleware.
`RedirectToLogout`	When a sign out causes a redirect in the cookie middleware.
`RedirectToReturnUrl`	When redirecting to a return URL.
`SignedIn`	When a cookie is created and a user is signed in.
`SigningIn`	When a cookie is created. Claims can be modified and added by overriding this method.
`SigningOut`	To do specific operations during a sign-out operation. For example, clearing up the session and so on.
`ValidatePrincipal`	Called each time when the request is validated. This can be used to verify the user from a database or external source based on the claims. For example, a cookie once set remains in the browser until a user signs out or the cookie expires. This can be used in conditions if we need to verify the user permissions for a specific page and navigate to the access denied page if that permission is not assigned.

Events can be specified as follows, where options are the instance of `CookieAuthenticationEvents`:

```
options.Events = new Microsoft.AspNetCore.Authentication.
Cookies.CookieAuthenticationEvents
{
    OnValidatePrincipal = CookieEvents
    .ValidateUserPermissions
};
```

`CookieEvents` is a custom class that contains a static method named `ValidateUserPermissions`, which can be specified through the `OnValidatePrincipal` property.

Here is the code of the `CookieEvents` class:

```
public class CookieEvents
{
    public static async Task ValidateUserPermissions(
        CookieValidatePrincipalContext context)
```

```
    {
        bool pathExist = CheckIfPageExist(
          context.HttpContext.Request.Path.Value,
            context.HttpContext.User.Claims);
        if (!pathExist)
        {
            context.HttpContext.Response.Redirect(
              "/Account/AccessDenied");
        }

    }
  }
```

Once the user is authenticated and the cookie is set, this method will be called every time when the request is made. In the preceding code we are passing the request path to the `CheckIfPageExist` method that checks if the user has an access to a particular resource and redirects it to the access denied page on a deny case. There are various other scenarios in which this can be overridden, such as if you want to check if the user is still active in the system and sign out in case a user is deactivated.

Implementing external authentication in ASP.NET Core applications

Many applications these days have implemented external authentication on their websites. This enables users to use their existing login credentials of Twitter, Facebook, Hotmail, or any other and register on a website. This type of authentication provides several benefits to the user registering on a website. It facilitates users to use their existing credentials and avoid themselves from going through a lengthy registration process and remembering the credentials they have created.

ASP.NET Core provides a very easy and quick solution to configure external authentication using OAuth 2.0.

OAuth architecture and basic components are explained in the following section:

Configuring external authentication in ASP.NET Core

In this section, we will implement external authentication with a Facebook authentication provider.

Creating a web application project

We can start by creating a web application ASP.NET Core project and selecting individual accounts as the authentication mode. This option actually creates the application project containing all the boilerplate code available to start using authentication using ASP.NET Core Identity.

Configuring apps on Facebook

To use of OAuth provider, we have to create an application first to obtain the client ID and client secret keys. We can then use these keys to authenticate our ASP.NET application by adding a middleware and specify them as discussed in the section as follows. Here are the steps to register a new application on Facebook:

1. Create an app by navigating to `http://developers.facebook.com/apps` and log in with your user registered Facebook ID.
2. Click on the **Add a new App** option and select **Website (WWW)**.
3. Specify your app name and click on **Create New Facebook App ID**.
4. Specify **display name**, **category**, and **Contact Email** and click on **Create App ID**.
5. Once the application is created, you have to go through some tabs to specify basic information.
6. Specify your website URL and proceed:

7. Go to your account settings and copy the App ID and App Secret that can be used for authorization:

To authenticate with Facebook or any other external provider, we need to provide the Application ID and secret key for authorization of our application. ASP.NET Core.

Enabling Facebook middleware

ASP.NET Core comes up with some out-of-the-box external authentication middleware to authenticate users from Facebook, Twitter, Microsoft account, and Google. To implement Facebook authentication, we have to add a NuGet package--
MicrosoftAspNetCore.Authentication.Facebook

Then, add the following code snippet to the Configure method of the Startup class:

```
app.UseFacebookAuthentication(new FacebookOptions()
{
    AppId = Configuration["your_app_id"],
      AppSecret = Configuration["your_app_secret"]
});
```

In the preceding code snippet, we are setting the Facebook App ID and Facebook Secret Key using the `FacebookOptions` object.

Now, when you run your application, it will show the Facebook button, as shown in the following screenshot:

Clicking on the **Facebook** button will get the authentication code from Facebook and render the Facebook authentication page where a user can specify the login credentials and proceed.

It will ask you to allow to access the profile information and on allowing, redirects to the website. Finally, it prompts you to complete the registration:

On clicking on **Register**, it will create the user in the ASP.NET Identity database. For Identity user you can specify any other username as well and use that credential to log in next time with local Identity authentication.

Two-factor authentication

Two-factor authentication, also known as 2FA, provides two-step verification of the user authentication in the system. Usually, with one-step authentication, we require the user to specify the username and password. With this type of authentication mechanism, instead of only asking the username and password, we require another piece of information, which is particular to that user only for authentication. For example, we can implement two-factor authentication on a website that requires the user to specify the username and password at the first step and then send a code through an SMS which will be used to authenticate the user at the second step.

In this section, we will show how to implement two-factor authentication using SMS.

Setting up an SMS account

The ASP.NET Core web application project templates provide a boilerplate of all the authentication mechanisms that you wanted to implement, which is provided in ASP.NET. It's a good choice to use the Web application project template and tweak based on your requirement.

`AuthMessageSender` is the main class that implements the interfaces, `IEmailSender` and `ISMSSender`, used to send SMS and e-mail. Specify the following code in the `SendSMSAsync` method that uses the Twilio API:

```
string AccountSid = "AC5ef872f6da5a21de157d80997a64bd33";
    string AuthToken = "[AuthToken]";
    var twilio = new TwilioRestClient(AccountSid, AuthToken);
    return Task.FromResult(0);
```

Enabling two-factor authentication

Two-factor authentication can be enabled in an ASP.NET Core web application by uncommenting the following code that comes with the ASP.NET Core web application project template. You can use the same or equivalent logic when working with an empty project template. To store your phone number where the application will send the code to perform the second step of authentication can be done by uncommenting the following code snippet from the Index view page of `ManageController`.

Here is the code of `Manage/Index.cshtml`:

```
@(Model.PhoneNumber ?? "None")
@if (Model.PhoneNumber != null)
{
    <br />
    <a asp-controller="Manage"
    asp-action="AddPhoneNumber"
    class="btn-bracketed">Change</a>
    <form asp-controller="Manage"
      asp-action="RemovePhoneNumber"
      method="post"> [<button type="submit"
      class="btn-link">Remove</button>]
    </form>
}
else
{
    <a asp-controller="Manage"
      asp-action="AddPhoneNumber"
      class="btn-bracketed">Add</a>
}
```

Enable Two-factor authentication by uncommenting the following code:

```
@if (Model.TwoFactor)
{
    <form asp-controller="Manage"
      asp-action="DisableTwoFactorAuthentication"
      method="post" class="form-horizontal">
      Enabled <button type="submit" class="btn-link
        btn-bracketed">Disable</button>
    </form>
}
else
{
    <form asp-controller="Manage"
      asp-action="EnableTwoFactorAuthentication"
      method="post" class="form-horizontal">
      <button type="submit" class="btn-link
      btn-bracketed">Enable</button> Disabled
    </form>
}
```

Once the user is registered, you can go to the user settings and enable **Two-Factor Authentication** and specify the mobile number where the SMS code will be sent, as shown in the following screenshot:

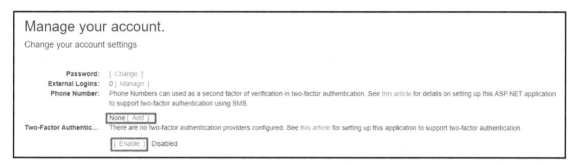

When you add the phone number and submit, it will send you the code over SMS, which should be specified in the next screen to verify it:

Specify the code you receive and click on **Submit**. Once the code is verified, it will be redirected to the account settings page and show the number added, as follows:

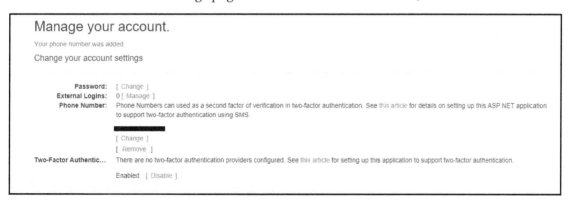

Now, when you try to log in again, it will ask you to select the **Two-Factor Authentication Provider**. As in the previous example, we have only enabled 2FA with Phone so we can select that and submit.

Security in an enterprise

In the preceding sections, we learnt about different authentication providers to authenticate users and manage them using Identity membership provider. Enterprise applications, however, consist of various APIs and those APIs should be protected so only authenticated users can access them. OAuth is widely used to protect APIs or resources deployed on a server and it provides them with a uniform interface by accepting an access token from consumers and based on its validity, returns a response. OAuth is not good for authentication as anybody having the same access token can access resources. To overcome this scenario, **OpenID Connect** (**OIDC**) is introduced, which adds an extension to OAuth and makes it more secure. IdentityServer4 provides the middleware to implement these scenarios in an easy and straightforward way, which we will discuss next.

Getting started with IdentityServer4

IdentityServer4 is the framework and hostable component that was created by the developers at Thinktecture, but now it is the recommended approach by Microsoft for providing single sign-on, federation gateway, and access control features to modern web applications and APIs using OpenID Connect and OAuth 2.0 protocols. It is highly optimized to address the security problems and provide certain APIs to implement your own STS (Secure Token Service) provider that generates access tokens for your client and the resource owners who wanted to access resource servers. It is a successor of IdentityServer3 and is completely developed on top of .NET Core. Moreover, it is also part of .NET foundation, and you can learn more about this at `https://identityserver.github.io`.

With IdentityServer4, we can implement the following features:

Feature	Description
Authentication as a Service (AaaS)	Centralized authentication service to which all applications can authenticate
Single Sign-in/Sign-out	Single sign-in and sign-out feature that can span to multiple applications
Access control for APIs	Issue Access Token to various consumers to consume Web APIs, which includes servers to server communication, web applications, native mobile apps, and desktop applications
Federation Gateway	Provides external authentication providers such as Facebook, Google, Microsoft, Twitter, Azure AD (Active Directory), and many more

Apart from the preceding features, we can also customize IdentityServer4 based on our needs.

Understanding OAuth

In a typical scenario of a web application, a user navigates to the website, specifies the username and password, which is then verified by the website by comparing the username and password stored in a database. Once the user is authenticated, a cookie is stored in the browser, which can be used for subsequent requests to access protected resources.

In the modern application scenario, applications consist of several services (Web APIs) and the number of consumers also varies. Moreover, many applications don't have their own authentication provider and they use an external authentication provider such as Google, Facebook, and Microsoft to authenticate users. In this case the typical identity scenario would not work.

OAuth is an open authorization standard that provides a key known as a token to access particular resources on websites. Tokens can be achieved by sharing a secret, which could be a user password or an application ID, and the user can use that token to gain access to resources (Web APIs) without revealing their secrets.

To elaborate, let's take an example of a hotel where a person needs a key to access a particular room. That key is actually an access token in the OAuth world and it can be used to access limited areas such as fitness clubs, rooms, and pool areas, whereas the other sensitive areas are still not accessible:

 An access token is just like a door key where any person having the key can enter into the room without providing any sensitive information, such as a username or password.

OAuth provides an access token that can be used to access the protected resources (Web APIs) of any application.

Actors in OAuth

OAuth contains the following actors:

Actors	Description
Resource Owner	End user who accesses the resource hosted on the resource server
Client	A web application or a mobile application that is authorized to access the resource on behalf of the resource owner
Authorization Server	Authorization server where the client application is registered and returns the access token
Resource Server	Web API or web service that provides access to the data
User Agent	Browser or any device that runs the application

Following is the logical representation of OAuth flow:

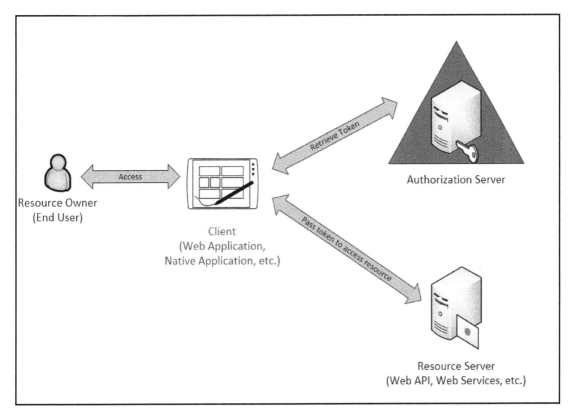

The resource owner is the end user who wanted to access the resource (API) from the resource server. Resources hosted inside the resource server are protected resources and the resource server needs an access token from the client accessing the resources. Client responsibility is to pass the access token on every request when accessing the resource where the access token can be retrieved from an authorization server.

 There are two types of clients; confidential clients and public clients. A web application is an example of a confidential client that maintains the client ID and client secret on the server. Whereas public clients are native mobile applications that install on each device, or a user agent-based application that uses JavaScript to access resources and stores client ID, and client secrets in the JavaScript itself.

Flows of OAuth 2.0

OAuth 2.0 provides four types of flows:

- Client credentials
- Implicit
- Authorization code
- Resource owner password credentials

Client credentials flow

This type of flow is used for server-to-server communication. It does not require any user interaction and only requires the client credentials such as client ID and client secret to get the access token:

1. Client sends the client credentials, namely client ID and client secret, to the authorization server.
2. Authorization verifies and returns the access token.
3. Client then passes the access token to the resource server to access the API.

Client credentials should not be used with the JavaScript or native mobile applications as, with these, both the client ID and client secret residing on the client side itself can easily be forged. In server-to-server communication, we can store the client ID and client secret on some safe storage and they can only be accessible by the application running on the server.

Implicit flow

Unlike client credentials flow, which is only recommended to be used in server-to-server communication, implicit flow is a highly secured flow that can be used for public clients. Implicit flow does not provide client authentication, as public clients cannot store the client ID and client secret on the public client itself:

1. Process starts when the client (for example, MVC app) redirects the resource owner's user agent (browser) to the authorization endpoint.
2. The client passes its client credentials (client ID and secret), scope, state, and redirection URI to the authorization server.
3. If the client is authorized, the authorization server will ask the resource owner to enter the resource owner credentials.

4. Authorization authenticates the resource owner via the user agent and establishes whether the resource owner grants or denies access to the client.

5. If the resource owner grants the permission to the client, the authorization server redirects the user back to the client through the redirection URI provided earlier and passes the access token in a URI fragment.

6. The user agent then makes the request to the web-hosted client resource without passing the fragment information.

7. Once the request is received by the web-hosted client resource, it will return the web page, typically an HTML document containing an embedded JavaScript that runs on the user agent, to extract the access token from the URI fragment.

8. Once the access token is extracted, it can be used for subsequent requests.

With this type of flow, the token is known by the user agent and the user agent can pass the token directly to the resource server to access the resource.

Authorization code flow

Authorization code flow is optimized for confidential clients, but it can be used for public clients as well. It is used to obtain access tokens and refresh tokens:

1. The process starts when the client (for example, the MVC app) redirects the user agent (browser) to the authorization server.

2. The client passes its client credentials (client ID and secret), scope, state, and redirection URI to the authorization server.

3. If the client is authorized, the authorization server will ask the resource owner to enter the resource owner credentials.

4. The authorization server takes the resource owner credentials and authenticates it.

5. If the resource owner is authenticated, the authorization server asks to either grant or deny permissions access to the client.

6. If the resource owner grants the permission to the client, the authorization server redirects the user back to the client through the redirection URI provided earlier.

7. The user agent then passes the authorization code followed with the redirection URI to retrieve the access token.

8. If the authorization server verifies the authorization code, it will return the access token to the redirection URI provided earlier.

9. This access token can be used by the application to authorize users on every subsequent request.

With this type of flow, access tokens are not known by the user agent and are only used by the client application. The user agent passes the authorization code to the client and the client uses the access token to access the resource server.

Resource owner password credentials flow

In resource owner password credentials flow, the client authenticates the user by taking the resource owner's username and password through a login interface. It can be used for both access tokens, and refresh tokens and it involves client authentication:

1. Resource owner enters the username and password in the client's app login screen.
2. Username and password are passed to the authorization server to authenticate the user.
3. If the user is authenticated, the authorization server returns the access token.
4. This access token can be used by the client to access authorized resources.

This type of flow is not recommended to be used for non-trusted sites, as user credentials are exposed to the client application.

Understanding OpenID Connect

OpenID Connect is a layer on top of OAuth introduced in 2015. The success of OpenID Connect is that it returns the simple **JSON-based identity tokens (JWT)** {pronounced as Jawt} signed by the **OpenID provider (OP)** through OAuth protocol to suit web, mobile, and browser-based applications. In comparison to OAuth, Open ID Connect actually tells about the user's identity information and instead of getting the access details, it tells exactly about the user accessing a resource. Consider the following diagram:

We can relate an Identity token to a driving license that contains driver information such as license number, license expiry, first name, last name, type of vehicle permitted, and so on.

The Identity token is encoded into the base 64 URL-safe string that contains information such as subject (sub), issuing authority (iss), audience (aud), and more. It may also contain some extra information about the user or custom claims in a set of scopes.

When the user is authenticated, the Identity token is returned to the client application in a secure manner and it can be used to retrieve the access token. The authorization server reads this identity token and verifies whether the user is valid to access the authorized resource and generate the access token.

Here is the sample JWT token representation:

```
{
    "typ": "JWT",
    "alg": "H5256"
},
    {
        "sub": "5c610ea3-2e19-4f1a-9c42-19f03539bad7",
        "aud":"ea",
        "iss":"https://ea/identity",
        "exp": 1554422985,
        "auth_time": 1554422985
        "given_name":"John",
        "family_Name":"Scott",
        "scope":["read","write"]

    }
```

It is not a good practice to store all the user claim information in the Identity Token, as it increases its size. The best way is to store some primary information of the user and use the access token to get the user info from a database by calling a protected Web API and passing the access token to access it.

You can learn more about OpenID Connect specification at `http://openid.net/specs/ope nid-connect-core-1_0.html`.

OpenID Connect flows

OpenID Connect provides three types of flows:

- Authorization code
- Implicit
- Hybrid

Authorization code flow

This is an extension of the authorization code flow, as shown previously in the OAuth 2.0 section. It is commonly used with web applications and native mobile applications. In this flow, the request is made to the **OP (OpenID provider)** to authenticate users and user consent, and client request the Identity token from the backend channel. With this type of flow, tokens are not exposed to the browser.

Implicit flow

This is highly used with JavaScript-based applications that do not have any server-side processing for communicating to the resources. In this flow, the Identity token is directly returned to the client from the OP.

Hybrid flow

This is the combination of authorization code and implicit flow, in which both frontend and server-side portions can access the Identity token from the OP.

Claims and scopes

Claims represent a single piece of user information, for example, `given_name` and `family_name` can be represented as user claims, whereas scopes are the collection of claims that represent a single piece of information.

There are two types of scopes, namely Identity scopes and Resource scopes.

- **Identity scopes**: Identity scopes represent the claims related to identity.

  For example, identity scopes can contain the set of claims that represents user basic information:

- **User scopes**: It may contain claims such as: given_name, family_name, first_name, middle_name, last_name, birthdate, gender
- **Phone scopes**: It may contain claims such as: phone_number, phone_number_verified
- **Resource scopes**: Resource scopes are related to the Web APIs, for example, a scope named subscription can represent the Subscription API that may contain methods such as `SubscribeUser, UnSubscribeUser,` and so on.

Endpoints

IdentityServer4 provides five types of endpoints to retrieve tokens.

Discovery endpoint

Used to retrieve metadata about IdentityServer, such as issuer name, supported scopes, key material, and so on.

Authorize endpoint

Used to retrieve tokens or authorization code via a browser and it involves user authentication.

Token endpoint

Used to request an access token by passing the client ID and secret.

UserInfo endpoint

Used to retrieve the user's identity information. It requires the valid access token and returns the user claims.

To learn more about endpoints, please refer to `http://docs.identityserver.io/`.

Developing a Centralized Authorization System using IdentityServer4

An enterprise consists of various applications that are running to serve specific needs. For example, there are web applications to which users interact with directly, Web APIs to which web applications, native mobile applications, desktop applications, or some server level applications communicate to access data, and so on. Security plays an important role to protect resources. One option is to implement security for each application and use simple Identity to authenticate users. With enterprise scenarios, keeping authentication separate to each application is a tedious process and centralizing it brings more benefits. Here, IdentityServer4 can be used to implement a Centralized Authentication System using OpenID Connect protocol:

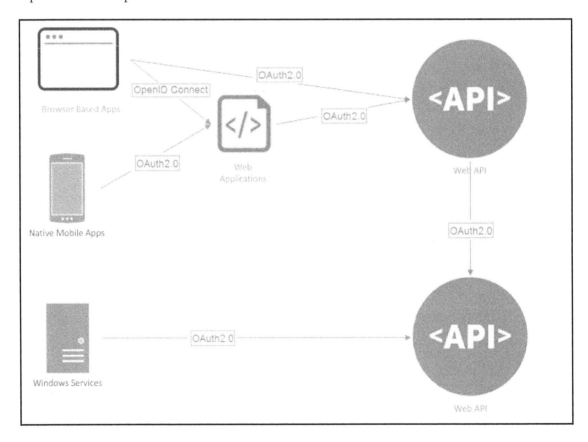

The preceding diagram shows various applications in an enterprise. There are Web APIs used by web applications and browser-based applications using JavaScript, native mobile applications, and Windows services that are using the Web API to access particular data, and so on.

Creating a Centralized Authentication Service/Authorization Server

To develop a Centralized Authentication Service, we will create an ASP.NET Core project. You can either create an empty project where you have to do everything from scratch or select the Web Application project that provides all the boilerplate code available, which can be further modified based on your requirement. The Web Application project also adds some extra code that you may not need in your particular business scenario. Therefore, choose the right project that suits your needs. We will go with the empty project.

Setting up IdentityServer4

Once the project is created, add the IdentityServer4 package in your authorization server through NuGet:

In the `ConfigureServices` method of the Startup class, we have to first add the Identity Server by calling the `AddIdentityServer` method as follows:

```
public void ConfigureServices(IServiceCollection services)
{
    services.AddIdentityServer();
}
```

Next, we will use the Identity Server by calling the `UseIdentityServer` method in the `Configure` method in the Startup class as follows:

```
public void Configure(IApplicationBuilder app,
  IHostingEnvironment env, ILoggerFactory loggerFactory)
{
    app.UseIdentityServer();
}
```

Defining scopes, clients and users

We can define a new class in the same project and name it `Config` class, and create test users, scopes, and clients to test our flow.

Scopes are the collection of claims and are mandatory to be defined, so the claims can be sent out in the response from authorization servers as part of a token. Claims are heavily used when dealing with the authorization scenario.

Scopes are modelled as resources and divided into two types, namely Identity and API. Identity scopes represent any claim, such as role, name, email, or custom claim values, whereas API scopes are used to access the protected resources, particularly APIs.

Identity scopes can be defined as follows in the `Config` class:

```
public static IEnumerable<IdentityResource> GetIdentityScopes()
{
    return new List<IdentityResource>
    {
        new IdentityResources.OpenId(),
        new IdentityResources.Profile(),
        new IdentityResources.Email(),
        new IdentityResource {
            Name = "role",
        }
    };
}
```

Whereas the API scopes can be defined as follows:

```
public static IEnumerable<ApiResource> GetApiScopes()
{
    return new List<ApiResource>
    {
        new ApiResource {
            Name = "vendorManagementAPI",
            DisplayName = "Vendor API",
            Description = "Vendor API scope",
        }
    };
}
```

Next, we will define the clients. When setting up the authorization server, we need to specify the clients so that the authorization can register them and return them the token on successful authentication. Once the client is defined, the client can communicate to the authorization and do the authentication and request tokens.

Here is the code snippet to define the client:

```
public static IEnumerable<Client> GetClients()
{
    return new List<Client>
    {
        new Client
        {
            ClientId = "client",
            ClientName ="MVC Client",
            AllowedGrantTypes= GrantTypes.Implicit,
            RedirectUris = {
                "http://localhost:5002/signin-oidc" },
            PostLogoutRedirectUris= {"http://localhost:5002"},
            Enabled=true,
            AccessTokenType=  AccessTokenType.Jwt,
            AllowedScopes =new List<string>
            {
                StandardScopes.OpenId,
                StandardScopes.Profile,
                StandardScopes.Email,
                StandardScopes.OfflineAccess,
                "role"
            },
        }
    };
}
```

`ClientID` is the unique ID of the client, whereas `ClientSecrets` are credentials to access the token endpoint. `AllowedScopes` are used to enroll the scopes eligible for the client. If the particular scope is not defined for the client's allowed scopes, the claims associated with that scope will not be enlisted as part of the token returned by the authorization server.

Lastly, we will define users. To understand the concepts, we will take a simple example and use test users that contain some hard-coded values.

To add the users, add the `GetUsers` method as follows:

```
public static List<TestUser> GetUsers()
{
    return new List<TestUser>
    {
        new TestUser
        {
            SubjectId = "1",
            Username = "scott",
            Password = "password",
```

```
                    Claims = new List<Claim>
                    {
                        new Claim("name", "scott"),
                        new Claim("given_name","scott edward"),
                        new Claim("family_name", "edward"),
                        new Claim("website", "www.scottdeveloper.com"),
                        new Claim("email", "scott@mailxyz.com"),
                        new Claim("role","admin"),

                    },
                },
                new TestUser
                {
                    SubjectId = "2",
                    Username = "richard",
                    Password = "password",
                    Claims = new List<Claim> {
                        new Claim("role","user")
                    }

                }
            };
        }
```

In the preceding code, we added two test users with claims. The user will be authenticated by the authorization server through the username and password specified, and the claims defined for each user will become part of the token if they are part of the allowed scopes.

Finally, we will modify the `AddIdentityServer` and add Scopes (Identity resources and API resources), Clients, and Users as follows:

```
services.AddIdentityServer()
    .AddInMemoryIdentityResources(Config.GetIdentityScopes())
    .AddInMemoryApiResources(Config.GetApiScopes())
    .AddInMemoryClients(Config.GetClients());
    .AddTestUsers(Config.GetUsers())
    .SetTemporarySigningCredential();
```

The default port to run the web application using `dotnet run` is 5000, and this can also be configured by calling UseUrls when defining the `WebHostBuilder` instance in your main `Program` class.

You can either run the application using the IISExpress option or through the .NET CLI command (`dotnet run`). For this section, we will run the authorization server through the `dotnet run` command. You can execute the following command to run the server:

```
dotnet run
```

Make sure to execute this command on the path where your project file resides.

Once the server is started, navigate to `http://localhost:5000/.well-known/openid-configuration` and you will see the discovery document.

Adding UI to enable authentication using OpenID Connect

Next, we will add UI so that users can enter their username and password to authenticate on Centralized Authentication Servers. IdentityServer4 provides complete support to use OpenID Connect protocol and it also provides a sample UI that contains MVC controllers, views, and boilerplate code to quick-start implement the authentication scenario.

In this section, we will use the quick-start UI repository and this can be further customized based on your requirement. The files can be downloaded from `https://github.com/IdentityServer/IdentityServer4.Quickstart.UI` or you can also run the PowerShell command. You can run the following command from the CAS application path:

```
iex ((New-Object
System.Net.WebClient).DownloadString('https://raw.githubusercontent.com/IdentityServer/IdentityServer4.Quickstart.UI/release/get.ps1'))
```

Once the files are downloaded, add the MVC and `StaticFiles` middleware in the `Startup` class as follows:

```
        app.UseStaticFiles();
        app.UseMvcWithDefaultRoute();
```

Now, run the authorization server and access `http://localhost:5000`.

The following page will be displayed:

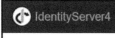

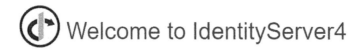

IdentityServer publishes a discovery document where you can find metadata and links to all the endpoints, key material, etc.

Here are links to the source code repository, and ready to use samples.

Creating an MVC web application project

In this section, we will create a simple MVC web application project that uses the authorization server to authenticate users and protect some action methods on controllers to see how authorization works. You can create an empty web application project and enable MVC by calling `AddMvc` in the `ConfigureServices` method and `UseMvcDefaultRoute` in the Configure method in the `Startup` class.

Adding OIDC and cookie middleware in HTTP pipeline

To use OpenID Connect Provider (OP), we need to add the middleware to our application's HTTP pipeline, so that unauthorized requests can be forwarded to the authorization server for user authentication.

Add cookie middleware and OIDC middleware as follows:

```
app.UseCookieAuthentication(new CookieAuthenticationOptions
{
    AuthenticationScheme = "Cookies"
});

app.UseOpenIdConnectAuthentication(
  new OpenIdConnectOptions
  {
      AuthenticationScheme = "oidc",
      ClientId = "client",
      Authority = "http://localhost:5000",
      RequireHttpsMetadata = false,
      SignInScheme = "Cookies",
      Scope = {"openid", "profile", "roles" },
      SaveTokens = true
  });
```

Both the middlewares should be added before the MVC middleware.

OpenID Connect contains some properties, such as `AuthentitcationScheme`, which represent the name of the middleware and `clientId` to represent the ID of the client, and it has to be matched with the one defined in the authorization server. The authority that represents the authorization server `URL`, `SignInScheme` holds the authentication scheme of the local middleware used to store the token once returned from the authorization server. In our case, it's cookie middleware. Scope is the important part that represents what scopes are allowed or contained in the token. In our case, we have defined `openid`, profile, and roles, which means the client ID, name, website and role, and others will be available in the token. For example, if we only specify the `openid` and profile, the roles will not be contained in the token and if you have used roles to authorize controllers or the action method that will not work, it will navigate you to the access denied page on authorization. Setting `SaveTokens` to `True` actually saves the tokens in the cookie. Tokens are stored inside the properties section of the cookie.

The easiest way to access them is through the extension methods as follows:

```
<p>
  @await ViewContext.HttpContext.Authentication
  .GetTokenAsync("access_token")
</p>
```

```
Or for Refresh token call this

<p>
  @await ViewContext.HttpContext.Authentication
  .GetTokenAsync("access_token")
</p>
```

To study more about what claims are part of each scope, please go through this link `https ://openid.net/specs/openid-connect-core-1_0.html#ScopeClaims`.

Enabling MVC and controller

Enable MVC in your MVC web application project, as done in the authorization server project and add Home controller. Here is the code of `HomeController`:

```
[Authorize]
  public IActionResult Index()
  {
    return View();
  }
```

Configure MVC web application on port `5002`.

You can configure the MVC web application on port `5002` by updating the `launchsettings.json` file and adding the `UseUri` in the `WebHostBuilder` object in the `Program` class.

Update the port to `5002` in the following entry:

```
"WebApp": {
  "commandName": "Project",
  "launchBrowser": true,
  "launchUrl": "http://localhost:5002",
  "environmentVariables": {
    "ASPNETCORE_ENVIRONMENT": "Development"
  }
}
```

Here is the code of the `Program` class:

```
public static void Main(string[] args)
{
    var host = new WebHostBuilder()
        .UseKestrel()
        .UseContentRoot(Directory.GetCurrentDirectory())
        .UseIISIntegration()
```

```
        .UseUrls("http://localhost:5002")
        .UseStartup<Startup>()
        .Build();

    host.Run();
    }
  }
}
```

Now build and run your web application through `dotnet run`. Once both the authorization server and MVC web application have started, and when you navigate to the MVC app at `http://localhost:5002`, you will be redirected to the authorization server login page:

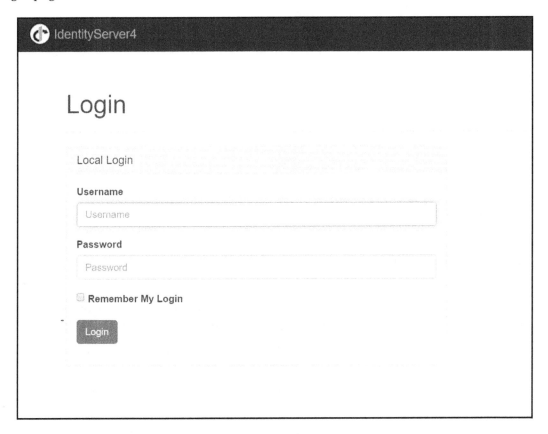

Log in with any of the users specified previously in the authorization server implementation and the authorization will show the consent screen, which confirms if the user allows the client application to access its scope claims:

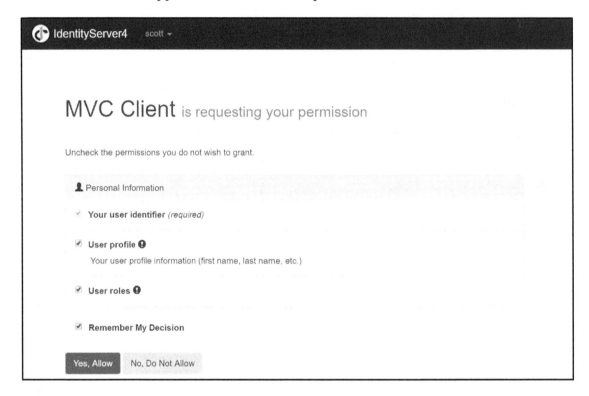

If you allow, it will send the token back to the MVC web application and the cookie middleware will store that in the browser's cookie store.

Now, let's modify our `HomeController` and add another method that we want to be accessible by the user having an admin role. Add the `ManageSite` method and its corresponding view in your MVC web application project:

```
[Authorize(Roles = "admin")]
    public IActionResult ManageSite()
    {
        return View();
    }
```

Now, if you run and access with `scott`, the page will be accessible. However, the other user `richard` does not have any admin role assigned, and in this case it will be redirected to the access denied page.

Adding a Web API

In the previous section, we implemented CAS and added an MVC web application. We used the implicit flow that returns the token to the client through the browser, which can be used by the client for further subsequent requests. However, APIs exposing the tokens over a browser channel is not a recommended approach, and there should be a mechanism that uses the client ID and secret to retrieve the access token and then use it to invoke secure methods.

IdentityServer4 introduces a new flow called Hybrid Flow, which is a combination of both OpenID and OAuth2.0 protocols. In this flow, the Identity token is transmitted via the browser channel on successful user authentication, whereas the access token is retrieved by the client through a backend channel.

In this section, we will modify the authorization server's grant type to `HybridAndClientCredentials` and add the client secret property. This client secret property will be used by the client, which can be used for subsequent API requests.

Here is the updated `GetClients` method, in which we have added the grant type to `HybridAndClientCredentials` for API clients and added two more properties, the client secret that denotes a password user by the client to retrieve the access token and a new scope of vendor API that we will use later in this section:

```
public static IEnumerable<Client> GetClients()
{
    return new List<Client>
    {
        new Client
        {
            ClientId = "client",
            ClientName ="MVC Client",
            AllowedGrantTypes= GrantTypes.Implicit,
            RedirectUris = { "http://localhost:5002/signin-oidc"
        },
        PostLogoutRedirectUris= {"http://localhost:5002"},
          Enabled=true,
          AccessTokenType=  AccessTokenType.Jwt,
          AllowedScopes =new List<string>
          {
              StandardScopes.OpenId,
              StandardScopes.Profile,
              StandardScopes.Email,
              StandardScopes.OfflineAccess,
              "role"
          }
```

```
            },

       new Client
       {
           ClientId = "clientApi",
           ClientName ="MVC Client API",
           ClientSecrets= { new Secret("secretkey".Sha256())},
           AllowedGrantTypes = GrantTypes.
           HybridAndClientCredentials,

           RedirectUris = {
             "http://localhost:5003/signin-oidc" },
             PostLogoutRedirectUris= {"http://localhost:5003"},
             Enabled=true,
             AccessTokenType=  AccessTokenType.Jwt,
             AllowedScopes =new List<string>
             {
                 StandardScopes.OpenId,
                 StandardScopes.Profile,
                 StandardScopes.Roles,
                 StandardScopes.OfflineAccess,
                 "vendorManagementAPI"
             }
         }
     };
 }
```

Once this is set up, add a new Web API project and create the `HomeController` (MVC controller) and `VendorManagementController` (API controller). Here is the sample `VendorManagementController` that contains some methods to get the list of all vendors, get vendor by ID, create vendor, update, and delete vendor:

```
[Route("api/[controller]")]
public class VendorManagementController : Controller
{
    [HttpGet]
    public IEnumerable<Vendor> GetVendors(){

      //Returning static values
        return new List<Vendor>
        {
            new Vendor { VendorID=1, Name="Bentley",
              Email="john@bent.com", PhoneNo="+12012020030",
              Website="www.bentley.com" },
            new Vendor { VendorID=2, Name="Mercedez",
              Email="william@benz.com", PhoneNo="+1201203300",
              Website="www.mercedez.com" },
```

```
            new Vendor { VendorID=3, Name="BMW",
              Email="scott@bmw.com", PhoneNo="+12014500030",
              Website="www.bmw.com" },
            new Vendor { VendorID=4, Name="Lamborghini",
              Email="tyson@lamborghini.com",
              PhoneNo="+12022220030",
              Website="www.lamborghini.com"
        },
          new Vendor { VendorID=5, Name="Nissan",
            Email="george@nissan.com", PhoneNo="+13312020030",
            Website="www.nissan.com" }
          };


    }

    [HttpGet("{id}")]
    public Vendor GetVendor(int id){ }

    [HttpPost]
    public int CreateVendor(Vendor vendor){return -1;}

    [HttpPut]
    public int UpdateVendor(Vendor vendor){return -1;}

    [HttpDelete]
    public int DeleteVendor(int vendorID){return -1;}
}
```

The HomeController is as follows. There are two methods, Index, which will display the page, and the CallAPI method which calls the VendorManagementController GetVendors method:

```
    public class HomeController : Controller
    {

        [Authorize]
        // GET: /<controller>/
        public async Task<IActionResult> Index()

        {
            return View();
        }


        [Authorize]
        public async Task<IActionResult> CallApi()
        {
```

```
var accessToken = await HttpContext.Authentication
.GetTokenAsync("access_token");

var client = new HttpClient();
client.SetBearerToken(accessToken);
var content = await client.GetStringAsync(
  "http://localhost:5003/api/vendormanagement");

ViewBag.Json = content;
return View();
        }
    }
```

Once we run the application, it will ask for the username and password and show the consent screen on successful authentication, as shown in the following screenshot:

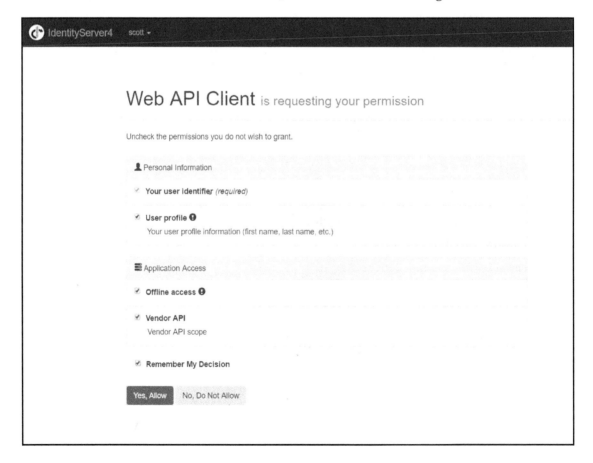

If you notice, on the consent screen, it asks you to allow offline access and Vendor API, which was added as the scope while defining the client on the authorization server. Finally, when we call `http://localhost:5003/Home/CallAPI` it will get the access token and access the `VendorManagementController` that returns the vendor list.

Authorization

As authentication is all about knowing the identity of the user and validating its credentials, authorization can be implemented to know what the user is authorized to do after authentication. In ASP.NET Core applications, authorization can be implemented using declarative and imperative methods.

Declarative authorization techniques

ASP.NET Core provides a simple declarative role and policy-based model where authorization can be defined using different criteria and gets evaluated based on the user claims.

Declarative authorization can be defined using attributes. Attributes such as `AuthorizeAttribute` and `AllowAnonymous` can be annotated on controllers and actions and validated when they are accessed by the security framework.

Basic authorization

Here is the example of annotating attributes on `EmployeeController`:

```
[Authorize]
[Route("api/[controller]")]
public class EmployeeController : Controller
{
    [HttpGet]
    public List<Employee> Get()
    {
        return GetEmployees();
    }

    [HttpPost]
    public bool Create(Employee employee)
    {
        return CreateEmployee(employee);
    }
}
```

```
        [HttpDelete]
        public bool Delete(int id)
        {
            return DeleteEmployee(id);
        }

        [HttpPut]
        public bool Update(Employee employee)
        {
            return UpdateEmployee(employee);
        }
    }
}
```

Annotating the authorize attribute on the Controller level will protect all the methods defined within it.

Alternatively, we can also apply the authorize attribute on the action level, as follows. In the following example, we have added the authorize attribute on Create, Update, and Delete operations:

```
        [Route("api/[controller]")]
        public class EmployeeController : Controller
        {
          [HttpGet]
          public List<Employee> Get()
          {
              return GetEmployees();
          }

          [Authorize]
          [HttpPost]
          public bool Create(Employee employee)
          {
              return CreateEmployee(employee);
          }

          [Authorize]
          [HttpDelete]
          public bool Delete(int id)
          {
              return DeleteEmployee(id);
          }

          [Authorize]
          [HttpPut]
          public bool Update(Employee employee)
          {
```

```
            return UpdateEmployee(employee);
        }
    }
}
```

Action level attributes override the controller attribute. For example, if our `EmployeeController` is protected by annotating `AuthorizeAttribute`, we can make particular actions non-protected by using `AllowAnonymousAttribute`, as follows:

```
[Authorize]
[Route("api/[controller]")]
public class EmployeeController : Controller
{
  [AllowAnonymous]
  [HttpGet]
  public List<Employee> Get()
  {
      return GetEmployees();
  }

  [HttpPost]
  public bool Create(Employee employee)
  {
      return CreateEmployee(employee);
  }

  [HttpDelete]
  public bool Delete(int id)
  {
      return DeleteEmployee(id);
  }

  [HttpPut]
  public bool Update(Employee employee)
  {
      return UpdateEmployee(employee);
  }
 }
}
```

Authorization filters

We can also filter using Authentication schemes, roles, and policies. `AuthorizeAttribute` provides some filters, such as `ActiveAuthenticationSchemes`, `Roles`, and `Policy` to filter authorization.

Filtering based on authentication schemes

Specifying the `AuthenticationSchemes` on the following controller will only allow users who are authenticated with the cookies authentication scheme:

```
[Route("api/[controller]")]
[Authorize(ActiveAuthenticationSchemes ="Cookies")]
public class EmployeeController : Controller
{
}
```

Filtering based on authorization

Here is how we can use roles. `EmployeeController` will only be accessible to users that have a claim type role, such as `Admin` or `Manager`:

```
[Route("api/[controller]")]
[Authorize(Roles = "Admin, Manager")]
public class EmployeeController : Controller
{
}
```

Filtering based on policy

Policy-based authorization is a little different than the first two. In this first step, you have to define a policy and then use it with the `AuthorizationAttribute`. Policies can be configured in the `ConfigureServices` method in the `Startup` class, and they can be used to define any criteria on user claims:

```
services.AddAuthorization(options =>
{
    options.AddPolicy("RequireManagerRole", policy =>
      policy.RequireRole("Manager"));
});
```

And we can use the `RequireManagerRole` policy as follows:

```
[Authorize(Policy ="RequireManagerRole")]
[HttpGet]
public List<Employee> Get()
{
    return GetEmployees();
}
```

Another example is by reading user claims. For example, if we only allow users to access the `EmployeeController`, if an `AccessAPI` claim is present, it can be implemented as follows:

```
services.AddAuthorization(options =>
{
    options.AddPolicy("RequireAPIAccess", policy =>
      policy.RequireClaim("AccessAPI"));
});
```

Controller can be annotated as follows:

```
[Route("api/[controller]")]
[Authorize(Policy ="RequireAPIAccess")]
public class EmployeeController : Controller
{
}
```

Multiple claims or roles can be defined as comma-separated. For example, the following example requires access to the `EmployeeController` if the user has `firstname` and `lastname` claims present:

```
services.AddAuthorization(options =>
{
    options.AddPolicy("RequireProfile", policy =>
      policy.RequireClaim("firstname", "lastname"));
});
```

Custom policies

Custom requirements can also be implemented to handle any requirement. We can define custom requirements by implementing the `IAuthorizationRequirement` interface. Here is our custom requirement that only allows users if they are based in GCC countries, namely Saudi Arabia, Kuwait, United Arab Emirates, Qatar, Bahrain, and Oman:

```
public class BaseLocationRequirement :
  Microsoft.AspNetCore.Authorization.IAuthorizationRequirement
{
    public BaseLocationRequirement(List<string> locations)
    {
        BaseLocation = locations;
    }

    public List<string> BaseLocation { get; set; }
}
```

Once the requirement is set up, we need to define the handler that evaluates the requirement:

```
public class BaseLocationHandler : Microsoft.AspNetCore
  .Authorization.AuthorizationHandler<BaseLocationRequirement>
{
    protected override Task
    HandleRequirementAsync(AuthorizationHandlerContext
    context, BaseLocationRequirement requirement)
    {
        if (!context.User.HasClaim(c => c.Type ==
          ClaimTypes.Country))
        {
            return Task.CompletedTask;
        }

        string country = context.User.FindFirst(
          c => c.Type == ClaimTypes.Country).Value;

        List<string> gccCountries = requirement.BaseLocation;

        if (gccCountries.Contains(country))
        {
            context.Succeed(requirement);
        }
        return Task.CompletedTask;

    }
}
```

The preceding code implements the `HandleRequirementAsync` method that evaluates the requirement and if the country lies within the GCC countries, the requirement will be succeeded.

This new custom requirement can be added in the `ConfigureServices` method as follows and can be used in the `AuthorizeAttribute` in controller or action level:

```
services.AddAuthorization(options =>
  options.AddPolicy("AnyGCCCountry",
    policy => policy.Requirements.Add(new
      BaseLocationRequirement(new List<string> {
        "Saudi Arabia", "Kuwait", "United Arab Emirates",
          "Qatar", "Bahrain", "Oman" }))));
```

Finally register the `BaseLocationHandler` with `AuthorizationHandler` using **Dependency Injection (DI)**.

Imperative authorization techniques

Declarative authorization is executed before the controller or action method is executed, whereas sometimes it is needed to load the controllers or actions before the authorization is executed, and this can be done using imperative authorization or resource-based authorization. Let's take an example of university courses, where we need to show the course page to only those students who have paid their course fees.

To implement this authorization, we first have to add the overloaded constructor in our Course controller, as follows:

```
public class CourseController : Controller
{
    IAuthorizationService _authorizationService = null;
    public CourseController(IAuthorizationService
      authorizationService)
    {
        _authorizationService = authorizationService;
    }
```

Here is the action method that the user will invoke to load the course page:

```
public async Task<IActionResult> ViewCourse(string courseCode)
{
    Course course = GetCourseObject(courseCode);
    if(await _authorizationService
      .AuthorizeAsync(HttpContext.User,
        course, "PaidCourse"))
    {
        return View(course);
    }
    else
    {
        return new ChallengeResult();
    }
}
```

In the preceding code snippet, we have called the `AuthorizeAsync` method and passed User, course object, and the policy name that can be used to validate if the user has rights to view the course page.

Similarly, like `BaseLocation`, we can define the requirement for the course and define the `CoursePaidHandler` to evaluate the authorization. The course object that we have passed through the `AuthorizeAsync` method can be retrieved using the `context.Resource` object and its `IsPaid` property denotes whether the student has paid the course fees or not:

```
public class CoursePaidRequirement : Microsoft.AspNetCore
.Authorization.IAuthorizationRequirement
{
    public CoursePaidRequirement()
    {
    }
    public class CoursePaidHandler : Microsoft.AspNetCore
    .Authorization.AuthorizationHandler<CoursePaidRequirement>
    {
        protected override Task HandleRequirementAsync(
            Microsoft.AspNetCore.Authorization
            .AuthorizationHandlerContext context,
            CoursePaidRequirement requirement)
        {
            Course course=(Course) context.Resource;
            if (course.IsPaid)
            {
                context.Succeed(requirement);
            }

            return Task.CompletedTask;
        }
    }
}
```

Finally, we will add the following lines in our `Startup` class to register the policy and `CoursePaidHandler`:

```
services.AddAuthorization(options =>options.AddPolicy(
"CoursePaid", policy => policy.Requirements.Add(new
  CoursePaidRequirement())));
services.AddSingleton<IAuthorizationHandler,
  CoursePaidHandler>();
```

Likewise `AuthorizationAsync` on the controller level, we can also use it in the view to load/unload a particular section of the page, and it can be specified as follows:

```
@model Models.Course
@if (await AuthorizationService.AuthorizeAsync(User, Model,
  "CoursePaid"))
{
    <p>Course fees paid?  @Model.IsPaid</p>
}
```

Safe storage

Before the release of .NET Core, developers used to store keys, connection strings, and other secrets in application configuration files. .NET Core provides a wide range of storage options to store this information and developers are only restricted to storing this information in `web.config` files, and now the information can be stored in JSON-based `appsettings.json` files, XML-based configuration files, or environment variables, and so on. Sometimes, when there is a big team and multiple developers are working on the same project, we don't want those keys to be shared among them. A good example is an e-mail gateway where developers use a third-party gateway such as Google, Hotmail, or Yahoo and use their login credentials to test it out.

.NET Core provides a Secret Manager Tool to store application secrets. It protects the values by storing them in a separate JSON file on the following path, which differs for each OS (operating system).

Windows: `%APPDATA%\microsoft\UserSecrets\<userSecretsId>\secrets.json`

Linux: `~/.microsoft/usersecrets/<userSecretsId>/secrets.json`

Mac: `~/.microsoft/usersecrets/<userSecretsId>/secrets.json`

Secret Manager Tool can be used by adding the following NuGet package:

`Microsoft.Extensions.SecretManager.Tools`

It also requires the `userSecretsId`, which should be unique for each project running on that machine. The `userSecretsId` can be added as follows:

```
"userSecretsId": "aspnet-UserSecretSample-c5c2838b-7727
  -4242-9973-d2b79c40e636",
```

Finally, we can set up a builder and add user secrets by calling the `AddUserSecrets` method as follows:

```
public Startup(IHostingEnvironment env)
{
    var builder = new ConfigurationBuilder();

    if (env.IsDevelopment())
    {
        builder.AddUserSecrets();
    }
}
public IConfigurationRoot Configuration { get; }
```

This also requires the following package to be added to your project:

```
"Microsoft.Extensions.Configuration.UserSecrets":"1.0.0"
```

Storing and retrieving safe storage values

Safe storage values can be stored by calling a .NET CLI command. The following command adds the complex password to the key password:

```
dotnet user-secrets set password P@ssW0rd
```

You should run the preceding command from the root of your project.

We can access the password by passing the key name of the value stored through the `Configuration` object:

```
Var password = Configuration["password"];
```

Summary

In this chapter, we learnt about both the ASP.NET Core Identity and IdentityServer4 security frameworks to handle both easy and complex types of scenarios, how to customize and extend the existing Identity model using Entity Framework Core, and used middleware to authenticate users using Facebook, 2FA, and OpenID Connect. Moreover, we developed a basic **Central Authentication System** (**CAS**) that provides multiple applications to connect using the same protocol and enables single sign-on. We also learnt different techniques of securing Web API and MVC controllers and actions through attributes and imperatively by writing custom code. Finally, we discussed how to store application secrets using user secrets.

11
Modern AI Offerings by Microsoft

This is the last chapter of our book, and is probably quite interesting. We will try to cover many topics in this chapter, so as to keep ourselves updated and aware of the most recent trends in the IT world.

We'll start by covering some technology topics that are not only the basis for the modern cloud infrastructure services such as IaaS and PaaS, but have also simplified the management, development, and testability of software applications. We will then look into some software development practices which have become common due to these modern technologies.

Only time can tell which trends will truly take off, as in the software industry, things can change rather quickly. Here, we talk about the current hot trends in relation to the .NET Core platform. This chapter gives a high-level view of some of the recent market trends and practices and how they can be achieved with .NET Core and Microsoft's tools and technologies.

We will cover various topics in this chapter, which include the following:

- Virtual machine and containerization
- DevOps practices
- Introduction to CI and CD in the cloud
- Multi-container sample microservice in Azure using Docker
- Big Data and Microsoft
- Introduction to **Business Intelligence** (**BI**) and Big Data
- Introduction to **Artificial Intelligence** (**AI**) and machine learning

Virtual machines and containerization

Let's start first with the topic of virtual machines and containers; it's been the primary infrastructure technology since the advent of cloud computing. These are the enablers in the cloud for the infrastructure as service phenomena. Since these technologies are, basically, packed binary images, one can copy, paste, and replicate them anywhere, any number of times. These images represent a computing machine, an OS image which can be virtually executed, say, inside another super host, which is capable of virtually running, a number of machines and operating systems inside it.

Virtual machine

A virtual machine enables you to simulate a computing hardware in the form of a software.

A virtual machine is usually not just geared towards simulating a particular hardware with a particular software, but it commonly imitates a type of processor and the relevant execution of instructions.

Simulation

A simulation is a system that behaves (internally and externally) similar to some other original system and is implemented in a completely different way from the other system that it is simulating. The underlying mechanisms used to recreate the scenario may be the same or different from the original one.

It can also be said that a simulator is a device that imitates the operation of another device, as it basically models the underlying states of the target system to the best possible way it can simulate.

Emulation

Emulation is, generally, using a software to provide a different execution environment or architecture. Emulation mimics the externally observable behavior to match the target. The internal state of the emulation mechanism does not necessarily reflect the internal state of the target which it is emulating. Emulators emulate hardware without relying on the CPU being able to run the code directly. So it is more like a translation of one set of instructions into another.

For example, a PlayStation 2 emulator on a Windows machine enables you to play PS2 titles on your PC; an Android emulator lets you emulate an Android device on your PC or Mac.

Virtual machine implementation base

There are some implementations of a virtual machine engine that rely on the techniques of emulation. For example, they emulate the x86/x64 architecture by adding a translation layer at the guest OS level, which enables them to execute on different platform architectures like the PowerPC, as well as x86/x64. However, this additional layer slows down the virtual machine quite significantly.

Modern virtualization techniques implement the isolation and segregation of the virtual machine within system memory. With support from modern hardware that provides special instruction-set for virtualization, the virtual machine engine passes on the execution of the guest virtual machine directly to the native hardware. Thus, the performance of a modern virtualization based virtual machine implementation is much faster than older VMs due to native hardware support and faster than emulation-based VMs due to the absence of an additional translation layer.

There is another concept of virtual machines, for example, those that execute the Java or .NET code, but they are different and are limited and targeted in their scope. A **Java Virtual Machine (JVM)** provides a mechanism to execute the Java bytecode, and **Common Language Runtime (CLR)** provides mechanisms to execute the programs written for the .NET framework, regardless of the programming language. The specs do not mandate that the bytecodes are executed by the software or the hardware, or that the bytecode should be translated to machine code. This sort of VM implementation can do a combination of both using emulation or where appropriate and by using a **Just-In-Time (JIT)** compilation, where appropriate.

Some famous examples of virtual machines include Oracle VirtualBox, VMware vSphere, Microsoft Hyper-V, Xen (OSS), and KVM (OSS).

Containerization

Containers provide an isolated, resource-controlled, and portable operating environment within an existing running operating system and that hosting OS can itself be either running on a single physical machine or on a single virtual machine (VM).

A container is an isolated place created by forming a virtual boundary using the process and namespace isolation technology by the host operating system so that an application running inside the container can run without affecting the rest of the system and without the system affecting the application. An app inside a container would feel like it is running inside a freshly installed OS (and the required prerequisites) on a computer.

The idea of such a virtual environment was first proposed in 1999 by an MIPT professor. It was an improvement on the chroot model and had three main components, which were:

- Groups of processes with namespace isolation
- Filesystem to share the code, and thus, save memory on disk and RAM
- Provide resource isolation as well as management

Evolution of containerization concepts

Let's take a quick look at the various container-like virtualization technologies created in the history of computing according to the timeline.

Chroot

The chroot utility was first implemented by Bill Joy in 1982. A chroot on the Unix operating system is an operation (system call/wrapper program) that changes the root directory for the current running process and its children. A process in such a modified environment cannot access files outside the designated directory tree. Chroot provides the guest OS / process with its own, segregated file system to run in, allowing applications to run in a binary environment different from the host OS. The modified environment is called **chroot jail**.

FreeBSD Jails

In March 2000, jail was introduced with the release of FreeBSD 4.0 and the release note goes as follows:

"A new jail system call and admin command have been added for additional flexibility in creating secure process execution environments."

FreeBSD jails had three main goals--Virtualization, Security, and Ease of delegation.

Solaris Zones

Solaris pioneered container technology in **2004** with the introduction of Solaris Containers, commonly known as Solaris Zones. Oracle is now the owner of Solaris and is integrating Docker into Oracle Solaris, which allows enterprise customers to use the Docker platform to distribute applications that are built and deployed in Solaris Zones.

OpenVZ

In **2005**, OpenVZ started as an open source software which brought huge improvements on existing implementations with the concept of container-based virtualization for the Linux platform. It allows you to create multiple, secure, and isolated Linux containers on a single physical machine. An OpenVZ container executes like a standalone operating system i.e. the container with its own boundary that can even be rebooted independently. It has its own root access, users, IP addresses, memory, processes, files, applications, system libraries, and configuration files.

Cgroups

This project, started in **2006** by two Google engineers, was later released by the Linux community in January 2008. Cgroups (short form of Control groups) was then implemented as a Linux kernel feature that allows you to allocate resources such as CPU time, system memory, disk I/O, network bandwidth, and/or combinations of these resources to the user-defined groups of processes running on a system creating, a virtual boundary between regular OS processes and the cgroup-ed process group.

LXC

LXC (short form of Linux Containers) was first released in **2008** as an operating-system-level virtualization to run multiple isolated Linux systems (called as containers) on a host using a single Linux kernel. It basically combines the Cgroups functionality and adds support for the namespaces to provide an isolation boundary for given containerized applications.

Lmctfy

First released in October **2013**, lmctfy is an operating-system-level virtualization technology implemented as open source by Google engineers. "**Let Me Contain That For You (LMCTFY)**". It is based on the Linux kernel's cgroups functionality. It has been managing Google's resource isolation needs since 2007. As it provides functionality similar to LXC and Docker, but at a lower level, the developers of this container technology have joined their efforts on the `libcontainer` library of the Docker and stopped maintaining the lmctfy open source repository since 2015.

Docker

Docker was first released in March 2013. The initial commit of docker consisted of a light wrapper written in the Go language to set up, manage, and execute LXC containers in Linux.

Docker is now an open platform for developing, shipping, and running applications. It allows you to build, run, test, and deploy distributed applications inside software containers.

Docker provides an additional layer of abstraction and automation on OS-level virtualization in Linux, and now, on Windows as well. It uses the resource isolation features of the Linux kernel cgroups and namespaces, and a union-capable file system, UnionFS (for example: AUFS, btrfs, vfs, and DeviceMapper).

Docker now includes its own `libcontainer` library to use the virtualization facilities from the Linux kernel in addition to using abstracted virtualization interfaces via libvirt, LXC, and `systemd-nspawn`.

From the Docker website - *Docker provides tooling and a platform to manage the lifecycle of your containers*:

- Encapsulate your applications (and supporting components) into Docker containers
- Distribute and ship those containers to your teams for further development and testing
- Deploy those applications to your production environment, whether it is in a local data center or the Cloud

Modern container fundamentals

With container-based development, deployment, and the whole ecosystem, following are the key concepts to understand the modern day containerization:.

- **Container host**: An operating system on a physical machine (bare metal), or a virtual machine configured with the container support.
- **Container OS image**: Containers are deployed from images in the form of layers as they stack up. The container OS image is the first layer in potentially many image layers for the given container. This image provides the basic required operating system environment for the desired application.

- **Container image**: A container image is primarily for the intended application, and it contains the base operating system, application, and all application dependencies in the form of container layers, as well as essential configurations that are needed to deploy a container.
- **Container registry**: Container registry is the placeholder for the container images which can be downloaded on demand. For example:
  - Docker Hub
  - Amazon EC2 Container Registry
  - Azure Container Registry
- **Container repository**: Container repository is a collection of different, but related, container images with different tags used to identify different versions of the same application or service.
- **Configuration**: Container configuration file is used to automate the creation of container images. It can, for example, specify the required base images, directory mappings, and required files before the given container is executed. For Docker-based container images, it is Dockerfile for all platforms.
- **Container orchestration**: When you deploy tens, hundreds, or thousands of containers that make up an application, tracking and managing the deployment requires sophistication in both management and orchestration of those containers. Container orchestrators are assigned a pool of servers in a cluster and the respective schedule to deploy containers onto those servers. Some orchestrators configure networking between containers on different servers, while some may also include load balancing, rolling updates, extensibility, and more. Examples of popular container orchestrators include the following:
  - Docker Compose / Docker Swarm
  - Kubernetes
  - Mesos / DCOS

Docker components

Docker is no more just a container or a mere container technology. It's a full platform with its various components, as well as a built ecosystem around it. Let's have a quick view of the main components of the Docker platform.

Docker Engine

Docker Engine is the core application that is deployed on the operating system, which becomes a host for the Docker containers. It is a client-server application which has a **server** (which is a background-running process called as a **daemon process**); a REST API exposing the interface (which programs can use to talk to the daemon); and a **Command Line Interface** (**CLI**) client. Most of the things that you would need to do with installing, configuring, and using containers on a container host are achieved via the Docker Eengine:

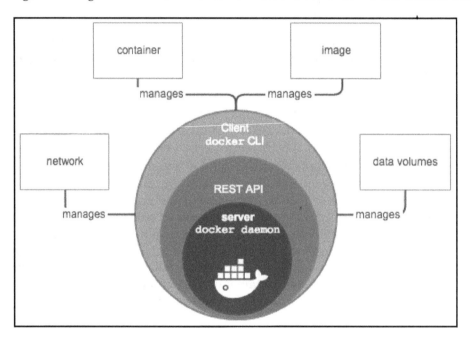

Docker Engine (courtesy of docs.docker.com)

Docker Engine has two editions, which are available for desktops, servers, or cloud providers:

- The **Docker Community edition** (**Docker CE**): Designed for enterprise teams who build, ship, and run business critical applications in production at scale
- The **Docker Enterprise edition** (**Docker EE**): It is ideal for developers and small teams, and is available on many platforms, from desktop to cloud

Cloud supported Docker EE includes--AWS, MS Azure, IBM SoftLayer, DigitalOcean, and more.

Docker Compose

Docker Compose is a tool for defining and running multi-container Docker-based applications. It provides you a with compose file (`docker-compose.yml`) to configure your application's services.

Using Compose is a three-step process, which includes the following:

1. Having a Dockerfile.
2. Defining services in `docker-compose.yml`, as they make up your app and run together in their own isolated environment.
3. Running `docker-compose` up in the end so that Docker Compose starts your entire application together.

Docker Machine

The primary purpose or benefit of Docker Machine is to enable the provisioning and managing remote Docker containers. Docker Engine runs locally, while Docker Machine runs remotely.

Docker Machine has its own CLI client, docker-machine, that lets you install Docker Engine on virtual hosts, and manage the hosts with docker-machine commands.

You can use machine to create Docker hosts on your local computer, on your data center, or on cloud providers such as AWS or Azure.

Docker registry

A Docker registry stores Docker-based container images. After building a Docker-based container image, you can push it to a public container registry such as a Docker Hub, to a private registry on cloud, or on-premise.

You also have the facility to search for existing public images, and pull them from the registry to your own host.

Docker Hub is a public Docker registry, which serves a huge collection (probably the largest) of existing images, and allows you to push your own. In addition to that, Docker also provides **Docker Trusted Registry**, which can be installed on-premises, or on a cloud. It allows you to store your Docker images, privately and securely, behind your firewall. There are also cloud-based private registry providers which you can use within your cloud environment, such as AWS EC2 registry and Azure container registry.

Docker Kitematic

Kitematic is a simple application to be used on desktops or DEV machines for managing Docker containers on Mac, Linux, and Windows.

Docker Swarm

Docker Swarm is a clustering solution for Docker-based containers by the Docker. It enables (for load balancing and failover) you to use the pool of Docker hosts into a single, virtual Docker host.

Docker Swarm is a standalone product, and there is a Swarm mode within a Docker Engine as well.

The cluster management and orchestration features are built in the Docker Engine using SwarmKit.

Swarm mode

When Docker engines are running in a cluster, they are said to be in a swarm mode. You can enable the swarm mode for a Docker Engine by initializing a swarm, or by joining an existing swarm.

A swarm is a cluster of Docker engines or nodes where your application services are running. When in swarm mode, the Docker Engine CLI and API include commands to manage the swarm nodes (like add or remove nodes), and deploy and orchestrate the services across the swarm. When you run a docker Docker without using the swarm mode, you are executing container commands directly, and when you run a Docker in the swarm mode, you orchestrate your services.

For more information on the swarm mode, go through the Docker documentation for swarm mode at
`https://docs.docker.com/engine/swarm`

Docker Cloud

Docker Cloud provides a hosted registry service (with private options) with build and testing facilities. It provides you with the tools to help you set up and manage host infrastructure and application life cycle features to automate the deployment of your containers.

The core set of Docker Cloud includes the following:

- Support for teams and organizations
- Management of builds and images
- Support for private image repositories
- Support for Continuous Integration
- Management of swarm clusters Management and distribution of Docker nodes and the respective Docker Cloud infrastructure

Docker containerization in Windows

Windows Containers are supported in Windows 10 Professional edition and up, as well as in Windows Server 2016.

Docker for Windows

Docker for Windows supports Docker Engine (server and client) with REST API, as well as CLI. It contains a docker GUI to control and configure the various aspects. You can also use Docker CLI, PowerShell, and Azure-related commands. There is an Azure Docker VM extension as well, which allows you to install and configure the Docker daemon, Docker client, and Docker Compose in your Linux virtual machine.

Windows Containers

Windows Containers include these two different types of containers:

- **Windows Server Container**: A Windows server container shares a kernel with the container host and all other Windows Containers running on the same host. It provides the application with an isolation boundary through the process and namespace isolation technology.

- **Hyper-V Container**: The Hyper-V container expands the application isolation by providing the optimized Hyper-V virtual machine on Windows. In this configuration, the kernel of the container host is not shared with other Hyper-V Containers. This type of Windows Container is most suited to Linux-based containers on Windows-based hosts.

> Head on to `https://docs.microsoft.com/en-us/virtualization/windowscontainers/` for more documentation regarding Windows Containers.
> Also see `https://docs.docker.com/docker-for-windows/` to have a first time hands-on with Docker for Windows.

Modern development

Modern day infrastructures are based on clouds, virtual machines, and containers, and form the base of the topics in this book as well. Therefore, let's call our modern day development environment, and set up where we are working around these technologies so we have a few of differences to the traditional mode of development.

Development editors

With the popularity of loads of JavaScript-based frameworks, SPA, and Node.js-based development setups in the web development world, a number of light-weight, cross-platform, and open source editors have become popular with a number of extensions around to help you work in a modern-day infrastructure. With such a scene, these are the top IDEs to consider along with their correct integration options offered by the extensions/plugins:

- Visual Studio Code
- GitHub Atom
- Sublime
- VIM

However, with the modern PaaS and **Backend As A Service** (**Baas**) offerings with tiny microservices models, we now see another set of editors, which are suitable for web development; these editors, themselves, are cloud-based, and run directly out of your browser. In addition to just being an editor, most of them have the ability to directly integrate with Git repositories and cloud-based deployments (with respect to CI and CD) for your app. These are called cloud editors, and the most famous of them include the following:

- Cloud9 (c9.io)
- Codenvy
- Koding
- codeanywhere

Development environment setup

No matter whether you use a fully-fledged development editor, a lightweight, or a cloud-based one, you need a development environment setup with a database and other collaborating servers that make up your application, and you need the development environment setup and ready to go in minutes. Traditionally, setting up the environment takes at least a day, if not a week. And modern day development welcomes remote development not just from office machines, but from your own computer as well. Thus, there is a demand Here comes the demand for the need for portable development environments.

You can have a showcase development machine with all tools installed, all the shortcuts setup, have it binary imaged as ISO or other tool-related formats, and burn them. With this, you can have your development machine ready in minutes. Even if you have destroyed the environment, you can rebuild it quickly.

With the advent of cloud, most of the development and testing has become focused on virtual machines. Here comes the Vagrant.

Vagrant

Vagrant is a software engine which takes a configuration file, and builds a VM out of it. You can have a VM or a combination of VMs (multi-machine) with the required OS, IDE, configuration, tools, and servers all installed on it. Since it's a VM, it is portable as a USB key. Use it and recreate it just by copy-paste, and identical copies will be ready in seconds or minutes.

Vagrant primarily supports VirtualBox and VMware, as well as AWS. Vagrant has unified the creation and recreation of such development environments, and has provided an online public repository of such machines that you can build and share, or use an existing one.

The following is an excerpt from the Vagrant website (`https://www.vagrantup.com/docs/why-vagrant/`):

> *Vagrant provides easy to configure, reproducible, and portable work environments built on top of industry-standard technology and controlled by a single consistent workflow to help maximize the productivity and flexibility of you and your team.*
> *To achieve its magic, Vagrant stands on the shoulders of giants. Machines are provisioned on top of VirtualBox, VMware, AWS, or any other provider. Then, industry-standard provisioning tools such as shell scripts, Chef, or Puppet, can be used to automatically install and configure software on the machine.*

Cloud development and test environment

In modern cloud-based applications, automation of development and testability in cloud arises with portability, heavy traffic, data, and performance requirements. DevOps can define the Developer VMs or environments with a set of limitations as well as VMs or setup for testable environment for various kinds of testing, all in the same cloud (but different network segment) where the production systems are running. This not just allows a the realistic feel, but also provides the flexibility to create environments in minutes instead of weeks by the infrastructure as a code paradigm with various cloud infrastructure providers.

In AWS, you have a number of predefined templates available to quickly create your development and test environments on the cloud. Once you have consumed them, you can then destroy them, since you can easily and quickly recreate them. This allows you to keep the cost under control, as well as keep your in-house infrastructure safe, secure, and undisturbed.

With similar goals, Microsoft Azure provides a dedicated optimized DevTest environment for pre-production development, a test setup where VMs can be created, started, stopped, and destroyed easily, and to frequently keep the cost under control.

Azure's feature is called **Azure DevTest Labs** , and has the following main points listed on their website:

- Fast, easy, and lean dev-test environments
- Quickly provision development and test environments
- Minimize waste with quotas and policies

- Set automated shutdowns to minimize costs
- Build Windows and Linux environments

 Browse over to
`https://azure.microsoft.com/en-us/services/devtest-lab/` for more information on Azure DevTest labs.

DevOps

The Dev in DevOps stands for development and Ops stands for operations. DevOps tries to minimize the gap between development and operations. Agile software development has minimized the gap and improved collaboration between requirements analysis, testing, and development, whereas, the DevOps movement encourages collaboration between development and operations.

The exact definition of DevOps varies from business to business, but, in essence, DevOps is all about minimizing the challenges of shipping, rapidly iterating, and securing software applications.

The Culture

Similar to agile software development, DevOps is just another buzzword even with the best tools if you don't have the right culture. In 2010, John Willis and Damon Edwards coined the term **CAMS** (**Culture**, **Automation**, **Measurement**, and **Sharing**). Over the time, this seems to be a more relevant definition of DevOps. The culture of DevOps is about the following:

- Communication and sharing responsibility
- Accepting failure rather than blaming faults
- Cross-functional alignment, that is, working together for a common goal
- Empathy, as in, teams with close ties

Key motivational aspects

DevOps has the following key aspects, which should be implemented when setting up the DevOps processes in your organization.

Sharing

This involves shared responsibility of the development and operations pipelines. It also includes sharing of code, tooling, and processes between the Ops and Dev teams.

The Development team helps improve the Operations team code and tooling, while the Ops security team helps ensure that best practices are used during development. Security typically falls to dedicated roles, but ultimately, it involves all other teams working together to deliver the application.

Sharing between autonomous teams mandates the techniques of self-testing-code (which comes in Continuous Integration) and continuous deployment (as already set up in close collaboration and improvement between the Dev and Ops teams).

Automation

It is almost impossible to have DevOps processes set up without the automation of processes using the appropriate tools, configurations, and team collaboration. Automation of tasks like testing, configuration, and deployment frees up people to let them focus on other more valuable tasks in the project. It also reduces the chances of human error by continuous improvement in the automation processes. At a higher level, automation includes the following:

- Automated testing
- **Continuous Integration (CI)**
- Infrastructure as a Code
- **Continuous Delivery (CD)**

Measurement

Measurement of a team's performance, artifacts delivery, performance of code, performance, and reliability of infrastructure are some of the very important functions of an IT team of any business to deliver its promise, sustain, and support growth. It's not only required by the Dev and Ops teams, but is an essential part of the project management community, which eventually helps to provide the running business with a visibility to management. Automation in DevOps enables a far more reliable measurement than the traditional models. Measurement includes, at least, the following:

- Tasks and deliverables visibility
- Visibility on build metrics

- Visibility of tests metrics
- Visibility on deployments in Dev, Test, and Prod environments
- Improves visibility of real project costs
- Logging of apps and infrastructure
- Monitoring of apps and infrastructure

Software development and delivery process

There is no single DevOps tool to achieve all the required target steps--rather, it is called the as DevOps toolchain. The toolchain fits into one or more of the phases of software development and the delivery process, as if they work in collaboration between the Dev and Ops teams.

The phases in development and delivery could be like the following, but every organization can have their own version. Note that these phases are also helpful to establish the CI and CD pipeline.

Phases	General Description
Code	Dev environment, IDE, version control
Build	Continuous Integration
Test	Automated and manual tests and related infrastructure
Package	Deployment packages, containers, packages repositories
Release	Change and release management processes
Configure and Provision	Infrastructure configuration and management, infrastructure as a code
Deploy	Deployment of packages, containers, VMS on to the infrastructure
Monitor	Application and infrastructure monitoring

Continuous Integration

The subject of **Continuous Integration** (**CI**) does not have to be linked to DevOps processes, as it is an independent activity by itself. CI promotes automated development into a testable package, which can then perform automated testing. The primary starting point for such self-testing code is **Test Driven Development** (**TDD**), so that you define the test cases and test scenarios beforehand or in parallel with the development activities of such types of testing--unit testing, integration testing, system testing, and stress and performance testing. CI is usually implemented as a separate CI server, which is integrated with your source control. The following types of testing, for example, can be configured to run as Automated Tests: unit testing, integration testing, system testing, and stress and performance testing. CI is usually implemented via a separate CI server that is integrated to your source control. **Visual Studio Team Services** (**VSTS**) is one of the good CI servers around, which not only integrates with the MS **Team Foundation Server** (**TFS**) source version control, but also with Git. It also supports multiple build and testing agents, which are available on multiple platforms--Windows, Mac, and Linux.

Best practices

Some of the best practices for the CI process, well outlined by Martin Fowler, include the following:

- Maintaining a (single) source repository
- Automating of the build process
- Having a self-testing build / automated testing--Automation also enables test metrics
- Everyone committing to the baseline everyday--Reduces conflicts, improves frequent communication
- Every commit to the main baseline should be built
- Keeping the build fast--Fast building process to provide rapid feedback
- Fixing the broken builds immediately--This also encourages the fixing of potential bugs before writing new code
- Testing in a clone of the production environment--More realistic tests
- Making it easy to get the latest deliverables--Reduce rework in the sense that builds are readily available to stakeholders and testers
- Maintaining visibility of builds and tests failure(s)--Everyone can see what's happening: Visibility of builds and tests failure(s)
- Automating deployment (for example Continuous Delivery)

Benefits of CI

There are a number of benefits when you opt for the CI processes, which include the following:

Improvement in Developer productivity

Continuous Integration helps teams to be more productive by freeing the developers of manual tasks, which also helps to reduce the number of errors and bugs in earlier stages.

Quick identification and addressing of bugs

Frequent automated testing (based on commits) enables the developers to discover and address bugs earlier, before they grow into larger problems later. This also provides feedback on, for example, system-wide impact of local changes. It ensures constant availability of a current build for testing or release purposes.

Faster Updates Delivery

With the essence of Agile software development, CI helps teams deliver frequent and faster updates to their customers.

Continuous Delivery

Continuous Delivery is not necessarily associated with the DevOps processes, but it is one of the primary automation activities in these processes. Continuous Delivery is, basically, a software development practice where you build software such that a software release can be deployed to the production at any time. Continuous Delivery is enabled through the pipeline in which Continuous Integration, automated testing, and automated deployment capabilities allow the software to be developed and deployed rapidly, reliably, and repeatedly, with minimal manual efforts.

With Continuous Delivery, your software is always ready to be deployed to production, but to push it into production requires a business decision, therefore, the final deployment is a manual step. Continuous deployment is the next step of Continuous Delivery--Every working version of the application is automatically pushed to production. Continuous deployment mandates Continuous Delivery, but the opposite is not required.

Continuous Delivery Pipeline

While the Continuous Delivery Pipeline may vary from company to company depending on the different processes, but a typical delivery pipeline looks like the following:

Continuous Delivery Pipeline

If we replace the only manual step in the preceding diagram, then this diagram will become the continuous deployment pipeline.

DevOps toolchain

Here, we will provide just a short list of tools that are generally available for the respective steps and tasks in the DevOps processes. Note that this is just a suggestive list; there could be better ones out there, and we have no commercial or non-commercial association with them.

Continuous Integration and Continuous Delivery:

- Jenkins
- TeamCity / Octopus Deploy
- Visual Studio Team Services
- Atlassian's Bitbucket
- Codeship, Travis CI, and more

Configuration and Infrastructure as a Code:

- Ansible
- Chef
- Puppet
- SaltStack

A sample microservices application based on Docker containers

You have so far learnt about **Service Oriented aArchitecture** (**SOA**) and microservices as key enterprise application architectures, and have also learnt the ideas behind the containerization, especially, how well it fits with the microservices architecture. Along the way, you've also gotten equipped with the Azure cloud offerings around the modern services oriented architecture, which fits according to our needs. We will now get a hands-on experience with a very basic application having two simple microservices based on Docker containers and we will then deploy them to Azure Container Service.

The sample application

Let's begin with dissecting our application in a step-by-step process, with a direct and no-nonsense approach.

Problem statement

Our problem is that we need a web application which can perform, let's say, an addition operation. The user will interact with the frontend of our application by providing the required inputs, and the application will render the answer as a result of the operation.

High-level architecture

Assuming that we are now happy and mature solution architects, based on our experience, we decide to take the service-oriented architecture approach, thereby exposing our addition operation as a service. This will easily allows us in future to have multiple types of front-end clients, and we can expose the service to the world as we desire. It will also allow us to have our front end(s) and our backend, that is, the service, to change independently.

So, we decide that we will have one service which will expose our addition operation capabilities, and another application package which will expose our frontend. For now, we will have only one simple web-based frontend application.

Let's call our software, *Math Application* or *MathApp* in short:

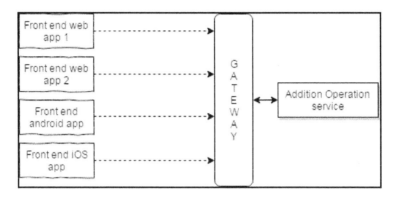

High level architecture of MathApp

Application architecture

Our Math Application, which is in focus as of today, has a requirement to have only one frontend interface. Therefore, our application architecture suggests that it will consist of two microservices. One microservice will contain our API Service, and the other will carry our frontend application. Now, as an architectural practice in our organization, we decide to use Docker-based containers for all types of microservices in our enterprise:

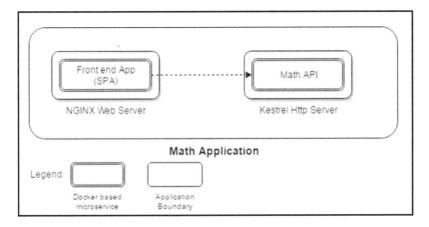

Application architecture for MathApp

Technical architecture

Our technical implementation architecture (or detailed Application Architecture) is based on Docker containers providing us with our microservices. We will be hosting our containers on the Microsoft Azure cloud platform using the **Azure Container Service** (**ACS**). We will use Docker Hub to host our container images as a public container registry, though we have an option to use the Azure container registry as well.

Setup in Azure Container Service

We will use the Azure portal (`portal.azure.com`) to create our environment for ACS. When creating our containers-based application environment, we will have the option to choose the required container orchestrator, and we choose Docker Swarm. We select one master node and two agent nodes for our container cluster managed by Docker Swarm. This means we will have two VMs for agent nodes and one VM for the master node in the docker swarm setup. When using the Azure portal for creating our ACS, it will drive us through the **Azure Resource Manager (ARM)** template for the ACS cluster, and choosing Swarm for orchestrator will follow this way of setting up our environment.

We will see more detailed and fundamental screens for the ACS and Docker image setup in later sections. For step-by-step guidance, please follow the link as mentioned in the later part of the section *Hands-on prerequisites*.

Architecture diagram

Let's finalize our technical architecture, which is one of the most important deliverables:

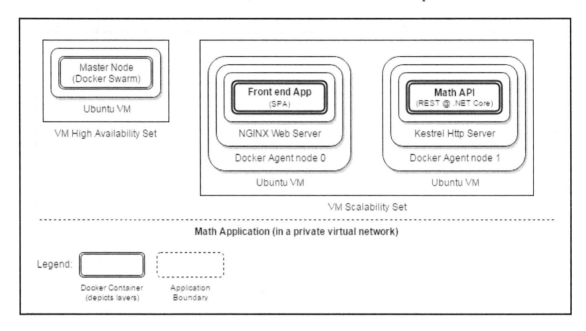

Technical Architecture for MathApp

 We can use ARM visualizer @ ArmViz.io/designer to be able to visualize and edit the Azure ARM templates for our project. Additionally, we can make use of many free-to-use Azure Quickstart templates @ `https://azure.microsoft.com/en-us/resources/templates/`, which are not just to give a quick start, but sometimes contains the complete ideal setup for our next Azure-based application.

Network architecture

The network architecture diagram focuses on the network infrastructure setup for our application. When using Azure ARM for ACS using the Docker Swarm as a cluster with a given master and agent nodes, the following is the network design that Azure ACS provides.

Since the setup remains the same in Azure with respect to the IP, ports, VMs, and load balancers, So we quote the same diagram as mentioned on the Azure website:

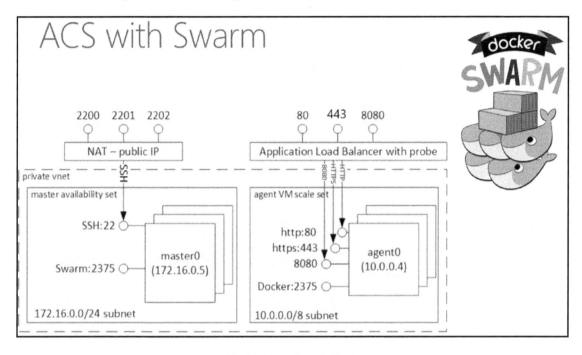

Network Architecture diagram for MathApp

What is visible in this diagram?

In the preceding diagram, you can see that the nodes, master node(s), and agent node(s), are distinctly visible, and are present in separate VMs. The ACS arm has minimal VM configuration already defined for the master node, while for the agent node, you can select the VM plan to reduce its processing and memory capacity according to the desired or expected load, performance, and cost.

The master node(s) remain in the Azure VM availability set to ensure high availability and failover scenarios, and the agent node(s) remain in the Azure VM scale set to ensure load balancing and auto scaling (of identical VMs) depending on your performance demands.

Virtual network, Subnets--NAT IPs, Agent IPs, and SSH-Docker-HTTP ports--are all preconfigured by default and opened in firewall, but you will need to enable ports in the firewall to gain access from public IP. Load balancers for both the master set and agent set are also set up and are basically assigned to the public IP.

Hands-on prerequisites

If you are doing the hands-on yourself, and want to repeat the steps, you will need the following:

- Active Microsoft Azure subscription
- Windows Users--PuTTY (basically `putty.exe` and `puttygen.exe`) and WinSCP (for file transfer)
- Visual Studio with Docker tools (works for both VS 2015 CE and VS2017 CE)
- Docker Client or Docker Engine CLI - Docker Toolbox if you do not have Hyper-V / VirtualBox

For step-by-step screenshots and directions for each activity to be performed, please follow the follow this tutorial: *Getting Started with Docker and Azure Container Services*:
`https://blogs.msdn.microsoft.com/uk_faculty_connection/2016/09/2`
`3/getting-started-with-docker-and-container-services/`

The tutorial will guide you through each step in a way similar to when we need to interact with the Azure portal and SSH console login to our respective VM. In this way, we can avoid one screenshot per page of the book, save time and resources, and focus on the important points.

Why Azure Container Service?

Azure offers multiple options when we want to work using Container-based applications. All the options satisfy a certain case, and you can choose what as best suits your needs. To evaluate which could be the better option for your case depending on the type of application, the containers it uses, and the cost model that fits your budget, you will first need to kn

ow what is actually is offered by Azure. We will list here the popular Azure options for container-based applications as of the first quarter of 2017. Instead of going into details, we will have a very brief look at each offering.

Azure App Service (on) Linux

This is called Azure App Service Linux from within Visual Studio 2017, and is one of the publishing targets. When you access this from the Azure portal, it is called as Web App On Linux.

How it works:

1. Create an ASP.NET Core web application project in VS 2017.
2. Add Docker support from within VS.
3. Publish: Select the publishing target as Azure App Service Linux; In a later step, it allows you to create an App Service directly to your Azure subscription.

 From within a VS 2017 project, you have an option to configure Continuous Delivery, and voila! You have your release pipeline up and running.

This is probably the simplest and quickest way to put your app in a container under a Linux VM on the Azure cloud. You might have realized that it is a very good option if you have a single-container application. But in our example, we need a multi-container app in a microservices architecture.

Creating VM directly on Azure

You can create a VM on Azure from the following:

- The Azure portal
- The Azure CLI
- Docker, using Docker Machine

Once you have a VM ready on Azure, you can, for example, use Docker Machine to install and configure Docker Engine on a remote machine, and publish Docker images from the Dev machine to the VM on Azure.

Not the cool way to leverage containerized applications on Azure; it's limited, and there's not much to explore in the context of the simple yet complete microservice architecture example in this book. That's why we skipped it.

Azure Service Fabric (ASF)

Azure Service Fabric offers a number of features out-of-the-box, which include the ones listed next:

- With ASF, you are not just limited to container-based applications but much more
- A number of Microsoft's own services are running on ASF, for example, Azure Event Hubs and, Azure SQL Database
- It gives you features to easily tune your microservice as stateless or stateful
- Some of the core infrastructure features are already built in, like scalability and low latency
- ASF offers Reliable Services or Actor Model (good for IoT solutions, for example, BMW implementation)
- It has a good Visual Studio Integration (build, test, debug, deploy, and so on)

All of the preceding features come at the cost of using Azure SDK using its own full-blown programming model. It means my architecture will be using yet another special or specific technology. I smell a vendor tie-in. Additionally, it has the potential to remove the focus from general cloud and container-based architecture to something specific to Microsoft Windows. Therefore, for our example project, we toss it up.

Azure Container Service (ACS)

Azure Container Service seems to provide the neatest framework to boot your application, which has a container-based microservices architecture. It offers an optimized container hosting solution, along with the following benefits:

- Container is open technology with a great community backing (no cloud vendor tie-in)
- ACS offers orchestrators like Docker Swarm, DC/OS, and Kubernetes
- It is well-suited for multi-container (and multi-VM) applications
- It sets up Infrastructure elements automatically with the provided ARM template, which saves lot of time and tuning
- It's all open source

We want to use the docker container technology for our simplest microservices-architecture-based application. We also wish to use .NET Core technology's cross-platform feature, thereby the need for the Linux-based VM and containers. This is why ACS is our best choice.

Implementing the Math app

We have a problem and we have architected its solution using containerized microservices. Now it's time to do the implementation.

Implementation approach

We will take a ground-up approach; in this way, we'll learn more, which, as a developer, is always helpful at the time of debugging. We will use Visual Studio Community edition (Free) with Docker support tools installed separately, and will not use the extra features of VS 2017.

> VS2017 provides a seamless integration with Docker, even with multi-container apps, and a smooth integration with the VSTS CI/CD pipeline directly to the VM. For a quick introduction to VS2017 with Docker, watch this short video by Steve Lasker at@
> `https://channel9.msdn.com/Events/Visual-Studio/Visual-Studio-201`
> `7-Launch/T111.`

Our frontend microservice is a simple single-page static (HTML + JS) application, which we've decided to host on the NGINX web server in a Linux-based container.

Our backend microservice is a simple REST API application, which is based on ASP.NET Core hosted on the Kestrel HTTP web server inside a Linux-based container.

For a richer experience, we will install both containers on a CentOS Linux, and test the *Math App* by interacting with the frontend SPA from a browser in Windows. Once we have achieved this successfully, we will push our docker container images to Docker Hub, the public docker images repository. We will pull these images, and then execute them inside our containers created using the ACS.

Following this approach, you'll not only understand the implementation of our architecture better, but also get the more fine-grained process of implementing the multi-container-based microservices architecture, which you would not grasp completely if you followed a VS 2017-based docker container implementation as your first application. In addition to that, it makes you cloud agnostic; you will be able to deploy container-based applications, locally on Dev machine(s), on-premises servers, or other popular cloud infrastructure providers.

Implementation Steps

By now, we have a clear design and architecture ready and we have also defined our approach to implementing the solution. We will now follow the step-by-step approach towards achieving each artifact according to our defined architecture. You should follow each step carefully and move on to the next step only after the current and all previous steps are completed successfully.

Installing the Hypervisor

We will install hypervisor for playing with the virtual machines locally. We select Oracle VirtualBox for executing our virtual machines.

Download and Install VirtualBox as follows:

- From `https://www.virtualbox.org/wiki/Downloads`
- Also download and install, when required, the Oracle VM VirtualBox Extension Pack

CentOS virtual machine

We now need our VM where we will install and execute our containers locally instead of in the cloud or on our own DEV machine to avoid cluttering and to explore.

Instead of downloading and installing the OS on a newly created VM image, we will download a pre-built VM image for VirtualBox, which is available for free. We will use a CentOS version 7 Base image. It has minimal packages installed, yet most of the basic libraries are already available. It does not have a graphical interface; we do not need one-- we will SSH into it.

1. Download the CentOS VM image from `https://virtualboxes.org/images/centos/`
2. Select CentOS 7.0 Base to download
3. Add and import the VM image into your VirtualBox
4. You should be up and running soon--the ID/PWD for the image is published on the download page

You might be thinking that it would be better to install docker on Windows and use the container in the VM from there. Surely, it would save time, but remember that Windows 10 Home does not have hyper-V, so you can't run Linux containers. Moreover, you will need Docker Toolbox, which will eventually install VirtualBox. The scene is the same for Windows 7; if you have Windows 10 Pro or greater, you can then play around with Docker easily.

CentOS configuration

We will mention here all the commands that we executed so that our OS in the VM is fully prepared.

First of all, if required, you can use the `loadkeys` command to set the keyboard language locale in your VM.

Next, in your VirtualBox, you can expose the ports (port forwarding) from inside the VM to the host environment so that they become accessible. For example, I exposed port 22 of CentOS VM outside, and mapped it to the host OS on port 3302 locally.

With this, I am now using PuTTY to SSH into my CentOS VM, as I type better on PuTTY over Windows.

Note that I am also using WinSCP for file transfers from the Windows host to the VM over SSH. WinSCP uses the same connection settings as PuTTY for secure file transfer.

Port Forwarding

The following screenshot shows all the exposed and mapped ports, which we will be needing sooner or later, to be accessible on the host OS. Please also enable other ports at your end:

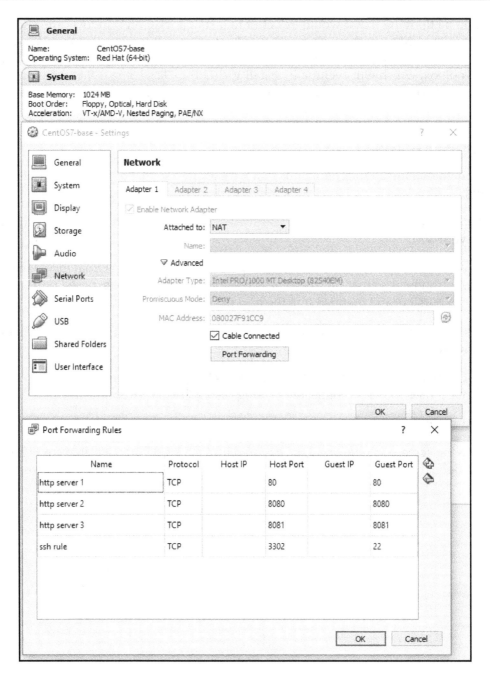

Port Forwarding rules for CentOS VM

The general VM configuration is also visible in the last screenshot, which was basically the default when I imported the image into the VirtualBox. Also, the steps to reach the final screen are pretty much visible: you need to go to the VM settings, followed by then **Network**, and then click on the **Port Forwarding** button.

Packages installation

Basically, there are two main packages that we want to install on our CentOS VM:

- Docker Engine
- Azure CLI

First of all, we need to install GCC and the C++ compiler, which will be used by other packages later. Execute the following command on your CentOS terminal:

```
yum install -y gcc-c++ make
```

Docker installation

To have full information on installing Docker on CentOS, please visit https://docs.docker.com/engine/installation/linux/centos/.

Execute the following commands under CentOS (either on the terminal in the VirtualBox window or in PuTTY) in the same order as displayed here:

```
sudo yum install -y yum-utils
sudo yum-config-manager --add-repo
https://download.docker.com/linux/centos/docker-ce.repo
sudo yum makecache fast
sudo yum -y install docker-engine (This is older command but still working)
sudo yum install docker-ce (This is a newer command)
```

Note that Docker runs as a privileged process, so you have to execute Docker commands as a root user, or perform the following steps to let your user added in a special Docker group on Linux:

```
sudo groupadd docker
sudo gpasswd -a coreos docker
sudo service docker restart
```

logout and then login again.

Now start the Docker daemon, the Docker service on the VM, by executing the following command:

```
sudo systemctl start docker
```

Your Docker is now installed and running. You can execute a tiny containerized application to test if it is successful:

```
docker run hello-world
```

It's a hello-world containerized application. See the output of the command; it confirms successful installation.

Azure CLI (command-line interface) Installation

We will now install the Azure CLI, and in order to do so, we first need to install NPM.

Login as root (for example, `sudo bash`), and execute the following command; notice the "-" in the end:

```
curl -sL https://rpm.nodesource.com/setup_7.x | bash -
```

You may now exit the root session, coming back to normal user, for example, centos (in my case), and execute the following command to install node.js so that the npm package manager becomes available:

```
sudo yum install -y nodejs
```

We are now ready to install the Azure CLI, so execute the following command, and we are done for now:

```
npm install -g azure-cli
```

Container installation and execution

We need to install and run two containers, one for the frontend and another for the backend. The frontend one is a static application, and does not need to be compiled, so we will get it directly from the Git repository, but you can just copy-paste the directory as well. For the backend project, you get the source code, and build it with dotnet core using `dotnet publish`.

When we have our package ready, either static pages or compiled binaries (as a result of `dotnet publish`, for example), we need to first build the Docker images for the new container. Then, we need to run the newly built docker image as a running container.

Running the frontend container

To run a new container, here, we will first download the source code from source control. In this example, we are cloning a Git repository, building the docker image and then executing the docker container based on the image we just built. Follow these steps in order to run our frontend container.

Note that I have generated my RSA private key, and added it online to my bitbucket login as well as in the SSH in the VM, using the `ssh-keygen` and `ssh-add` commands. If you want to simulate the same steps on your own repository, then please see more information here:
`https://confluence.atlassian.com/bitbucket/set-up-ssh-for-git-728138079.html`:

1. You can download the source code or do a Git clone.
2. Current directory: `/home/centos/containerization/app`.
3. Online Git repository:
   `https://bitbucket.org/packt_ea_net_core/chapter11_cc_fe`.
4. Git clone--`git@bitbucket.org:packt_ea_net_core/chapter11_cc_fe.git`
   `fe`.
5. We named the newly created folder/directory named as `fe`.
6. In the `index.html` page, remember to change the URL inside the html file from
   `http://eaaagents.eastus.cloudapp.azure.com:8081` to
   `http://localhost:8081` so that it's accessible to be tested locally from the local (port forwarded) VM.
7. Build the Docker image like this:

   ```
   docker build . -t mathappfe
   ```

8. Run the Docker container from the image just built as follows:

   ```
   docker run --name mathappfe-container -p 8080:80 mathappfe
   ```

9. You can now access `http://localhost:8080` on your host machine hosting the VM, and you will see the response (as we have already forwarded this port in VirtualBox), as seen in this screenshot:

Output of a frontend microservice container

Running the backend container

Again, to run a new container we will first clone the Git repository, build the image and execute the container. Here, since our backend container is a .NET Core based code, we will need to compile the C# code as well. Follow these steps in order to run our backend container:

1. You can download the source code or do a Git clone.
2. Current directory: `/home/centos/containerization/app`
3. Online Git repository: https://bitbucket.org/packt_ea_net_core/chapter11_cc_be
4. Clone the git repository using the following command git clone: `hqureshi@bitbucket.org:packt_ea_net_core/chapter11_cc_be.git be`
5. We named the new folder name be, and all the source can be found at: `/home/centos/containerization/app/be`.
6. For the backend case, the source code is C# based on .NET Core, and we did not install the .NET core build environment on our VM; so, in this case, we will build our source code in to the binary package from within Windows (host machine) with visual studio CE 2015 installed (though, in my case, I have VS also installed in a separate Windows VM).
7. Now run the following command under the project directory:

```
dotnet publish
```

Note that, from the source code, you could see the presence of the Docker file; for this to publish from within Visual Studio, you need to have Docker client installed on the same machine; otherwise, like me, you create a published package from the CLI.

8. In this case, we published the folder to the Windows host, and transferred to our VM using WinSCP at this location:
   `/home/centos/containerization/app/dynamic/mathwebapi_publish`

9. The flow of these commands looks as seen in the following screenshot:

```
centos@localhost:~/containerization/app/dynamic
[centos@localhost ~]$ cd containerization/app/dynamic/
[centos@localhost dynamic]$ ls
mathwebapi_publish  mathwebapi_publish.zip
[centos@localhost dynamic]$ rm -rf mathwebapi_publish.zip
[centos@localhost dynamic]$ ls
mathwebapi_publish
[centos@localhost dynamic]$ clear
[centos@localhost dynamic]$ docker images
REPOSITORY        TAG         IMAGE ID        CREATED        SIZE
hello-world       latest      48b5124b2768    4 weeks ago    1.84 kB
[centos@localhost dynamic]$ docker ps
CONTAINER ID     IMAGE        COMMAND         CREATED        STATUS        PORTS        NAMES
[centos@localhost dynamic]$ pwd
/home/centos/containerization/app/dynamic
[centos@localhost dynamic]$ ls
mathwebapi_publish
[centos@localhost dynamic]$ docker build mathwebapi_publish -t mathwebapi
Sending build context to Docker daemon 7.576 MB
Step 1/6 : FROM microsoft/aspnetcore:1.0.1
1.0.1: Pulling from microsoft/aspnetcore
386a066cd84a: Pull complete
```

Building the Docker container image from dotnet published directory

10. From the preceding screenshot, you can notice that `docker images` resulted in only one image, which is installed in this VM. Executing the `docker build` will create a new docker container image for our .NET Core-based backend WebAPI microservice:

    docker build -t mathwebapi mathwebapi_publish

    Take a look at the following screenshot:

```
[centos@localhost dynamic]$ docker images
REPOSITORY              TAG         IMAGE ID        CREATED          SIZE
mathwebapi              latest      1786f7451938    3 minutes ago    274 MB
hello-world             latest      48b5124b2768    4 weeks ago      1.84 kB
microsoft/aspnetcore    1.0.1       2c7bbc508bb2    8 weeks ago      267 MB
[centos@localhost dynamic]$
```

Building the docker container image from dotnet published directory

11. Run the docker container from the image just built, as follows:

```
docker run -it -d -p 8081:80 mathwebapi
```

Take a look at the following screenshot:

```
[centos@localhost dynamic]$ docker run -it -d -p 8080:80 mathwebapi
8c22f2bcb2d1b16c92a70b20d2c47d3cb39aba02c6bd1c131201e83f1f89a260
[centos@localhost dynamic]$ docker ps
CONTAINER ID    IMAGE         COMMAND             CREATED        STATUS         PORTS                    NAMES
8c22f2bcb2d1    mathwebapi    "dotnet MathWebAPI..."  6 seconds ago  Up 4 seconds   0.0.0.0:8080->80/tcp     pedantic_albatt
```

Output from docker run command

You can now access `http://localhost:8080` on your host machine (which hosts the VM), and you will see the response (as we have already forwarded this port in VirtualBox).

You can also verify the output using `curl`, which will basically call the API directly, as follows:

```
curl "http://localhost:8081/api/math?a=1&b=11"
```

Executing our two static and .NET Core-based microservices inside the two Docker containers that are inside Linux VM, we get an output similar to this screenshot:

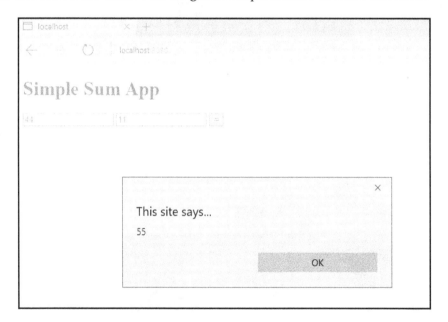

Successful output of executing two microservices (locally)

We have now successfully verified executing both the containers locally. The next step is to prepare and achieve the same results from the Azure cloud.

Uploading container images to container registry

We now want to upload the Docker-based container images that we have created in the previous steps to a container registry.

Why:

- We want to execute container images on the Azure cloud as facilitated by ACS
- In order for us to run the containers on ACS, we need to push them
- Either we push the container binaries manually, or have them uploaded and stored on some public or private container registry over the Internet.
- So, we will first push our images from our local (DEV) VM to (our selected) Docker Hub, which is a public container registry available to be used for free for public containers
- The next step will be to pull the images from Docker Hub to ACS, then install and execute them

First of all, create a Docker Hub account for free; my Docker Hub account, for example, is *habibcs*. Then, we create a repository in our account with the name `eea-spa`, which appears in Docker Hhub as seen in the following screenshot shown as follows in the docker hub:

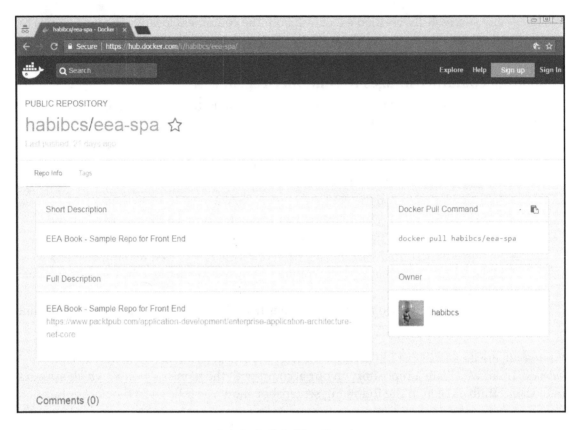

A repository in a Docker Hub container registry

We now want to push our image to this repository. Run the `docker images` command on your CentOS VM to see the list of images installed on the machine (or call it a docker node). The names we gave to our frontend container and backend containers were `mathappfe`, and `the backend container was mathwebapi` respectively, which will appear as the output of the command beside other images:

```
[centos@localhost static]$ docker images
REPOSITORY          TAG          IMAGE ID        CREATED            SIZE
mathappfe           latest       8e4917865c26    About an hour ago  182 MB
mathwebapi          latest       80a458cc5a04    About an hour ago  274 MB
```

List of images available on the machine

To push our frontend image successfully to Docker Hub, we need to execute the following command to log in to your Docker account via Docker CLI:

```
docker login
```

Execute the following command to tag the container image:

```
docker tag 8e4917865c26 habibcs/eea-spa
```

We tag our existing container image using its IMAGE_ID with the repository name we want to push to:

```
docker push habibcs/eea-spa
```

We push the image to our repository on Docker Hub:

```
docker container rm 46c07d651266
```

We now remove the container installed locally by using its CONTAINER_ID; 46c07d651266 in my case:

```
docker rmi -f 8e4917865c26
```

We now remove the image by using the Image_ ID.

To test whether our operations worked successfully, we execute the following command:

```
docker run --name eea-spa-container -t -d -p 8080:80 habibcs/eea-spa
```

This will download the image-- **habibcs/eea-spa** from Docker Hub, since it has been removed from our system, and then create a container instance of it with the name of eea-spa-container, and execute it by exposing internal port 80 to port 8080 on the host VM. After that, the final behavior will be exactly the same as what we have done before with the locally built Docker image.

We repeat the same steps to upload our backend microservice image once after creating the eea-be-mathwebapi repository on the Docker Hhub.

Creating Azure Container Service

We now begin to transfer our microservices-based application to the Azure cloud utilizing its Azure Container Service offerings.

Azure subscription

First of all, we need to have an Azure subscription, so, if you do not have one, create one. You can have 200$ free to use for one month on anything on Azure the first time you create your Azure account. If you are a Visual Studio subscriber, you can have 50$ to 150$ per month of Azure credit to spend on. Similarly, if you are an MSDN platform subscriber, you get 100$ per month of Azure credit.

In addition to some of the afore mentioned options, there is also a plan called Visual Studio Dev Essentials. This plan is basically to attract non-Microsoft developers to try various MS tools, and it gives you a 25$ monthly credit to try on Azure for a year.

25$ is more than enough to try our ACS sample application; be sure to destroy all of your ACS resources once you have successfully completed your experimentation. If, for some reason, you do not want to destroy the ACS resources immediately, then you can stop and deallocate all the VMs allocated in your ACS service using, for example, the Azure Portal. In our example, we will have 3 VMs allocated.

Monthly Azure credit for Visual Studio subscribers `https://azure.micro soft.com/en-us/pricing/member-offers/msdn-benefits-details`
Monthly Azure credit for MSDN Platforms subscribers `https://azure.mi crosoft.com/en-us/offers/ms-azr-0062p`
Visual Studio Dev Essentials
`https://azure.microsoft.com/en-us/pricing/member-offers/vs-dev-e ssentials`

Creating Azure Container Service

Now we need the Azure Container Service to execute our microservices containers.

For our sample in ACS, we create a Docker Swarm-based orchestrator with one master node and two agent nodes. Please follow the instructions given earlier in the section *Setup in Azure Container Service* under *Technical Architecture* to create the ACS for our sample. Although creating ACS via the Azure portal is self-explanatory, you can additionally follow the step-by-step guide as mentioned previously in the *Hands-on Prerequisites* section.

It takes a few minutes to create your ACS resources. For our sample, we name our Azure resource group as `RG_ACS_EABook_Example`. After the ACS is created successfully, it looks similar to the screenshot here:

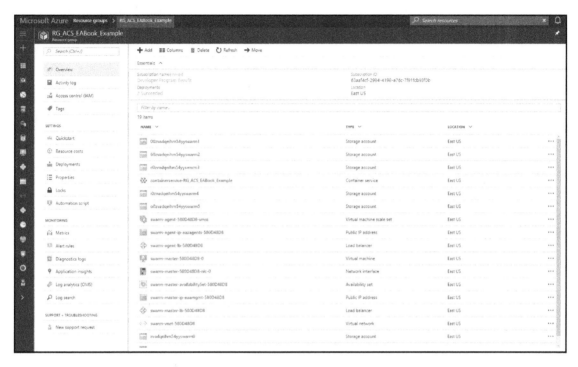

Resources in our Azure Container Service

Note that the resources you see in this screenshot are mentioned nicely and explained a bit in the *Network Architecture* section previously. Please refer to it now to have a fresh picture again in your head.

In the last screenshot, you can see **Deployment History**, which is shown right after your successful ACS deployment, or you can have the same view when you go to the **Deployment** option in your newly created resource group. The name of the deployment usually looks something like `microsoft.acs-2017123456789`. It may look a little different for you depending on the names given by you, but the private network, internal IPs, ports, and general accessibility look the same as mentioned in the preceding Network Diagram:

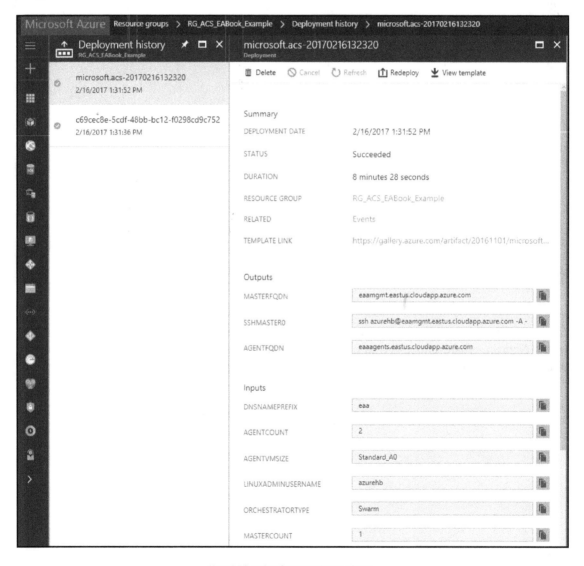

Network information of our Azure Container Service

Container installation and execution on ACS

To install, and later execute our containers on ACS, we need a shell to log in. We can retrieve the FQDN information (fully qualified domain name) of our (Ubuntu Linux-based) VMs (docker swarm nodes), which hold our containers from the deployment information as shown in the last diagram.

These VMs are installed with Ubuntu Linux with Docker Engine. The agent docker nodes and the master node are stringed together by the virtual of Docker Swarm orchestration, which is why we now call them Docker Swarm Nodes instead of just docker nodes.

In your ACS deployment, and in the last screenshot, there is a field called **SSHMASTER0**, from where you can get the SSH settings to log in to the secure shell. You will need to use your private key, which you have supplied when creating the ACS resources to log in via SSH.

In our example case, this is the FQDN and port number to log in via SSH, `eaamgmt.eastus.cloudapp.azure.com:2200`

Using this information along with our certificate key, we can successfully log in to our master node in the ACS. Once logged in, you can execute the command `docker info`, and it gives an output as shown in this screenshot:

```
azurehb@swarm-master-580D48D8-0:~$ docker info
Containers: 2
 Running: 2
 Paused: 0
 Stopped: 0
Images: 2
Server Version: 1.13.1
Storage Driver: aufs
 Root Dir: /var/lib/docker/aufs
 Backing Filesystem: extfs
 Dirs: 25
 Dirperm1 Supported: true
Logging Driver: json-file
Cgroup Driver: cgroupfs
Plugins:
 Volume: local
 Network: bridge host macvlan null overlay
Swarm: inactive
Runtimes: runc
Default Runtime: runc
Init Binary: docker-init
containerd version: aa8187dbd3b7ad67d8e5e3a15115d3eef43a7ed1
runc version: 9df8b306d01f59d3a8029be411de015b7304dd8f
init version: 949e6fa
Security Options:
 apparmor
Kernel Version: 3.19.0-65-generic
Operating System: Ubuntu 14.04.4 LTS
OSType: linux
Architecture: x86_64
CPUs: 2
Total Memory: 6.805 GiB
Name: swarm-master-580D48D8-0
ID: ZVNF:TMRA:IHVY:SHSF:BVHM:45BJ:4YJM:TYLU:ALCI:BICM:J7EW:77LM
Docker Root Dir: /var/lib/docker
Debug Mode (client): false
Debug Mode (server): false
Registry: https://index.docker.io/v1/
WARNING: No swap limit support
Experimental: false
Insecure Registries:
 127.0.0.0/8
Live Restore Enabled: false
```

View of docker info command on master node

Now, from within the terminal, type this command:

```
export DOCKER_HOST=tcp://127.0.0.1:2375
```

With this last command in your terminal session, your Docker commands will be redirected to `2375`, on which Docker Swarm is listening. Running `docker info` now gives a different output, as shown in this screenshot:

```
azurehb@swarm-master-580D48D8-0:~$ export DOCKER_HOST=tcp://127.0.0.1:2375
azurehb@swarm-master-580D48D8-0:~$ docker info
Containers: 2
 Running: 0
 Paused: 0
 Stopped: 2
Images: 4
Role: primary
Strategy: spread
Filters: health, port, dependency, affinity, constraint
Nodes: 2
 swarm-agent-580D48D8000000: 10.0.0.4:2375
  L Status: Healthy
  L Containers: 1
  L Reserved CPUs: 0 / 1
  L Reserved Memory: 0 B / 702 MiB
  L Labels: executiondriver=<not supported>, kernelversion=3.19.0-65-generic, operatingsystem=Ubuntu 14.04.4 LTS, storagedriver=aufs
  L Error: (none)
  L UpdatedAt: 2017-03-12T16:25:07Z
 swarm-agent-580D48D8000002: 10.0.0.6:2375
  L Status: Healthy
  L Containers: 1
  L Reserved CPUs: 0 / 1
  L Reserved Memory: 0 B / 702 MiB
  L Labels: executiondriver=<not supported>, kernelversion=3.19.0-65-generic, operatingsystem=Ubuntu 14.04.4 LTS, storagedriver=aufs
  L Error: (none)
  L UpdatedAt: 2017-03-12T16:24:55Z
Plugins:
 Volume:
 Network:
Swarm:
 NodeID:
 Is Manager: false
 Node Address:
Kernel Version: 3.19.0-65-generic
Operating System: linux
Architecture: amd64
CPUs: 2
Total Memory: 1.371 GiB
Name: 9d951f333a17
Docker Root Dir:
Debug Mode (client): false
Debug Mode (server): false
WARNING: No kernel memory limit support
Experimental: false
Live Restore Enabled: false
```

View of docker info command on master node from Docker Swarm

In this preceding screenshot, now you can see that `docker info` displays clearly the status of the two agents connected.

After exporting the docker port, that is, now using docker swarm, running the Docker commands will be executed on the docker agent nodes. Type the following commands:

```
docker run –name eea-spa-container –t –d –p 8080:80 habibcs/eea-spa
docker run –name eea-be-container –t –d –p 8081:80 habibcs/eea-be-
mathwebapi
```

Running these commands means that Docker will pull the images from the docker hub public registry, install them, and execute the containers from these images, instructing to redirect port 80 to 8080, and to redirect from 80 to 8081 for the backend container. Remember, our index.html page in the frontend SPA container has the URL http://eaaagents.eastus.cloudapp.azure.com:8081. This is the URL to invoke the backend hosted in a container on the Azure Container Service. Since the docker swarm is in control, it automatically runs the containers on the agent nodes, and decides automatically which node(s) to run the given container. The frontend is now accessible over ACS, which we can use to test at http://eaaagents.eastus.cloudapp.azure.com:8080/.

But before we continue to test, we need to allow one of our ports to be accessed publicly. The ports which are opened by default on VMs are 80, 443, and 8080. So, we need to allow port 8081 to be opened as well so that our API can be accessed over this port. To do this, we need to go to the Azure Resource group for our ACS, which, in this case, is RG_ACS_EABook_Example; in the resource group, locate the load balancer for the agent nodes (in my case--**swarm-agent-lb-580D48D8**), select it, then go to **Health Probes**, and add the new HTTP port 8081. In addition to that, we also need to add a new **load balancing rule** in the load balancer for the newly added port:

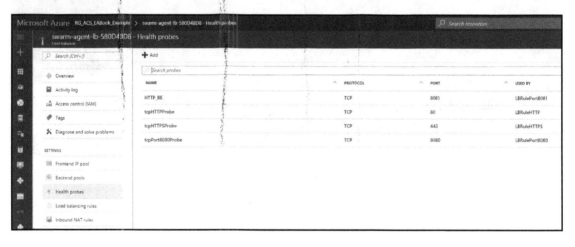

Add a new rule to open a port (Load balancer - Health probes)

The following image shows the newly added load balancing rule for port `8081` in our load balancer for ACS:

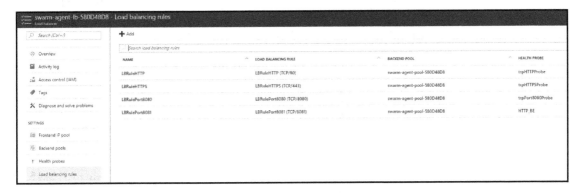

Add a new load balancer rule (Load balancer - Load balancing rules)

Finally, we can execute our sample microservices-based *Math Application* from Docker containers, orchestrated by Docker Swarm, hosted by the Azure Container Service on the Azure cloud, and it looks like this:

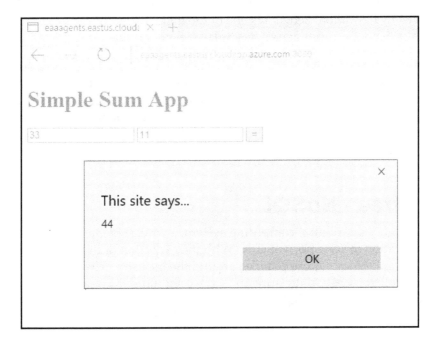

Final view of app running from Azure Container Service

Big Data and Microsoft

With the complexity of the disruptive Big Data technology, it is hard to conclude a single solution as the silver bullet for every problem. At the same time, Big Data fundamentals have not changed since Google's 2004 White Paper publications.

With two decades of hands-on experience, computing fundamentals have never changed in spite of the upcoming technologies like Big Data, Cloud, Internet of Things, digitization, and so on. I feel that easy user interaction makes a product innovative in our industry.

For example, WhatsApp was built with two key fundamentals, namely, real-time messaging and device-embedded authorization. Real-time messaging with traditional sign-on application was quite common in the last decade. The key difference is the mobile-enabled automatic sign-in in WhatsApp. In this era of customer satisfaction, this technology has been well received by the end users for the product's success.

Definition of Schema

As the word **Schema** is quite popular in the RDBMS world, let us take a minute to assess what Schema is. By definition, Schema is one of the many different types of structured data used to leverage the data carrier across multiple layers of enterprise application.

In simple terms, Schema is the skeleton of the data structure to be used in an enterprise application. As an example, a banking application might represent the customer details in some prescribed layout, which is termed as **Customer schema** of the banking application. In the RDBMS context, a predefined structure is essential for efficient database management in the storage layer. Also, it helps to build and search the relationship between the different objects of the underlying database tables.

Schema free - NoSQL

In the modern highly distributed computing system, a strict schema data store restricts the enterprise application to scale horizontally. With the evolution of the Big Data technologies, schema-free design becomes more popular around the industry. The Big Data industry refers to a term called NoSQL data store. In fact, we should not literally interpret the word NoSQL; actually, it is Not Only SQL.

As the name itself explains, schema-free is built on a data model/design without any strict schema. Data structure is highly runtime dynamic, that is, the data store schema is altered during the execution of the application. So, there is no need to define the upfront frozen data design in an enterprise software development cycle.

Fixed vs no schema

In the fundamental design, no schema does not design the application data store based on the relationship between data entities (like fixed schema). Rather, the design of the data store is flexible and dynamic based on the end user query/request against the enterprise application.

Let us illustrate this with a real-time example to understand it in a better way. In a traditional application, say the customer has been advised to share their data feed in a prescribed format, such as comma-separated, excel-based file, and the like. Here, the end customer is forced to send the input data layout strictly in the predefined format, required by the built enterprise application. On deviation from this fixed schema of input file, the system will reject the source abruptly.

In modern applications, this is completely reversed. For example, the Facebook application allows the end user to post/host their messages in whatever format they want. FB never instructs the end user to feed their input data using a predefined format. The FB users can post their input data in audio, video, message, images, of literally any format. Even within the image upload, FB allows the user to host the snapshot of any image format like JPG, BMP, GIF, PNG, and so on. For the end user of FB, this concept of no schema for input feed provides great flexibility.

We hope that these real-life examples of the traditional fixed schema and modern no-schema models clarify the key differences between them.

To illustrate more precisely, a matrix has been drafted with the x-axis representing **Fixed Schema** and **No Schema** along with y-axis as **Flat Layout** and **Complex Layout**. Four commonly used input feed sources like **CSV**, **Avro**, **HBase**, and **JSON** are categorized in the appropriate quadrants of the matrix, as shown in the following diagram:

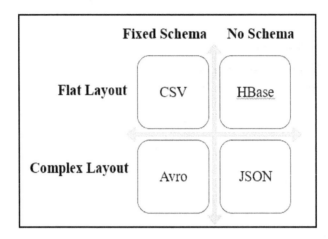

The main strength of no-schema databases becomes known when using them in an object-oriented context with inheritance.

The key advantage of a schema-free database is that we can store the data as it is. By doing schema-free design, it will be challenging to impose the database structure rules. A good example is that of the flexibility to post any type of content (like audio, video, image, and others) on the Facebook wall.

Another advantage of a no-schema database is that it gives additional agility during development. It easily allows you to try new features without having to restructure your database during the later phases of the software development life cycle in the enterprise environment.

On the flipside of no schema usage, metadata is a vital component to interpret the meaning of the actual data store.

NoSQL types

So far, you've got a clear idea on schema-free NoSQL data store for the model highly distributed computing application. Let us take a deep dive into the various types of NoSQL data store. Broadly speaking, a NoSQL data store is categorized into four areas, namely:

- Key Value
- Column
- Document
- Graph

A few samples of these four categories of NoSQL data stores are depicted in the following image:

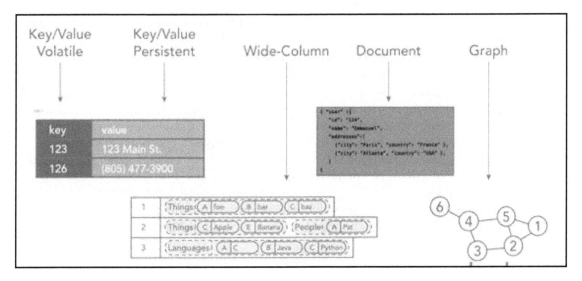

Let us explore the four types of NoSQL data stores:

- **Key Value**: As per the principles of data management, Key is a primary value used to seek the content of the associated record. As self-defined, Key Value databases pair keys to values. A classic example is employee ID, which is the key element to map the employment details of an associate in a firm. Well-known examples of Key Value NoSQL databases are Microsoft Azure Table and Amazon Dynamo DB.

- **Column**: In a traditional RDBMS, an entire record is persisted in the underlying disk at the table-row level. It helps the RDBMS table to retrieve a particular row faster. Therefore, RDBMSs are termed as row-based databases. In contrast, the modern column-family NoSQL databases store all the values of a particular column together on-disk. Apparently, it makes data retrieval of a large amount of a specific attribute faster. As a result, this approach helps the end user to aggregate queries and analytics scenarios in which the intention is to execute the data retrieval based on a particular field of the record. This type of NoSQL is the perfect solution for any query-based modern distributed application. In my own experience in the development of financial products, I had an opportunity to swim the depth and breadth of column family stores like Cassandra and Vertical.
- **Document**: By design, these types of NoSQLs consider documents as a record of its storage. In simple terms, a document is generally defined as a grouping of key-value pairs (as referred in the first category of NoSQL). The major difference lies in the Value section of a Document NoSQL on comparison with a Key Value NoSQL. Actually, the document value can be nested to arbitrary depths, which leads each document to carry its own schema. The most popular Document NoSQL industry database is MongoDB.
- **Graph**: Graph data structure is the fundamental design here. As we know, Graph is a network model with a unique feature to traverse more than one path using uni- and bi-directional paths/edges between nodes. Connections between nodes are termed as edges in graph theory. The strength of a graph database is in traversing the connections between the nodes. However, they generally require all the data to fit on one machine, limiting their scalability. Graph NoSQL is the best suitable data structure in the modern social computing connectivity model. In fact, LinkedIn connections (with all permutations and combinations) are derived using the industry popular Neo4j graph database.

Architectural best practices

Traditionally, **Scale up** methods are used to increase the power of an enterprise server. Here, concurrent programming methodology is leveraged using multi-core architecture in the context of a single application in an enterprise world.

In the modern world, **Scale out** design is followed to implement the scalability of any enterprise infrastructure. Highly distributed programming is the foundation for this model, which works by distributing the given job across the connected machines throughout the network:

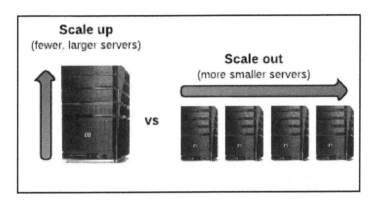

Legacy mainframe and modern Hadoop processing are the best suitable examples for the Scale up and Scale out designs respectively. It will be easy to understand the fundamental design change with the right example.

During mainframe days, the vertical scaling/scale up was used to upgrade the capacity of the existing server by adding more processors and memory. This process was not only costlier, but also could not scale beyond a threshold. On the other hand, horizontal scaling/scale out refers to adding more servers with less processors and memory. Usually, Scale out is not only cheaper in terms of the overall cost, but can also, literally, scale infinitely without any limitation.

To make the comparison clear, the following table lists the differences between Scale up and Scale out, based on the fundamental design concepts and implementation specifications of an enterprise application:

S.No.	Design element	Scale up	Scale out
1	Fault tolerance	Great risk	Easy by design
2	Upgrade mechanism	High effort	Easy to implement
3	Elasticity (on demand)	Remote chance	Easy to build
4	**TCO (Total Cost of Ownership)**	Large	Medium
5	Adaptation to the modern cloud model	Difficult	Easy

6	Utility cost (electricity and cooling charges)	Relatively less	High
7	Network equipment like switches and routers	Medium	High
8	License quantity	Moderate	High
9	Agile methodology	Challenge to follow	Easy adoption

Based on your enterprise need, limitations, and so on, it is highly recommended to choose either Scale up or Scale out as the right fit. It should be a wise and careful decision taken by the infrastructure and enterprise architects of the firm.

Microsoft HDInsight

Big Data is creating a tsunami in the current IT world. Every firm / product company is investing heavily in this space. Microsoft is not an excuse in the race of open sourced big data technology platform.

As Microsoft shifted their strategy towards open source in recent years, they focused their Big Data efforts with Hortonworks. The resultant product is named as HDInsight ,with general availability since October 2013:

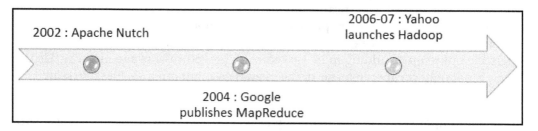

On reviewing the history, Google published its trade secret in 2004 using the MapReduce research paper. Then, it was available for everyone to use as an open source. On similar lines, Doug Cutting used to work on the Apache Nutch project as the open source. Inspired by Google's research paper, Doug released the Hadoop framework with the support of Yahoo. Since then, Big Data framework has been quite popular in the industry.

As Microsoft was already ahead in Cloud space using Microsoft Azure, it became easy to launch their Big Data suite HDInsight using its own cloud platform:

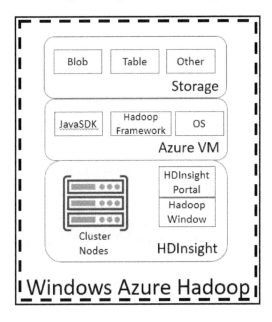

As depicted in the preceding diagram, Hadoop is hosted in the cloud-based virtual boxes on the Microsoft Azure platform by leveraging either Windows or Linux distribution. There are three layers in this HDInsight design, which are as follows:

- Storage (top layer of Azure storage elements)
- Infrastructure (middle layer of Windows Azure VM)
- Process (HDInsight HaaS Hadoop as a Service)

In any computing theory, Process and Storage are the two fundamental blocks by design. The underlying platform is termed as Infrastructure. In this section, we are going to analyze three items:

- **Storage**: Traditional RDBMS persists the content in the Table object, if it is structured. In case of unstructured content, the data is stored in the Blob object. As per the design, there are two core storage models supported by the HDInsight ecosystem, namely Azure Storage System and Hadoop Distributed File System. As Hadoop is the industry-popular stack, HDFS content is accessible using interoperable HDFS API. Though Azure storage is a separate element, **WASB (Windows Azure Storage Blob)** is designed for storage interoperability between HDFS and Azure Blob.

- **Infrastructure**: In terms of Infrastructure, Microsoft provides a powerful industry adopted cloud platform namely Azure. Architecture and design of Azure platform is capable to support the next generation scalable Big Data platform.
- **Process**: In terms of processing, HDInsight service is completely built based on the Apache Foundation Hadoop software, which is designed on the open source concept. By doing so, the HDInsight ecosystem leverages the standard and open source Hadoop concepts and technologies. In turn, it helps the end user to learn and deploy in the system easily. On top of that, HDInsight supports Windows PowerShell scripting for better deployment. Fundamentally, the ecosystem is implemented by the elastic business needs of the end customer using Microsoft's cloud-based Azure.

HDInsight ecosystem

In my experience, big data solution requires several products and technologies, because no single product in the market delivers an end-to-end solution. There is no single silver bullet to resolve all the Big Data challenges. On similar lines, Hadoop and HDInsight are critical technologies in a modern Big Data solution. There are three essential elements in HDInsight platform, which are described as follows:

- **Data management**: It is considered as the initial layer of the HDInsight ecosystem. It extracts and loads the source data feed with built-in tools like Microsoft Sqoop. If the business use case has the real-time feed, Microsoft StreamInsight is the live data-streaming engine to ingest the source feed into the main application.
- **Data enrichment**: Its key objective is to improve the raw source data into understandable quality data. Microsoft's SQL Server has a **DQS** (**Data Quality Services**) component, which cleans the data from multiple sources for analysis.
- **Data analytics**: Technology needs to enable the business. To achieve this, a big data solution must deliver actionable insights through a rich set of analytical tools including **Business Intelligence** (**BI**), advanced analytics using data mining, machine learning, graph mining, and others.

As an enterprise Big Data system, the ideal end-to-end solution is proposed in the following design diagram:

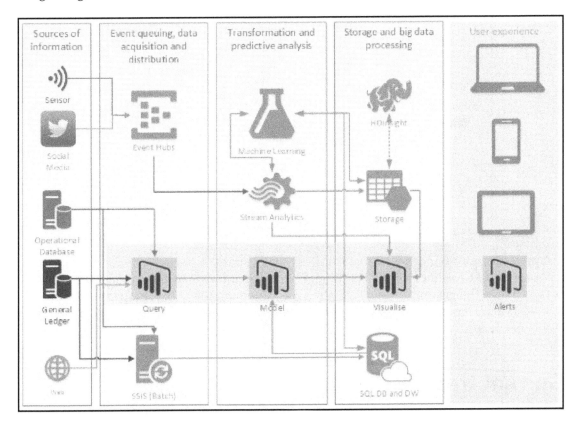

Briefly, HDInsight is a powerful Hadoop distribution, which opens up new opportunities for developing Hadoop applications in the Microsoft cloud platform, Azure. With HDInsight, the user can easily deploy a Hadoop platform in less than 20 minutes, which is impressive. Also, it supports pretty much all the common languages such as Java, .NET, and the like, to develop Hadoop applications in a quick and powerful way.

Introduction to Business Intelligence (BI)

On analyzing the history of the computing industry, BI was initialized at Lyons Electronic Office during the early 1950s. Interestingly, in those days, the system was built using thousands of vacuum tubes. It is termed as meeting business needs through actionable information.

The following is a graph depicting the business value of BI against the time factor:

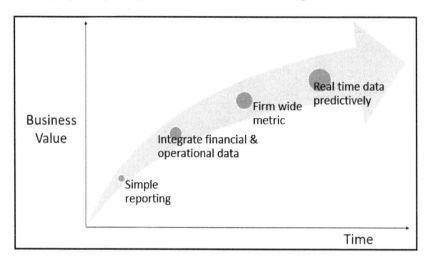

The preceding graph indicates a major shift in the BI space. It started with the simple reporting of text-based content. With time, BI integrated the financial and operational perspective in their output. Then, it covered the system metric at the company level to add business value. Now, BI generates the predictive analysis-based report with real-time data of the business.

Current trend

In today's Big Data world, BI has matured to a greater level with four major classifications, namely:

- Descriptive
- Diagnostic
- Predictive
- Prescriptive

With the available raw source data, BI helps to build meaningful information to act and decide using one of the aforementioned models. Let us illustrate them in detail with the real life scenario of being an end customer of a mobile service provider.

Descriptive: The core theme of a descriptive report is, What happened to source data? Being the mobile user, we are sent the monthly usage/billing report by the service provider. The monthly report shares the billing details with the associated transactions of mobile calls/usage during the specified period. Therefore, it gives a perspective on what happened to my mobile usage during the last month.

Diagnostic: A diagnostic report responds to the question, Why did it happen? In the same scenario, the mobile service provider can send the monthly usage report along with reasons for the usage spike (if any). Assume that the data consumption was quite high for a few days due to the local seasonal festival. It might be the reason for the usage spike in the monthly report.

Predictive: The core theme of a predictive report is, What will happen inferred from the source data? With this type of report, the mobile service provider will be in a position to predict the upcoming usage spike based on the historical usage and social media seasonal feeds. For the end user, the monthly usage report will be delivered along with the predictive usage for the upcoming days.

Prescriptive: A prescriptive report is an advanced action-oriented report with the theme, What should I do as a corrective action?. In the discussed use case, the prescriptive report shares some beneficial action with customer as well as the service provider. As an example, the prescriptive report may share the insight to promote the existing mobile plan into a beneficiary plan based on the earlier prediction. Ultimately, it adds value for both the stakeholders. It is a win-win situation for the end customer and the mobile service provider. Hence, this advanced action oriented prescription is in high demand for modern business execution.

Road map

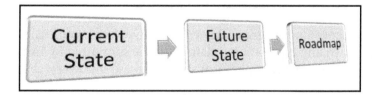

In any IT company, there are the following two key strategies:

- Change the business
- Run the business

With advanced BI in place, research indicates that 80% of all enterprise reporting will be based on modern business intelligence and analytics platforms; the remaining 20% will still be on IT-centric operational reports. Key drivers are 80% towards change strategy and the remaining on run the business. Therefore, BI strategy is considered the key business success criteria, going forward.

As per the Gartner report, the BI market has shifted to a more user-driven, agile development of visual, interactive dashboards with data from a broader range of sources. With my rich experience of building the financial enterprise data hub, I can sense the breadth and depth of the *broader range of sources*.

Power BI architecture

Power BI is a self-service BI platform, launched by Microsoft ahead in the race, during the 2010 Microsoft Excel product release. It was initiated with the name *Power Pivot for Microsoft Excel*. However, the initial launch did not pick up with the BI end customers, so, Microsoft gathered user feedback, and carefully constructed the current version of Power BI.

The following diagram depicts the Power BI architecture:

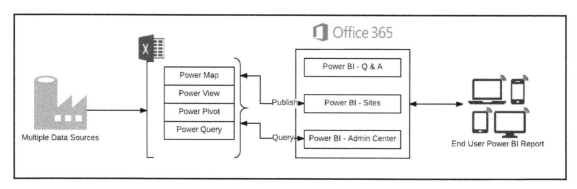

As described in the preceding diagram, Power BI has two key layers, namely, Excel, and Office 365. Pretty much any type of input data source is supported by Excel. At the same time, Power BI report has common platform support like Windows, web, and mobile-based end user experience.

Power BI is an evolution of the add-ins previously available in Microsoft Excel, like Power Pivot, Power Query, and Power View. Let us explore the functionality of these components.

PowerPivot is placed as a data analysis tool. For customer convenience, it can be easily used within the Excel product rather than a standalone tool. Moreover, this tool helps the end customer to ingest the data literally from any kind of data source without much restriction. In turn, it adds a degree of flexibility in the ecosystem. In terms of output, PowerPivot generates end custom reports based on data insights, data analysis, collaboration, and so on.

Power Query is used for the purpose of data discovery; it can be easily embedded in an Excel add-in. It helps the end user to reshape the data and to combine the data coming from different sources. Power Query is supplied as a plug-in product from Microsoft Power BI self-service solution. It is considered the common **ETL** (**Extract Transform Load**) tool component. It has an intuitive and interactive user interface, which can be used to search, discover, acquire, combine, refine, transform, and enrich the data.

Power View is a vital output component. It enables the end user to build interactive data exploration and visualization. The Power View product promotes intuitive ad hoc reporting using enterprise data sets. As data visualizations are dynamic in nature, it is easy for the end user to produce a single consolidated report.

Power BI layers

As you know, Power BI supports the end user to create personalized dashboards to monitor their most important data on-premise and from cloud-born enterprise critical data points.

In terms of system layers, Power BI Desktop and Power BI are two sides of the same coin. Power BI Desktop is a Windows application running on your PC, whereas, Power BI is a cloud service that you use through the web browser:

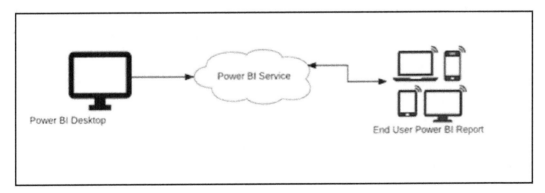

Power BI is a cloud service, which provides tools to perform analysis of data, and gain insights from your numbers. It is quite easy to create visualizations by using natural-language queries, Quick Insights, or full reports.

In terms of the reporting process, the end user can access the enterprise dashboards and reports on mobile devices by using native apps. Most importantly, the end user experience is the same across multiple platforms.

Visualization plays a key role in promoting the success score for the end user. Additionally, it adds business value for all stakeholders. In the modern world, the end user expects intuitive, informative, and interactive reports.

Let us illustrate with a perfect example. Our use case is corporate travel analysis and its consequences. As every firm marches towards cost-reduction initiatives, travel is a hanging fruit for the senior management.

To make a decision on this strategic cost initiative, the system is expected to share the data points in different dimensions. In our use case, travel data is analyzed with a region-wise split, quarterly sales, trips segregation based on purpose, types of booking like rush, normal, seasonal, and so on. On plotting the various business analysis using Power BI, the user community can easily proceed to make business decisions with multiple dimensions of the source data:

Few highlights of the Power BI products are as follows:

- **Real-time support**: It has the facility to update data not only scheduled refresh, but also live-stream data
- **Office Integration**: Power BI has a seamless easy integration with Microsoft Office product suite
- **Data Security**: Power BI has a data access mechanism for specific users with row-level security
- **Next Gen Service Availability**: Coordinated with the industry evolution, Power BI exposes the business functionality using the REST API mode

Artificial intelligence (AI)

In recent times, a few words such as Robotics, Artificial intelligence, Analytics, Data mining, Machine learning, and so on are powerful in the current IT industry.

In this highly competitive world, it is extremely important for any software engineer to understand the concepts and usage of the emerging fields. It is essential to survive in the rapid-growth IT industry.

Core components

AI is a broad term referring to computers and systems that are capable of, essentially, coming up with solutions to problems on their own. The solutions are not hardcoded into the program; instead, the information needed to get to the solution is coded, and AI (used often in medical diagnostics) uses the data and calculations to come up with a solution on its own.

One of the daily-life AI examples is seen on online portals like Amazon, Netflix, and others. AI accomplishes a useful task by recommending music and movies based on the interests you have expressed and judgments you have made in the past. By monitoring the choices you make and inserting them into a learning algorithm, these apps recommend that which you are likely to be interested in:

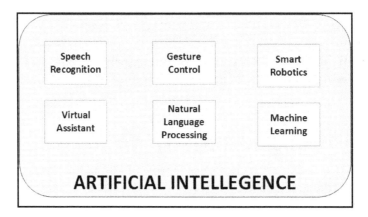

As depicted in the preceding diagram, AI is the superset of the listed components, and so, it's a vast area to explore.

Machine learning (ML)

Often confused with Artificial intelligence, machine learning actually takes the process one step further by offering the data necessary for a machine to learn and adapt when exposed to new data. I would define it as the self-learning capability of the machines by modern computing principles. Fundamentally, it is designed and built by reading mined data, creating a new algorithm through AI, and then updating the current algorithms in a highly dynamic fashion according to the newly learnt task. In turn, the self learning matures with time and with more experience/executions.

ML has the following few fundamental capabilities:

- Generalizing information from large data sets
- Detecting and extrapolating the data patterns
- Applying derived information to the needy solutions
- Executing the appropriate actions

By design, the preceding execution steps are based on self-intelligent algorithms. Obviously, certain parameters must be set up at the beginning of the machine learning process so that the machine is able to find, assess, and act upon new data.

Data mining

Data mining is an integral part of coding programs with the information, statistics, and data necessary for AI to create a solution:

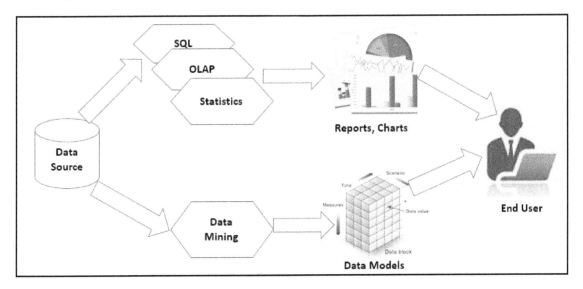

In the traditional reporting model, the data source is retrospective, and looks back to examine the exposure of the existing information.

However, in the case of data mining, as the name implies, the same data source is described. This method summarizes the raw data, and makes it something that is interpretable by humans. They are analytics that describe the past. The past refers to any point of time when an event has occurred, whether it was one minute or one year ago. Descriptive analytics are useful, because they allow us to learn from past behaviors, and to understand how they might influence future outcomes.

Interconnectivity

On connecting the dots of the aforementioned platforms, Artificial Intelligence is the foundation that is followed by Machine learning, Statistics, and Data mining, chronologically. In simple terms, AI is the superset of all paradigms, which is represented in the following diagram:

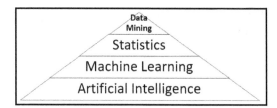

Artificial intelligence is a science to develop a system or software to mimic humans in response and behavior in a given circumstance. As the business benefits, AI provides effective execution by increased automation, with a reduced defect rate for enterprise applications.

AI at Microsoft

As AI is the foundation of next generation Robotics, Machine learning, Data mining, and so on, there are lots of attractions in this space in industry and institutes.

At Microsoft, research plays a crucial role in driving those breakthroughs. The Microsoft research team has influenced virtually every released product in the past three decades, including Cortana, Azure ML, Office, Xbox, HoloLens, Skype, and Windows. Microsoft researchers believe in sharing these fundamentals through Project Oxford and CNTK, and through partnerships with leading universities and research organizations.

Industry Bots

Bot is the short form of Robot. What is a Bot?

By definition, it is a software program that operates as an agent for a user or another program, or simulates a human activity. The best common industry-used example is the Internet crawler program. It accesses websites and gathers their content for search engine indexes.

Microsoft open source strategy

Satya Nadella could not have found a better way to tell the IT world there is a new sheriff in town than when he said these three words: *Microsoft loves Linux*.

It's a complete contradiction of what Ballmer said in June 2001: *Linux is a cancer that attaches itself in an intellectual property sense to everything it touches*.

In this process, Microsoft is partnering with open source companies such as *Canonical Ltd*. to enable Windows Server to run as a guest OS on Ubuntu and OpenStack.

Hot core development platform, .NET Framework, is being migrated into open source as .NET Core with cross platform (Windows, Linux, Mac, and others).

Cognitive Services

With Open Source Strategy, Microsoft initiated Cognitive Services, which expands on Microsoft's evolving portfolio of machine learning APIs, and enables developers to easily add intelligent features such as emotion and video detection, facial, speech, and vision recognition, and speech and language understanding into their applications.

Microsoft Cognitive Services (formerly, Project Oxford) are a set of APIs, SDKs, and services available for developers to make their applications more intelligent, engaging, and discoverable. These APIs of Cognitive Services are hosted on Microsoft-managed data centers.

Microsoft Bot

Microsoft Bot Framework is a comprehensive offering to build and deploy high quality bots for users to enjoy in their favorite conversation experiences.

Bot Framework provides just what you need to build, connect, manage, and publish intelligent bots, which interact naturally wherever your users are talking from text/sms to Skype, Slack, Facebook Messenger, Kik, Office 365 mail, and other popular services.

A chatbot can be easily built into any major commonly used chat product like Facebook Messenger or Slack. On analyzing where people really spend time, you will probably get details about where users are.

Summary

In this chapter, you learned about virtual machines and containers, and understood the difference between containers and VMs, various containerization technologies, and how the containerization fundamentals in today's world make up the full ecosystem, especially docker-based containers.

You also learned about the core of DevOps, practices including the CI and CD processes, and how it is becoming common in modern cloud-based development and deployment scenarios. Along the way, we also gave recommendations on the most popular tools for the right job in today's market. Now, the reader will be able to learn the emerging Architecture practices of the industry in a succinct and concise way with the .NET Core environment.

We went on to implement a sample microservices-containers-based application, something which we chose to skip in the Chapter 9, *Microservices Architecture*, and decided to demonstrate it when explaining containerization. We not only implement, our sample microservices application locally, but also successfully deployed our multi-container app on the Azure cloud using Azure container services. We discussed some of the internal aspects of Azure and its offerings for container-based applications. We also deployed our application on to ACS, which demonstrates how easy and flexible today's cloud infrastructure like Azure and AWS have become.

Index

Z